Secularizing the Faith

*Canadian Protestant Clergy and the
Crisis of Belief, 1850–1940*

The intellectual ferment of the Victorian era posed a substantial challenge to religious institutions. In Canada as elsewhere the focus of religious belief, especially in the Protestant sects, shifted perceptibly away from spiritual concerns. David B. Marshall explores the ways in which the clergy responded to these changes.

Faced with war, depression, and the absence of religious revival in the twentieth century, a crisis in theology emerged: the church and religion seemed 'marginal.' Ministers strained to find a 'preachable gospel.' Sensing that their congregations were growing indifferent to spiritual homilies and references to the supernatural, ministers spoke of the Christian mission in the world with growing reference to morality and the obligation to create social justice. God ceased to be a transcendent being and Jesus became a historical man actively engaged in the concerns of the world rather than the son of God showing the way to personal salvation. Clergymen no longer led their congregations in a quest to understand the mysterious or supernatural.

The process of secularization during this time took place throughout much of the Western world. In exploring its course in Canadian Protestantism, Marshall sheds light on a key development in Canadian religious and intellectual history.

DAVID B. MARSHALL is a member of the Department of History at the University of Calgary.

Secularizing the Faith

Canadian Protestant Clergy and the Crisis of Belief, 1850–1940

DAVID B. MARSHALL

UNIVERSITY OF TORONTO PRESS
Toronto Buffalo London

© University of Toronto Press 1992
Toronto Buffalo London
Printed in Canada

ISBN 0-8020-5938-4 (cloth)
ISBN 0-8020-6879-0 (paper)

Printed on acid-free paper

Canadian Cataloguing in Publication Data

Marshall, David B. (David Brian), 1954–
Secularizing the faith

Includes index.
ISBN 0-8020-5938-4 (bound) ISBN 0-8020-6879-0 (pbk.)

1. Methodist Church – Canada – History.
2. Presbyterian Church – Canada – History.
3. Liberalism (Religion) – Methodist Church – History.
4. Liberalism (Religion) – Presbyterian Church – History.
5. Secularization (Theology) – History.
6. Liberalism (Religion) – Canada – History.   I. Title.

BX8251.M37 1992   287′.0971   C92–093478–1

All photographs are courtesy of The United Church of Canada/Victoria
University Archives, Toronto, except for Charles Gordon, and the Gordon &
Gulch Bookstall, Melbourne, Australia, which are courtesy of the Department
of Archives and Special Collections of the University of Manitoba, Winnipeg.

This book has been published with the help of a grant from the Canadian
Federation for the Humanities, using funds provided by the Social Sciences
and Humanities Research Council of Canada.

Contents

ACKNOWLEDGMENTS   vii

Introduction: Secularization and the Writing of
Canadian Religious History   3

1 Clergymen and the Problem of Religious Doubt   25

2 The Emergence of Liberal Theology: A New Certainty?   49

3 Salvaging the Bible and the Evangelical Tradition   72

4 The False Promise of Missions   99

5 Stemming the Tide of Secularization, 1890–1914   127

6 Battling with the Great War   156

7 The 1920s: An Era of Drift   181

8 'Why No Revival?'   205

9 Stumbling towards a Theological Reformulation   228

Conclusion   249

NOTES   257

NOTE ON THE SOURCES   305

INDEX   313

Acknowledgments

A great deal of the research for this book was done in the United Church/Victoria University Archives at the University of Toronto. The staff of this superb archive unfailingly provided assistance and responded to what for them must have seemed to be a never-ending series of demands. There is nothing quite like working on the history of religion in Canada with the imposing portraits of the fathers of Canadian Methodism and Presbyterianism staring down at one. The portraits of Egerton Ryerson, George Pidgeon, and James Robertson remain vivid images. In particular, I would like to thank Glenn Lucas, now retired, and Neil Semple, who generously shared their vast knowledge of the various collections and their insights into the church history of Canada. The staff of the Emmanuel College Library at Victoria University and the Caven Library of Knox College, both in the University of Toronto, were also most helpful in opening up their vast holdings in rare books by Canadian clergymen. I have also had the privilege of working at the Department of Archives and Special Collections of the Elizabeth Dafoe Library of the University of Manitoba, and there my research into the C.W. Gordon papers was generously facilitated by Richard Bennett. Finally, the members of the University of Calgary Library's inter-library loans division and microform division have constantly responded to my demands.

During the thesis stage my work was directed by Michael Bliss of the University of Toronto. He gave me an immense amount of freedom to pursue this topic, while providing good advice, asking tough and challenging questions, and giving me much-needed encouragement when my faith in this project was declining. His dedication and enthusiasm for history have remained an inspiration. Also, the members of the thesis defence committee forced me to refine many of my arguments. While I was a graduate student, my research was funded by the University of Toronto, the Social Sciences and Humanities Research Council of Canada, and the government of Ontario.

In the transition of this work from thesis to book, I benefited from my association with the University of Calgary. The members of the Department of History, especially the recent head, Chris Archer, have been supportive and patient. At the University of Toronto Press, Gerry Hallowell and Laura Macleod have been primarily responsible for guiding me through the writing of this book, and their constant encouragement enabled me to complete it. I am particularly grateful to Gerry for his dedication to sound scholarship and good books. This book was also strengthened by the insightful assessments it received from the anonymous readers of the University of Toronto Press and the Social Science Federation of Canada. One reader in particular helped me to sharpen the analysis. Of course, none of these individuals or institutions is in any way responsible for the interpretations I make in this book, or for any errors of fact that may appear. For both the contents and shortcomings of this work I am solely responsible.

Finally, and most importantly, I would like to acknowledge my wife, Diane, and two daughters, Bria and Simone, for putting up with me and my obsession over the past years. They made many valiant efforts, too often stubbornly resisted, to distract me from my work and get me out of my study. Somehow, I am sure, their insistence that I spend more time with them has led to a better book. Mostly, I thank them for their emotional support, love, and companionship.

This book is dedicated to the memory of my parents, Brian and Marnie Marshall, who died about a decade ago, while I was embarking on this project. I believe that they would have concurred, although reluctantly, with what I have written.

Edward Hartley Dewart, editor of *Christian Guardian*, 1869–95

Daniel James Macdonnell, Presbyterian minister charged with heresy
in the 1870s

Albert Carman, general superintendent of Methodist church, 1884–1910,
pictured here in 1859 while principal of
the Belleville Seminary

Francis Huston Wallace, professor of New Testament theology,
Victoria College, Cobourg and Toronto, Ontario

The Grimsby camp-meeting site in 1859, when the emphasis was on conversions

The Grimsby camp-meeting site in 1889, a recreational retreat for the respectable middle classes

Thomas Crossley, popular urban revivalist in the Dwight Moody style

Alexander Sutherland, author and general secretary of the
Methodist church's Board of Missions

James Robertson, superintendent, Home Mission Committee,
Presbyterian Church of Canada, 1882–1902

Charles W. Gordon, late 1890s, when he launched his literary career
as 'Ralph Connor'

Major George Fallis, chaplain, Methodist Church of Canada,
during the First World War

Testament to popularity: Gordon & Gulch Bookstall, Flinder's Station,
Prince's Bridge, Melbourne, Australia. The poster advertises
Ralph Connor's book *Corporal Cameron* (1907). His earlier
novels are on the right side of the stall.

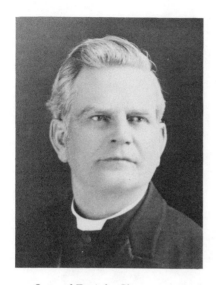

Samuel Dwight Chown, general superintendent, Methodist Church of
Canada, 1910–25

George Campbell Pidgeon, first moderator of the United Church of Canada,
1925–6

Edmund H. Oliver, principal, Presbyterian (St Andrew's) College,
Saskatoon; overseas chaplain during the First World War; and moderator,
United Church of Canada, 1932–4

Richard Roberts, moderator, United Church of Canada, 1934–6,
pictured here in 1925, his first year in Canada

Secularizing the Faith

Introduction

Secularization and the Writing of Canadian Religious History

In a widely distributed manual on Christian morals for Canadian families and schools Egerton Ryerson, the Methodist architect of Ontario's education system, cautioned that those who rejected the Bible 'have no certain standard of faith and morals ... having nothing but the shifting sands of expediency, and that blown about by every wind of passion, as the rule of their practice; are irregular in life and miserable in death.'[1] Ryerson's stern warning was no idle observation. A few years later, in 1878, another prominent Methodist clergyman, E.H. Dewart, the editor of the *Christian Guardian*, rang the alarm bells more loudly. In his investigation of the rise of scepticism he concluded that there was serious questioning about 'whether there is any human soul, any God, or any future state at all. The assailing army of unbelief repudiates all teaching that implies any supernatural power, a spiritual existence whatever.' He explained that since people are most religious in situations in which powerlessness, uncertainty, and material insecurity are most apparent, then the affluence of the industrial economies and the growing capability of advanced societies to manipulate the environment depresses religious sensibilities. 'The nations,' he explained, 'in which Christianity occupies the most prominent place among the moulding forces of social and personal life, are those in which the useful arts have been the most successful in promoting the growth of wealth. Yet this very accumulation of wealth promotes irreligion and worldliness.' Thinking that societies such as Canada were trapped in something like an iron law of secularization, Dewart prophesied the creation of 'a breach between modern culture and devout faith.'[2]

The impact of secularization on Canadian society was one of the most pressing issues of the day. The prospect of a society in which religious beliefs and institutions were in decline was disturbing for most, since Christianity was regarded as the foundation for the moral and social order. Family life, educational institutions, many philanthropic and voluntary organizations, the drive for moral and social reform, and the understanding of civilization and human nature were all somehow dependent on Christianity.[3] Even those who willingly surrendered belief in those elements of Christianity they considered to be untenable and irrational and challenged others to disregard what was apparently immoral and unnatural in the Bible regarded the prospect of a society lacking the foundation of Christianity with grave concern.[4]

Dewart's assessment of the rise of doubt and unbelief in Canada was not a traditional clerical jeremiad expressing concern about a sinful and materialistic world. In his view the process of secularization included the attempt by religious institutions to accommodate themselves to secular society. He argued that the 'progress of doubt and unbelief has not been by direct and open assault; but by a slow and steady undermining of the foundation principles of revealed religion.' There was constant pressure 'to reconcile Christianity with modern culture, by renouncing all that is essential and characteristic of religion.' Dewart's considerable alarm was based on his belief that 'within the Church itself ... the appointed expounders and defenders of religious truth have adopted and propagated theories that, at one time, would have been regarded as ... utterly inconsistent with the historic faith of the Christian Church.' Dewart's stunning conclusion was that secularization was taking place within the church and its ministry.[5]

It is the purpose of this book to demonstrate that the dominant trend in Canadian Protestant history from some time during the Victorian era has been the accommodation of the clergy and churches to a society growing more secular, not a march of progress towards the Kingdom of God. People were not willing to submit to what they considered to be standards too exacting, responsibilities too demanding, and doctrines too other-worldly, and consequently the churches were forced to accept a relaxed standard of membership in order to maintain their adherents. Responding to the 'crisis of plausibility' confronting Christianity, ministers strained to find a 'preachable gospel.' Sensing that their congregations were growing indifferent to spiritual homilies and references to the supernatural, ministers spoke of the Christian mission in the world with growing reference to morality and the obligation to create social justice. Clergymen no longer led their congregations in a quest to understand the mysterious or supernatural. Their message lost the essential supernatural context, and the evangelical imperative to show the way to personal salvation was neglected.

The clergy were confronted by a culture in which they had to compete with a host of ideas, values, and activities that challenged religious beliefs and worship practices. They attempted to keep the gospel a central force in Canadian culture by developing forms of worship, styles of preaching, and a Christian message that would be appealing in an increasingly consumer-oriented society. In the transition from the pioneer to the settled and industrial stage of development in Canada many people no longer simply struggled for subsistence but enjoyed some personal wealth and leisure time. Religion and the churches did not hold a monopoly. People experienced an expanding array of choice regarding not only how they spent their time but also what values would dominate their activities, whether they be spiritual ones or material ones. Mass revivalism, unconventional forms of sermonizing, such as the novel or popular gospel tunes, and moral rearmament or 'therapeutic mind cure' were some of the ways in which the clergy attempted to make religion an attractive commodity. These alternatives represented a secularization of the gospel message and worship practices, and they did not lead to a renewal of religion or church life in Canadian society. People still drifted away from religious belief and worship. The clergy failed to find a gospel that an increasingly secularized society would listen to, except for one that was stripped of theological content and was based largely on sentimental emotionalism and moral platitudes. Religion became an empty shell; the church's mission became secularized.

A distinction must be made between changes in the fundamental elements of religion and Christian belief, which indicate a process of secularization, and mere developments in understanding, which represent a modernization of belief without substantially affecting the essentials of the Christian faith. Defining religion is extraordinarily difficult and controversial; but it is necessary because religion can be described in ways that completely rule out the concept of secularization. For example, definitions which either consider important human concerns to be religious or relate things that inspire a sense of wonder to a form of religious worship are too imprecise and inclusive. All-encompassing definitions of religion lead to the assertion that only change, never decline, is possible. A clear distinction must be drawn between religion and other phenomena, such as political ideologies or faith in science, which can, like religion, provide a framework for understanding the human condition and gather a large and devoted following. These secular faiths, however, are different from religion in one crucial respect: a supernatural or miraculous element is not necessarily present.

The notion of the supernatural is religion's essential and distinguishing feature. Religion is a system of beliefs, values, and rituals acknowledging a form of being which transcends the world and a level of reality beyond what is observable to human beings. Religious people and institutions hold that the supernatural is a living, effective, and intrusive force in the natural world and in human history. As Owen Chadwick has recently explained, belief in the miraculous touches 'some vital root-canal of religious power over men's minds and hearts.' Loss of conviction about the existence of the supernatural or possibility of miracles can not be 'wholly separable or distinct from a process of secularization,' Chadwick concludes. 'For this very axiom, *miracles do not happen*, comes near the heart of that elusive shift in the ... mind we seek.'[6]

In Christianity faith has been concentrated on one transcendent historic miracle: the revelation of God and his Word in the life and resurrection of Jesus Christ. This and other specific religious ideas – God the Creator and some form of personal immortality – are essential to Christianity. It must be stressed, however, that no definition of the Christian faith can be final, for Christian belief and worship are forever changing. There are also great tensions within Christianity, which are made most clear by the prevailing concepts surrounding God and Jesus Christ. On the one hand, God is the Father Almighty, maker of heaven and earth. This view emphasizes God the Creator, outside the world and human history. On the other hand, God is an actor in the world – the most significant transforming power in history and individual lives. This view emphasizes the incarnation and Christ's sacrifice on the cross. Jesus Christ is considered both divine, the Son of God who was resurrected from the dead, and human, the man who was tempted, suffered, and was crucified on the cross. In Christianity both these views are of vital importance.

Secularization is best understood in the context of how religious beliefs and institutions adapt to social, cultural, and intellectual change.[7] It involves the interplay of a number of historical forces, such as the emergence of science and critical inquiry, a rising standard of living, improvements in medicine and health, better education, mobility and urbanization, more leisure time, and the rise of the mass media and the entertainment industry. There are also profound changes in human values that directly relate to secularization, such as the rise of individualism, a growing sense of personal freedom, and greater tolerance for diversity.

The process of secularization itself is complex. There is disenchantment about the world. Religious or supernatural explanations are replaced with natural and scientific ones. Secularization also involves what commentators have termed the laicization of social institutions and functions, such as schools and welfare. Religious values and clerical control are superseded by concerns about good citizenship and the imposition of bureaucratic or state control. Here lies a central dynamic in the process of secularization. Religion and the churches lose their monopoly position as social and intellectual life becomes more pluralistic. They are thrust into a competitive situation in which they are forced to accommodate an increasingly secular world. Secularization also involves religious change or the modernization of belief and worship practices in a fashion that undermines the essential supernatural or other-worldly aspects of the faith. Finally, secularization involves a decline in church involvement. Churches lose their central role in society and individual lives. Exactly how these different elements of the process of secularization are related is difficult for the historian to be precise about.

Many of the issues relating to the secularization of Canadian society can best be examined by exploring the ideas, attitudes, and activities of clergymen. Through their writing, preaching, worship services, pastoral work, dedication to missions, and quest to foster a religious revival, ministers seek to gather a congregation. The extent to which they are able to attract and hold a following or are rejected and dismissed is one way for the historian to capture a sense of people's religious faith and commitment. Moreover, the fact that clergymen take ordination vows promising to bear witness to the Christian gospel, lead congregations in worship, and uphold the doctrines of the church places them in a unique position. In order to spread Christianity throughout society the ministry must remain an effective social

institution and a vibrant intellectual force. This task compels clergymen
to make some accommodation with the secular world so as to make
certain that the Christian message and discipline are always present
and relevant in society. At the same time, however, the secular world
is something to be resisted. This is the fundamental dilemma facing
the church and its ministry: how to maintain Christianity as an effective force in secular society without sacrificing its cardinal principles
to a more secularized outlook. It is in the interaction of the church
and its ministry with society that some of the central themes of secularization can be discovered. Clergymen in Canada unwittingly contributed to the process of secularization in their quest to make religion conform to the needs and demands of the modern world.

Unlike other recent studies on secularization in Canadian society
this one focuses on the clergy's struggle to find a preachable gospel in
an increasingly secular society. More attention is paid to those clergymen who concentrated on reaching congregations than the leading
theologians who were cloistered in the colleges. This does not mean
that theologians or clerical leaders in the colleges are ignored, for
theology is an important aspect of the story. But the religious ideas
and worship practices of men and women in the churches are central.
The intricate relationship between the sacred and the secular cannot
be fully grasped by focusing exclusively on theology or religious
ideas.[8] What happened to religion at a popular level or in society is
crucial to an understanding of secularization. Ironically, in writing
about popular religion the focus of this work is on the elite; not
necessarily the theologians, but rather those clergymen who gathered
a large following and rose to prominence in churches and religious
movements.[9] The clerical elite is critically important in understanding
the social history of religion in Canada.

This study, therefore, concerns the difficult question of the relationship between the clergy and the people. It rejects the concept of
two distinct religious traditions – one rooted in folklore and popular
beliefs and the other the preserve of a highly educated clergy. The
clergy have been the object of satire and criticism in Canadian popular
culture, as, for example, some of the characters in Stephen Leacock's
fiction suggest; but there has not been a tradition of anti-clericalism in
the Canadian Protestant community. The clergy have been instrumental in shaping popular religion. They have had a prominent role
in forming people's religious beliefs and worship practices since they
continuously espoused certain ideas in their writing and especially

their sermons and constantly led people in worship and other important religious rituals, such as baptism, confirmation, marriage, and funeral services.

Indeed, the clergy have shared a great deal in common with their parishioners, and they have sought to identify closely with them. The Rev. Robert Falconer stressed to the theology students at Pine Hill College that a minister must be 'a friend and comrade ... a director of youth, an adviser for the tempted, a comforter for the sorrowing, weeping with those who weep, rejoicing with those who rejoice.'[10] Many clergy were able to portray the hopes, aspirations, doubts, anger, and fears of the people in their congregations in the most compelling terms. Most preaching was characterized by its plainness. The Christian message was delivered in terms that most people could readily understand. Vivid images as well as parables derived from everyday experiences were frequently employed. By likening worship to farming, the Rev. C.W. Hawkins was able to explain to his rural congregation the importance of worshipping regularly instead of relying upon occasional revival meetings for spiritual sustenance. 'It is not as though the farmer should, after four or five weeks of arduous toil in the spring-time putting in his grain, neglect to take care of them. Weeds might grow, fences be blown down, cattle might trample on his grain, meanwhile he would look on with folded arms, and perhaps lament the desolation, but do nothing until the time to make a special effort again.'[11] Moreover, many sermons and theological addresses were published, especially in the nineteenth century, as a result of public demand or at least the request of members of congregations. Strong clerical leadership, however, did not mean that lay persons were not instrumental and innovative in shaping religion in Protestant Canada.

This book does not attempt to be comprehensive in covering all Protestant denominations. It is primarily concerned with Methodist, Presbyterian, and, after 1925, United church clergymen. In terms of theology, church polity, liturgy, and worship practices Methodism and Presbyterianism were based on different foundations; but their experiences in Canadian society drove them closer together. By the late nineteenth century they were cooperating on a number of fronts. As this book will demonstrate, a great deal of this cooperation was rooted in the realization by the clergy of both these denominations that they were facing a more hostile environment of growing religious pluralism and secularity in which their mission to establish 'His Dominion' across Canada was slipping further away from their grasp. By 1902 serious discussion about union between these two churches was under way.[12] The Baptists also cooperated on a number of fronts with the other evangelical churches and responded in ways broadly similar to the Methodists and Presbyterians to the forces of secularization. But throughout the period under study, the Baptists remained fiercely independent and consistently set themselves apart from the other Protestant denominations.[13] Full integration of the Baptist story would have led to a much longer study; and so discussion of the Baptists' broad-ranging response to the problem of secularization is confined to certain points of comparison.[14] All denominations or faiths have been engaged in a struggle with secularizing pressures; but exactly how they responded has been dependent on a whole range of factors, including theological background, social teaching, church polity, and forms of worship.[15]

Methodists and Presbyterians were the two largest Protestant denominations in Canada. In 1871 there were 578,161 Methodists and 574,577 Presbyterians. Each denomination comprised 15.6 per cent of the total Canadian population. At the turn of the century, in 1901, there were 916,866 Methodists comprising 17.1 per cent of the population and 842,531 Presbyterians comprising 15.7 per cent of the population. In 1921, prior to the 1925 Church Union, there were 1,159,993 Methodists and 1,409,406 Presbyterians, respectively 13 and 16 per cent of the Canadian population. In 1931 the ranks of the United Church of Canada, which included Methodists, Presbyterians, and approximately 30,000 Congregationalists, totalled 2,021,065, which was 19.4 per cent of the total population. The non-concurring Presbyterians numbered 872,428 in 1931, and this amounted to 8.4 per cent of the population. During this period the Roman Catholic church remained the largest Christian church in Canada. The Anglican church's numbers ranged from 501,269 in 1871 to 1,639,075 in 1931, while the Baptists grew from 234,714 adherents in 1871 to 443,944 in 1931. The landscape of Protestantism was also filled with many new denominations during this period. These religious movements tended to be evangelical, such as the Salvation Army, or fundamentalist, such as the Pentecostals, but they did not gather a following large enough to become major denominations. In 1931 there were 30,733 members of the Salvation Army and 26,349 Pentecostals according to the census of Canada.

It should be noted, however, that drawing conclusions regarding religious commitment from statistics must be done cautiously. Fluctuations in church membership, Sunday school enrolment, and church donations depend on many factors besides secularization. Statistics depend on the churches' definitions of membership, which have never been precise or constant; and also how zealously they have been in collecting accurate records. Churches attract the very pious as well as the nominally Christian. In Victorian Canada the church was the centre of some people's lives. They attended Sunday worship regularly, were active in teaching Sunday school, and attended mid-week Bible study classes as well as other church-related activities such as temperance meetings and socials.[16] Other people attended church intermittently. Attendance at church could depend on the calendar year. There might be greater attendance at Thanksgiving, Christmas, and Easter, and in rural communities church attendance probably depended on the demands of agriculture. The stages in people's lives could have an impact on their beliefs. There might be greater willingness to worship with the arrival of children and during old age; whereas other stages might be characterized by indifference. The rites of passage, particularly baptism, confirmation, marriage, and death, were important in the religious life of a family. Moreover, statistics do not indicate the presence of worship in the privacy of the home. Activities such as family prayer or Bible study, singing popular hymns, reading devotional literature or religious fiction, and the purchasing of religious ornaments were an integral part of religious life for many.[17] Census returns and even church membership statistics do not capture the tremendous range of religious practice and commitment. Despite these many shortcomings the churches paid close attention to statistics. They provided a sense of how effective efforts at evangelization were. Statistics had an impact on church policies and strategies.

Perhaps the most interesting figures in the census returns for religion were the numbers indicating 'no religion.' The returns for 1901 and 1911 were particularly significant. In 1901, 6,193 people stated that they had no religion, and one decade later 26,893 people stated that they fell into this category. According to the census return this figure included 10,770 agnostics and 4,450 atheists. This dramatic increase probably reflects an important change in Canadian social attitudes as opposed to a sudden conversion of many to the atheistic or agnostic position. Perhaps people who had been quietly harbouring secularist ideas were more willing to confess their unorthodox position. During the Victorian era any public pronouncement of religious disbelief was a challenge to the convention that all respectable citizens led pious lives, and it brought a certain degree of social exclusion.[18] Disapproval of those holding iconoclastic beliefs was being eased by the late-Victorian period as it became increasingly evident that Christian beliefs no longer held a monopoly in Canada. As Ramsay Cook has demonstrated, late-Victorian Canada was populated by an array of outspoken and colourful free-thinkers, spiritualists, and secularists as well as labour advocates and social reformers who had abandoned much of orthodox Christianity and had left the confines of the church to pursue the goal of constructing a Christian social order.[19] The prominence of such individuals indicated the degree to which unbelief was a credible alternative to Christian belief and the extent to which such ideas were being tolerated in Canadian society.

Until very recently the writing of Canadian Protestant religious history has been dominated by the theme of progress and growth as opposed to decline and secularization. Few Canadian church historians pursued Dewart's observations about the role of the clergy and the churches in the rise of scepticism and secularization. Throughout the Victorian age the idea of Providence was central to the understanding of history. The Rev. Alexander Sutherland's explanation for the success of the Canadian Methodist church's missionary effort was typical. Methodism, he explained, was 'the child of Providence. No elaborate plans were formulated in advance ... men who had felt the constraining power of the love of Christ ... went forth at the call of God, exhorting men everywhere to repent and believe the Gospel.'[20] Events were interpreted within the context of an outpouring of the Holy Spirit or in terms of God's unfolding design. It was thought that God intervened directly in the lives of individuals as well as the affairs of society and the churches for the purposes of reward, edification, or chastisement. The growth of the churches was understood to be a result of divine favour. For example, the Rev. Thomas Webster suggested that the growth of the Methodist Episcopal church in Upper Canada could only be explained by God's approval, since this church was a branch of Methodism with roots in the United States and consequently it was constantly subjected to the 'malicious slander' that it was 'disloyal' and under 'foreign ecclesiastical control.'[21] These historians considered the church to be a unique institution with a history that somehow transcended secular developments.

Denominational development was the organizing principle of most histories. The accounts glorified the exploits of heroic figures who forged religious institutions in 'uncivilized areas.' A common technique employed to document the progress of a denomination was to record the growing number of churches, mission posts, and ministers. It was assumed that church membership, in particular, provided concrete evidence of the increasing commitment to Christianity. Sunday schools, universities, denominational newspapers, and religious and devotional literature were regarded as evidence of the churches' ongoing progress.[22]

In the late nineteenth century church historians did not sound any notes of trouble. There was no hint of the difficulties confronting the churches. The challenge of science and critical inquiry was not analysed; the struggle that clergymen had in maintaining their adherence to orthodox standards, made public by a number of heresy trials, was not mentioned; and finally, the problem of attracting the urban masses to the churches was overlooked as part of the story. Even Dewart, who was pessimistic about the church's prospects in his essays and editorials, succumbed to a progressive interpretation in his historical writing. In an essay on the Methodist Church of Canada between 1874 and 1884 he emphasized the theme of progress and suggested that the history of the period was uneventful as a result. He approvingly cited Lord Macaulay's statement that 'the time of a country's greatest prosperity is the time of least historic interest. This is certainly true with regard to Church history. Periods when no striking event happens, and no great controversy stirs the community, may be times of great spiritual progress; and yet there may be nothing very remarkable to record.'[23] Those arguing the opposite, such as Goldwin Smith in his pessimistic essay on the future of religion, 'The Prospect of a Moral Interregnum,' were dismissed as 'Cassandra-like prophets of evil' and 'apostles of complaint and despondency.'[24] Perhaps Dewart and other chroniclers of the progress of the church and religion were taking comfort from a nostalgic view of the recent past because of their growing concern.[25]

E.H. Oliver's *The Winning of the Frontier* (1930) is considered 'the first serious attempt to submit the church history of the nation to historical analysis.'[26] Oliver was an ordained Presbyterian minister who had been trained as a scientific historian at Columbia University in the first decade of the twentieth century. Like many other historians writing in the 1920s and 1930s Oliver was deeply influenced by Frederick Jackson Turner's 'frontier thesis.' His analysis of Canadian Protestant churches was a major development, for it was shaped by the canons of secular historiography rather than a sense of Providence. He was aware of the relationship between church history and secular forces, but he did not abandon the progressive or heroic tradition of Canadian Protestant historiography. Oliver was also influenced by the works of the missionary chroniclers writing in the first decades of the twentieth century, such as Alexander Sutherland, C.W. Gordon, and James Woodsworth.[27] He was particularly influenced by Sutherland's dramatic account of Canadian Methodist missions published in 1904. It helped to persuade him to become a student missionary for the Presbyterian church in Saskatchewan.[28] *The Winning of the Frontier* concentrated on areas of church growth and phases of successful missionary enterprise. Once an area had passed out of its frontier stage and its churches had become established, Oliver's attention passed to the next frontier and another period of heroic missionary activity and energetic church building. The narrative concluded by discussing the West, which he indicated was the present source of energy and renewal for the churches. It was the example of church life on the Prairies, Oliver stressed, that had inspired Canadian Protestantism's greatest achievement, the Church Union of 1925.

One indication of how deeply rooted this theme of progress has been was the response to S.D. Clark's classic study, *Church and Sect in Canada* (1948), which was the antithesis of the progressive or heroic tradition.[29] Clark argued that Canadian religious life was characterized by two antithetical trends, both determined by the complex interplay of economic and social factors. In new social settings or frontiers sectarian religion, which was evangelical and other-worldly in character, flourished while in more developed areas, especially urban centres, sectarian religion retreated and was replaced with the 'territorial church' which identified itself with the dominant ethos of secular society. By 1860 the conditions necessary to support evangelical religious values no longer existed, according to Clark. There was a 'strengthening of worldly attitudes and outlook,' and the secular values of business ruled church policies. The best example of this secularization was the Church Union of 1925. Clark employed the metaphor of the market-place to explain that competition among the churches had become keener as the appeal of religion became more restricted. Ultimately this competition had become so wasteful that consolidation of effort and service through union was adopted 'as a means of cutting down overhead costs.'[30] For Clark, church union movements were evidence of the decline of religion as opposed to an indication of progress towards the reunification of Christianity.

Not surprisingly, church historians sharply criticized Clark's analysis of religious decline. H.H. Walsh set the tone when he attacked Clark for making Christianity the product of social and economic forces while ignoring the essential point that the history of Christianity was rooted in the historic fact of Christ's mysterious resurrection.[31] This hostile reaction to Clark's study was part of a general sense of crisis among church historians who were faced with the immensely difficult task of developing a critical narrative of the Christian past based on the scientific standards of modern historiography without completely undermining a sense of Providence.[32] This concept could not be completely abandoned by the church historian without sacrificing a major premise of the Christian faith: God's real presence in human history. But church historians could no longer assume that the church was an institution that somehow completely transcended secular influences. The issue of whether change in religious beliefs and institutions was merely the result of social and economic pressures or was also the product of an inner search for spiritual truth had to be confronted.

A new school of church historians, eager to integrate Canadian church history with the story of Canadian national development, emerged in the 1950s and 1960s. They documented the positive influence religion and the churches had upon Canadian national life, demonstrated how church history reflected broader social and political developments, and identified the uniqueness of Canadian church life.[33] The hand of Providence was fading into the background of analysis. On the issue of secularization this nationalist school denied the presence of significant decline or crisis of religious faith. That secularization was a process deeply rooted in the intellectual life, consumer culture, and emerging urban industrial society of Victorian Canada was not seriously contemplated.

In one of the most important books from this school, *The Church in the Canadian Era: The First Century of Confederation*, John Webster Grant concluded that the 1960s brought about 'the passing of Christian Canada.' Secularization was presented as a very recent and sudden event, strictly the result of the turbulent 1960s, when the 'God is dead' argument seemed to be winning many converts. According to Grant, the 1960s was the first era in which the Christianization of Canada was interrupted. But even this admission of real crisis in the churches could not shake Grant's confidence in ongoing religious progress. He thought that the secularization of the 1960s was transitory, speculating that it was a preparation for the further Christianizing of Canada. 'A period of exile to the periphery of power,' Grant suggested, 'might well release Christian energies that had been smothered for centuries.'[34] The prospect of secular forces becoming victorious could not be integrated into the traditional interpretation of Canadian religious history. The outlook of this important nationalist school is well summarized by John Moir in his preface to *Enduring Witness*:

> Certainly in the history of this country the servants of the church have always stood in the front ranks of its cultural and social development ... Religion has played a central role in shaping the Canadian character and making the Canadian experience. In obvious, but also in subtle, almost indefinable ways, the influence of the Christian church has made Canadians into religiously motivated individuals. The whole Judeo-Christian tradition is so deeply infused into the fabric of Canadian life that even modern secularists have unconsciously accepted its values and its forms of expression.[35]

This nationalist school marked the end of a cloistered church history. No longer was the study of religion in Canadian society confined to the sanctuary of church history.

Historians who were determined to make church and religious history a part of the mainstream began to explore the complex relation between the sacred and the secular. All have agreed that secular society posed tremendous challenges for the churches in Canada, but whether they have met the challenge and survived in tact has become a tremendously controversial issue. The first study to investigate these questions was also the most direct attack on S.D. Clark's thesis of religious disintegration. In *The Social Passion: Religion and Social Reform in Canada, 1914–1928* Richard Allen argued that urban-industrial society fostered a new Christianity, one that was instilled with a social conscience. This social gospel provided a framework for the Protestant church's ability to thrive in modern Canadian society.[36] While Allen argued that the churches were renewed and religion was on the vanguard of a new social ethic, others were suggesting that a scientific world-view was replacing the Christian one and that in urban-industrial society there were numerous indications of decline in the moral authority of the churches and in religious commitment.[37] A number of historians studying various aspects of cultural, social, and intellectual

life in late-nineteenth- and early twentieth-century Canada, most notably Brian McKillop, Ramsay Cook, and William Westfall, have argued that secularization was a dominant trend in modern Canada.[38]
Indeed a new orthodoxy seems to be emerging in Canadian historiography: the outcome of the quest to stem the tide of secularization
and to redeem and transform the secular world into the Kingdom of
God, ironically, has been the triumph of the forces of secularization.

This interpretation, however, has not remained unchallenged. In
his masterly study, *A Profusion of Spires: Religion in Nineteenth-Century
Ontario*, J.W. Grant considered the work of these historians and concluded 'that the churches were subject to stresses that belied their
triumphal language.' But he wondered whether it is correct to interpret
the confusion and doubt regarding essential questions, such as the
nature of the authority of the Bible, as evidence of decline. He acknowledged that industrialization and urbanization had a weakening
effect on religious institutions but concluded that 'social developments
over which the churches had little control, rather than their response
to them, were the most significant precursors of twentieth-century
secularization.'[39] Contrary to what E.H. Dewart was suggesting a
century ago, Grant argued that secularization was something that
primarily happened to religion and the church, rather than being a
process in which the churches and clergy played an direct and integral
role.

In his various studies of evangelicalism and Baptist higher education George Rawlyk has suggested that secularization is best understood as a process of 'internal decay' rather than 'external attacks'
and has departed from the traditional emphasis on Darwinian evolution, critical biblical scholarship, and the emergence of comparative
religion as the most important forces in 'shattering' the evangelical
faith. Instead he has suggested that 'consumerism may have had a far
greater impact on the nineteenth century consensus.'[40] There is also
more fundamental questioning about whether secularization exists
and to what extent religious beliefs and institutions themselves have
become secularized.[41] The thrust of Marguerite Van Die's study of the
Methodist divine Nathanael Burwash was to challenge the secularization thesis on the grounds that there has been an essential continu-
ity in evangelical religion in Canada from the mid-Victorian period to
1918. The change within Methodism from initially emphasizing personal salvation to focusing subsequently on social regeneration was
not an indication of secularization, she argues, but rather a way for it

to remain prophetic within changing cultural and social conditions.[42]

That there is such controversy is hardly surprising, for the process of secularization is extremely complex and subtle. To argue that society is becoming increasingly secular does not mean that religious faith and institutions disappear. Beliefs linger, people still worship, congregations persist, and churches survive. Religion continues to influence individuals and a variety of institutions, social movements, and ideals; but it is no longer at the core of social, intellectual, or cultural life. Secularization cannot be viewed as a necessarily linear, irreversible, or inevitable process. Religious decline may also be halted, briefly, or temporarily reversed in an age of secularization. Religious revivals may occur in counteraction to the decay of faith. Moreover, in all societies there are tragedies and grim realities suggesting human powerlessness and, perhaps, sinfulness which may invigorate a religious quest for the supernatural. It is also important to stress that the secular should not be simply regarded as the opposite of religion. Ruth Brouwer's sensitive analysis of what compelled Presbyterian women to volunteer for foreign mission work demonstrates that it is impossible to separate the sacred from the secular in assessing motivation or actions.[43] In early twentieth-century Canada scientific-minded social work was rooted in a Christian-inspired social gospel and missionary impulse. Much of the investigation and analysis of social problems, despite the emphasis on the scientific method, was still influenced by religious concepts.[44] The sacred and the secular form a complex, somehow reciprocal, and interdependent relationship. These complexities make it often difficult to discern the process of secularization. Nevertheless, it has occurred.

There has been keen debate surrounding the question of when secularization became a significant factor in Canadian history. A crisis, serious break from the past, or a 'take-off point' for secularization has been identified by many authors. Brian McKillop's study of the rise of critical inquiry and Ramsay Cook's exploration of the emergence of social criticism identify a serious break from a past of religious certainty in the late nineteenth century. Michael Gauvreau's recent study argues that the tenets of evangelical religion were remarkably resistant throughout the nineteenth century. Despite his sustained attack on the secularization thesis he suggests that there was a serious crisis in which theologians lost their intellectual and moral influence in Canadian life and the colleges were separated from the congregations. This break from the nineteenth-century evangelical consensus,

Gauvreau estimates, occurred during 1905–14 and was caused by the emergence of 'historical relativism.'[45] Such narrow precision about the chronology of the loss of certainty in religion and theology overlooks the complex interplay of long-standing forces that contributed to secularization. When clergymen were confronted by new challenges to religious faith, they often characterized the times as being at a critical point, with religion and the church in peril of being over-whelmed by secular activities and material concerns. The constant sense of crisis expressed by the clergy suggests that there was not any one crisis that can be identified as a turning point, but rather a whole series of deeply rooted trends that were challenging religion and the churches.

This book argues that there was not a crisis or a serious rupture from a religious past. The process of secularization in Canada, for the most part, was slow and at times almost imperceptible. Throughout the nineteenth century the churches flourished, and evangelicalism remained a part of the religious life of many Canadians; but there were significant social and political pressures as well as cultural and intellectual challenges that were undermining the evangelical con-sensus and the churches' dominant role in society. As a result, nu-merous accommodations were made by the churches and clergy to the demands of popular culture, which in subtle ways had the effect of secularizing the faith from within. There was neither a great break from a religious past nor an enduring and unyielding evangelical tradition. Compromises were made within the evangelical creed which transformed its message and character to something that was more concerned with this world and more attuned to the tastes and de-mands of consumer culture. This study pushes back to the 1840s and 1850s, when there were clear signs of secularization pressures from the political arena with respect to central institutions in Canadian society, and then beyond the Great War to the 1920s and 1930s, when many of the trends that were only emerging in the late nineteenth century had become much clearer. Secularization is something that ran deep in the Canadian experience. It was not just a crisis experienced by the late-Victorian generation or by those touched by the Great War. By necessity a chronology of secularization in Canada must remain imprecise, for like other major changes in the structure of society, such as industrialization or urbanization, its genesis is far too complex and its course much too varied.

To suggest that secularization was underway throughout the nineteenth century does not indicate that a 'golden age' of religiosity previously existed. Both Methodism and Presbyterianism in Canada were part of a broader transatlantic evangelical culture, a religious movement that began in the eighteenth century to counter the strong secularizing pressures that were overtaking Christianity.[46] Evangelicalism was a revolt against indifference and, in particular, an overly rational faith that was insensitive to the emotional and mysterious elements in religion. Evangelicals were determined to revitalize 'the dry bones of the Church' and to reform 'the godless ways of contemporary society.'[47]

In pioneer British North American society preachers frequently denounced the lack of religious piety as they travelled through the backwoods of the colonies. Drinking, dancing, gambling, and horseracing seemed to be common pastimes. Sunday was likely to be a day for amusements, not religious edification and worship. In 1809 William Case, an itinerant Methodist preacher, wrote the following of the Thames River area of Upper Canada:

> This country, perhaps, is the most wicked and dissipated of any part of America ... The holy Sabbath has no preference over any other day, except that they make choice of it as a day of wicked amusements, visiting in parties, often dancing, hunting, fishing, &c. For drunkenness and fornication I suppose no place is more noted ... Many of the people know little of the Bible, having never learned to read. And some of these who can read have had no Bible in their families; nor did they think they needed any, for some have openly blasphemed the name of the Lord Jesus, and spoke of the Virgin Mary in a manner too shocking to repeat.[48]

Some of this rhetoric was, perhaps, more reflective of the evangelical ethos than actual conditions in Upper Canada, for evangelicalism had a strong other-worldly emphasis which constantly called for conversion. One way to encourage a religious revival was to exaggerate the immoral conduct of the sin-stricken, materialistic world.

By 1821, however, Case was claiming that Upper Canada was a regenerate society. He observed that as a result of the many conversions 'we are prospering finely in this country ... Churches are crowded with hearers. Youth and children, instead of wandering the fields, or loitering in the streets are in many places, thronging to the schools, books in hand, and learning to read the book of God.'[49] The numerous moral and social reform movements in British North American society, such as those for temperance, education, relief of the poor, sabbath observance, abolition of slavery, and prison reform, were often spearheaded by the evangelicals. The clergy could well claim that they were instrumental in rescuing British North America from spiritual ruin; but they clearly were interacting with a society in which many were preoccupied with secular affairs and were to a significant degree indifferent to religious beliefs and authority.

The most significant characteristic about religious life in the formative period of Canadian history was that the landscape of the early nineteenth-century British North American colonies was cluttered with a great variety of denominations.[50] Religious pluralism required some degree of tolerance for the differing religious beliefs and forms of worship that were flourishing in Canadian soil. The Baptists, who were staunch advocates of the separation of church and state and believed in the independent self-government of each congregation over which no temporal or church authority could be imposed, were most clear about the necessity and justice of 'liberty of conscience.' The Rev. E.W. Dadson, one-time editor of the *Canadian Baptist*, wrote that 'every man has the right to believe what he pleases, without interference or proscription; and when, because of that belief, the State denies him privileges which are freely accorded to those who believe otherwise, violence is done to that part of him over which God, and He alone, has any controlling right.'[51] In British North America there was intense competition for souls, conflict over church-state relations, and keen debate over the most fundamental questions.[52] As no one denomination was dominant there could not be an established religious faith; and so 'official' religious toleration was legislated in the 1840s and 1850s to deal with the Protestant-Catholic duality and the quest of the many dissenting denominations for equality. As John Moir has pointed out, the dismantling of the established church was not a matter of religious decline, but rather a political solution to the social and religious realities of Canadian life.[53]

Nevertheless, the disestablishment of religion has proven to be an essential precondition in the process of secularization. Egerton Ryerson seemed to be keenly aware of the broader implications of the principle of civil and religious liberty in Canada. He suggested that without the established church 'the Holy Scriptures [were] the only source of authority in matters of religion' and that everyone had gained 'undeniable and inviolable right of private judgement in all matters of religious faith and duty, irrespective of civil governmental authority.'[54]

Without an established religion there is no single authority, and as a result diverse beliefs, practices, and institutions flourish. D.A. MacGregor, a prominent Baptist educator, confronted the implications of religious tolerance and liberty by explaining in his 1878 valedictory address at Woodstock College that there was a growing popular perception that if 'the fundamental doctrines held by one denomination are flatly denied by another ... the beliefs of both cannot be true.' The dangerous result, he warned, could be 'an epidemic of loose-reined speculation ... in reference to fundamental doctrines.'[55] 'Toleration,' Herbert Butterfield has written, 'by paths almost too intricate to trace,' has led to religious liberty and in its train 'that whole tendency which the historian likes to call the process of secularization.'[56]

According to Owen Chadwick, a liberal society tends to develop in the direction of a secular society, since 'a free market in opinions becomes a reality; on grounds of right of conscience, and duty of toleration, and principles of equity and expediency in a world of disagreement.' Such freedom had to be extended to irreligious opinion as well as the numerous dissenting forms of Christian faith. Such diversity in religious beliefs and practices would lead to debate, an essential prerequisite for the development of doubt. Chadwick suggested that J.S. Mill's *On Liberty* was as symbolically important to an understanding of secularization as Charles Darwin's *Origin of Species*, the book usually associated with the dawning of the age of religious doubt.[57]

Accompanying this recognition of the necessity of religious toleration were profound changes in the status of religion in major Canadian institutions, especially in the schools. Prior to the 1840s the Upper Canadian school system was dominated by the churches and clergy, and the use of the Bible in the classroom was explicitly sanctioned and encouraged. Religious diversity made the continuation of this system impossible, for it was thought that sectarian controversy in the schools should be avoided. The reforms that Ryerson introduced in 1846 ended the use of the Bible as a textbook. A truly secular education, however, was unthinkable. Ryerson's influential 1846 *Report on a System of Public Elementary Instruction* stressed 'the absolute necessity of making Christianity the basis and cement of the structure of public education.' The Lord's Prayer and the Ten Commandments were recited and there were readings from the Scriptures. Ryerson was able to defend the presence of the Bible in the schools as a 'symbol of right and liberty dear to the heart of every Protestant freeman, to every lover of civil and religious liberty – a standard of truth and morals, the foundation of Protestant faith, and the rule of Protestant morals.' The religious instruction that was allowed in the schools was based on Ryerson's notion of 'common Christianity,' which emphasized morality and cited the Bible as an authoritative guide for good citizenship. An equally important principle within the school legislation was the protection of the freedom of conscience of all students. It was stipulated in the School Acts that no pupil shall be required 'to read or study in or from any religious book or join in any exercise of devotion or religion objected to.'[58] In the Ontario schools, therefore, religious instruction emphasized moral and social utility as opposed to its evangelical doctrines, and even this relaxed Christianity was not imposed.

By the 1850s the churches and clergy were losing their central role in the schools. Clergymen ceased to be teachers in the classrooms as they were replaced by professionals, and clergymen-trustees became a minority. Under Ryerson's reforms the schools became civil institutions. According to the authors of a recent study of secondary education in Ontario, this secularization – or laicization – of the schools did not happen dramatically but nevertheless 'represented one more step in the larger story of the secularization of nineteenth century society.'[59] The modern liberal state was emerging in Canadian society. The principle of toleration was established, and the churches in Canada were no longer protected. Religion could not be imposed, and adherence to any particular faith was voluntary. Churches had to compete with each other and with secular institutions, such as the schools and the bureaucratic state. Religion, therefore, had many rivals for the attention of the people.

During this early period there were also significant developments in the material and cultural life of Canadians. William Westfall has pointed out that a powerful new social ethic gained currency in British North America: an ethic which regarded economic development and material progress, rather than religion, as the foundation for a stable social order.[60] The 1840s and 1850s marked the dawning of the intertwining industrial and consumer revolutions. As Rosalind Williams has argued, the consumer revolution was 'a pivotal historical moment ... for the first time in history, many people have considerable choice in what to consume, how, and how much, and in addition have the leisure, education, and health to ponder these questions. The consumer revolution brought both the opportunity and the need to reassess values.'[61] Pinpointing the beginnings of the consumer revolution in Canada is impossible; but the diaries and letters of pioneer families often paid a great deal of attention to the acquisition of material goods and luxury items.[62] In the eyes of many clergymen 'the love of gain' was becoming the dominant value and activity in the colonies.[63] What is important in relation to this study is that consumer culture gave people an ever-growing variety of choices. In terms of what institutions and activities would attract peoples' time and resources the churches were far from the only alternative. Secularization, then, involves much more than changing beliefs and thought; it also involves changes in the choices people make regarding their daily life. It is as much a matter of social and cultural history as it is of intellectual history. In a modern liberal society such as Canada the key to understanding the process of secularization rests in the fact that religion and the churches are part of a pluralistic society and are thrust into a market-place of competing ideas, values, activities, and institutions.[64]

1

Clergymen and the Problem of Religious Doubt

The one thing that Methodist and Presbyterian clergymen in Canada were certain of during the latter half of the nineteenth century was that they were living in an age of religious doubt. They sensed a disturbing lack of 'anchorage' in people's religious faith, and their own writings gave witness to a pressing burden of religious turmoil. The whole range of Christian faith and practice was brought into question. Is God present? Is there a divine purpose? Is the Bible divinely inspired and infallible? Is Christianity a true religion? Is there life after death? Is what the churches preach moral? Many clergymen well understood, through their own experience, that such doubts could ultimately lead to greater understanding and deeper piety. Nevertheless, the widespread currency of these questions was the source of their persistent concern. Although a complete loss of faith was rare, a constant struggle and sense of despair often resulted. It is more accurate to describe the Victorian age in Canada as one of much serious thought and debate about religion rather than one of unquestioning faith and great piety.

The source of many clergymen's profound disquiet was growing doubt regarding the major tenets of evangelical Christianity. Constant reference to the fallen state, emphasis on the need for personal conversion, and the reaffirmation of God's saving grace characterized evangelical worship. But this orthodox evangelicalism had become so commonplace – and in some cases hackneyed – that it was losing its power and effectiveness. Notions of human depravity and vivid depiction of the horrors of damnation or consequences of sin often stimulated emotions no stronger than indifference. When stated too boldly or directly, the response could be flat denial instead of penitent conversion.

The Methodist, Presbyterian, and Baptist traditions in Canada were based on evangelical Christianity.[1] The distinguishing feature of the evangelical faith was its emphasis on becoming aware of God in the depths of the heart. Evangelicals were convinced that God was constantly rewarding, admonishing, and punishing individuals. It was believed that God directly created fears, desires, hopes, and assurances regarding personal salvation. One prolific Presbyterian layman explained that 'providential dispensations, by severe bodily complaints – by dangers and deliverances – deaths of relatives or friends, are also divinely made to produce ... awakening and salutary effects.'[2] During the cholera epidemic of 1832 Thomas Webster 'felt calm, trusting to God, and I resolved that I would not run into danger ... I had a slight attack of cholera but through the mercy of God soon recovered.' According to Webster, who became an itinerant preacher with the Methodist Episcopal church in 1838, those who died of the cholera were the 'profane and intemperate.'[3]

For many living in the early and mid-nineteenth century the world was a dangerous place in which drought, storms, crop failure, fires, epidemics, and countless other afflictions threatened one's precarious existence. There seemed to be few explanations for events, and therefore many occurrences seemed to be the result of the supernatural or some form of divine intervention. For example, George Young experienced a series of inexplicable events during his boyhood in Upper Canada, which for him was direct evidence of divine Providence. One morning he was in the basement of the barn feeding the cattle when 'a terrific wind storm, a veritable tornado, struck the building, and by its marvelous force crushed the entire structure to the earth, as if it had been a child's playhouse.' Young recalled that when he heard the crash of the falling and breaking timbers, he 'was instantly prompted to fall on my knees and pray. Responding immediately to the prompting, the prayer of the penitent publican was earnestly uttered, and I fully believe, instantly answered.' Apparently, if he had not been kneeling to pray the falling beams and timber would have 'crushed [him] to death.' According to Young there was only one explanation for this good fortune:

Had I been disobedient to the prompting and remained standing, I must have been instantly killed. Whence came that prompting to kneel and pray – was it from within or from above? ... Of the many who came that day to view the ruins all seemed, as they took in the situation, to regard my escape as miraculous and many unhesitatingly declared it to be so. How could they do otherwise? ... I believe in God as Preserver as well as Creator, and that it was He and He alone that 'redeemed my life from destruction.'[4]

All events, even everyday ones, were considered by many to be harbingers of God's will.

Central to the evangelical faith was the belief that humankind was sunk in original sin and that the soul stood in peril of eternal death and damnation. There could be salvation, however, since Christ had died on the cross for sinfulness. If one allowed God's grace to enter the soul and recognized that Christ was Saviour, then one would be restored to divine favour and receive life everlasting. Individual conversion – to be 'born again' – was essential. Evangelicals insisted that the individual was unable to achieve salvation without God's merciful love and sacrifice. These religious beliefs were sanctioned by the divinely inspired Scriptures, which evangelicals insisted were the very Word of God. This doctrine of divine inspiration did not imply a mechanical process of dictation to the scribes. Rather, as one Canadian Methodist explained, 'by inspiration we mean the Holy Ghost so controlling and directing the mind as to preclude all error, prompting the agent to state only the truth.'[5]

The major tenets of the evangelical faith were impressed upon congregations with intense zeal. Most evangelical sermons were preached extemporaneously. It was thought that the preacher delivering a spontaneous sermon or exhortation was guided by the Holy Spirit. The consequences of remaining in sin or refusing to join in the fellowship of Christian converts were outlined in dramatic, sensational, and even frightening terms. 'Sin,' a Niagara Conference circuit preacher affirmed, 'carries with it a sense of shame and degradation. By it, communion with God has been broken off; peace banished from his bosom; pain darkens both mental and moral, misery and despair have taken the place, and finally if persisted in, eternal destruction from the presence of God [sic].'[6] This disjointed but descriptive imagery was designed to impress its listeners with the im-

perative of conversion. There was always an element of warning in
evangelical preaching for the prospect of damnation provided incentive for conversion. For example, shortly after George Young escaped
certain death, he experienced conversion. The occasion was the funeral
service of a friend. At the burial service an exhorter warned those
present that they should become reconciled to God immediately before
they also were 'suddenly stricken out of life.'[7] But, as most evangelical clergy insisted, it was the hope of life everlasting that led people
through conversion. The objective of conversion was not escape from
sin and guilt, but rather to secure 'eternal salvation and happiness.'
Ultimately evangelicalism emphasized the assurance of salvation. It
was a religion of hope rather than despair.[8]

Although subscription to certain doctrines was an important element
in the evangelical faith, a vivid and compelling religious experience
and a sense of God's abiding presence were paramount. As J.E.
Sanderson noted in his history of Methodism in Canada, 'repentance,
the new birth, pardon and holiness were not preached as forms or
professions, but as blessed realities, experienced and attested.'[9]
Evangelicals stressed experience and religious sensation or feeling.
Without the experience of regeneration and salvation, one Presbyterian
warned, religion was 'merely ceremonial or formal and heartless.'[10]
Repentance, Egerton Ryerson explained, 'is the sorrowful consciousness of guilt, and a throbbing desire for forgiveness.'[11] Evangelicals
understood that sinfulness was a condition in which one's consciousness of God was faint and grew ever weaker; redemption was a
condition in which one's sense of God remained vivid, strong, and
capable of growth.

For many living in mid-Victorian Canada, however, the experience
of a dramatic conversion was full of doubt, and the sense of God's
direct and guiding role in their lives was not entirely certain. Albert
Carman was forced to come to terms with his God during a particularly
disruptive period in his life. Carman was born on 27 June 1833 into a
prominent family from Iroquois, Upper Canada, on the shores of the
St Lawrence River. In 1855, after graduating from the Methodist
church's Victoria College in Cobourg, he returned to his hometown
and became headmaster of the county grammar school. As one of the
better-educated townsfolk, he gave public lectures on the virtues of
temperance and self-improvement as well as the uplifting influence
of religion on the social fabric.[12] Then on 9 May 1856 he was autho-
rized to serve as a local preacher on the Matilda circuit of the Methodist

Episcopal church. He had hardly begun his itinerancy when the Belleville Seminary, the newly established college of the Methodist Episcopal church, appointed him instructor in mathematics. After the first year of operation, in which controversy raged over debt, sources of funding, codes of discipline, and the largely American origin of the faculty, Carman was appointed principal.

During this period of upheaval and challenge in his life, Carman 'consecrated himself wholly to God.' In confiding letters to his father he outlined his experience. 'The Heavenly Comforter and Guide led me by a way which I knew not ... I knew not why the Holy Spirit was feeling around in the soil of my inner nature and the roots of sin, laying hold of them and extracting them one by one till my bleeding lacerated heart lay on the foot of the Cross. I understand not why I was shown what it is to live by faith ... Now I see it all. I believe myself to be here by Divine direction.' Initially, this experience was accompanied by an exultant sense of release from a sinful past and a strong feeling that after much struggle a close relationship with God had been established. Carman clearly felt that he could overcome the obstacles in his way since 'the Heavenly Father hath given me grace sufficient for my day and in His strength I stand.'[13]

Shortly after this conversion experience Carman recorded his personal covenant with God: 'it is my unceasing duty to devote all I have and am to His service.' Hoping that God was constantly near, he prayed that he would be granted the strength, wisdom, and grace to fulfil the obligation of the covenant, for he understood that he was 'so weak and worldly and temptations were so strong ... that unless Thou sustain me I shall fall: my mind and heart are so corrupted by sin that unless Thou purify them and lift me up out of myself, evil thoughts and motives will creep into even this decision and action, which I really wish to be pure and conformable to the spotless requirements of the Holy Word.'[14] This crucial period in Carman's life was characterized by agonizing periods of self-examination and soul searching. In a fashion typical of the evangelical temperament Carman had grave doubts about the validity of his religious experience since in his view it was not sufficiently powerful or emotional, and he worried about whether his commitment to a Christian life would be sustained.

It was necessary for earnest evangelicals to develop methods of self-examination and to chart their spiritual progress for they were obsessed with the Divine Judgment which awaited them at death.

Constant vigilance against backsliding had to be maintained as evangelicals were keenly aware of the dreadful consequences of failing to lead a useful and Christian life. According to the evangelical creed, salvation entailed much more than a conversion experience, and adherence to religious doctrine was more than a solemn intellectual pastime. Within evangelicalism there was no clear-cut dichotomy between one's personal relation with God and commitment to building a social order based on Christian principles; they were integrally related. The evangelical faith was an 'active faith'; and therefore one had to account for the way in which one lived. The Methodists designed the weekly class meeting with these concerns in mind. Another way to keep account of one's spiritual condition was to keep a diary. Many Methodists kept spiritual journals following the advice of John Wesley. William Case recorded a journal while he was an itinerant minister in Upper Canada between 1803 and 1807, and it provides fascinating insights into his many spiritual visions and dreams and his unshakable conviction that he was being directed by God in his arduous labours in the backwoods.[15]

The journals and diaries of the evangelical clergy are particularly illuminating in uncovering their inner world of religious beliefs and doubts. For example, William Cochrane had kept a diary since 1840. Shortly after his ordination in 1859 he abandoned his diary, and he did not return to it until 1870, when he had been called to the ministry at the thriving Zion Presbyterian Church in Brantford, Ontario. It seems that Cochrane resumed his diary as a means to keep an account of his Christian stewardship. 'I begin again', he wrote, 'trusting for grace ... I hope it may assist me in being more diligent in my Master's work ... that I may be shamed into a more perfect consecration of myself.' Cochrane's diary frequently took the form of a list of his clerical pursuits: devotional study, sermon writing, attending church meetings, mission work, and pastoral visitation. Despite this evidence of a pious life in which ministerial responsibilities were faithfully carried out, he continually expressed doubts about his devotion. On 31 December 1893 he reflected on his year's work: 'the record has been to me a humbling one ... what of the results – good from an outside view, but spiritually not so comforting. Oh for greater zeal, faith, and unselfish work.'[16]

Similarly, John Mockett Cramp, the prominent Baptist author who became president of Acadia College in Wolfville, Nova Scotia, referred to his meditations and prayers in his diary:

1. How is my heart affected in prayer? Is there a spirit of adoption?
2. Do I realize the presence and the character of God?
3. Do I feel a sense of my insignificance and vileness? ... Am I watchful over my besetting sin? Do I cultivate those virtues and graces in which I am most deficient?
4. What have I read lately, and with what spiritual advantage? Have I had any edifying intercourse with my Christian brethren?[17]

Cramp's diary suggests that he struggled to lead a Christian life, and he possessed a grim determination and solemn resolve to do good. Such earnest and melancholic introspection, as revealed in the Cochrane and Cramp diaries, was typical of the evangelical temperament.

Spiritual autobiographies by clergymen show that there were grave doubts about the emotional requirements and central notions of orthodox evangelicalism. There was an element of 'literary formula' in evangelical writings, especially those that chronicled the struggle from sin to redemption and outlined the challenge in leading a devout life. But the fact that this story or framework dominated much of the literature, whether it be in the form of diary, letters, unpublished memoir, published autobiography, or religious fiction, indicates that such religious experiences were central to many people's beliefs and understanding of their religious condition. Some form of doubt, therefore, was at the heart of popular religion.

Typical of this struggle was Nathanael Burwash's religious development in the 1850s. Burwash was raised in an Upper Canadian family in which the Methodist faith was the ruling force. Marguerite Van Die's recent study emphasizes that family worship, especially under the guidance of his mother, Anne Taylor, was much more formative than Sunday school, itinerant preachers, or camp meetings in shaping Burwash's evangelical faith.[18] One of Burwash's contemporaries recalled that while growing up in a Scottish Baptist community in the Ottawa Valley 'every dinner table was a theological class, and with the pork and potatoes went the Calvinism and Arminianism in due course. The Bible was the family hand-book, and handled reverently, it was the arbiter of the daily discussion.'[19]

Burwash remembered that during family worship, after Scripture reading, reciting the Catechism, and hymn singing, 'came the talk about sin and its awful consequences.' Two things had become clear to the young Burwash: 'I was a sinner; and I needed, must have,

forgiveness if I would escape the terrible punishment of sin.' Wanting to know whether God had forgiven his sins caused terrible anguish
for Burwash. He prayed earnestly and continued to attend the meetings
led by Methodist exhorters, but became discouraged as all he heard
was that he must 'believe in order to get the blessing.' This only left
him perplexed for 'what faith meant, and how to believe was still a
mystery.' God seemed difficult to reach for he seemed to be 'a holy
God before whom sin was an awful thing.'[20]

When Burwash entered Victoria College at Cobourg in 1852, there
was intense religious activity among the students and in the town.
The students held daily prayer meetings and organized weekly fellowship meetings for the unconverted. According to Burwash these
services were interrupted by 'the boldest and most riotous boys of the
College' who pelted the candles with marbles and then fled from the
darkened room. Nevertheless, the revival 'spread with great power'
in the college. Lectures were suspended, and the professors 'were
holding meetings for deeply distressed inquirers.'[21] Burwash had difficulty during the revival. He attended class meetings, where he was
pressured to confess his sins and declare his faith. But still all he
could utter was 'the cry and tears of a broken penitent.' Something
was holding him back from entering into a dramatic and emotional
conversion and fervently proclaiming a renewed faith in Christ and
assurance of personal salvation. At one protracted meeting Burwash
recalled that he 'stood in the pew trembling ... when in a moment like
a flash of light I saw that God was declared to be gracious and
merciful through Christ, forgiving inequity, transgression and sin
and I began to claim that mercy as mine.' But this experience lacked
the sense of a great break with the unregenerate past and the absolute
conviction of a renewed life that typified many accounts of conversions.[22] He was full of uncertainty, for his religious experience did
not follow the traditional pattern – sin, despair, conviction, conversion, regeneration, sanctification – that was outlined in advice and
devotional literature and countless sermons. 'I did not call this faith.
I did not call it conversion ... I made no public profession, and did not
give up my name as a candidate for church membership. I had my
new experience. In a little time I began to question its reality as the
great change which I had sought. Was I really born-again?'

Burwash was not assured that this awareness of his sinfulness and
God's mercy encompassed all that was required to be a true Christian.
Indeed this occasion was only the beginning of his struggle for deeper

religious understanding and a purer spiritual condition. At Victoria College his faith developed further. He led a Sunday school class, joined a club pledged to holding weekly prayer meetings and working daily to bring the unconverted to God, and he attended Bible classes.[23] This was a period of growing faith but continued uncertainty for Burwash.

Many of Burwash's doubts concerning his own spiritual condition were resolved by the doctrine of Christian Perfection, one of the most distinctive aspects of Wesleyan theology. According to John Wesley, the conversion experience was the crucial beginning of Christian life but was insufficient to ensure salvation. Wesley understood that the intense emotion of conversion could not be sustained indefinitely. Conversion had to be followed by growth in Christian understanding, moral sensibility, stewardship, and service to God. Burwash realized that 'though trusting in God's mercy for forgiveness, I was still beset by unholy desires, often falling under the power of temptation and continually coming back to the mercy seat for forgiveness of fresh trespasses.' Repentance towards God was not a single act ending at conversion, but a continual life. Burwash understood that he had to struggle constantly for deliverance from the 'power and indwelling as well as the guilt of sin.'[24] An individual's Christian faith was in recurrent crisis, and the struggle to lead a Christian life was neverending. Burwash's faith was evolutionary in character. It was in need of constant nurturing and subject to gradual improvement. It was the product of education, reverential study, earnest worship, and discipline rather than the instance of sudden regeneration at a revival meeting.

The notion of Christian Perfection liberated Burwash and other earnest Methodists, such as Albert Carman, from the sense that they must experience an emotional conversion. It did not, however, signify a departure from the evangelical dependence on 'new birth.' To abandon repentance as a central experience in evangelization would mean that religious life was merely a matter of education.[25] Christian Perfection, however, provided a great deal of scope for the development of a personal Christian faith, reflecting the age's optimistic faith in progress and human abilities. In very large measure, whether one attained Christian Perfection or not was dependent on one's own efforts.

Burwash's spiritual odyssey was evidence of an important development in Canadian Methodism. During the pioneer era the instantaneous experience of conversion had been the major focus of religious

life for many Methodists. There was little emphasis on further spiritual growth or Christian nurture. To an extent this emphasis on revivals
reflected pioneer social conditions. Forced to rely on an itinerant
ministry for religious sustenance, Methodists had little choice but to
rely on revivals and other forms of spontaneous religious activity.
But by the 1850s social conditions were changing abruptly. The Rev.
Nathan Bangs, a saddlebag preacher who had arrived in Upper Canada
before the War of 1812, was awestruck when he visited his old mission field. It was barely recognizable. He remarked to a fellow itinerant preacher from the earliest days in Canadian Methodism: 'What
scenes and changes have passed in review since we commenced our
ministry! ... Once we addressed the few in private dwellings, large
assemblies were congregated in barns, for churches were few and far
between! We now preach to thousands; churches have arisen, large
and numerous in our cities, towns, and circuits!'[26] Mass revivals and
intense conversion experiences, based on a sudden conviction of personal sinfulness, were no longer as necessary and were in decline.

Moreover, there was serious questioning about the religious impact
of revival services. According to Egerton Ryerson, 'these phenomena
... have not always been followed by a religious life; they are no
criteria of a genuine conversion, the proof which must be sought in
its fruits.'[27] The presence of a settled pastorate and permanent churches
gave the clergy an opportunity to cultivate or nurture the religious
faith and piety of their congregations. Methodists could worship
regularly in churches, and this allowed for less emphasis on revivals
to promote and maintain religious commitment. The ordinary means
of grace, hearing the Word of God, taking the sacraments, and prayer,
could be relied upon and in many cases was preferred by congregations that were better educated and increasingly concerned about
respectability.[28] One observant Methodist itinerant preacher concluded
that 'the penitent form is held in great abhorrence.'[29]

Similar tension between evangelical orthodoxy and a more liberal
religious consciousness was experienced by Presbyterians. Francis
Huston Wallace resolved his difficulties with what struck him as the
harsh condemnatory aspects of Calvinism by ultimately joining the
Methodist church. Wallace was the son of a Presbyterian clergyman
from the evangelical Free church tradition. His father's sermons made
a powerful impression upon him for they constantly stressed 'the
absolute necessity of a great conscious change called conversion, the
new birth, in order to escape hell and gain heaven.' Wallace recalled

in his unpublished memoir that 'the idea of judgement and punishment used to haunt me even in my dreams, and I would awake in terror from nightmares of convulsion, amid the thunder and lightnings of the awful day of Judgement.' According to orthodox Calvinist teaching, there was nothing anyone could do to ensure salvation until God called one to regeneration and placed one into his service – the responsibility and capacity was the Almighty God's alone. Wallace was paralyzed by wondering whether he was one of the eternally elect. As a result, he resisted his father's entreaties to enter studies for the Presbyterian ministry at Knox College in Toronto, 'feeling that it would be desecration of so high and holy an office for so sinful a man as I to enter it, that it would be hypocrisy for me to preach to others a religion which I had not experienced myself.'[30]

In the autumn of 1870 Wallace decided to prepare for law at Knox College, but his inability to experience conversion continued to create great anxiety. He started attending prayer meetings at Queen Street Methodist Church. When he went up and knelt with others at the communion rail hoping to be converted, he 'got no relief, no light, no help!' The confusion of the Methodist meeting, with many praying and much singing and exhorting, disturbed Wallace's 'staid Presbyterian spirit' since he felt that 'salvation was a thing directly between the soul and God.' This only deepened Wallace's despondency. He became so obsessed with 'getting right with God' that he stopped attending law classes at Knox.

Then, on 11 March 1871, after attending another Methodist meeting, a Primitive Methodist layman explained to Wallace that he 'was holding back from trusting Christ until I could *feel* that I trusted Him and that I was saved. My will needed to be exerted.' Presbyterian doctrine had taught Wallace to wait 'for some extraordinary, irresistible divine action that should come like a torrent' sweeping him into a new experience. Now he was being told that to some extent his spiritual regeneration would come from his own actions, not God's alone. Acknowledging the sinner's role in bringing about repentance and conversion challenged the orthodox Calvinist doctrine of predestination. Wallace began to understand that to a certain extent the individual had responsibility for accepting or rejecting God, although regeneration could not occur without the grace of God. This harmonizing of the doctrine of election with the concept of free will helped to assure Wallace that things were right between himself and God, and he was now able to proclaim his faith in Christ.[31]

With this assurance Wallace joined the Presbyterian church and became actively engaged in Christian work. He led prayer meetings at his father's church, distributed religious tracts for the YMCA and conducted worship services in a mission hall in downtown Toronto. He had not, however, broken away from his Calvinist roots. At a prayer meeting he led at his father's church he reminded those present that they stood 'depraved by nature, condemned for our sins, & hurrying on to Hell and Destruction, we are helpless, hopeless, doomed on the brink of ruin.' Those seeking conversion were told that they would remain 'wallowing' in the 'dark-pit of sinful pleasure with a hollow and aching heart' unless they were 'born-again.' He stressed that only God was sufficient to conquer the burden of despair brought by sinfulness and that belief in the Lord Jesus Christ was the only way to obtain full assurance of salvation. At the climactic moment in his address Wallace portrayed the nature of God's covenant with fallen humanity in a fashion that aroused the congregation's sense of the drama of Christ's atonement: 'now that you know that you are a sinner, you know that you can't erase the dark record of your sins yourself; you know that Jesus died in Calvary & that His pressed and bloody hand will be drawn across the page and blot out with His own crimson blood the writing against all those who put their trust in Him.'[32] This imagery was designed to move people to a strong emotional conversion.

Wallace was still deeply troubled by matters of faith, and during the summer of 1871 he experienced a radical change in his theological attitudes. He read Watson's *Theological Institutes*, a standard work that was widely used as a text in theology courses for the Methodist ministry. This book cited numerous Scripture passages which elaborated the notion of universal redemption for all believers and explicitly countered orthodox Calvinist doctrines of predestination, which seemed to restrict the salvation gained through Christ's sacrifice to those who were the elect and clearly limited God's love. Scripture made it clear that Christ died for all humanity. Whether one would indeed be saved depended on the response to Christ's offer of salvation. If one failed to gain salvation, it was the fault of one's own opposing will, rather than the result of not being chosen by the Almighty. 'All the evasions and subterfuges which had helped to reconcile me to Calvinism,' Wallace concluded, 'were swept away by the arguments against Calvinism.' When he turned to Calvinistic books, Wallace recoiled with an 'ever deepening horror of the Theology which taught the rigid and unworthy conception of an arbitrary divine sovereign, an unconditional election, an atonement limited to the elect ... and an eternal damnation of those not elected for a disobedience that they could not help.' His religious and moral conscience forced him to reject the apparent inhumanity of Calvinism. He could no longer honestly subscribe to the Westminster Confession of Faith or become a Presbyterian minister.[33]

In the autumn of 1871 Wallace began attending Methodist class meetings. During that time he wrote a sermon which confronted the Calvinism he had been struggling with. 'The Spirit will not believe for you,' he argued. 'Don't bide your time till you feel some extraordinary moving, some sensible impulsion of the Spirit. Don't expect that such an intoxication of feeling is to take possession of you as will hurry you on blindly into faith & love & pardon.'[34] Wallace was acquiring a more confident faith in the capacity of people to 'believe intelligently' and 'take actively' the pardon offered by the grace of God for salvation. Humankind was not completely reliant on an all-powerful God. At class meetings Wallace found that his faith was constantly strengthened; he was 'growing in grace.' In January 1873 he joined Queen Street Methodist Church and soon after became a 'local preacher.' He had attained a new understanding that 'God was no longer an abstraction far away, but a Heavenly father close at hand.' In analysing this formative period in his life, Wallace wrote that this revelation of 'God's tender mercies ... shaped my thought of the relation of all men to God' and 'broadened and humanized and Christianized my theology.'[35] Consistent with the romantic spirit of the age a harsh and judgmental God was being replaced in the imagination of many by a God of love.

By the 1870s many aspects of orthodox Calvinism were being disregarded. For example, the strict aspects of the Calvinist heritage within the Maritime Baptist churches were being slowly abandoned. Beginning in the 1850s, there was less reliance on the use of discipline, whether it be public admonition, or suspension or exclusion from the church, as a means to maintain a regenerate church membership of believers.[36] More profound was the difficulty of reconciling the doctrine of election with the evangelical quest for all to be converted. Many Presbyterian ministers preached that everyone could attain salvation, not just the elect. The Rev. J.M. Gibson must have stunned the more orthodox by proclaiming: 'We know that the death of the Son of God is a sufficient atonement for all. We know that the

offer of mercy is addressed to all without exception. We know that
the Holy Spirit is promised to all who ask Him.'[37] It was also difficult
for evangelists to exhort people to become 'born again,' while
preaching that individuals had no capacity to bring about their salvation. Many Presbyterian clergymen therefore stressed that the only
way for the 'desperate inquirer ... to shake off the incubus of doubt
and fear is to strike out vigorously. Action will break the spell, and
when that is done, the living soul will be its own best witness to the
grace of God.'[38] John George Marshall, a learned lawyer from Nova
Scotia of a strong Puritan background who wrote numerous pamphlets
on the religious questions of the day, was able to reconcile certain
traditional aspects of Calvinism with the modern emphasis on the
human role in attaining salvation. He understood that 'there is no
ground or reason for concluding ... that we must *silently* and *quietly*
wait until the Lord, in some powerful and irresistible manner, operates
in or *upon* us, and brings us into the requisite state of conversion,
faith, and salvation.' According to Marshall, 'the Lord will not compel
sinners to accept salvation, for He has created mankind as free or
voluntary beings.' Regeneration and the attainment of eternal salvation
involved two distinct powers: 'the one power being *divine*, the other
human and *personal*.'[39]

Orthodox notions were challenged more dramatically and found to
be wanting in the foreign mission fields. One of the first overseas
missions sponsored by a Canadian church was the New Hebrides
field established by the Presbyterian Synod of Nova Scotia in 1846. The
Rev. John Geddie was the first missionary sent to the Pacific islands,
and he was followed by three others, including the Rev. George
Gordon, who was stationed at the outpost of Eromanga Island. One
of Gordon's letters detailed how he preached 'the doctrine of retribu-
tive Providence with unusual earnestness" in an attempt to bring
about an end to the natives' 'idolatrous and wicked practices' and
shock them into conversion. He warned the natives of 'the wrath to
come' in 'the shape of temporal punishments.' Unfortunately, a few
weeks later there was a deadly outbreak of the measles. The natives
believed that Gordon had prayed for their destruction and murdered
him and his wife. For John Geddie there was an important lesson in
these tragic events. He questioned the wisdom of Gordon's emphasis
on a punishing God. Writing a report on the incident to the secretary
of the Mission Board, Geddie concluded that the 'Gospel is a message
of mercy and love, and should be addressed to the heathen in its most
attractive form.'[40]

It is impossible to tell precisely when the doctrines of election and predestination began to be less frequently heard from Presbyterian and Baptist pulpits and the more evangelical emphasis on God's offer of free grace to all who repented began to triumph. The decline of orthodox Calvinism was never complete in the nineteenth century. It proved to have a tenacious hold on many. According to William Gregg, clergymen continued to preach the doctrine of original sin and inherent depravity of humankind. They remained convinced that people could not resist temptation whenever left to their own devices, and they continued to argue that sin brought divine wrath in this life and eternal punishment in the next.[41] For example, as late as 1895, at St James Presbyterian Church in Toronto, the Rev. W.G. Jordan presented the congregation with a vivid but gloomy picture of evil. The devil, according to a reporter who was reviewing the church service, was depicted by Jordan as a 'real malign intelligence' of such power and cunning that it was almost impossible to escape his clutches.[42]

Nevertheless, Wallace soon encountered further religious difficulties. Throughout his struggles with orthodox Calvinism his absolute confidence in the Bible as the infallible Word of God had not been shattered. Chilling doubts darkened his outlook, however, as he read Hesiod's *Works and Days* and noticed the parallels between Greek mythology and the stories of Genesis. He wondered if the book of Genesis was true, and this caused him to contemplate whether there was a God. Such doubt raised a pressing question for Wallace: 'how can I, racked with such doubts, preach the Gospel to others?' He answered that since he had not arrived at a conclusion denying God and Christianity and had experienced 'something ... with renewing and elevating power,' he would continue as a preacher. According to the account in his 'Memoirs,' this period of religious doubt lasted for several years, but Wallace had decided to 'do nothing to unsettle the minds of others, for that unsettlement is far too powerful to be lightly caused.'[43]

Clergymen, more than others, had to confront their religious doubts because they were constantly challenged by the problem of what to preach. Could, for instance, a minister openly express questions about doctrine and the Bible and still remain a spokesman for the Christian church? Could doubt be expressed in the pulpit without unsettling the faith of congregations? Furthermore, could a church allow its ministers the freedom and independence to interpret the Holy Scriptures according to his own investigations and convictions without sacrificing the authority of the church? Could a minister openly

question the doctrines, teaching, and discipline of his church and
remain true to his ordination vows? The possibility of further unsettling faith made this a difficult position for a minister and a potentially
schismatic one for the Protestant churches in Victorian Canada.[44]

Exactly this dilemma was confronted by the Rev. D.J. Macdonnell
and the newly formed Presbyterian Church in Canada in 1875.
Macdonnell, born in January 1843 in Bathurst, New Brunswick, was
the son of a Presbyterian minister. Between 1855 and 1858 he studied
at Queen's University, and during his stay in Kingston he boarded in
the manse of the Rev. Dr John Machar, whose 'breadth of mind' and
'practical Christian wisdom' greatly influenced the young student.[45]
After receiving his BA, he served as assistant headmaster of Queen's
Preparatory School and began studying theology at the university.

In the autumn of 1863 he sailed for Scotland to continue his theological studies. At Glasgow University he was exposed to the spirit of
modern inquiry, which assumed that finality in the search for Christian
truth had not been reached. Macdonnell encountered further liberalizing influences while studying in Germany. There, in the theological
curriculum, 'everything was tested by the touchstone of historical
evidence and intellectual criticism.'[46] During this period the influence
of Albrecht Ritschl, the New Testament critic, was beginning to be
felt in Germany's universities. Ritschl was sharply critical of orthodox
evangelical theology because of its concentration on the doctrine of
original sin and God's wrath. Too great a chasm between humanity
and God had been created by such preaching, he argued. For Ritschl
the experience of the gracious will and love of God was the essence of
Christianity. In his teaching, he focused on Christ's message of divine
forgiveness and redemption.

Macdonnell's experience overseas did not lead him to a radical
position, as he maintained that 'we must not, in rebelliousness against
chains and fetters, ignore what is great and good in the past.' But it
did cause him considerable difficulty in accepting the doctrines set
forth in the Westminster Confession of Faith without reservation.
Macdonnell's correspondence during the spring of 1866 suggested that
he was tormented by the question of whether he could subscribe to
the Confession. 'There have been times,' he wrote, 'when I have
almost vowed not to enter the church, not to come under obligations
which I could not honestly take, not to put myself in a position in
which I might be accused of dishonesty if I dared to say what I really
thought.' He noted that the Confession 'remains word for word as it

was drawn up more than two hundred years ago' and that the Presbyterian church asserted that the statements of the Westminster divines were 'fixed and unalterable.' He had hoped that the church would adopt a less intransigent attitude towards the matter of subscription to the Confession, for he was convinced that absolute insistence on the very words of the Confession caused 'more harm than good' and 'torment[ed] the conscientious men.' In the end, his father counselled him by suggesting that the principle of comprehensiveness had limits and that many clergymen with reservations had subscribed to the Confession honestly 'as the best thing they could do in the circumstances.' This pragmatism persuaded Macdonnell, and he proclaimed his adherence to the Westminster Confession and was ordained on 14 June 1866 in Glasgow.[47]

After the ordination Macdonnell returned to Canada and on 20 November was called to St Andrew's Church in Peterborough. Portents of trouble, however, quickly appeared. Macdonnell had not resolved his theological difficulties, and they became more troublesome as he undertook the responsibilities of the ministry. In a 1874 sermon he hinted at his ongoing difficulties with the Westminster Confession. 'It is nearly as great a mistake to try to build the Church on the foundation of theological dogmatism as to try to build it on philosophical speculation,' he stated. The true foundation of the church was the preaching of Christ and the testimony of the apostles and prophets concerning Christ.[48] Macdonnell found it difficult to preach doctrines which he doubted. As a result, he avoided preaching on difficult theological topics and instead spoke on issues such as temperance and busied himself with pastoral activity. 'It is a great thing to have definite practical work to do,' he commented, for 'it prevents too much speculation, which is for me, at least, not a terrible thing. I think there must be much in a minister's work, when earnestly gone about, that tends to correct the evils of theological study.'[49] In Peterborough Macdonnell was torn between his desire to preach his own sense of Christian truth and his appreciation of the proper role of a minister of the Presbyterian church.

Macdonnell seemed to become bolder after he was called to St Andrew's Presbyterian Church in Toronto. One late September Sunday in 1875 some journalists happened to be present at St Andrew's. The sermon, on the text Romans 5:12–21, excited them, for in his impassioned discourse Macdonnell aired his difficulties and doubts concerning the idea of the eternity of future punishment, one of the most

controversial topics in theological discourse during the 1870s.[50]
Macdonnell was known as one of the more logical and forthright
preachers in Toronto; but he was also powerful and passionate. One
observer concluded that 'he has ... the fire that flashes into the soul
and vivid lightning which at one stroke makes a man care whether
there really is a God or not: whether he has a soul to save or if it is
worth while.'[51]

According to reports, Macdonnell expressed his 'moral confusion'
over the apparent irreconcilability of a God who meted out 'eternal
torments' and 'everlasting punishment' and a God of love and mercy.[52]
Macdonnell boldly proclaimed to his congregation that he was 'not
bound by the Confession of Faith when it conflicts with the Bible ...
The question is, What is the truth of God? Let us get that and live and
die on it.' The Confession, he argued, was 'a human account ... not the
Gospel truth'; it should be considered 'subordinate to the Word of
God.' He cautioned, however, that he was not in sympathy with the
notion of universalism which advocated the abolition of any distinction
between sin and righteousness. 'If there is universal salvation taught
in the Bible,' he explained, 'it is not that a man can go on sinning all
his life. The question is not is there a hell – for there is; it is not about
punishment, but about the eternity of it.   It is not the question of
suffering for our sins beyond the grave, for we shall suffer.' But
Macdonnell insisted 'there is nothing dangerous in telling poor sinners
that men will have a chance to gain life beyond the grave.'[53] A sum-
mary of this daring sermon also appeared in the evangelical Protestant
daily, the *Montreal Witness*, under the sensational and misleading
headline 'Universal Salvation.'[54]

Macdonnell had challenged the Presbyterian church in Canada's
doctrinal standards. The Presbytery of Toronto called upon him to
explain his position. Macdonnell indicated that while the reports on
his sermon were largely correct, they did create the false impression
that he accepted the doctrine of the 'final restoration of all' and had
flatly denied the eternity of future punishment. He told church officials
that he had merely stated his difficulties in coming to any conclusions
regarding the idea of eternal punishment. Many passages of Scripture
'appeared to teach,' he explained, 'that there would come a time ...
when all things should be reconciled, when God should be all in all,
and when consequently punishment should come to an end.'

During his defence Macdonnell outlined the dilemma of the modern
minister whose mind was frequently 'in a state of uncertainty and

perplexity' with respect to the teachings of the church. What is a preacher to do about a difficult passage in the Bible, he asked? 'Pass it over? or give a superficial explanation that left the difficulty exactly where it was? or make the best I could of it after honest and prayerful study?' To be silent on controversial matters struck Macdonnell as the wrong course, for he was opposed to the view that ministers should only preach about matters 'on which no doubt can be entertained.' Macdonnell concluded by asserting that he was doing his congregation 'a real service in leading them to think for themselves.' He was convinced that such encouragement of debate and independent inquiry and less insistence on doctrine would 'make it possible to embrace within one Church a larger body of believing men.' In an age of critical inquiry, churches had to be more tolerant, or they would become much too exclusive.[55] This position reflected the increasingly liberal or tolerant spirit of the Victorian age. Finally, Macdonnell submitted a written statement in which he indicated that he adhered to the teachings of the Confession of Faith on the question of the eternity of future punishment only in so far as they were consistent with Holy Scripture.

The Presbytery of Toronto found this much too controversial and declined to accept Macdonnell's written statement. Attempts were made to find a compromise, but in the end Macdonnell's 'fastidious conscience' made it impossible for him to cover up the full extent of his doubt. If he accepted the doctrine of the absolute, unconditional, and eternal nature of future punishment, then he would be forced to deny the righteousness of a loving God, and this he could not do.[56] It was a troubling time for Presbyterianism, and the response to Macdonnell's sermon reflected the confusion within the Canadian church. The more orthodox argued that absolute adherence to the Westminster Confession was essential, and they pushed the General Assembly to start a formal heresy trial for Macdonnell had clearly wavered from the church's standards.

Many Presbyterians were torn by the issues raised by the Macdonnell controversy. For example, the Rev. George Grant, the young minister of St Matthew's Church in Halifax, was deeply disturbed by Macdonnell's position. Grant had established a reputation for religious toleration. The question of instrumental music had erupted in his church in the early 1870s, and he argued that it was wrong for those angrily opposed to instrumental music to refuse any accommodation to those wishing to place an organ in the church 'because no one dreams of even asking them to change their usages; all that is asked is liberty for those who think differently.' He explained that 'in a large and historic church there cannot be ... absolute uniformity in things indifferent, and though personally all my taste and prejudices are opposed to instrumental music in churches, I shall never sanction any narrowing of congregational liberty, which, I believe, we possess.'[57] To be successful in the emerging urban communities, it was prudent, Grant understood, for ministers to be pragmatic, practical, and liberal-minded in order to accommodate different theological views and religious temperaments within the parish. Consistent with this quest for tolerance was Grant's disapproval of the attempts to drive Macdonnell out of the church.[58] Such action would only undermine efforts to build unity within the Presbyterian church.

This desire for greater liberty in the church, however, was severely tested by Macdonnell's position. Grant had trouble accepting his actions because he viewed them as being indiscreet. He explained to Agnes Machar that a minister's duty in the pulpit was 'to announce God's truth, not to indulge in speculations. Any part of God's truth we are not clear upon ... we had better keep for study, for further thought, for discussion with trusted friends.'[59] The diplomatic Grant sensed that the tenuous state of the Presbyterian union made the battle being waged by Macdonnell a risky one. He dreaded the General Assembly discussion on the subject of eternal punishment since it was not a doctrine 'for light remarks on the street, or heated discussion in church courts or church assemblies.' Even Macdonnell was concerned about the tide of doubt which seemed to be unsettling many as a result of his comments. While defending himself before the General Assembly, he expressed 'grief' over his remarks, since he had been proclaimed 'a champion' by 'the godless, the careless, the unbelieving, the worldly, and the vicious.' By openly stating his difficulties with the doctrine of eternal punishment, Macdonnell acknowledged that there had been 'harm done to the Church and the cause of Christ.'[60]

Moderate opinion prevailed during the Macdonnell controversy. Ultimately a compromise was struck between Macdonnell and the Presbyterian Church of Canada during the General Assembly of 1877. The following resolution was agreed to by Macdonnell and accepted by the General Assembly: 'I consider myself as under subscription to the Confession of Faith in accordance with my ordination vows, and I therefore adhere to the teaching of the Church as contained therein on the doctrine of the eternity or endless duration of the future punishment of the wicked, notwithstanding doubts or difficulties which perplex my mind.'[61] Still, the church insisted that ministers remain loyal to the Confession. Doctrinal standards had to be maintained as protection against more serious doubt and speculation which would lead to error or outright disbelief as well as cause divisiveness in the church. Macdonnell remained concerned about the tide of doubt which seemed to be unsettling ministers and congregations alike. After his trial he wrote to Agnes Machar: 'I confess that I wonder less at men growing skeptical and unbelieving when I find how many things are perplexing to myself.'[62] Even the most daring of the clergy recognized that the path of greater liberalism in religious thought and practice was a perilous one. Nevertheless, this compromise was significant for in dismissing the charges that Macdonnell's utterances were heretical, the Presbyterian church was acknowledging that a spirit of toleration and some degree of liberality in thought, albeit circumspect, were necessary.

The origins of religious doubt during the Victorian era are difficult to determine. Traditionally, it has been attributed to intellectual factors, especially the rise of science and history. The Christian faith was especially vulnerable to the discoveries of science because the arguments of natural theology held great sway in the Victorian era.[63] It was thought that the design of the natural world was direct evidence of the existence of God. Discoveries in the fields of geology and biology created an unavoidable conflict with orthodox Christianity. Geologists' conclusions about the age of rocks and fossils contradicted the chronology of Genesis, and biologists' claim that humans were a product of an evolutionary process, rather than the children of a special creative act of God, could not be readily reconciled with biblical accounts or the accepted Christian view of humanity. The application of historical techniques to the books of the Bible also undermined faith. The gospel narratives were critically examined, according to insights gained from history, literary and linguistic studies, and the sciences. A major implication of this approach was that the Bible was not necessarily a divinely inspired factual record, but was often composed of legends and myths expressing human ideas of Christianity or understanding of spiritual truth. According to the most challenging critics, the Bible should be read 'like any other book.'

These challenges were becoming well known in learned circles by the 1830s. Sir Charles Lyell's *Principles of Geology* (1830) showed that the antiquity of the earth was much greater than biblical chronology indicated and implied that geological change on earth was not the result of divine intervention. In 1835 the German theologian D.F. Straus published *Leben Jesu*, which critically examined the gospel account of the life of Jesus Christ. By the 1860s the doubts about Christianity raised by science and history were gaining wider currency. Books such as Charles Darwin's *Origin of Species* (1859) greatly increased bewilderment concerning the truth of Christianity; but its importance was also symbolic of the age's loss of religious assurance. As Owen Chadwick wrote, 'Darwin was only a sign of a movement bigger than Darwin, bigger than biological science, bigger than intellectual inquiry.'[64] By the 1860s doubts about Christianity had gained currency that was much wider than the debates occurring within the educated elite.

It was rare for a sudden revelation or thunderbolt from science or history to cause complete despair or abandonment of faith. According to Macdonnell's biographer, there was 'no violent wrenching of his mental development ... at any stage of the process ... nothing sudden, nothing single.' His perplexity grew out of deliberate and independent 'pondering upon the mysteries of divine government and human destiny.'[65] He was unable to reconcile certain aspects of orthodox doctrine with the concept of a God of love. While a minister in Belleville in the mid-1860s, Burwash faced a direct challenge to his faith when he read a copy of Bishop Colenso's *Pentateuch* (1864), which criticized Mosaic history as it was written in the Bible. He recalled 'feel[ing] all certain ground sinking from under my feet.' But he did not become despondent or flirt with agnosticism. This intellectual challenge sent him on a quest for 'the true foundation of all certainty in religion.'[66] And in his inaugural address as Professor of Natural Science at Victoria College, he admitted that 'it cost me many a painful struggle when I came to see that I could not harmonize ... science in all its teachings with the general interpretations of scriptures.' His strong religious upbringing and his 'inner assurance of faith,' however, allowed him to withstand the claims of speculative science.[67] In Burwash's case, then, struggle with the emotional demands and certain moral concepts of orthodoxy and revivalism caused greater turmoil and doubt than grappling with the disturbing implications of science and history. Similarly F.H. Wallace's misgivings were intensified, not begun, by his comparison of biblical accounts with classical history and mythology. What initially disturbed him was that there was little room for an individual's own will or desire for improvement within the harsh dictates of Calvinist theology. The doubts experienced by Burwash, Wallace, and Macdonnell were the result of an inner spiritual quest to reach an understanding of God and their own religious experience.

Much of this inner spiritual quest was prompted by changing moral and social values. Orthodox dogma which stated that God would cast the unrepentant into hell-fire and keep them there in indescribable torment forever was increasingly regarded as morally outrageous by many Victorians. It could not be reconciled with the sense of God's fatherly love, mercy, and eternal justice. Refinements were being made to what seemed erroneous or too harsh in orthodox Christianity. Rather than the gloomy emphasis on human depravity, the idea of Christian love became dominant, a notion that reflected the optimistic and romantic spirit of the mid-Victorian era. What disturbed those struggling with their Christian faith was not so much the truth of Genesis or the possibility of miracles, but orthodox doctrines. The orthodox view of atonement, which viewed Christ's death on the cross as a sign of God's harsh righteousness rather than an unconditional gift of love, was assailed for its lack of justice, and predestination was questioned for its inequity and its denial of human freedom. To many, certain aspects of Christianity seemed wrong – not scientifically or historically – but morally. Ethical concern and moral feeling were probably more responsible than critical inquiry or intellectual problems for unsettling the faith of clergymen and their congregations.

The struggle with orthodoxy and the emergence of a more liberal and temperate faith also reflected a broader transformation in Canadian society. In mid-Victorian Canada evidence of progress abounded. A transportation system of roads, canals, and railroads was constantly expanding, and communication was improving with the rise of the telegraph and newspapers. In the growing towns, schools and denominational colleges were established, and institutions that promoted advances in the sciences and technology were being fostered. In this culture, people were not as willing to accept that their lot was strictly the result of uncontrollable forces or Divine Providence. Scientific knowledge, in particular, convinced people that they could control their destiny and expand their horizons.[68] A gospel of the 'self-made man' was emerging in which individual capabilities were emphasized.[69] Progress was the result of human initiative and endeavour, and disasters could be explained by natural causes. This maturing faith in human potential was accompanied by a decline of belief in the supernatural and in religious explanations of worldly events.[70]

One perceptive commentator on the implication of this growing faith in human sufficiency was the Baptist educator D.A. MacGregor. The theme of one his notable sermons was an exploration of the questioning about God's promises. Commenting on the prayer debate, MacGregor noted that the doubts that had emerged with respect to the efficacy of prayer rested, not on the limitations of human knowledge or piety, but upon human sufficiency or a sense that prayer was no longer necessary. Equally troubling, in his estimation, was that those who still did pray or worship seemed to do so for worldly ends and not for holiness. There seemed to be disillusionment about prayer because God did not grant whatever was asked during prayer. He asked his audience: 'Have not God's people often, in tearful anxiety, prayed for the recovery of a loved one from death and yet no recovery came? Have not his people often in perplexity in the business of life, asked him to help them through a financial crisis and yet they have become insolvent even in the midst of their asking.'[71] There was a hint in this despondent analysis that the secular ethics of a consumer culture, especially the quest for self-fulfilment and immediate gratification, were penetrating the most important aspects of religious life such as prayer.[72]

A culture with different religious ideas and needs emerged in mid-nineteenth-century Canada. It was a culture that was, perhaps, more secular because a greater role for individuals in their own material and religious lives was now acknowledged. The evangelical worldview was by no means bankrupt, but it was increasingly difficult for Victorians to adhere strictly to its tenets.

2

The Emergence of Liberal Theology: A New Certainty?

The primary task of many clergymen in the late nineteenth century was to counter the drift away from the Christian faith and find a firm foundation for the resurrection of religious certainty. They understood that they would not be able to inspire a confident Christian faith if they remained unsettled in their own faith and uneasy with respect to the church's doctrines and teachings. There was a consensus that a new religious understanding had to be developed for Protestantism to remain a vital force in Canadian thought and society. Much of the pressure for change came from the clergy in response to growing disillusionment on the part of their congregations. Many who attended church considered worship services dull and lifeless, objected to the traditional forms of scriptural exposition, and criticized ministers who preached on the fundamental doctrines of evangelical Christianity. Members of the clergy admitted that they easily became 'addicted' to traditional forms of expression and old systems of doctrine. The result was a 'superstitious reverence' for dogma which proved altogether unsuited for a successful ministry and fatal to religious progress. The more discerning clergy realized the church was 'fatally deceiving itself regarding its true condition if it argued that growing numbers meant inner strength.'[1] There was little question that a modernized Christianity was required to combat the progress of doubt and unbelief, and to provide a foundation for a revival of religion.

Many clergymen in Canada accommodated their Christian beliefs to modern social and intellectual trends, those forces that were partially responsible for undermining faith. Christianity was refashioned into a religion that accepted the discoveries of science and principles of history, incorporated the results of reverent biblical criticism, and was sensitive to the moral issues and social concerns of the times. Many liberal-thinking clergy were confident that this new Christianity would foster greater faith and a stronger presence of the Christian church in Canadian society. Any reconciliation of Christianity with modern knowledge and values, however, had to be carefully constructed, so that what was essential and characteristic of the Christian religion was not sacrificed, renounced, or forgotten. In establishing a new Christianity, based on the insights of science and history, clergymen were aware that they had to tread carefully.

One of the leading Canadian churchmen responsible for trying to establish Christianity on a more certain foundation was the Rev. E.H. Dewart. He was an important figure because as editor of the *Christian Guardian* his thought gained wide exposure. To an extent, Dewart was an official voice of Canadian Methodism. In many respects his career was typical of the mid-nineteenth-century Canadian Methodist ministry.

Edward Hartley Dewart was born in the County of Cavan, Ireland, in 1828 and immigrated with his family to the County of Peterborough, Upper Canada, in 1834. The Dewart household was 'always stocked' with useful literature, and the young Edward acquired extensive knowledge of Scripture. At age nineteen Dewart became a student at the Normal School in Toronto and then taught in Dunville, Ontario. He also began to teach Sunday school at the local Wesleyan Methodist church and deliver addresses for the Sons of Temperance. These accomplishments made him a logical candidate for the ministry, and Methodist officials invited him to become a local preacher. Previously he had resisted such requests for he was unsure of his own faith. But this invitation 'produced a serious mental crisis. It seemed as if coming to Dunville I had, like Jonah, fled from the presence of the Lord; but to be offered a circuit ... I could not but deem a providential call that I ought not to disregard.' Delivering his first sermon 'seemed to break all the chains that had held me back, and set me free to give myself fully to the work of preaching the unsearchable riches of Christ.'[2] In 1851 he was received on probation by the Wesleyan Methodist church. For two years he was junior preacher on the St Thomas circuit, and then he served on the Port Hope and Thorold circuit. This completed his four-year probation, and Dewart was ordained in London in 1855.

He had received no formal theological training. Like most Methodist preachers, Dewart's ministry was characterized by brief appointments on numerous circuits and constant transfer.

What was outstanding about Dewart was his literary talent. His most notable contribution to a burgeoning Canadian literature was the anthology *Selections from Canadian Poets; with Occasional Critical and Biographical Notes, and an Introductory Essay on Canadian Poetry* (1864). He also published two volumes of his own poetry, *Broken Reeds* and *Songs of Life*. In these literary endeavours, Dewart's purpose was largely religious or devotional as well as being nationalistic. He wanted to foster a Canadian literature, but it had to be uplifting and inspiring. Like most Victorians concerned about respectability Dewart was concerned about the impact of worldly literature, especially fiction. He thought that poetry was a medium for conveying God and his design in nature. If a poem happened to preach scepticism or 'praise licentiousness,' it was false to its mission. Dewart made sure that his anthology fixed 'the soul with noble and holy purpose' by organizing many of his selections around the theme 'Sacred and Reflective.' His own poetry was dominated by two themes: the glory and majesty of God in nature; and God's abiding love and guidance in the lives of all believing Christians.

In his devotional poetry Dewart always affirmed his faith in God; but some of his poems, such as 'Questionings' and 'A Plea for Liberty,' suggested that he was troubled by religious doubts. The opening poem in the devotional section of *Songs of Life*, 'Through the Shadow,' indicated that Dewart's faith in Christianity was being shaken: 'The truths I thought would aye abide. / Totter and reel at every side. / In doubt and gloom I grope / My rough and toilsome way / Hoping with anxious trembling hope.' At the end of this poem Dewart pronounced his faith in God, but his lingering doubts remained. They are not fully resolved. He concluded: 'Though doubts perplex and shadows lower, / I'll trust His wisdom, love, and power.'[3]

During the 1860s Dewart was developing his skills as an essayist, and he began writing on the major religious questions of the day. In an widely read essay published in 1866 he argued that F.W. Robertson of Brighton, a prominent Anglican clergyman in England, 'was a representative man' for the age, illustrating the 'tendency to freer thought and a greater latitude of opinion in theology.' What impressed Dewart about Robertson was that his writings contained a 'most vivid description' of the struggles of one drifting away from Christian faith. He thought that the following passage by Robertson captured the ominous doubts and despair that many were encountering: 'It is an awful hour ... when this life has lost its meaning ... when the grave appears to be the end of all human goodness ... and the sky above this universe a dead expanse, black with the void from which God himself has disappeared!'[4] There was a danger, Dewart thought, that if such 'hideous uncertainty' was not met by the Christian church with a believable gospel, then many would follow the same dark course as Robertson had. This alarmed Dewart, for in his estimation Robertson had abandoned all sacred meaning in Christianity. As Dewart stressed, in Robertson's thinking 'the great scriptural truth, that Christ died for our sins and that we have redemption through His blood, is dissolved into airy mist and supplanted by fanciful and baseless speculation the meaning of which is very hazy.' Equally distressing was that Robertson had argued against the claim that the Bible was the Word of God, opposed the concept of biblical authority for the Christian observance of the Sabbath, and had suggested that the expectation that God would answer prayer by direct interposition was futile. If Robertson's spiritual descent was representative, then Christianity was in danger of becoming a 'simple landmark of morality,' bereft of anything that could inspire religious devotion.

Dewart's accomplishments as an essayist contributed to his selection as editor of the Methodist church's newspaper, the *Christian Guardian*, in 1869. Much of his editorial commentary over the first decade was consolidated in a book entitled *Living Epistles; or, Christ's Witness to the World* (1878). His outlook was pessimistic, for the theme of this book and indeed many of his editorials was discussion of the question why the Christian church had not achieved 'the object of her great mission in the world, as the Divine promises would lead us to expect.' Christian influence in society, he concluded, was 'feeble and ineffective.' In one of his first editorials Dewart suggested that the churches were failing to reach every level of society. 'There is, even in our Canadian cities, a rapidly increasing class who are not reached by ordinary Church agencies. The people who occupy seats in our city churches are mostly the well-to-do respectable middle-class. There is a large number who never come to any church and who are not reached by any church service. They are too low down in the pit to be reached by the rope let down by the churches in ordinary cases.' According to Dewart, the church was confronted with a general indifference to its moral teaching, spiritual message, and mission to the world. There was great indifference within the churches also, which was apparent by the failure of church members to go forth like the disciples and bring others to Christ.[5]

This indifference on the part of churchgoers in Dewart's estimation was at the root of the church's weakness, for he believed that people brought the 'standards of religious life down to the level of their own experience.' He argued in an uncompromising fashion that 'the tone of the Church, as an organized society, must sink to the level of the members who compose it. The notion that because of its orthodox creed ... or its graceful ritual, a Church can be bright with the beauty of holiness, while its members are unholy and worldly is a delusive falsehood.' Moreover, it was the weakness within the church, Dewart contended, that gave power to Christianity's enemies. Without 'holiness' – the conformity of the soul to the will and image of God – people were unable to resist the temptations of the world or the doubts generated by sceptical thought. The rise of worldliness and scepticism in Canada, therefore, was a direct result of the indifferent faith of church members and clergy.[6]

Like most other clergymen he identified scientific materialism as a major opponent of religion.[7] Christianity was faced with growing faith in a scientific world-view which assumed that matter was 'capable of producing all the phenomena of life and thought.' This raised questions regarding the existence of the human soul, miracles, God, and a future state. According to Dewart, 'the battle of our day must be fought out on the question, whether the attested revelations of physical science are, or are not, irreconcilable with the basal doctrine and fact of the Christian religion.' Displaying a deeply conservative concern for the social and religious order, Dewart explained that just 'as political liberty has sometimes degenerated into reckless license and the lawless tyranny of mob rule, so may intellectual freedom drift into egotistic independence' in which the standards of Christian faith are ignored and broken down.[8] In this highly speculative atmosphere it was imperative for the church to present Christianity in a vital form. In Dewart's estimation the future of Christianity was tied up in the challenge that science and the critical spirit posed to its central beliefs. The church's response clearly was crucial.

Initially Canadian clergymen greeted the rationalistic temper of modern thought and the materialistic foundation of science with horror. As Brian McKillop has demonstrated, the pages of the *Christian Guardian* during the 1860s and early 1870s were full of editorials, articles, and correspondence discussing the threat speculative science and irreverent philosophy and history posed for Christianity.⁹ Similar attention was paid to the dangers of modern infidelity in the Presbyterian press. Typically the *Presbyterian Witness* argued that the Darwinian theory of the origins of life destroyed the doctrines of creation and design. 'There can be no wisdom manifested in this endless and awful struggle – no adapting of means to beneficent ends,' the *Witness* argued. 'All naure becomes but one dread battlefield without an intelligent power, purpose, or end. God is excluded from the world.'¹⁰ Theories which denied the efficacy of prayer, rejected the possibility of miracles, discounted divine inspiration, or dismissed the existence and Providence of God were attacked. Methodists and Presbyterians alike explained that the materialistic theory of nature and history could not account for the religious, ethical, and artistic dimension of humankind. Only the existence of God could; and so the reality and significance of Christian revelation were emphasized in defence against materialistic speculation.

By the mid-1870s, however, many clergymen were beginning to reach a degree of accommodation with modern thought. The torrent of protest levelled against Darwinian evolution, Huxley's agnosticism, and Tyndall's criticism of the physical efficacy of prayer subsided. A calmer mood prevailed as the compatibility of science and Christian doctrine was acknowledged. James R. Moore has recently demonstrated in *The Post-Darwinian Controversies* that 'the military metaphor must be abandoned to achieve historical understanding' of the relation between science and religion.¹¹ Christianity had been cast as a reactionary and repressive force in modern thought and society due to the initial vehement opposition by leading churchmen to the new discoveries of scientific inquiry. Nervous ecclesiastical officials anxiously mocked anything which questioned traditional Christian doctrines, including the new sciences.

This depiction of staunch church opposition to scientific advances was soundly criticized by the clergy. W.S. Blackstock was a learned Methodist minister stationed in Napanee, Ontario. He reviewed for the *Canadian Methodist Magazine* John William Draper's *History of the Conflict between Religion and Science* (1874), a book which contended the church stood vehemently against all scientific advance and established the idea of warfare between science and religion. Blackstock charged that Draper's account of the conflict between science and religion was 'overdrawn and exaggerated.' He thought that those who had contempt for religion and 'ignorant and narrow-minded clergy' were responsible for making the breach between science and religion unnecessarily wider. Contrary to the popular notion, Blackstock concluded, the Christian religion was a patron and promoter of science. Each successive step in the progress of scientific discovery and improvement of biblical interpretation would lead to the final and complete reconciliation of science and religion.[12]

To demonstrate the existence of harmony rather than discord, concerned clergymen were fond of pointing to the religious devotion of scientists as well as the scientific achievements of deeply religious men. The meeting of the British Association for the Advancement of Science was held in Montreal in 1884. In Canadian church circles this event was regarded as 'a practical living refutation of the somewhat common error, that science and religion are in any sense antagonistic to each other, or that an earnest piety is any disqualification for scientific culture of the highest type.' The Rev. William Harrison reported that a large number of the association's members attended religious services and noted that many of the scientists stressed the religious character of their work by acknowledging 'the Divine Creator and guidance.' For example, the president of the association, in recognizing the existence of the supernatural world as well as the limitations of science, proclaimed that 'the higher mysteries of being, if at all penetrable by the human intellect, require other weapons than those of calculation and experiment.'[13] Such scientific opinion, it was claimed, represented a rebuke of materialism and confirmation of the position held by Christian apologists. Quite possibly, scientists who rejected doctrines essential to Christianity as a result of their investigations were nominal Christians before encountering the corrosive effects of scientific inquiry.[14]

Hidden by the noisy rhetoric of the science versus religion debate, there were many clergymen groping for a reconciliation of Christian revelation with the new scientific discoveries. During Burwash's inaugural lecture as professor of natural science at Victoria College he remarked that there were 'apparent conflicts between the teachings of science and revelation.' He admitted that 'it cost me many a painful struggle when I came to see that I could not harmonize ... science in all its teachings with the general interpretations of scriptures.' Burwash's 'inner assurance' that both nature and the Bible were 'from one perfect God,' however, gave him confidence that proper understanding of the natural world and the Bible would make clear that there was no conflict between science and Christianity.[15] After the initial shock and confusion when confronted by the most recent advances in scientific knowledge, there was growing confidence that God would be better understood and Christianity would be strengthened as a result of proper scientific investigation. The relationship that the Christian religion had with science and modern thought was much closer and more intricate than the image of polarization, irreconcilability, or the victory of one over the other would suggest.

In responding to the question Is evolution consistent with Christianity? clergymen answered that it depended upon what was meant by evolution. Some of the implications of Darwinian science, such as the idea of mutability of species, could be fairly easily conceded without sacrificing anything essential to Christianity. And similarly, except for those who tenaciously held to the doctrine of the plenary inspiration of the Bible, the reinterpretation of the Genesis account of creation from the literal to the symbolic was admitted. There were other aspects of Darwinian thought that could not be accepted without fundamentally undermining Christianity. What disturbed many Christians was the tendency to argue an all-sufficient evolution which assumed that all things of nature were the product of material forces alone. As Dewart pointed out, the claim that all beings have evolved by a brutal process of natural selection 'from some extremely low primordial forms of life ... dethrones God, and tells us that the evidence for His existence is not sufficient to warrant belief.'[16] The materialistic view of nature could not be reconciled with the notion of God the Creator whose Providence was a living force in the origin and fate of all beings. These beliefs could not be easily altered or given up without seriously jeopardizing Christianity. There was loud protest against the view that evolution was the supreme creative power.

E.H. Dewart was seriously torn by the issues raised by science. He was aware that some accommodation of religion with new scientific understanding was necessary as a basis for the urgent reconstruction of Christian theology. But evolution presented him with major difficulties, for as he acknowledged in the Christian Guardian 'the results of modern scientific research have thrown doubt upon the soundness of some interpretations of the Bible.'[17] The degree of predetermination implicit in Darwinian evolution was objectionable to Dewart, since Methodism was a faith which minimized the idea of the governing laws of God and allowed maximum scope for freewill. As Dewart explained, the modern theory of evolution 'denies to men the freedom of choice which is the basis of all personal moral responsibility, and without which praise and blame cannot be awarded to human actions.' The spiritual, moral, and intellectual faculties of human beings, Dewart believed, could not have evolved by the ordinary forces of nature. 'The chain of lineal descent, which the theory supposes, is nowhere to be found. All attempts to complete such a chain have been utterly lame and defective.' Humanity, he insisted, was the product of direct supernatural intervention, a divine creation. Like the other critics of Darwinian thought Dewart particularly objected to the materialistic and atheistic implications of Darwinian thought.[18]

Of greater significance than this attack were the aspects of evolutionary thought that Dewart was compelled to accept. The evidence supporting evolution, in some form, was extensive enough to force him to admit that complete denunciation was unwise and dangerous to the cause of Christianity. 'No one,' he wrote, 'can deny that evolution is one of the methods of nature. The world did not spring at one bound from nothing into its present state of completeness ... Every intelligent Christian will candidly admit that evolution is one of God's modes of working in the universe.' Dewart, therefore, was forced to make Christianity consistent with evolution without sacrificing the concept of divine revelation. To do this, Dewart followed the arguments of Dr James McCosh, one of the leading Protestant theologians in the United States. The discovery of evolution as the 'efficient cause' of things did not preclude the existence of a final cause.[19]

Others, having less difficulty than Dewart in accommodating scientific ideas with their Christian beliefs, argued that the Darwinian theory simply meant that what was thought to have been done 'directly and at once was done indirectly and successively.' God was forever present in evolution. Typical of the growing mood of reconciliation, the editor of the *Presbyterian Witness* announced that 'the derivation of man from inferior species need give the student of the Bible no trouble of mind provided in connection with it, a divine act is admitted to have been present, both physically and spiritually in the new creation.'[20] On the condition that God was acknowledged to be the imponderable yet supreme power overseeing the natural law of evolution, many were able to admit the idea of evolution without greatly upsetting their religious beliefs.

The response of Baptists in Canada to evolutionary thought indicates a similar spirit of accommodation and openness. A liberal spirit was central to the Baptist heritage. The Baptists did not have a standard set of doctrines to defend, for they were a denomination that cherished the notions of independent thought and democracy. The only authority that could be exercised over a Baptist congregation was the word of Christ derived from the Bible.[21] The Rev. R.A. Fyfe, a leading Baptist educator and one of the founders of the Canadian Literary Institute in Woodstock, Ontario, captured the Baptists' outlook by insisting that in establishing what is religious truth 'we must distinguish between what is merely incidental ... what God positively requires, and what is merely a way in which some good people suppose they are carrying out the spirit of the Heavenly Father's instruction.' Fyfe suggested that while traditional Baptist practices regarding adult baptism were essential and clearly biblical in their foundation, the New Testament did not mention missionary societies, Bible societies, or temperance organizations. These voluntary societies were important but not essential.[22]

In his study of Acadia College in Nova Scotia Barry Moody explained that the response to Darwin was 'calm temperate debate from which hysterical over-reaction seems largely absent.' He suggested that a variety of opinions were expressed; moreover, the principal of Acadia, John Mockett Cramp, was fascinated with scientific discovery. To the 1867 graduating class Cramp proclaimed that 'the discoveries and researches of modern times had shed light on the divine record, and removed numerous obscurities which have long been impenetrable.' This open attitude, according to Moody, was not merely confined to Baptist intellectuals or faculty members.[23]

For evangelical clergymen to be able to accept evolution, they had to refashion it into a natural process that was designed by and dependent upon God's active supernatural power. Divine agency, therefore, was imposed on evolutionary theory. They also minimized the emphasis given to evolution as an explanation for the origin of species. Instead they regarded evolution as a description of the divine method of perpetuating or improving species; it explained natural development. Since clergymen remained convinced that the world was the outcome of God's design, the Darwinian notion of nature 'red in tooth and claw,' characterized by struggle, cruelty, and destruction, by necessity, was replaced by the view that the world was a place of orderly growth and beneficent development. Christian evolution embraced the concept of 'universal progressive providence; it meant inevitable material, social, moral and spiritual advance.'[24] In concert with the optimistic spirit of the Victorian age evolution was interpreted as a fact of history, nature, and Providence. Evolution, then, had become a metaphysical doctrine, Christian in inspiration, rather than a strictly scientific theory.

In accomplishing this reconciliation, clergymen had managed to interpret Darwinian evolution in a manner which seemingly provided greater assurance of the truth of Christianity. 'Evolution,' proclaimed the Rev. Daniel Miner Gordon during his inaugural lecture at Presbyterian College in Halifax, 'with its conception of growth rather than mechanism, of life working from within rather than a power constructing from without, helps further to illustrate the method of Him who is the life of all that lives.'[25] Seen in this way, evolution gave evidence of God's existence and watchful Providence; it revealed that the Creator was omniscient and omnipresent. Christian evolution implied a God of immanence, a God who dwelled within and constantly guided the natural world. This contrasted sharply with the orthodox view of a transcendent God who ruled the world from afar and touched it only by the occasional intervention in nature or history – a miracle. It now seemed that God was within nature and history, and close to human kind. Moreover, God the harsh judge had been banished by scientific understanding. It was understood that God was an active benevolent spirit. Some of the mystery had been lifted. Evolution had cast new light upon nature, the destiny of humanity, and the ways of God. It seemed to have provided a more inspiring and certain Christian world-view. Ironically, the clergy could base their arguments regarding the existence and nature of God on science, the source of so much doubt regarding the truth of Christianity.

The acceptance of the idea of universal evolution directed by God laid the foundation for many developments in Protestant thought in late-Victorian Canada. Soon after Dewart had made peace with evolution he delivered a ground-breaking lecture on the development and history of Christian doctrine before the Theological Union of Victoria College. Indeed F.H. Wallace remembered that in the winter of 1876, during a private conversation, Dewart talked approvingly of the modern historical view of the Bible.[26] One of Dewart's younger colleagues, the Rev. S.P. Rose, pointed out that the image of Dewart one received through his editorial writing did not fully reflect the character of his thought. 'I shall surprise those who knew him only through *The Christian Guardian*, as the vigorous defender of the old theology (that is the older theology of Methodism) against evolutionists and sponsors of higher criticism, when I express the mature opinion that at first, at least at heart, he was a radical, and that if he had followed his earlier instincts he would have been a leader of those whose positions he afterward assailed.'[27]

Dewart's arguments regarding the development of doctrine were based on the premise that evolution was the 'divine mode of operation' in the spiritual realm as well as the natural order. He noted that within Scriptures there was an 'increase of religious knowledge.' New truths were 'revealed by the Prophets and Apostles, and by the Great Teacher Himself.' This was evidence of 'progressive Revelation.' Furthermore, humanity's understanding of Christian revelation was imperfect and subject to improvement over time. The early Christians, he pointed out, 'held the central verities of the Gospel with the assurance of a strong conviction'; but 'the theological remains' from this period show that the first Christians had 'an imperfect grasp of the doctrines of Christianity ... There were mines of truth in the Bible, whose wealth they had not discovered. Their discussion did not embrace the whole range of doctrinal truth.' In rejecting the errors of Rome, the Protestant reformers were compelled to undertake closer study of the Bible. Theological inquiry was enriched with a 'broader and sounder interpretation of the teaching of the Word of God.' According to Dewart, the Protestant Reformation represented a 'fuller and more explicit statement of the doctrines of Christianity bequeathed to the world in the inspired writings.' Similarly Wesley's exposition of free grace and Christian Perfection was a fuller development of biblical truth. These doctrines were given a prominence and power in Wesley's sermons that had been previously lacking. The history of Methodism, Dewart claimed, illustrated the reality of the development of understanding of Christian doctrine.[28]

This argument had profound implications for religion because it led to the conclusion that the human understanding of Christian revelation was imperfect and subject to improvement. Central to Dewart's new outlook was a confident conviction that progress in human knowledge would lead to greater Christian faith. He wrote: 'as Christian theologians become better acquainted with the literature and times of the languages in which the Scriptures were written – as they grow in knowledge of the facts of the created universe, and of their relation to spiritual truth – and understand more perfectly the laws and power of the human mind, they interpret the Word of God more correctly, and thus discover new truths and richer meanings in the teaching of the old Book.'[29] History had shown that Christian doctrine was moulded by the thought and social circumstances of the times. The idea of evolution suggested a new way to read the Bible, interpret doctrine, and comprehend revelation.

Dewart attributed his breaking away from the orthodox view of the fixity of doctrine to the influence of historical research. The biography of Jesus Christ had been recently written by a number of scholars to determine the indisputable facts of his life and what such facts revealed of his character, teaching, and mission. 'This widely-prevailing spirit of historical criticism,' Dewart explained, 'prompts us to trace the story of those doctrinal statements of truth, which have so largely become the guiding stars of Christendom.'[30] Dewart demonstrated that there was abundant historical evidence for the development of doctrine during biblical times and then further development throughout history by tracing the modifications in the doctrine of atonement. Unlike the most daring critics, however, Dewart was not willing to abandon the doctrinal foundation of Christianity. Development of doctrine did not imply that doctrines were necessarily false or that they inevitably hampered Christian understanding. On the contrary, according to Dewart, God was the guiding spirit of humanity's improving religious understanding and the development of doctrine. This more modern understanding provided Dewart with a sense of greater certainty for it seemed that the development of doctrine was another powerful indication of God's immanence. He was a spiritual force within nature and history.

Only a short time ago, Dewart acknowledged, it was deemed a serious heresy to argue that Christian doctrines had a historical development. The idea of development of Christian doctrine directly challenged some orthodox notions of the character of the Bible. All Scripture was understood as the Word of God, written under the inspiration of the Holy Spirit, and therefore free of any error in language, fact, or doctrine. Those holding a strictly orthodox view thought that the theory of development of doctrine implied the insufficiency of divine revelation and error in Scripture. In his lecture Dewart endeavoured to show that his modern point of view neither conflicted with the notion of divine authority of the Holy Scriptures, nor disparaged the value of definite doctrinal statements. He pointed out that there was an important distinction to be made between the infallible and unchangeable Word of God and the modifications in human understanding of it. Evolution of doctrine and understanding was possible, but not of Christianity itself. Revelation was complete, and Christianity was the final and complete expression of religious truth. Dewart was careful to explain that Christianity was not subject to 'the mutations and modifications of other sciences.' The Word of God was 'a Divine legacy to the Church and the world,' not the product of nature or history or human discovery. Any attempt to explain Christianity as the result of the evolution of civilization's religious consciousness was incorrect and dangerous, according to Dewart. He insisted that evolution could not explain the person, the teaching, or the life of Christ. Christianity arose not because of humanity's greater understanding of things spiritual but because of the miraculous intervention of God in history.

Although the idea of development of doctrine was a significant departure from orthodoxy, it was consistent with Methodist beliefs. The Methodist doctrine of Christian Perfection held that good Methodists would be constantly striving to improve their faith. Both Methodism and the nineteenth-century idea of history stressed that there was development through time, usually to a better state, and that this was moulded by experience. This affinity between Methodism and the modern approach to religion assisted clergymen like Dewart in accepting the perspective of science and historical criticism. Modern thought had been successfully remoulded into a Christian-based perspective. A sudden break from the religious past that many feared modern thought would bring, therefore, did not occur.

There was similar exploration of modern ideas and historical criticism of the Bible in Canadian Presbyterian circles. The much-publicized heresy trial of D.J. Macdonnell as well as controversies in Scotland alerted many to the currents of new thought.[31] William Caven was the principal and professor of biblical studies at Knox College in Toronto. He was instrumental in working out a compromise during the Macdonnell trial and wrote a number of pamphlets on the subject of doctrinal standards. He suggested that the church 'may not claim infallibility in interpretation of Scripture,' for he realized that progress in science and biblical criticism required some changes in the Westminster Confession. He did not feel threatened by the prospect of some revision because in his estimation none of the essential standards of the Christian faith were open to question. This acknowledgment of the wisdom of some liberality was tempered by his insistence that the Presbyterian standards had to be upheld against the 'age's eagerness ... to have the Church set free from the restraint of Confessions and Doctrinal Formularies altogether.' There must be resistance, he asserted, to any attempt to have doctrinal standards fundamentally revised in the cause of freedom of belief. He was convinced that the doctrines that formed the basis of evangelical Christianity, such as the trinity, divinity of the Lord, fall of humanity, as well as the atonement, regeneration, and salvation could 'never need fundamental revision.'[32]

Dr Caven was noted for his cautiousness. Rather than being on the cutting edge of biblical inquiry, he preferred to lead the students at Knox College to a deeper appreciation of the truth of Christianity. Keenly aware of the responsibility resting on the teachers of the Presbyterian church's ministry, Caven insisted that it would be scandalous for any student's belief in the authority of the Scripture and the central doctrines of the church to be undermined in the college classroom. In an age when there was fundamental and often intense and controversial questioning of Christian doctrine, he attempted to maintain a balanced view by being 'conservative of everything good which has come down to us, while ... seek[ing] by careful investigation to enlarge the boundaries of ascertained truth and to purge away errors and mistakes.' The Rev. Principal Gordon of Queen's University observed that 'he did not readily accept new views or methods, for he was conservative in his habits of thought; and yet he was always open to new disclosures of truth, ready to receive them after careful and sufficient test.'[33] Steadfast opposition to a critical approach to the Bible, Caven realized, could hinder proper interpretation of Scripture. There was scope for new and better understanding. This careful position dictated how Caven and many other Canadian Presbyterians responded to biblical criticism.

The degree to which Caven advocated a progressive stance was revealed in his sermon on the text 'All scripture is given by inspiration of God,' which he preached before the General Assembly of the Presbyterian Church at Brantford in 1893. He affirmed that the Bible was the 'inspired Word of God'; but also rejected the traditional view that the sacred writers were 'merely penmen of the Spirit, whose task was the purely mechanical one of setting down the words which were given to them.' With the exception of the Ten Commandments, according to Caven, the Scriptures were written by men. Most striking to Caven was the individuality of style and thought found in the Bible, including the New Testament. 'Isaiah's language and thought are easily distinguished from those of Jeremiah or Ezekiel,' he proclaimed. 'Little penetration is required to discern the difference between the vehement logic of Paul and the contemplative spirituality of John, to see wherein Luke is both like and unlike Paul, or to note in the Epistle of James striking features not found in any other part of the New Testament.' Differences in Scripture were not contradictions; but rather the distinctive ways in which writers of varying moral sensibility, intellectual outlook, and spirituality portrayed truth and revelation. Indeed, in Caven's view, God had selected different writers precisely because of their different 'aptitudes.' The variety of sacred writers served God's many purposes.

Caven affirmed that the Bible was 'most surely the Word of God.' He explained: 'God speaks *in* and *through* it. Its thoughts are God's thoughts, and its words are God's words. The human writer cannot strictly be termed the author of scripture, for this designation can belong only to Him who deigns to employ the writer for the delivery of His message.' Caven harmonized the critical approach with the Presbyterian belief that the Bible was the Word of God. According to Caven, the doctrines, narratives, prophecies, songs, and prayers in the Bible are forms of human speech employed by God to reveal himself. The Bible, therefore, was 'throughout human and throughout divine.' The authority of Scriptures could not be assailed. Biblical criticism understood in this way, he asserted, would only 'strengthen faith in God, the soul, redemption and immortality.'[34] Caven confidently believed that the insights gained through historical criticism would not alter 'the great lines of evangelical doctrine.'

Not surprisingly, the leading exponents of the new understanding of Christianity were those who had valiantly struggled with orthodoxy. In Methodist circles Nathanael Burwash and F.H. Wallace were two of the more vigorous advocates of liberal Christianity. In 1873 Burwash was appointed the dean of the new Faculty of Theology at Victoria College. This appointment signalled the commitment of the college and Methodist leadership to reconciling Christianity to science and modern thought for Burwash had been the professor of natural science and chemistry.[35] He was an early convert to biblical criticism, for he believed that a scientific theology would put an end to the numerous misconceptions and errors in human understanding that, in his view, were at the root of dogmatism and sectarianism, both very destructive of true Christianity. While he insisted that 'all scripture is given by inspiration of God,' he admitted that the words and books of the Bible were 'but the earthen vessel which but imperfectly contains the heavenly treasure.' What is divine in Scripture, he pointed out, should not be confused with the rhetoric and grammar of the Bible, which was determined by the time and place in which the Scripture was written as well as the personality of the writer himself. Burwash was determined to apply scientific principles to the Bible as a means to gain a deeper understanding of the Word of God.[36]

Along with Burwash, Wallace was a leading exponent of biblical criticism in Canada. He was one of the few Canadian clergymen who had direct contact with Harnack and Ritschl, the boldest and most speculative German biblical critics.[37] After his theological education Wallace served in Methodist parishes in Toronto, Cobourg, and Peterborough. In 1887 he was appointed professor of New Testament literature and exegesis at Victoria College. Wallace was convinced that an historical understanding of the Bible confirmed rather than undermined the divine origins and historical reliability of the New Testament. He emphasized, however, that the idea of plenary inspiration could not be maintained. Historical principles taught readers of the New Testament 'to give due prominence to the individuality of the various writers and to the development of thought.' The New Testament, Wallace wrote, was 'alive with the experiences, difficulties, struggles, antagonisms, heresies, arguments, appeals ... of the men and times to whom Christ spake and to whom he committed the special charge of founding the Church and of expounding His truth.' Jesus Christ was variously apprehended by different men in accordance with their backgrounds, temperaments, and circumstances.[38]

Wallace outlined the four separate perspectives, contained in the New Testament, that defined the major developments in human knowledge of Christ and understanding of divine revelation. First, there were the events and teachings of Jesus' life according to the synoptic Gospels. Second, there was the Apostles' representation of Christ's person, work, and teaching. Third was the theology of St Paul, which emphasized universal sin and salvation, the experience of conversion, and the missionary ideal. Finally, there was the theology of St John as it appeared in his gospel and epistles as well as the Book of Revelation, which according to Wallace's historical interpretation belonged to a time and stage of development different from the other parts of the New Testament. John, he pointed out, preached the truth of eternal life. Historical study, Wallace concluded, brought people closer to 'the living realities of the Bible and Christian experience' for it allowed them 'to behold the Divine Providence' guiding the growth of religious truth.[39]

Dewart was very cautious and Caven was defensive in approaching the modern understanding of Christianity, while Burwash and Wallace were much more open. Despite this important difference in their acceptance of critical inquiry, they agreed that the modern understanding of the Bible provided the foundation for greater assurance regarding the major tenets and cardinal beliefs of Christianity. The idea of development of doctrine, in particular, seemed to indicate that there were many ideas associated with Christianity that were the product of a particular time and place which probably obscured the faith. If these transitory ideas were recognized through critical inquiry, then what was truly essential in Christianity would be clear.

One of the major reasons why clergymen were receptive to the new liberal theology was that it assisted them in dealing with those aspects of Christianity which had struck them as immoral or no longer tenable and had caused many in their congregations to doubt the truth of Christianity. The historical understanding of the Bible liberated clergymen from many of the repressive characteristics of orthodoxy. For example, what struck many as being immoral or perhaps false in the Bible, such as the stories which taught that those who held irreverent views of God would be fined, imprisoned, or killed, could now be dismissed as part of the human element of the Bible, not to be confused with divine revelation or the Word of God.[40]

Clergymen could now more confidently defend the Bible against those who wondered whether it was a divine document. The Old Testament, in particular, had been subject to severe attack. There was serious question concerning its historic truthfulness, its scientific accuracy, its literary merit, and its moral standards. Also, critics pointed out that there were huge discrepancies between the Old and New Testament and concluded that both could not be the inspired and authoritative Word of God. They contrasted Jesus' teaching, which emphasized love and forgiveness, with the harsh Old Testament maxims of retaliation and revenge and felt 'compelled to cast away the old.' Clergymen were able to defend the Old Testament according to the principles of the development and growth of Scripture. The Rev. G.H. Wells, the minister of the American Presbyterian Church in Montreal, countered that 'the New Testament is different from the Old, not in the sense of denying or opposing it, but in the meaning of completing and of making it more full and clear. The Evangelists are wiser than the Prophets, and Christ is a better teacher and higher moralist than Moses.' Wells explicitly applied the idea of progress as

the key to reading the Bible properly. He explained that the harshness
of the Old Testament was an integral part of God's unfolding revelation. People had to learn the principle of justice, the danger and
enormity of sin, and the necessity of atonement before God could
reveal his mercy and forgiveness to them through the redeeming
work of Christ.[41]

One of the most hard-hitting and controversial attacks on the Old
Testament was Goldwin Smith's charge that it was 'Christianity's
Millstone.' Indeed he suggested that for the sake of Christianity the
Old Testament should be discarded because of its crude morality and
its unworthy religious and social ideas. Many, including Nathanael
Burwash and E.H. Dewart, severely criticized Smith's position on the
grounds that it had failed to make the 'enlightened distinction' between
what were the human elements in Scripture and what was the Word
of God. They charged Smith with failing to place the Old Testament
in its literary and historical context and instead presenting it in a
literal, mechanical, and old-fashioned manner which no competent
theologian would now be prepared to accept. Employing the new
historical and critical method, Dewart pointed out that a distinction
had to be made between events that occurred in Old Testament times
that were recounted in Scripture and the moral standard of the Old
Testament. He concluded that the Old Testament representations of
the majesty and glory of God, its denunciations of oppression and
injustice, its depiction of personal righteousness, its sympathy for the
poor and downtrodden, and especially its predictions of the Redeemer
'disprove, as with a voice from heaven, the unjust allegation that the
moral teaching of the Old Testament is "low and crude."'[42] The moral
questions pertaining to Christianity that had been so troublesome for
earnest clergymen at mid-century were largely answered for those
who embraced the tenets of liberal theology. History and biblical
criticism had become the basis for a new Christian apologetic, dem-
onstrating the degree to which the new understanding verged on
becoming the new orthodoxy.

This new orthodoxy seemed to liberate clergymen from many of
the problems and struggles they had been encountering. Harsh doctrinal standards were the source of much personal difficulty for many
clergymen. So long as preachers emphasized orthodox doctrine in
their sermons, they failed to attract the working masses and the educated in society. If, wrote one critic, the churchgoer only heard of sin
and its consequences Sunday after Sunday 'built upon isolated texts

of doubtful meaning, vain theological pretensions and so-called infallibilities of rite of doctrine,' then 'who is to blame if the once familiar pew sees him less than of old and the family becomes a backslider?' Holding up the 'great platitudes' of evangelism – sin, God's judgment, and death – in 'relentless images' only caused the pulpit to 'degenerate into a mere machine.'[43] A person's creed or belief in specific doctrines was now of little consequence.

If preaching was no longer to be doctrinal, then clergymen were faced with an urgent question, What shall we preach? One of the most far-reaching implications of liberal theology was the emphasis placed on Christianity as a moral system, instead of as a system of doctrine. 'Not only does the Bible reveal Christ and salvation,' Caven pointed out, 'but the whole duty of a Christian man is therein clearly set forth. The true code of morals is in the Bible.'[44] The Old Testament prophets were viewed as 'preachers for the times' since their ministry, as well as predicting the arrival of the Redeemer, condemned the personal and social evils of their society.[45] Jesus was interpreted in historical, ethical, and social terms as opposed to miraculous and spiritual ones. Attention was paid to his moral example and social teachings rather than to the meaning of the atonement and resurrection.

This social orientation in Christianity was a response to both the social and spiritual difficulties of the age. Albert Carman, now the general superintendent of the Methodist Church in Canada, outlined what he thought should be the new message and mission of the church in a ground-breaking sermon 'The Gospel of Justice.' He was struck by the contrast between Jesus' great appeal among the 'common people' and the cry of the modern church: 'How shall we reach the masses?' He wondered if the problem was rooted in the fact that the modern church's message was 'simply a spiritual one, teaching but the way to heaven.' Jesus, he pointed out, brought a gospel of hope as well as salvation. 'Christ's method,' he explained, 'seems to have been to crush the wrong, and thus make room for the spontaneous growth of the right. He found the temple a den of thieves; and he simply drove them out. He found the Scribes and the Pharisees oppressors of the people; and He ... scourged them with the whip of His divine wrath.'

Carman pointed out that in modern society, even though the landscape was 'covered with a forest of church spires, there are hideous wrongs, mighty injustice and cruel dishonesty.' In particular, there was great disparity in wealth between most working people and a small group of industrialists, landowners, and capitalists. The 'industrious, honest, capable' wage earners in Canadian cities were not paid enough to afford to furnish their homes, educate their children, pay their taxes, or pursue any kind of self-improving leisure activities, he charged. It seemed that the church's position with regard to these social conditions was non-interference. The modern church 'stands with open eyes and closed lips before the giant system of robbery, and assures the robbed that the Gospel has nothing for them but the droppings of charity from the ... rich, and a heaven of bliss if they bear with patience and meekness their wrongs on earth.' By the 1890s there was a widespread disposition to criticize this social conservatism that dominated preaching. The traditional evangelical approach – saving souls – was deemed inadequate in the face of society's ills. 'We are following the senile methods of the old temperance societies,' Carman wrote, 'which saved the drunkards but never thought of closing the saloons.'

Like the Old Testament prophets and the reform-minded Jesus clergymen would have to claim the rights of justice and brotherhood for the workers and the poor to enable the Christian message to have any meaning in a modern setting. It was thought the Christ who 'unsheathed the sword of the Gospel' against all moral and social wrongs should be the standard-bearer for the modern church. This social emphasis in preaching seemed to be unassailable under the scrutiny of historical criticism. It was based on an image of Jesus clearly outlined in the gospel accounts and the recent biographical studies of his life. Many clergymen reinterpreted Scripture and emphasized economic, social, and political themes in their sermons. The reconstruction of society, not the renewal of the individual soul, was increasingly emphasized. The moral and social improvement of society became the chief article of Christianity, while altruism became a Christian's highest calling. Carman's plea that the modern churches adopt a 'Gospel of Justice' was designed as a defence against the appeal of secular socialism among the urban masses. It was thought that if the churches preached a social gospel, based on the example of the Sermon on the Mount, which offered hope, then once again the 'common people' would flock to hear the Christian message.[46]

What had been a stumbling block for many mid-Victorian clergy, the moral and social teaching of the church, now had become the inspiration for the reform of the Christian message and mission. The theological foundation for this new orientation rested on the idea of the development of doctrine and the results of reverential biblical criticism. Liberal theology allowed the clergy the luxury of thinking that by emphasizing Christ's moral and social teaching they were, in essence, preaching a more enlightened Christianity.

Christian beliefs had been profoundly transformed in the period between the 1870s and the 1890s. By locating God in nature and history, instead of outside and beyond, traditional ideas of transcendence and eternity were undermined. This understanding had potentially powerful secular implications, since it led to the conclusion that God worked through natural and historical means instead of miraculous ones. Since modern thought had cast so much doubt upon spiritual realities, morality came to be identified with the Christian faith. As a consequence there was a tendency to render spiritual facts, such as the message of the Old Testament prophets and New Testament apostles, the life of Christ, and the Providence of God in terms of moral truths and ethical development. Furthermore, the Bible was understood in different terms. A distinction was drawn between divine revelation and the record of revelation as it appeared in the Bible. This new liberal theology marked a significant accommodation of Protestantism with the social and intellectual tendencies of the age. The Christian faith had been adjusted to the discoveries of science and history and the conclusions of biblical criticism. A strong sense of the miraculous or supernatural was being lost. Potentially this represented a powerful secularization of Christianity.

A daunting question arose: Did this modernization amount to the renewed certainty of belief and rejuvenation of faith that the clergy had been seeking? Liberal-thinking Christians placed emphasis on individual moral conscience over doctrine. In 1887 Macdonnell delivered a sermon which questioned the role of doctrinal standards much more profoundly than he had in the sermon that prompted the heresy trial in 1875. In discussing who may be full communicants in the church, he denied that candidates should believe in the doctrine of the trinity, the atonement, 'or the opinions handed down from the church fathers concerning future punishment.' What was important, Macdonnell concluded, was for communicants to believe in Jesus Christ as saviour from sin and to seek to obey his teaching.[47] In the more liberal theological atmosphere of the 1880s this more daring rejection of Presbyterian doctrine was not met with opposition or controversy. Doctrinal standards were no longer considered firm statements of truth; they were attempts to define the meaning of Christian revelation.

Furthermore, there was always the prospect of further development of Christian understanding. This commitment to perpetual change or greater understanding meant that Christianity was subject to constant reformation. There was no objective authoritative principle of belief. The most progressive liberal Protestants tended to base their religious understanding on science, history, empirical fact, and contemporary philosophy. In the quest for renewed certainty through the accommodation of Christianity with modern thought the era of certainty in matters of Christian faith had passed.

No doubt, the new Christianity saved many from completely losing their religious faith. God was no longer the remote, exacting judge for he had become a benevolent immanent Father, and Jesus was not the divine incarnation but the 'Perfect Man.' But this softening of orthodox evangelical doctrine marked an important development in the secularization of people's religion. Rather than trying to understand God being outside history and beyond human comprehension, those struggling with their faith, in a sense, wrestled God down to earth, making him understandable in human terms and conformable to the needs and demands of society. Humanitarian and moral concerns began to dictate people's understanding of the nature of God. Conceptions of God were being based, in part, on what people would like God to be.

3

Salvaging the Bible and the Evangelical Tradition

Below the surface of the successful accommodation of Christianity with modern thought there were serious cracks in the foundations of Protestantism in Canada. For some clergymen the outlook for the church was precarious at best. Superintendent Carman of the Methodist church, despite his advocacy of the gospel of justice, wondered if the modernists would do as well in saving people and fostering the church as the evangelicals who had brought 'their pure Bible and their pure faith and Gospel before the people.'[1] There was significant concern that the modern understanding of the Word of God advocated by the more liberal clergy robbed Christianity of its fundamental simplicity and appeal. Many clergymen commented that the genius of Jesus Christ the evangelist was that he preached the gospel in a 'plain' straightforward style. Frequently they cited Jesus' use of parables or the Sermon on the Mount to emphasize the importance of preaching directly to the people. Employing everyday language and illustrations was thought to be essential. In an address to the theology students of Knox College, Principal Caven emphasized that 'the Simplicity and Directness of Scripture should ever be the pattern of preaching.'[2]

Moreover, during this period of social and intellectual turmoil there was a growing realization regarding the necessity for united action in defence of the foundations of evangelical Christianity. There arose a number of evangelists who espoused a simple faith, did not stray from stating the main doctrines of Christianity, emphasized personal conversions, and insisted that the Bible was the Word of God. They attracted great support from people who received little spiritual sustenance or assurance from the learned discourses of the modern clergymen. In Canada the Crossley-Hunter urban revival team was symbolic of an important element within Protestantism that refused to abandon evangelicalism in favour of modern theology or the social gospel. This renewed emphasis on evangelicalism was not a return to the past; rather, it was an attempt to redefine what was thought to be the traditional foundation for the growth of Christianity and to rediscover the gospel message uncluttered by the complexities of transitory modern concerns. Ironically, however, these urban religious crusades were also very modern, particularly in the methods employed to gain new converts.

In many ways the Crossley-Hunter team made religion an attractive commodity for the masses of Canada's burgeoning towns and cities. This seemed essential for religion to remain central to the activities, concerns, and values of a culture that was undergoing massive change. A more pluralistic society was emerging in the wake of industrialization and urbanization. Many working people were looking to labour politics and the secular utopia of socialism to deal with the conditions that confronted them. A new middle class – including a growing number of retailers, clerks, professionals, managers, and business people – was also emerging. Many of these new urban citizens, whether they were labourers or well-off people in the middle ranks of the new social order, had migrated to the cities and towns from rural society. For the first time they were separated from the family home and the local church, regarded as the buttresses of religious life in the nineteenth century. Urban revivalism was designed to bring the mobile, rootless urban masses into fellowship in a church.[3] In the anonymity of city life pressure to attend church out of concern about one's image of respectability was not as compelling. To be successful urban revivalism had to attract the attention of the masses, who were experiencing an ever-growing choice of leisure activities, consumer items, and life styles.

Liberal theology proved to be shaky ground. Even the proponents of the modern outlook had certain reservations and worried about the passing of the evangelical tradition. Without rejecting the liberal spirit's social concern or open-mindedness to science, history, and biblical criticism, many clergymen still maintained that preaching personal salvation had to remain the church's primary mission.

Moreover, they realized that the foundation of Protestant Christianity, the divinely inspired Bible, had to be defended against the more speculative criticism that was being advanced from within church circles. Opposition to certain tenets of liberal theology emerged which were based on the fear that Christianity was being seriously compromised by powerful secular forces and consequently was becoming less distinctive and vital. There was concern about the future of many evangelical doctrines; but most worrisome to Protestant clergymen was the fate of people's understanding and appreciation of the Bible.

Protestants were a people of the Book; they insisted that Scripture alone was authoritative. The source for doctrine, church government, practice of the sacraments, ceremonies of worship, and hymnody was the Bible. It also was a proof text for systems of government and moral instruction as well as a guide to understanding the human experience. Principal MacVicar of Presbyterian College, Montreal, explained this overwhelming faith in the Word in matters of faith and worship: 'What do we know about the sacraments, their nature and efficacy, apart from the Word? What do we know about good works, wherein they consist and how they are to be performed, aside from the Bible? How can we engage in meditation and prayer unless we ·have revealed truth to direct our thoughts and teach us what to pray for?' Only through the Bible could one get close to God, for 'the written Word must be our medium of knowledge of the Incarnate Word.' It was the Word of God, MacVicar asserted, that brought people into 'living connection with Christian truth.' The gospel was a potent example of Christ's transforming power.[4] Before the beginnings of critical inquiry, most Protestants believed that the Bible was a book unlike any other. The Holy Scriptures were perceived as being uncorrupted by translation or print; they were the product of a miracle. To read or hear the Gospels was to come into direct contact with the Holy Spirit. A Bible that seemed accessible and easy to comprehend, therefore, was crucial to the strength of Protestantism. Indeed so much of the edifice of Protestantism was based on faith in the Bible as the Word of God and ultimate authority in both sacred and secular matters that if confidence in the Bible was undermined there was little to prevent the crumbling of the Protestant faith.[5] It was not surprising, therefore, that a great deal of the discussion within the Methodist and Presbyterian churches was ultimately focused on the nature and authority of the Bible.

Awareness that the Bible was subject to interpretation and that its text was subject to questioning and amendment became widespread with the publication of the Revised Version of the New Testament in 1881.[6] In Canadian dailies quotations from the Revised Version were compared with the text of the well-known and immensely popular King James Version, and the denominational press gave the revisions detailed and considered attention. Whether the revisions undermined the Christian faith was the most pressing question. In the *Christian Guardian* Nathanael Burwash confidently concluded that what was essential to Christianity remained intact. 'The authority and inspiration of the Scripture, the unity and spirituality of God, the person and work of Christ ... and the doctrines that concern the sin and salvation of man all find here most definite and satisfactory expression.'[7] Others were not so sanguine about the impact of the Revised Version on the popular mind. That the Bible was not necessarily the very Word of God was unsettling to clergy and laity. F.H. Wallace recalled that he stirred great controversy in his congregation when he read Scriptures from the revised New Testament.[8] The Rev. S.P. Rose pointed out that the Revised Version 'gave a great shock to popular belief in the verbal inerrancy of Holy Scripture.' He stressed that 'the growing loss of faith in the absolute inerrancy of Scripture, means a season of peril to multitudes. We have been trained to speak of the Bible as the religion of Protestants.'[9]

Leaders in the Methodist and Presbyterian churches identified the issue of whether the biblical writers were divinely inspired as the most important line of defence in their efforts to protect the Christian faith. At the 1893 meeting of the General Assembly of the Presbyterian Church of Canada, Principal Caven warned: 'We Protestant Christians should never forget how surely the maintenance of evangelical Christianity and freedom is bound up with the defence of the Bible. Let scripture lose its place of reverence and authority – let its authority be seriously impaired – and we shall inevitably suffer ... Our zeal for the circulation of the scriptures would soon decline.'[10] Albert Carman was equally outspoken in his defence of the Bible. 'Take away the Divine inspiration of the Holy Scriptures, which is to take away their infallibility, their sovereignty, and their sufficiency as a rule of faith and practice, and you take away the heart and life-blood of Christianity.' In Carman's view all the important doctrines that were indispensable to the Christian work of converting individuals and society were dependent on the overriding fact that the Bible was the revealed Word of God.[11]

It was the more speculative criticism which denied that the Bible was divinely inspired that alarmed the clergy. To use John S. Moir's apt phrasing, the course of biblical studies in Canada has been 'sane and tactful' or 'mildewed with discretion.'[12] Certainly Dewart and Caven and the even more liberal-thinking Wallace and Burwash were careful not to upset belief that the Bible contained the Word of God. Indeed the studies pursued by Canadian critics affirmed the authoritative role and divine inspiration of Scripture. The leading clergy in the Canadian Methodist and Presbyterian churches did not follow the more speculative criticism that rejected the notion of divine inspiration and suggested that any miraculous or supernatural act described in the Bible was of dubious historical validity. Perhaps typical of the consistently reverential and ever-cautious approach in the Canadian churches was the Rev. D. Ross's conclusion that speculation wielded an 'axe at the root of the fundamental truths of Christianity with savage vehemence,' for it did not regard the Bible as an account of God's actions throughout history and the record of His Word.[13] To deny divine inspiration of the Bible was to doubt the existence of the supernatural and the possibility of miracles, and therefore Christianity itself.

This insistence regarding the divine inspiration of the Bible led to highly publicized heresy trials in both the Methodist and Presbyterian churches in the 1890s. George C. Workman started teaching metaphysics and theology at Victoria College in 1882. Two years later he went to Germany to study Old Testament theology, and he came under the powerful influence of the most speculative higher critics. When Workman returned to Victoria College to resume his teaching duties in 1890, he was invited to give the annual lecture to the Theological Union. He delivered a paper on 'Messianic Prophecy,' in which he boldly argued that 'while ... portions of Hebrew Scripture abound with Messianic Prophecy there is no passage in the Old Testament that refers directly and predictively to Jesus Christ; that there is no passage in which the future Messiah stood objectively before the writer's mind, or in which the prophet made particular personal reference to the historic Christ.' Old Testament predictions of the coming of the Messiah were expressions of the traditional Judaic hope for a saviour-king, according to Workman. For Workman the significance of the prophets was that they were moral reformers and they paved the way for Christ and his message of personal religion, moral perfection, and faith in God. They 'were pre-eminently religious teachers, whose duty it was, as preachers of righteousness, to denounce sin, to command repentance, and to enforce obedience. In these respects, they were pioneers of Christianity.'[14] Workman's approach was a strictly historical one. There was little room in his interpretation for elements of the miraculous or supernatural. In his view God had not spoken directly to the prophets about the coming of Christ.

This lecture touched off great controversy. Charges were made that Victoria College was harbouring heretical teaching. The attack against Workman was led by E.H. Dewart, who quickly responded in the press and in *Jesus the Messiah in Prophecy and Fulfillment: A Review and Refutation of the Negative Theory of Messianic Prophecy.* By the 1890s the materialistic and speculative aspects of modern criticism were pushing Dewart into an increasingly conservative stance.[15] He assailed Workman for rejecting Christ's historic place in the prophecies of the Old Testament and for robbing the Old Testament prophets of their role as God's messengers. 'The knowledge of divine truth and future events which God supernaturally revealed to the Prophets was their crowning distinction. It lifted them out of the ranks of ordinary men and invested them with a mysterious authority in declaring "the word of the Lord" to the people.' The fulfilment of the prophecies in the New Testament vindicated the supernatural origin of the Old Testament, according to Dewart. What disturbed Dewart was the speculation which denied the supernatural role of divine power in human affairs and the Bible.[16] Workman's speculation only confirmed Dewart's long-held conviction that the church and clergy were partially responsible for the rising tide of unbelief in modern society.

Dewart was not repudiating the position he outlined in his groundbreaking address on 'The Development of Doctrine.' His criticism was consistent with the limits he had defined for the application of evolutionary principles to Christian understanding. The Messianic idea did not gradually develop by natural evolution as Workman had claimed; it was the outcome of the divine teaching received by the prophets. Dewart still espoused his approval for a modern approach to the contents of the Bible. He admitted that the human personality of the prophets could be seen in their revelations and that 'there is generally something in the prophecy adopted to the condition of the people of the prophet's time, and often a local coloring, if not local application.' He continued to defend the necessity of reverential biblical criticism. 'Dogmas and themes which cannot be proved by proper evidence, must give place to something better.'[17]

Dewart was convinced that the higher critics were casting the doctrines of evangelical Christianity aside instead of placing them in a
stronger and clearer light.[18] He had become so alarmed that he used
the pages of the *Christian Guardian* as a mouthpiece for his attack on
modern criticism. His insistence on unwavering belief in the verities
of evangelical Christianity placed him within a growing minority in
the church, and the *Guardian* no longer reflected the church's liberal
outlook. Dewart's increasingly strident position led to his dismissal
from the editorship of the denominational paper. The final words of
his last editorial indicate the degree to which he had fallen out of step
with a church that was open to reverential criticism and eager to
pursue a social gospel. He concluded: 'No modern culture can be
safely substituted for the fire and faith of the early Methodists. Nothing is so essential to the success of a Church as a genuine experience
of salvation.'[19] It is important to stress that Dewart clearly was not
drifting into the emerging fundamentalist camp. He dissociated his
position from that of the premillennial school, which applied Old and
New Testament prophecies to signs of the times and the imminent
second coming of Christ. The more speculative materialistic biblical
criticism had moved Dewart into an increasingly conservative stance
within evangelicalism.[20]

The questions raised by the Workman trial were terribly perplexing
ones for many Methodists. The division in the Methodist church was
not a clean-cut matter of one side publicly denying that Workman's
teaching had 'a baneful effect upon spiritual life,' and the other side
refusing to accept higher criticism.[21] Even some of the most liberal-
thinking clergy in the Methodist church could not support Workman.
For instance, F.H. Wallace found it difficult to take a position for he
believed in liberty and freedom of expression, but also in 'theological
honesty.' Wallace knew Workman well and was familiar with his
views, which were regarded as being highly speculative. The 'wreck-
age' of Christian beliefs such as human sinfulness, Christ's sacrifice,
and the atonement was a hopeful sign for Christianity, Workman
boldly proclaimed, for they were an obstacle to religious understanding. All that was necessary for Christian faith was belief in God,
immortality, and Christ.[22] Wallace found Workman to be 'opinion-
ative and dogmatic' as well as lacking in 'richness of imagination, or
grace of style' and concluded that his theology was 'essentially Uni-
tarian and inconsistent with his position as a Methodist minister and
professor.'[23] He was compelled to stand with those pressing for a

charge of heresy and Workman's dismissal. For Wallace, however, the issue was not one of heresy; rather, it was a question of the proper responsibilities of an ordained Methodist. Theological education had to be according to the church's 'own acknowledged and historical principles,' and Workman's teaching was clearly not within the Methodist discipline.

This view was echoed by Superintendent Carman. 'It would be a misfortune, an unpardonable blunder,' he told the 1896 convocation audience at Victoria College, 'for a young man to be sent out from a Presbyterian or Methodist theological school with loose ideas or no ideas at all of the divine inspiration of the Holy Scriptures.' As a basic principle, Carman insisted, anyone unwilling to teach Methodist doctrine should not receive Methodist money. This policy, he added, should apply to professors in Methodist faculties of theology as well as to ordained clergy.[24] In the end, Victoria College's Board of Regents decided, by a vote of ten to eight, to change Workman's appointment from the Faculty of Theology to the Faculty of Arts. In response, Workman resigned.[25]

A similar incident occurred in the Presbyterian church in 1893. The Presbytery of Montreal charged the Rev. John Campbell, professor of church history and apologetics at Presbyterian College of Montreal, with heresy. At issue was a lecture on 'The Perfect Book and the Perfect Father,' which was delivered to the Queen's theological alumni and student body. Campbell's lecture, although boldly phrased in sections, sought to make the same point that many other liberal-thinking Protestants had been advancing. The Bible was not infallible; it contained much that was faulty and human. He claimed that the Old Testament writers did not always portray the character of God in a true light; and therefore Jesus was sent to reveal him. The New Testament, he said, was the authoritative and supreme rule of faith, worship, and morality. In a more controversial vein, he proclaimed, 'We do not worship the book written or printed ... We worship God and hold the saving power of the book to be nil if it does not lead to Him ... It is of infinitely more importance to believe in an infallible God than an infallible book. The latter is vulgar idolatry, the worship and service of the creature more than the Creator.' Campbell went so far as to claim that his reason and moral sensibility told him as much about God as the Bible. For instance, he had concluded that despite what many Old Testament scribes had indicated, God did not sit in judgment and the 'penalty of sin' was not part of his perfect nature.[26]

This liberal doctrine was reminiscent of D.J. Macdonnell's speculations. Campbell's musings challenged the orthodox view that Scripture was inerrant in all matters of doctrine and fact because it was written under the inspiration of God.

That Campbell was charged with heresy revealed how vulnerable many felt the authority of Scriptures as the Word of God was becoming. The Presbytery of Montreal found Campbell guilty. But this judgment was overturned on appeal to the Synod of the Presbyterian Church of Canada, for Campbell's arguments did not border on the extreme secularist position. It was clear that Campbell considered the Bible to be a holy book which contained revelations from God and therefore had divine authority. Indeed, during the address in question Campbell stressed that 'without the printed book, I should never have known the heart of God, I cannot afford to undervalue the Bible, to put it on a level with reason or nature or with any other book in the world. It gives me truth, the objective and real as contrasted with the subjective and ideal God.'[27] These heresy proceedings were 'unpleasant' in Campbell's estimation for all he had done was indicate that 'ethical imperfections' existed in certain passages or accounts in the Old Testament. Yet he had been 'dragged into publicity, tossed about and baited in church courts' by an 'unjust, slanderous, abusive, and cruel' campaign.[28] In the end, in yet another compromise between the Presbyterian church and one of its bolder ministers, Campbell agreed that 'the statements of the Old Testament writers as to the character of God were true as far as they went, but in a few cases were not the whole truth.'[29]

For many concerned clergymen' the modernist disposition to minimize the divine element in the Bible was potentially much more dangerous to Christianity than the orthodox insistence on minimizing the human element in Scripture. Criticism and speculation, unchecked by the Christian apologetic, would lead to a decline of piety, which was the beginning, many feared, of the slippery descent into scepticism, worldliness, immorality, and atheism. For the Methodist and Presbyterian churches there was a fine line between reverential criticism and an understanding of the Bible that was dangerously sceptical and worldly.

These heresy trials and the bitterness surrounding them reflected growing concern about the implications the modern outlook had for the prospects of Christianity. The critical approach to the Bible and the realization that the Holy Spirit was not the actual author of every

word in Scriptures severely tested the liberal outlook of many clergymen. On one occasion Principal Grant confessed that he had held his
'own judgement in suspense for years, partly because the problem is
a very complicated one, partly because of natural reluctance to abandon a traditional view, and partly ... because of the philosophic pre-
suppositions of unbelieving critics.'[30] Ultimately, Grant concluded that
historical criticism did not harm Christianity provided it insisted on
the divine inspiration of the biblical writers. His later discussions of
the contents of the Bible were distinctly modern. He did not stress the
divine truths revealed supernaturally to the writers of Scripture. Instead he emphasized those things that were not matters of revelation
in the Bible, such as the history, morality, and ordinary experience of
biblical times.[31]

It was no coincidence that there were stirrings of the fundamentalist position in Canada during this period. Some Baptist and Presbyterian clergymen with a strong Calvinist background began to challenge
the prevailing post-millennial notion that the Kingdom of God would
be established after a long process of continual progress and before
Christ's second coming. This optimistic view was consistent with the
evangelical creed, liberal theology, and social gospel outlook that
dominated the late-nineteenth-century Protestant churches of Canada.
The dissenting premillennial view was at odds with this mainstream,
for it held to a gloomy view of the future.[32] At the Prophetic Bible
Conferences held at Niagara, Ontario, in 1885 the Rev. Joshua Denovan,
widely known as a 'hardshell Baptist' preacher, gave an address on
the second coming of Christ, in which he questioned many of the
assumptions of a generation convinced that the Kingdom of God was
closer to realization as a result of the moral and spiritual improvements
brought about by recent enlightened developments in human thought
and action. In Denovan's typically bleak premillennial view the establishment of the Kingdom of God was becoming more remote, and
Christ would have to intervene suddenly to rescue the redeemed
from the ever more sinful and wicked world:

Nowhere does Scripture say the human race is destined to be converted
by the Gospel. On the contrary, Jesus Christ repeatedly assures us that
at His return even the Christian world will resemble the Ten Virgins –
one half deluded and unprepared, the other half weary and slumbering.
With all the religious enterprise, with all the denominational competition
of these latter days 'when the Son of man cometh will He find faith in

the earth?' Nay, but as to the world in general when Jesus returns it will
be as it was in the days of Noah and Lot, the vast majority totally
wrapped and lost in godliness, worldliness, and ruinous sin.[33]

This reading of Christ's second coming was based on a literal or
mechanical approach to the Bible. The emergence of this viewpoint
was highly significant for not only did it indicate the beginnings of
the breakdown of the shaky evangelical consensus; it also indicated
that the Bible and how to read it were becoming very difficult and
controversial matters. The bedrock of the Protestant faith, therefore,
was on the verge of becoming the subject of a debate even more
divisive than the controversy over the proper boundaries of biblical
criticism revealed by the Workman and Campbell heresy trials.

What was perhaps most alarming to the Protestant clergy was that
the Bible no longer seemed to be readily understandable. Indeed,
George Grant felt compelled to deliver a series of addresses to the
Queen's Theological Alumni on 'How to Read the Bible.' He acknowledged that the Book was becoming difficult for Christian believers. Grant posed the question of whether the modern critical approach to Scriptures 'may not rob the plain man of the old Bible that
has hitherto sustained his spiritual life?' Most lay people were not
acquainted with history or criticism, and Grant feared that the new
insights into the Word of God were not easily accessible. Grant opened
his discussion by commenting that the Bible was no longer read as
extensively or with the same devotion as it had been in the past. He
noted that previously Bible reading was pursued eagerly, its contents
were considered interesting, the language of the day was biblical, and
indeed the Bible had 'great charm' in people's imagination. Such
reverence and enthusiasm for the Bible, Grant lamented, no longer
existed 'either in home, or church, or anywhere else.' Instead people
eagerly pored over the daily newspaper and 'other scrappy literature.'
Enthusiastic and attentive crowds were attracted to political speeches,
not to sermons containing the Word of God.[34] The Bible was losing its
place in popular culture.

Some explanation for this decline in Bible reading was provided by
Grant himself. For many the modern approach to the Bible had robbed
the Scriptures of their simplicity. For the Bible to be readily understood
the aid of historians, literary critics, and biblical commentators was
necessary. The critical approach to the Bible seemed to have created a
great distance or a barrier between the Word and its audience. The

Bible was becoming a scholar's book, not a holy book for everyone. The Word of God no longer seemed self-evident or immediately available. Furthermore, the critical method deprived the Bible of its uniqueness as the special revelation from God by placing it on the same level as other literature. Indeed, Grant probably stripped the Bible of some of its divine mystique, himself, during these addresses. In a statement that must have distressed the more devout in the Kingston audience, he said that 'we know from the New Testament what kind of men the Scribes were and we cannot accept them as trustworthy critics or infallible witnesses.' Even more shocking, perhaps, was Grant's declaration that 'the Book as the joint product of paper, ink, and leather-makers, of printers, binders, and publishers is nothing more than a piece of handiwork.' He went on to affirm that 'the spiritual truth it contains is what makes it precious and that is precious only as it is received into the soil of honest hearts and so becomes to them living truth.' But nevertheless the Bible was not as sacred or awe-inspiring as it had been for Protestants in the past; in the hands of some critics and clergy it was a book like many others.

Parish ministers were required to treat historical and literary criticism of the Bible in a different manner than theologians stationed in universities or clergy holding office in church bureaucracies or the editorial chair of a denominational paper because their calling was largely pastoral and their purpose was to affirm people's faith. In the pulpit ministers refrained from in-depth presentations or discussions of biblical criticism. To do so would make sermons too technical and worship too controversial for congregations seeking religious sustenance. But biblical criticism could not be completely ignored in the pulpit since it was leading many to call into question the authority of the Bible as the Word of God. Speculation concerning the nature of the Bible could not remain unanswered by clergymen. Otherwise, one Methodist preacher wrote, there was a danger 'in every man sitting in judgement upon the Bible, choosing such portions as he prefers, and rejecting the rest as not consistent with his reason or sentiment. It leads to the incoherent mass of opinions which, in the last fifteen years, have been in their variety like Falstaff's recruits, ... opinions which are in harmony neither with each other nor with the Bible.'[35] The approach of the 'busy pastor' to the challenge of biblical criticism was suggested by the Rev. S.P. Rose. Ministers had to admit the human element of the sacred writings in their sermons, he concluded; but they also had to preach that the Bible remained infallible for the purpose of making people knowledgeable about Christ and bringing them closer to God.[36]

Throughout the 1880s and 1890s many clergymen were convinced that the pulpit was losing its power.[37] There was a note of concern in the 1888 report of the Methodist church's Committee on the State of the Church: 'While our ministry is increasing in culture and accept-ability to the refined is it quite as powerful as of old in the awakening and conversion of the outcast and degraded?' Sermons that were informed by the most learned biblical theories or most recent social commentaries might meet the intellectual challenges of the day, but it was a matter of keen debate concerning the ability of such pulpit discourses to meet the evangelical imperative of claiming souls for Christ. In the *Canadian Baptist* E.W. Dadson eloquently editorialized that those listening to the sermons of the day

> must be struck with the marked absence of any conception of a God who demands anything, and who stands ready to exact the fulfillment of His will. We have the beauty of His compassion, the patience of His long suffering, and His mercy which endureth forever, plentifully set forth, but we miss mention of His compelling power and the conse-quences of not yielding implicit obedience to His will ... the fatherhood which reveals the stern face and the unequivocal rebuke not unaccompanied by the rod is conspicuous by its absence.[38]

A contributor to the *Knox College Monthly* summarized the concern that many held regarding the changes that were occurring in preaching. 'If in former times the pulpit was too dogmatic and given over to abstract doctrinal preaching, the pendulum has swung over to the other side, and now we have much preaching without doctrine, without teaching, without certainty, and consequently without power or spiritual results.'[39] The decline of preaching that was based on the doctrines of evangelicalism – something that had been looked for-ward to as the means of liberating Christianity from an oppressive dogmatism – was viewed with certain misgivings.

Such commentary was also advanced by observers from outside the churches. The editor of *Saturday Night* magazine, E.E. Sheppard, who was hardly an exponent of doctrinal orthodoxy, was also quite critical of what he considered to be the secularization of the pulpit. It seemed clear that the churches were losing their hold on the masses; but this was not because the masses were losing their religious faith, according to Sheppard. Instead, ministers were largely responsible for they no longer preached the gospel which emphasized the power of God to deliver salvation to everyone who had faith. While at Knox Presbyterian Church he heard the Rev. Dr Parsons deliver a sermon 'with the charm of cultured expression and theological expertness' on the question of salvation. But it had no effect. The congregation was left groping in the dark. In his critique Sheppard confronted the preacher: 'How? When? Where? Was there a soul within sound of your voice who did not desire the priceless gift! No. Why did they not reach out and take it? Because they could not see the hand or appreciate the gift! ... Did you tell us? Not a word.' This failure to reach the congregation was not just a shortcoming of one minister. After having listened to sixteen different preachers in Toronto, Sheppard concluded that he had 'not yet heard an answer to the jailer's question, "What shall I do to be saved?"' Even more indicative of the worldly spirit that was entering the church was the fact that if anyone had cried out that question from the pew, such an outpouring of contrition would be regarded as an embarrassment. 'Read one another's sermons,' Sheppard implored the ministry; 'read your own religious journals and see what they talk about and let me ask you this serious question: Is religion losing its hold on the preachers?' It was difficult for people to find religion at the church.[40]

For the churches there seemed to be plenty of evidence to suggest that if they deviated too far from the traditions of evangelical Christianity, then their ability to attract new converts or to maintain adherents was seriously diminished. One of the first indications of this was the success of the Salvation Army in Canada's cities and towns throughout the 1880s and early 1890s.[41] What impressed Agnes Machar, one of the most informed Presbyterians in Canada, was that the Salvation Army preached 'the simple gospel of Jesus Christ ... – no mere outward obedience to an organization, no complicated system of theology, but the simple elementary truths, acknowledged by all evangelical Christians, that sinful men need a Saviour, and that Christ is the saviour they need, to deliver them from guilt and the power of sin.' She approved of the Army's meetings in which recent converts gave testimony 'as to the joy and strength which they have received in the *great salvation* from sin and bondage' and outlined the change in their daily lives that had been wrought. The 'occasional grotesqueness' of the language or hymns employed in the services did not disturb her. She was convinced that the churches should embrace the zeal of 'these Red Cross Knights' as the means of 'grappling with an unbelieving world.'[42]

Response to the Salvation Army by the Methodist church was particularly revealing. The *Christian Guardian* acknowledged that the Salvation Army was doing work that the Protestant churches were failing to do. The Army's concentration on promoting the salvation of sinners and its ability to enlist new converts into active Christian work were impressive; whereas Methodism seemed to be lacking in vitality. So that worldliness would not continue to creep into the church, the *Guardian* called for the adoption of the Salvation Army's evangelical spirit.[43]

The successful revival campaigns waged by the American 'professional evangelists,' Dwight L. Moody and Sam Jones, perhaps, had a greater impact on the Methodist and Presbyterian churches in Canada.[44] In 1884 ministers from Toronto's evangelical churches, including E.H. Dewart and D.J. Macdonnell, organized an interdenominational Christian Convention, at which Dwight Moody was to be the keynote speaker. There was great anticipation regarding the arrival of the era's most successful evangelist. The Toronto publishing firm Hunter Rose reprinted many of Moody's volumes of sermons, such as *Heaven*, *The Way of God*, and *To the Work*, in its inexpensive pocket library series that was designed for the mass market. For church officials Moody was a great attraction because they were convinced that he was instrumental in modernizing the methods of the churches, in reaching the urban masses, and, most important, adding numbers to communicant rolls. Moody always worked in cooperation with the churches. As early as 1874, during the Moody-Sankey revival crusade in England, one minister pleaded for the adoption of Moody's systematic evangelistic work in the Canada Presbyterian Church.[45] The appeal of Moody's method was that he preached the gospel of 'the power of God unto salvation.' Such preaching seemed the only way for the clergy to be able to compete in an increasingly secular world in which hearing the Word of God by attending church seemed a very low priority. A half-hour sermon each week, it was recognized, was "a meagre opportunity for all we need to do ... For what can we expect to do in such a short space of time, for six days before, the minds of our hearers have been made a common thoroughfare by the concerns of worldly business. When we have them before us there is a worldly attitude of mind to rectify, an earthly crust to be broken through, before we can fairly reach them.'[46]

The major theme for discussion at the convention was 'How to Promote Spiritual Life in the Churches.' That such a theme was featured implied religious declension according to the *Christian Guardian*. In his opening address Moody declared that the only way people became spiritually quickened was by hearing God speak through the Bible. During his more detailed discussions he explained that modern preaching had strayed from the necessity of preaching Christ. 'Many ministers preached everything else but Christ,' he declared. Moody laid particular emphasis on the importance of believing in the inspiration of all the of Scriptures. Once confidence in the Bible as the Word of God was lost there would be a flood of backsliding, he warned. According to Moody, one of the largest barriers to spiritual life in the churches was that 'men did not seek the Lord with their hearts; a good many men were searching for the Lord with their intellects. It was a matter of revelation, not investigation. It was not necessary to go to find Christ. He was right there in His Word and they would find him if they searched for him with their hearts.' Neglect of the Word of God and a lack of effort for the conversion of souls were the causes of many difficulties for the churches, according to the convention. 'The world has gone into the church,' it was argued, 'moved right in and taken possession and that is the reason why we have little power.'[47]

While in Toronto, Moody led revival services during the evenings at Metropolitan Methodist Church. In the audience was a large proportion of young men, including artisans, mechanics, and 'toilers' as well as businessmen, professionals, and store clerks. The service had all the characteristics of a mass entertainment scene. The reporter for the *Toronto Evening News* observed that

> before the cathedral clock had chimed the hour of seven o'clock last evening the Metropolitan church was not simply crowded but packed ... by that time hundreds were being turned away, much to their discomfiture and disappointment; the gates were fully secured by chains and pickets were posted in every corner in the vain attempt to keep the immense throng from gaining admission to the grounds, but although this precaution was mainly successful there were nevertheless those whose impatience led them to scale the high iron fence with the thought that once within the grounds entrance to the church was comparatively easy, but in this they were mistaken, for every door was locked and picketed, and the last vestige of a chance to hear and see what was going

on inside was cut off, and the seeker was finally compelled to give up in despair. Before 7:30 thousands had turned their steps to the overflow meetings in Knox Church and Shaftesbury Hall.

Inside the cathedral, following hymn singing and before the exhortation for all to accept Christ, Moody sermonized that the greatest sin and the root of all other sins was unbelief. When he asked who was ready to come to Christ, 'up jumped several. Cries of "I will," came from all over the church ... amid the excitement young men got up and said "I will."' Moody then led those seeking conversion into the inquiry rooms, where he and his co-workers read from the Bible, explained in measured tones the need for immediate conversion, and encouraged the inquirers to repent.[48]

Toronto's ministers were convinced that the reasons for Moody's success were his stress on personal salvation, effective use of Scripture, facility for illustrations, and his plain style.[49] Moreover, Moody expressed no doubts regarding his religious convictions. These were the very features of worship that the Protestant churches under the influence of modern liberal theology were moving away from. Indeed, the Rev. John Potts suggested that although Moody and Sankey had done tremendous work in converting thousands, 'their chief work has been in the Churches – awakening drowsy professors into a quickening spirituality, and leading them out of the wilderness of doubt and barrenness into the promised land of abiding faith and unceasing fruitfulness ... I incline to the opinion that Mr. Moody has done good service in opening the eyes of ministers to see that hearty, earnest sermons are better than dry, elaborate discourses, or polished essays upon general topics of Scripture.'[50]

Sam Jones's revival campaign lasted for three weeks during October of 1886. The *Christian Guardian* reported that 'no such numbers ever before attended any religious services in Toronto.'[51] His preaching stressed something liberal ministers seldom mentioned: the importance of forsaking sin. The Rev. John Potts observed that 'never in the history of this city was there a more fearless denunciation of sin – of sin in its public and wide-spread manifestations – than by this simple, unostentatious, heroic soldier of the Lord Jesus Christ. While unusual attention was given to the bitter consequences of sin in this life as well as in eternity, never was the saving power of the Gospel more effectively proclaimed to listening multitudes.'[52] The necessity of repentance, the renouncing of all forms of ungodliness or immoral behaviour, and obedience to Christ were themes that dominated his addresses. Jones's preaching was emotional and personal in its appeal and sensational in its rhetoric. In his opening Toronto sermon he explained that he did not 'like to see a preacher who has one voice for the pulpit and another for the street.' Indeed, reliance on 'slang expressions' was the one thing that the Toronto Methodist establishment seemed to 'regret' about Jones's preaching.[53] Typically, Jones proclaimed: 'Every wrong road leads to hell, no matter how small it is, and how little you go into it. A little piece out of harmony with God, and you are altogether in harmony with hell.'[54] Jones's services closed with a call for all who desired to be saved and follow the Lord to stand up. 'Persons rose in all parts of the house in response ... and at every meeting a large number profess to have found peace through believing in Christ.' This ended Jones's appeal; he did not lead those seeking salvation to an inquiry room for a crisis-filled conversion experience. These mass meetings were endorsed by the Methodist church as an 'excellent way to bring sinners from darkness to light.'[55]

There was concern that the churches might not directly benefit from the quickened spiritual life in the community resulting from these revivalists' efforts. Indeed, one of the issues that caused the keenest debate at the 1884 Christian Convention was whether revival work lasted beyond the period of initial enthusiasm. The task of the clergy, therefore, was to find a way to harness the religious enthusiasm that these evangelistic services created to a sustained commitment to worship in the church. The Methodist church decided to appoint ordained clergymen to conduct revivalistic services. These special evangelists represented a return to the Methodist system of itinerancy on a grander scale. Instead of preaching on a rural circuit of many small communities, urban revivalists travelled from city to city spending up to six weeks in each urban centre leading revival meetings. The most influential of these professional Methodist evangelists was the team of the Rev. Thomas Crossley and the Rev. John Edwin Hunter. Crossley was born on 19 November 1850 in King Township, Canada West. At the age of seventeen he was converted at a Methodist camp meeting. He attended Toronto Normal School and taught in Oxford County for four years. Then he responded to a call to preach the Word of God. After finishing his term on probation, he attended Victoria College in Cobourg. After being ordained in 1880, he served as pastor at Hannah Street Methodist Church in Hamilton and Oxford Street Methodist Church in Brantford. Hunter was born in Durham

County, Canada West, on 29 July 1856. He was raised in the Presbyterian church but became a Methodist at age sixteen, as he found
certain elements of Calvinism to be too harsh and exacting and Presbyterian services to be too restrictive and spiritless. Hunter was an
itinerant preacher before being ordained in the Methodist Church of
Canada in 1882. He was the minister at Dominion City, Manitoba,
prior to teaming up with Crossley.

This revival team's services followed the immensely successful
structure developed by Moody and Sankey. They were a mixture of
biblical exposition, hymn singing, and exhortation. The purpose of
the meetings was to gain converts, and the meetings ended in an
inquiry room. Responsibility for the preaching and hymn singing fell
to Crossley. According to one editorialist, his sermons were 'plain,
pointed, logical, persuasive, and powerful,' while he employed the
language of 'the home, the shop, the world, but perfectly free from
slang.' He had a baritone singing voice 'of wonderful power and
sweetness ... Every word is distinctly uttered, so that, while the music
opens the door, the words enter, and pierce the heart.[56]

Crossley claimed that his talks were 'in harmony with the fundamental doctrines and practical teachings of evangelical denominations.'[57] He stressed the basic ideas of human sinfulness, the necessity
of repentance, the atoning work of Christ, and the Methodist concept
of perfect love. Crossley's message was particularly well suited to the
needs of a church hoping to prevent its communicants from drifting
away and seeking to win new adherents. It was unencumbered by
biblical scholarship and sophisticated doctrinal expositions, while still
being scriptural in many of the examples it outlined. Numerous biblical
quotations to illustrate the major points of the talk were always provided. Furthermore, Crossley made no reference to the harsh and
exacting rite of passage in orthodox theology. Hell-fire and the wrath
of God were not preached. The fundamental doctrines of evangelism
– ruin by sin, redemption through Christ, and regeneration by the
Holy Spirit – were not denied, but they were expressed in gentle and
romantic terms. During the constant stress on the necessity of conversion, the love and trustworthiness of God were emphasized. The
decision to become a Christian was made an easy one. Salvation was
based on two simple conditions, Crossley preached: 'repentance toward God and faith toward our Lord Jesus Christ.'[58]

The team also eschewed many of the intellectual and social problems
of the age that were engaging so many other clergymen. Reference

was not made to the challenges posed by science and biblical criticism, and a social gospel was not espoused. Such matters distracted attention from the primary objective of evangelism, saving souls. Crossley and Hunter were traditionalists in that they rested their faith on the 'solid ground' of 'the unchangeable God and the immutable Word.' In dealing with the contemporary 'contagion' of religious doubt, they revealed an anti-intellectual bias that seemed to appeal to their enthusiastic followers. For example, the Rev. W.H. Hincks had become disenchanted with complex theology. He acknowledged that Burwash was a man of 'cyclopaedic theological lore' to whom 'God was ... a glowing reality'; but found his teaching 'heavy.' By contrast, the Crossley-Hunter team 'exercised ... spiritually hypnotic evangelism.'[59] A common source of doubt, they claimed, was the misguided quest for explanations of spiritual phenomena and divine mystery. 'Faith is natural, while doubt has to be learned,' Crossley argued.[60] The antidote for religious doubt was straightforward: 'first take God's infallible Word as the ground of your unfaltering faith; and second, know Christ dwelling in your heart as the all-sufficient Saviour; and third, be a Christian worker.'[61]

The singing of popular hymns and gospel tunes was an integral part of the Crossley-Hunter revival meetings, and in this they also patterned their meetings after the successful Moody-Sankey formula. Hymns opened and closed the service, and appropriate gospel tunes were interspersed between the different sections of the program.[62] Crossley was following the evangelical tradition of breaking away from the constraints of formal church music, first established in Canada by Henry Alline during the Great Awakening in Nova Scotia.[63] Exuberant hymn singing had always been central to revival meetings in Canada, and many hymns had become deeply embedded in popular memory.[64] The compilers of the Canadian *Methodist Hymn and Tune Book* recognized that 'the rich treasures of gospel truth and Christian experience, embodied in our noble Wesleyan hymns, have been among the most potent forces in the history of Methodism. These hymns have been a liturgy and a confession of faith; promoting the spirit of devotion and soundness of doctrine, among the people called Methodists.'[65] It was understood that singing the gospel could reach the heart in ways that preaching could not. In his assessment of great hymns and hymn writers the Rev. Duncan Morrison of Owen Sound suggested that if anything will move the heart of a recreant backslider it is the singing of popular hymns with simple verses set to rousing popular music. In his analysis Morrison suggested that hymns were a potent 'vehicle of instruction and preaching God's great ordinance,' because the 'charm' of their rhymes and tunes 'affects the popular ear and makes a way for itself to the popular heart.'[66]

By the late nineteenth century hymns and gospel tunes were a deeply entrenched aspect of Protestant popular culture, and there were a number of publications designed to meet the public's growing demand for sacred songs.[67] Analysis of the lyrics of the gospel songs is revealing for with the emphasis on singing repetitious refrains and rousing choruses they were designed for memorization and enthusiastic audience participation. The lyrics reflected the religious language and values of the late-Victorian age.[68] These gospel tunes were probably a much better expression of the piety of the age than doctrinal statements, theological tracts, or sermons.

The gospel songs utilized in the Crossley-Hunter meetings were collected in a volume entitled *Songs of Salvation*. The preface indicated that the collection included songs which were different from the hymns that were ordinarily sung in churches and Sunday schools.[69] A few of the songs were Crossley originals, but the vast majority were the most popular gospel songs of the day which were a part of the broader evangelical culture. For example, a great many of Fanny Crosby's popular gospel songs were included. They were free from theological complications and stressed pious religious feeling with a particular emphasis on the tenderness of Jesus. Generally, the selections in the Crossley-Hunter collection ranged from intensely personal testimonies of individual religious experiences to rousing marchlike songs of collective spiritual enthusiasm and from songs of bereavement to choruses of exaltation and Christian triumph.

The lyrics of the gospel tunes sung by Crossley were an important complement to the evangelical message of his talks. It was hoped that the songs would lead to conversions; and so, the tone of many of the songs was exhortative. One song inquired: 'Jesus is pleading with thy poor soul, Will you be saved tonight? / ... Will you go on the same old way, Or will you be saved to-night?' In many of the songs individuals were portrayed as suffering, beset by temptation and sin, and unable to find any solace. The world was pictured as a stormy place of 'strife,' 'temptation,' and 'gloom.' The sinner was helpless, but not alone for salvation from the sin-stricken world rested with Jesus Christ. 'Jesus my Lord to Thee I cry, Unless thou help me I must die; ... / Helpless I am and full of guilt, But yet for me Thy blood was spilt, ...

/ No preparation can I make, My best resolves I only break, ... / Spirit of God now breathe on me, The Saviour's glory makes me see.'[70]

Jesus was depicted as the saviour for the broken, burdened, and 'sin oppressed.' He was sympathetic to the plight of the human race, for he had been tempted, suffered terribly, and died on a old wooden cross. 'At the cross of Jesus Let thy burden fall, While he gently whispers, I'll bear it all.' The frequent images of the crucifixion reflected the evangelical emphasis on personal salvation through Christ's sacrifice. 'Jesus keep me near the Cross, / There a precious fountain, / Free to all, a healing stream – / Flows from Calvary's mountain.' Although references to sinfulness abounded, the songs always ended with an exultant confirmation of the promise of salvation brought by Christ. Moreover, the relationship between Christ and those seeking salvation was portrayed as an intimate one. Christ reached out in a manner that was comforting, gentle, and full of love; there was no anger or harshness. The chorus of 'Song of Trust' rejoiced: 'Safe in the arms of Jesus, / Safe on His gentle breast, / There by His love o'ershaded, / Sweetly my soul shall rest.' Idyllic pastoral or domestic images, which would appeal to a populace seeking some kind of a utopia where their worldly aspirations would finally be fulfilled, dominated the portrayals of heaven:

My Father's house is built on high,
Far, far above the starry sky;
When from this earthly prison free,
That heavenly mansion mine shall be,
CHORUS: I'm going home, I'm going home
        I'm going home to die no more.[71]

The images throughout *Songs of Salvation* were sentimental, and the mood was always reassuring and winning. More important, the redemptive process outlined in the gospel songs was deceptively simple. What was called for was not intellectual assent to theological principles, but, rather, acceptance of an intimate relation with the tender, suffering person of Jesus.

Hunter was responsible for leading people through the conversion experience. He delivered the Bible readings and prayers, offered consolation, and directed the exhortations at the after-meeting in the inquiry room. Most reporters commented on Hunter's ability to move and control the audiences. During prayer, 'at his request, the vast audience acts like an army of soldiers under command, all heads are bowed in prayer – or all instantly rise and sing – as Hunter gives the word.' It was towards the end of the meetings, after the singing of gospel tunes, that Hunter would make powerful appeals to the unsaved, requesting those who desired salvation to stand up so that they could be led into the inquiry room. In impassioned tones he pleaded for people to seek conversion immediately, for there was great danger in delay. According to one witness, he 'was penetrating driving the truth home to the conscience of the people, or pathetically moving them to tears.'[72]

Despite these warnings the seriousness of sin was softened by Crossley and Hunter. For them, sin was a series of moral offences, such as drinking, card-playing, attending parlour dances, and reading sensational novels, rather than fundamental alienation from God. Conversion therefore was much easier, for it was largely a matter of pledging to give up immoral behaviour. At the Crossley-Hunter meetings people were not made uncomfortable about their lack of piety. There was little confrontation. 'The style of these evangelists is pleasant,' *Acta Victoriana* concluded. 'They make you feel right at home; they want you to get acquainted; they never scold; they are happy, and want everybody else to be the same.'[73] The moral rather than spiritual aspects of Christianity were emphasized by the late-Victorian revivalists.

The Crossley-Hunter revival meetings were deeply rooted in evangelical heritage; but it is also clear that this professional revivalism was designed to appeal to and even manipulate the modern urban citizen. The methods employed by Crossley and Hunter were more suitable for an urban population intensely concerned about respectability and privacy. Outdoor camp meetings were replaced by mass gatherings in churches and auditoriums, and the highly visible anxious bench was replaced by the more confidential and secluded setting of the inquiry room. Indeed, the atmosphere in the inquiry room was very much like a family parlour as opposed to the anxious bench of the camp meeting. Perhaps the inquiry room was designed to substitute for the intimacy of family worship around the hearth, something many in the cities would no longer experience. The emotional intensity of the early Victorian revival, in which penitents experienced the extremes of agonizing confession and ecstatic deliverance from sin, was replaced by a more earnest and restrained evangelical meeting.

There was support within the Presbyterian church in favour of this

Methodist-inspired evangelism. The *Knox College Monthly* argued that 'one enthusiastic meeting of five hundred is worth more than ten meetings of fifty persons each ... Men are more easily moved in masses. The ablest preacher finds it a difficult thing to move men in their struggling congregations. There is a warmth and power of sympathy in numbers which greatly helps in evangelistic services.'[74] Indeed, the Presbyterian church had been wrestling with the stultified nature of its worship services since the 1870s. They were long and almost completely dominated by the spoken word and the minister. There was little meaningful congregational participation. Wishing to end their passive role during worship services, the Presbyterian laity pressured for reform. This movement was spearheaded by Sir Sandford Fleming, who advocated the introduction of congregational prayers as a regular part of worship. He suggested that a Book of Prayers or a 'treasury of common Christian devotions' including prayers of confession, supplication, thanksgiving, and intercession be adopted by the church.[75] The installation of organs and hymn singing were the most controversial and visible signs of the pressure to move away from a strict puritanical heritage in Presbyterian worship.

The Crossley-Hunter revivals were not strictly Methodist meetings. Ministers from all the evangelical churches joined the team on the platform and in the inquiry rooms. Moreover, the statistics quoted in local newspapers on the number of new members gained by the different churches during the team's campaigns indicate that the movement was broadly based and interdenominational. The meetings were often advertised as 'Union Revival Services.' In Kingston the local Methodist churches received 501 new converts during the revival period, the Presbyterian churches 183, the Church of England 131, the Congregational churches 87, the Baptists 22, and the Salvation Army 5. In Hamilton the Methodist churches gained the most new adherents by far. There were 587 new Methodist members, 98 additional Presbyterians, 58 Anglicans, and 36 Baptists. The revival was also very broadly based in Winnipeg. The Methodist churches received 308 new members, the Presbyterian churches 254, the Church of England 108, the Congregational churches 98, the Baptists 32, the Lutheran churches 12, and 5 new members joined the Catholic church.[76]

Not all clergy, however, were enthusiastic about the professional revivalists. Presbyterians, in particular, sensed that urban revivalism was making an accommodation with popular culture in a manner that robbed religion of its otherworldly or spiritual qualities. William

Caven reflected a traditional Presbyterian concern regarding the primacy of sound scriptural preaching in worship services in his commentary on modern preaching. There was a tendency towards a lack of seriousness, dignity, and reverence, he thought. It was difficult to detect a sense of divine presence in preaching styles that were primarily designed to amuse the congregation. Caven was despondent for it seemed that clergymen were succumbing to whatever happened to be fashionable. 'Many who stand to speak in God's name and to continue the work in which the prophets and apostles were engaged deliberately count upon their irreverent eccentricities, whether in selection of subjects or in their manner of speech, as an element of popularity.'[77] Entertainment was being substituted for devout communion with the Holy Spirit, in Caven's estimation.

William Cochrane was equally harsh. He noted that worship was being overwhelmed by 'a love for the beautiful – a fondness for pomp, and ostentatious display.' The rise of this sentimental religion was a direct reflection of the languishing of true piety and the decay of vital Christianity. The idea of preaching as a form of communion between God and faithful communicants, with the minister being an inspired medium, seemed to be disappearing. Sermons were no longer challenging for they did not lift people out of the mundane secular world. It appeared that true religion was being replaced by 'sentiment,' and 'mere outward emotion' was being mistaken for godly penitence and conversion. Such false piety meant that the boundary line between the church and the world was becoming 'less and less definite.'[78] A more measured assessment of the qualities of sentimental preaching came from the pen of E.E. Sheppard in his *Saturday Night* series on Toronto's prominent clergy. When he attended Jarvis Street Baptist Church, he heard the Rev. Dr Jesse Thomas deliver a sermon full of flowery rhetoric and references to holy things that lifted the congregation 'gently as the breeze moves the flowers that look up to God.' There was no question that Thomas had created a devotional atmosphere, Sheppard commented; but he wondered whether the sermon made a lasting impression that inspired people to good works, or whether it moved anyone beyond a mere 'feeling of goodness.'[79]

Mass evangelism, therefore, represented a very different response to the spiritual crisis of the age than the one advanced by liberal divines. The Crossley-Hunter worship services were designed to relieve the spiritual anxiety and religious doubt of the masses. By shunning theological controversy Crossley and Hunter set themselves apart from the more militant conservative position, and by softening evangelical doctrine they were consistent with the optimistic mood of the age. Like other leading Victorian evangelists, Crossley and Hunter were effective because, at least superficially, they appealed to the traditional and familiar in an age of uncertainty.

While their message may have been reminiscent of evangelicalism, their revival techniques or methods were unabashedly modern. Indeed, Crossley and Hunter seemed to realize that they were involved in intense competition with more secular forms of entertainment and leisure for the attention of the urban masses. Crossley's most oft-repeated lectures were his attacks against the social evils of modern leisure, such as frequenting saloons, ballroom dancing, card-playing, and reading sensational novels.[80] In their determination to compete with an ever-growing number of secular leisure pursuits, Crossley and Hunter subjected the Christian message to the standards of popular culture. Only in this way, it seemed, could the urban masses be reached and religion and the churches remain central to modern life.

At a popular level the evangelical tradition clearly had been affected by the social and intellectual turmoil of the era. To dismiss those elements in Crossley-Hunter revivalism that were clearly based on the evangelical tradition would be inaccurate; but to overlook those elements, especially in their techniques, that were clearly designed to appeal to a secular popular culture and mass consumer consciousness would also be inaccurate. What was disturbing was that the religion that seemed to appeal to the greatest number and attract a large following in the towns and cities was shorn of real substance or a sense of awe and reverence for the supernatural. As the *Presbyterian Review* lamented, 'the old, old story of the love of Jesus seems to have lost its charm; and so there must be something more spicy, for a religious public that seems to be acquiring a *depraved* taste.'[81]

The success of the Crossley-Hunter team and other urban revivalists in late-nineteenth-century Canada was an ironic indication that a great deal was being sacrificed in Protestant Christianity in order for it to compete successfully in the open market-place of modern society. The critics of modern preaching indicated there was a serious loss of substance in the gospel message as it was delivered by many popular revivalists. Indeed, what was demanded of people in terms of conversion experience and belief by the late-nineteenth-century clergy was much less substantial than what had been demanded in the earlier part of the century. The softening of the evangelical creed, the shallow nature of religious experience, the open debate about the contents of the Bible along with questioning of its authority, and the vague sense of the supernatural all pointed to a process of seculariza-tion occurring within the Protestant community.[82]

4

The False Promise
of Missions

The missionary impulse was one of the major features of late-Victorian society. In the records of the Presbyterian and Methodist churches more attention was given to missions than to any other topic or concern. Reports from the mission fields, especially foreign missions, captured the imagination of Canadians. It was thought that missionary activity marked a new and greater 'heroism in the army of Christian adventurers going to all lands, and proclaiming under King Jesus a war against sin and idolatry.'[1] The resources and the workforce dedicated to Christian missions represented an outpouring of the confident and optimistic spirit of the age. The 'evangelization of the world in this generation' was thought to be within reach. Missionary work was regarded as the ultimate act of dedication to the cause of Christianity, as it called for courageous surrender to the service of God on the part of missionaries and revealed an unusual degree of religious conviction. The missionary enterprises of Canadian churches were regarded as a measurement of their vigour and wealth, and the growing number of missionaries and especially converts was regarded as evidence of the truth and efficacy of Christianity.[2]

This perspective underestimated the forces compelling churches to look outward to new fields. To an extent, they were drawn to missions because attracting new converts close to home seemed to be increasingly difficult. The growing resistance to evangelical activity within Canadian society accounts for the flood-tide of Canadian missionary activity overseas and in the Northwest. The missionary fields seemed more promising for church expansion and growth. The Rev. William Withrow, editor of the *Canadian Methodist Magazine*, which dedicated many articles to missions overseas, wrote: 'when the citadel of our faith is attacked at home, let us go to our Missions to authenticate our theology, in these days of sad latitudinarianism, when spiritual religion is by many derided as a myth and a mockery, let us go to our Missions to authenticate our experience.'[3] The outpouring of missionary activity in late-Victorian Canada was as much a defensive reaction by the churches increasingly conscious of their declining fortunes as it was an indication of their strength. The supreme confidence and crusading spirit which underlay missions almost concealed – but not quite – the deeper currents of unrest and anxiety over the prospects for Christianity in Canada.

In the end the missionary experience, especially in the foreign fields, further undermined confidence in Christianity. The missionary experience did not 'authenticate' the religious experience of evangelicalism. The great difficulty in gaining converts through preaching the 'pure gospel' led to more serious questioning about Christianity. Moreover, contact with the religions of the world undermined the absolute confidence in the uniqueness and superiority of Christianity. Underneath the aggressive and confident outreach of foreign mission enthusiasm there was a deep sense of crisis brewing.

The interest in foreign missions was evident as early as the 1830s in Canada. R.E. Burpee, who under the sponsorship of the Baptist Associations of Nova Scotia and New Brunswick set sail for Burma in 1839, was the first Protestant foreign missionary to leave British North America. The first foreign mission field sponsored by the Presbyterians was the subject of much debate. The Free Church Synod of Nova Scotia comprised only thirty churches and around five thousand members. Many of the congregations were poorly organized and could barely support a local clergyman. When the prospect of sponsoring a mission field in the New Hebrides arose, many argued that a mission field could not be supported. The prevailing argument, however, insisted that a commitment to a mission field would promote the cause of religion and strengthen the church in Nova Scotia. John Geddie, who was destined to be appointed the missionary to the New Hebrides, argued that 'a wider beneficence which looked to the welfare of those beyond, would be returned in rich blessings upon the church in all her measures at home.'[4] This conviction that foreign missions were essential to the prosperity of the churches at home remained strong until the end of the century. There was a flood of promotional literature from the churches and the missionaries themselves emphasizing that the conversion of the 'heathen' has strengthened faith in 'the supernatural origin and truth of our religion.' Success in foreign missions, particularly conversions, was regarded as solid evidence of the truth and efficacy of Christianity.

Indeed the missionary movement was inspired, in part, by a belief in the universal application of Christianity to the spiritual needs of every human race. This supreme confidence was best demonstrated in the contemptuous attitude of the missionary promoters towards the other religions of the world. They were quickly dismissed as being inadequate in meeting the spiritual and moral requirements of their followers. Buddhism was dismissed as being 'utterly powerless to beget wisdom or virtue' and was regarded as being a form of atheism, leaving people without any hope in the world. Hinduism was rejected as idolatry in which the crudest things are 'converted into objects of superstitious reverence.' The rites of the Hindu faith were considered 'impure and sensual and ... utterly debasing.' Although it was acknowledged that the Islamic faith was not sunk in primitive idolatry and professed a reverence for a Supreme Being, it also was dismissed as being inadequate, for it did not meet the spiritual yearnings of the soul. For example, James Croil, the editor of the *Presbyterian Record* and an enthusiastic supporter of foreign missions, wrote that 'Mohammedanism ... recognizes no divine mediator between God and man.' In a fashion typical of the lack of sympathy and understanding of the day he continued: 'Maintained by the sword, it exercises a cruel and despotic sway over the minds of its votaries. It is remorselessly intolerant and persecuting, deprives men of liberty, upholds slavery and polygamy, and degrades women to the level of brutes.'[5]

In the encounter between Christianity and the 'heathen faiths,' it was believed there could be absolutely no modification of Christianity in response to the other faiths, for to do so would compromise Christianity with superstition and immoral ethics. The principal of Acadia College clearly set forth this understanding in his correspondence with Canadian Baptist missionaries in the Telugu field in India. 'The theological system you introduce,' he instructed, 'must be thoroughly *biblical*. The question is not what *we think*, but what *God teaches* and to that teaching their must be absolute submission.'[6]

Similarly, the reports from the mission fields contained an equally unenlightened view of world religions. There was heavy emphasis on what was regarded as the superstitious faith, immoral society, and backward culture of foreign people. Examples of compassion and understanding by the missionaries were frequently overwhelmed by a militant missionary language that continually insisted on the ability of the soul-winning gospel to uplift the 'wretched heathen.' John Geddie understood that a gospel message of mercy and love should be preached in every foreign mission field; but his attitude towards the natives of the New Hebredes outlined in his mission reports was insensitive and even ruthless.[7] The solution to what was considered the pervasive heathenism and immorality of foreign lands seemed crystal clear to the mid-Victorian Christian missionary. Reflecting a confident faith in the spiritual and moral superiority of Christianity, there was an overwhelming consensus that the gospel of salvation was the only remedy that could possibly uplift the heathen world.

This supreme confidence in Christianity was initially undermined in the mission fields themselves. Indeed from very early on missionaries privately reported that they were encountering great difficulty in gaining converts. In 1860 George Gordon wrote to the Board of Foreign Missions of the Presbyterian Church of Nova Scotia from the Pacific island of Eromanga that he could only report matters of 'secondary importance.' There was no evidence of the 'convincing and quickening power' of the Holy Spirit moving the 'heathen' to conversion. For the most part, these difficulties were mentioned in the missionary literature as a way of bringing attention to the necessity of gaining more support for the field. These struggles allowed the churches to dwell on the martyrdom inherent in the missionary calling. Somehow the struggles of the missionaries made their endeavours more heroic and therefore more appealing at home.

No doubt much of the disillusionment over the foreign missions rested in the unrealistic or utopian expectations regarding the power of the gospel. What is important for the purposes of this study is that the resistance the missionaries encountered in their attempts to establish Christianity in foreign fields compelled them to emphasize more secular or civilizing aspects of missionary work. Few were advocating the pure gospel approach to missionary work by the late nineteenth century. The evangelical emphasis on snatching the 'heathen' from the hell-fire of sinfulness was being replaced by an approach that emphasized long-term evangelization through education and social service. This shift does not indicate that, in the early stages, the missionary was motivated by religious concerns alone. Missionaries had always been intent on introducing Western morality and culture. For instance, John Geddie was concerned about the lack of formal education, native marriage practices, cannibalism, and what he thought was a brutal system of justice, and he hoped that introducing the gospel would change these 'barbaric customs.'[8]

Nevertheless, as missionaries continually faced dismal results in their attempts to extend the gospel of salvation and bring about conversions, their emphasis changed into a broader concern for the promotion of moral and social reform. Missionary work in schools and hospitals consumed a growing amount of the missionaries' efforts and enthusiasm. They hoped that this more secular missionary activity would open the door to the gospel; but the emphasis in their work clearly had changed. Mission fields were becoming crowded with laypersons, especially teachers and medical doctors, who did not preach and who measured successful missionary work in terms of the progress of education, the cure of disease, and the numbers of hospitals and schools built, not the number of souls saved or churches built.[9] As Ruth Brouwer has demonstrated in her work on Presbyterian women missionaries, this social service or civilizing orientation in missionary work was not rooted in a conscious secularization of the missionary impulse, but rather disappointment in the failure to bring about mass conversions.[10] The result, nevertheless, was mission work that was more secular in its objectives.

The emphasis on civilizing missionary work received powerful support from the increasingly liberal religious outlook of the Canadian churches, which tended to minimize the importance of doctrine and saving souls while emphasizing Christianity's role in promoting moral reform and social justice. George Grant made this new understanding clear in a review of missionary work he wrote for the Presbyterian church. Our aim, he argued, was not to convert individuals but to inspire societies with new life. It would be a waste, he added, to send out missionaries without furnishing them with all the 'appliances' that a Christian civilization offered, such as hospitals, dispensaries, printing presses, schools, and orphanages.[11] Instead of accounting for the low number of converts, many reports from the mission fields outlined the moral reform that stemmed from the missionary effort. Missionaries could point to the decline of the opium trade, temperance, restraint of practices, such as polygamy, adultery, and child-marriage, and the improved status of women, as well as the end of cannibalism and the slave trade as evidence of the fruits of Christianity. Their reports often became detailed accounts of successful orphanages and schools, better medical care and standards of health, and the introduction of improved agricultural techniques. It was the tangible impact that this more secular mission work was having, not the conversion of souls, that made the bold dream of the 'evangelization of the world in this generation' seem possible to many in the late nineteenth century and inspired continued confidence and support for missionary activity.[12]

Liberal Christianity also had a profound impact on how Christianity was understood in relation to the other religions of the world. The idea of the development of doctrine and the realization that interpretation of the Word of God was subject to social and cultural circumstances and was not final meant that establishing certainty about what was permanent and essential in Christianity was difficult. What was Christian truth and what was myth or merely the product of Western civilization could not be confidently discerned. There was questioning about the absolute supremacy of Christianity among the world religions. Total conversion to Christianity resulting in the complete disappearance of other religious faiths, therefore, could no longer be demanded. On the mission fields and in the mission board meetings in Canada there was a growing encouragement of native missionaries, who would combine what was best from their religious traditions with Christianity.[13]

In George Grant's influential and important study, *The Religions of the World* (1895), there are hints that his appreciation of other faiths was perhaps unnerving faith in the absolute moral and spiritual superiority of Christianity. This book demonstrated how significantly attitudes towards other religions had changed as a result of a generation of exposure to different cultural and religious traditions. At the beginning of his study Grant acknowledged that the earlier expectations of Christian 'victory' on the mission fields were naïve in the face of the sophistication of the other world religions. Moreover, he conceded that Christianity would have to learn certain things from the other religions in order to be successful in its missionary endeavours. In particular, he explained that there would have to be an appreciation of 'the spiritual and social needs' that other enduring world religions were able to meet. Christianity would have to assimilate these qualities if it ever was to realize its goal of becoming the universal faith of humankind.[14]

Throughout his study of comparative religion Grant made it clear that he still thought that Christianity was the superior faith. Indeed he used Christianity as the standard by which to compare the other religions. Not surprisingly, they came up short; but what was significant was the degree of tolerance that Grant demonstrated in his analysis. He undercut many of the confident beliefs in the unique spiritual and moral qualities of Christianity. He pointed out that the founder of Taoism 'taught the greatest of the New Testament precepts "Recompense evil with good."' Grant was perhaps most impressed by Hinduism. In citing a poem from the Bhagavad Gita, he noted 'how the great tenets of Hinduism are here enunciated; the eternity and immortality of the soul, the mortality and mutability of the body, the transmigration of the soul, and the existence of Supreme Spirit to whom the existence of the universe is to be ascribed, from which everything proceeds, and to which everything returns.' Despite these striking similarities to Christianity, Hinduism had some fatal defects, according to Grant. It did not establish the fact that God was separate from humankind, possessed a sovereign will, and was a righteous, pure, merciful, and loving spiritual presence.[15]

Grant's comparative study was most intriguing in relation to the Islamic faith. In this analysis he directly contradicted traditional Christian notions of the inferiority of Islam; moreover, he suggested that the history of Christianity, much like that of Islam, was not above reproach. He noted that while Muhammadanism sanctioned the use of the sword, 'Charlemagne's arms had more to do with the conversion of the Saxons than had the preaching of the missionaries.' And down to very recent times, he noted, the Bible has been cited for authority to draw the sword against the enemies of God and the church. Grant was willing to concede other similarities between the two historic faiths. He applied his knowledge of biblical criticism to his comparative study and concluded that both the Koran and the Old Testament were flawed records. The life and teachings of Muhammad as presented in the Koran, Grant indicated, were 'rudely and fortuitously put together ... with artless simplicity' with the result that the proper historical context was not known. But Grant cautioned, 'it is now understood that the scribes who compiled the sacred literature of Israel did their work with a similar unconscious lack of critical judgement. The proof is on the very face of the Old Testament. They separated the first five books from the sixth ... and they threw the twelve so-called minor prophets, including the earliest and the latest of the canonical prophets, pell-mell into one book.' The Bible was still superior, Grant insisted, for it contained the record of the life and resurrection of Jesus Christ, God's only revelation. One of the crucial areas where Islam differed from Christianity was in its understanding of God. In Islam, according to Grant, God was only sovereign. There was no concept of a loving merciful God. Moreover, there was not the historical experience of the Incarnation, and therefore 'no intimate and constant communion of the soul with God in Christ.' Without an historic event like Jesus' sacrifice on the cross, Grant suggested that Islam was only left with the uncertain foundation of Muhammad's word as it was reported in the Koran.[16]

In advocating this more open and tolerant response to the religions of the world, Grant was careful to dispute the more radical view that Christianity was merely one of many legitimate faiths that somehow met the spiritual yearnings of people and answered imponderable questions about the 'unseen.' He pointed out that 'the tendency on the part of hasty generalisers, is to assume that Christianity can have no special claim, and that the differences between it and other religions are merely accidental. It is even thought a sign of narrowness or intolerance to assert that Christianity is distinctive, and that it has its root not only in the spiritual nature of man, but also in a Special Revelation from God.'[17] Clearly, Grant did not share this view that placed the Christian faith on the same footing as Confucianism, Hinduism, Buddhism, and the Islamic faith. He was obviously concerned about the emergence of religious relativism that would undermine confident belief in Christianity. There was the possibility for people to choose those aspects of the different religions of the world that they found the most appealing.[18]

Such an understanding of comparative religion caused a serious stir in the Baptist church in 1909. By this time, controversy regarding teaching at McMaster University was reaching serious proportions as the more conservative members of the church worried that many of the professors were teaching heretical ideas. The Rev. Elmore Harris, the premillennial pastor of Walmer Road Baptist Church who had been long-involved in the Prophetic Bible movement, was alarmed by an address given by George Cross, who held the chair in history at McMaster, to the Canadian Club in Woodstock, Ontario. There had been growing concern in Baptist circles concerning Cross's elevation of the world's religions to a status similar to that of Christianity. What disturbed those who were concerned about the rising tide of doubt among Baptists were the reports that Cross advocated 'a desirable religion in the East that would perhaps drop some of the essential features of Christianity and ... assume some of the good points of Oriental religions and produce an amalgam ... religion that would ... be something better than anything we have had yet.'[19] The implications of this comparative or relative line of thinking were shocking and unacceptable for many. From a traditional evangelical perspective it equated the truth and uniqueness of Christianity with the myths and legends of heathenism. Moreover, it suggested that if various laudable elements of all faiths were selected, then a religion superior to Christianity would emerge.

There was an undercurrent of doubt or pessimism about the whole missionary enterprise that emerged in the late nineteenth century. The realization of the positive aspects of other religions, perhaps, eroded some of the urgency in missionary work. In George Grant's estimation the problem with missions was not so much with foreign peoples so sunk in heathenism and ignorance that it was impossible for Christian missionaries to be effective as it was with the lack of Christian faith of the congregations at home. According to Grant, the religion of many foreign peoples was exhausted, and the time was ripe for Christianity to establish itself as the universal religion. But he wondered 'whether Christianity can satisfy the demands of universal reason and conscience. Can it quicken the teeming millions of China and India with a new faith that will come as an indubitable message from the living God to their hearts? If it cannot do this, it is not what it professes to be.' The slow progress of Christianity in foreign lands, according to Grant, rested in the weak faith of the Canadian churches.[20] This note of pessimism stood in stark contrast to the supreme confidence of the earlier generation of missionary enthusiasts.

Dramatic events on the mission field made questioning about the missionary enterprise even sharper. For example, after the horrifying and bloody events of the Boxer Rebellion of 1900 notes of criticism about the missionary movement were sounded.[21] According to one missionary from China, Jonathan Goforth, there was less enthusiasm for traditional proselytizing. He had returned to Canada in 1909 to report about the large numbers of conversions and baptisms occurring at the North Honan mission field. There had only been a brief interruption of mission activity in China in the wake of the Boxer Rebellion. At the General Assembly of the Presbyterian church Goforth compared the religious activity in North Honan to a revival and gave specific details about 'the remarkable readiness of the converts to make confession of their faults one to another, and take higher spiritual ground in other directions as well, carrying the mind backward to the simplicity which was in Christ.' This account did not seem to excite or impress the Canadian audience. Goforth attributed this complacency to the influence of modernism upon church members. There was no longer absolute confidence in Christianity, he observed, and this dampened the response to mission work that was based on conversions.[22]

The missionary work that seemed to gain the most support in the early twentieth century was inspired by the social gospel, which had emerged as a powerful force in the early twentieth-century churches. After the Boxer Rebellion missionary work in China emphasized medicine and education. The social service emphasis in the mission fields, however, led to another difficult question about the legitimacy of the missionary enterprise. Were the missionaries exporting Christianity or Western secular values and institutions? For the missionary movement the more fundamental question of what was essential and enduring in Christianity became a pressing one as missionary work was more inclined towards a social gospel. Emphasizing social service was merely advocating the secular objectives of the Christian community or the moral equivalent to imperialism. There was a danger of making missions the equivalent of imposing transitory secular values on another society. The essential and enduring supernatural elements of Christianity – God's existence, the Incarnation, and life everlasting – were seriously jeopardized in any overly secularized understanding of Christ's teaching and mission. There was a growing conviction that Christianity was rooted in culture, not divine agency.

Between 1900 and 1914 recruitment and financial support for foreign missions continued to grow. Despite the persistence of missionary enthusiasm other concerns were growing in importance in the councils of the churches. Beginning in the 1890s, there was pressure on the churches from their missionaries in the Northwest to pay closer attention to home missions. These pleas hit a responsive chord as the churches recognized the considerable challenges facing them with the opening of the West and the influx of foreign immigrants. No longer were the heathen in overseas lands; they were knocking at the doors of Canada's port and railway centres and settling the West. As the West and foreign immigrants began to claim more attention in the final years of the 1890s, the churches rearranged their resources accordingly, and the denominational press devoted an ever-growing amount of attention to home missions throughout the Laurier years.

The home mission movement in the Methodist and Presbyterian churches also went through a process of disillusionment and secularization, although less dramatically and disturbingly than in the case of the foreign mission movement. Many clergymen were convinced that the only hope for the rejuvenation of Protestantism in Canada rested in the missionary effort in the unspoiled West. The West provided an opportunity to recreate the heroic age of evangelization in Canadian history. The late Victorians idealized the early Canadian missionaries in historical accounts, biographical sketches, and religious novels. According to these accounts, courageous missionaries, preaching the pure gospel of conversion and salvation and working against the tremendous obstacles present in pioneer society, had laid the foundations for the Protestant church in the Maritimes and Upper Canada. Similarly, throughout Canadian history, the bravest and most devout missionaries had risked and sacrificed everything in the noble attempt to convert the native peoples. There was an element of nostalgia in this. Many late-Victorian readers of this heroic missionary literature needed their faith in the power of the gospel and the possibility of significant Christian advance affirmed. They would have approved of the missionary effort after reading in the biography of George McDougall the following romantic passage about changes wrought in the native societies of the Northwest: 'Where once there was dissipation and wretchedness, there is now temperance and comfort. Instead of the dismal clatter of the pagan drum ... there is now heard the voice of prayer and praise.'[23] It was hoped that the accomplishments of the earlier generation of Protestant missionaries could be repeated in the West of the late nineteenth century. This missionary impulse was considered necessary for the survival of the Protestant faith in Canadian society.

A faith unencumbered by any accommodation with the demands of modern society could take root in the Western mission field. Only in a 'virgin society,' it was argued, could a Christian faith that was stripped down to its essential or purified form flourish. What was vital and unique about Christianity could be discerned from the example of the church in the West. Those in Central and Eastern Canada could find inspiration and the model for the rejuvenation of their faith and church, which had been compromised and undermined by modern society's secular forces. The West was considered a potential 'city upon the hill.' Just as it was serving as the source of hope for Canada's secular or material goals, so it also provided hope for Protestantism's sacred quest to create 'His Dominion.'[24]

The secretary of the Missionary Society of the Methodist Church of Canada was the Rev. Alexander Sutherland, a leading force in the church, who was convinced that planting Methodism in the Prairies was essential for religious renewal in Canada. Alexander Sutherland was born in the township of Guelph in September 1833. In 1847 he left the family farm and became an apprentice printer in the town of Guelph. There he became involved in the Methodist church as a Sunday school teacher and lay exhorter at revival meetings. In 1855 he was thrust onto a Methodist circuit as an itinerant preacher, and the following year was received on probation. He attended Victoria College for one year, but the demand for itinerant preachers was so great that he returned to circuit preaching. Sutherland was received into full connection in 1859. Like most Methodist ministers during this period he served in a number of churches and circuits.

In the 1870s Sutherland emerged as one of the most forceful preachers and more prolific writers in Canadian Methodism. His sermons explored the themes of human sinfulness, the necessity of conversion, and God's offer of salvation through Jesus Christ.[25] He wrote a number of pamphlets on important theological questions, as well as on the evils of alcohol. Sutherland was not a controversialist like Dewart and Carman; he was a mediator. His intention was to create a broad and clear understanding of Christianity. He dismissed both the 'monstrous perversion' of orthodoxy which made 'God a merciless tyrant' and 'man the helpless victim of the vindictive rage,' as well as the modern view which 'fought very shy of Scripture' by denying the central doctrines of evangelicalism. For example, on the controversial question of the final outcome of sin he clearly repudiated both extremes of the debate: the notion of total annihilation of sinners and the optimistic denial of the eternity of punishment. According to Sutherland, the result of sinfulness was punishment that lasted forever and took the form of banishment from God.[26] Clear exposition of Scripture as the means to preach the risen Christ and show that God cared about human suffering characterized Sutherland's writing. He remained within the orbit of evangelical Christianity, but was suffi-ciently influenced by the spirit of the times to reject the 'cast iron' theology of harsh orthodoxy.[27] Indeed, he took a progressive stand on the relation of children to the church, arguing that they were not

inherently evil and they could avoid falling into sinfulness if they
received a sound Christian and moral education.[28] He believed in
Christian nurture as opposed to sudden conversion as the best means
to create Christian fellowship and a strong church.

He also edited the Methodist review *Earnest Christianity: A Monthly
Magazine Devoted to the Revival of Religion and the Spread of Scriptural
Holiness*. The chief purpose of this review was to assist the Methodist
church 'in working out the problem' of 'enjoying a large measure of
worldly prosperity,' while 'preserving intact its spiritual vitality and
power.' To accomplish this, Sutherland sought 'short clear Scriptural
papers on the various phases of Christian life.' What was required 'to
drive back the tide of worldliness' and 'to save the church from
sinking into utter spiritual paralysis,' Sutherland editorialized, was
not new doctrines, but the old doctrines in 'new and living exposition.'[29] He was convinced that Methodism was failing in its task 'to
spread scriptural holiness throughout the land' because it lacked clarity
about the meaning of Scripture. *Earnest Christianity* was not a successful enterprise, and it ceased publication in 1876. Sutherland had
tremendous difficulty in getting the kind of article he sought contributed to the paper. The exclusive scriptural emphasis was abandoned,
and articles concerning church architecture, literature, and temperance
were included as well as regular columns devoted to 'Missionary
Work' and 'Topics of the Day.' The review could not fulfil its stated
devotional purpose. The paper's offices were amalgamated with those
of the *Methodist Magazine and Review*, which was a popular family
magazine and not a religious review, in Sutherland's estimation. The
fate of *Earnest Christianity* for Sutherland was an indication of the
decline of scripturally based Christianity in Canadian Methodism.
Because of this failure he was becoming increasingly despondent
about the prospects of the his church.[30]

After spending a 'summer on prairie land,' Sutherland concluded
that the West provided a great opportunity and challenge for Christianity. He published his impressions of the West in *A Summer in Prairie Land: Notes of a Tour through the North-West Territory* (1881). The
sketch was written for two audiences: prospective Ontario settlers,
and the churches 'who are just beginning to wake up to the fact that
they have now before them one of those grand opportunities which
may not occur again – the opportunity of working out the problems
of a Christian civilization on a purely virgin soil.' For Sutherland, the
prairie was a place where one could get closer to God. 'The very

isolation,' he explained in a fashion typical of nineteenth-century romantic notions of nature, 'seems to intensify the feeling of devotion, and the sense of utter dependence upon God becomes a felt reality. And in truth God himself seems nearer in these solitudes than "in the city full" for here is nothing to divert the attention or distract the mind.' He was particularly moved by what he observed in the native missions. To him, the 'conversion' and 'subsequent lives' of the Christian natives were evidence of the power of the Gospels in the pastoral setting of the West.[31]

Sutherland was not so sanguine when he observed the kind of society the new settlers were building. There were serious social problems emerging in Western society, particularly the liquor traffic, speculation in land, the ambition to acquire wealth, and corrupt politics. 'The spirit of reckless speculation,' he warned, 'has kindled the fires of an unrestrained avarice, which devours and destroys the spirit of simple piety and issues in utter shipwreck of faith and of a good conscience [sic].' He was alarmed by the 'general disregard of the Sabbath,' which was in his view the 'one great hindrance to the spread of religion.' This was made apparent to Sutherland when he visited Battleford, where there was no regular Protestant service. Such examples of worldliness convinced Sutherland of the urgent necessity for missionary work out West. 'If the great evangelical churches of this land work diligently and wisely, not in building up their respective denominational interests, merely, but in spreading broadly among the people the principles of New Testament Christianity ... these problems will be solved.'[32] In his journeys to Prince Albert and Birtle he encountered many Methodist families from Ontario who gave assurances that if a pastor was sent, they would provide a manse and build a church without delay. As Sutherland indicated to the 1882 meeting of the Toronto Conference: 'We cannot close our eyes to the fact that the ages have unconsciously waited for the opening of the golden gateways of our great North West. Brilliant opportunities invite forward, but awful dangers threaten the advance.'[33]

During this period the missionary effort in the Northwest was undergoing an important transformation as homesteaders began to dominate Prairie society and the Indians moved from the range to the confines of the reserve. Instead of concentrating on converting native peoples to Christianity, the primary object of missions was to establish churches in settled communities. For those with experience in the West this task seemed far easier than the conversion of the natives.[34]

A sense that the missionary effort was successful could be derived from the creation of self-sustaining churches. Such physical evidence of progress was necessary for maintaining the missionary effort. A new type of missionary, therefore, came to the West. 'No longer was there the call for pioneering skills and the spirit of reckless adventure. Instead the demand was for steady pastors and diplomatic administrators.'[35]

Symbolic of this new order was the Rev. James Robertson, the superintendent of missions for the Presbyterian Church of Canada, a new office created in 1881. Robertson was born in 1839 in the highland district of Dull, Scotland. His family immigrated to Canada West in 1855. James Robertson began teaching in East Zorra and at the same time became actively involved in Chalmers Presbyterian Church in Woodstock. Between 1863 and 1866 Robertson attended the University of Toronto and served in the University Corps of the Queen's Own Rifles, which helped to quell the Fenian uprising of 1866. Robertson was involved in the Battle of Ridgeway, after which he wrote, 'I passed through all safe, however, and now how thankful I should be; amidst dangers I was protected ... by God's providence.'[36] After graduating from the University of Toronto, Robertson decided to enter theology. During this period the teaching at Knox College in Toronto was encountering heavy criticism from the students; and so Robertson decided to go to Princeton, where Charles Hodge was a dominant force.[37] Hodge was an orthodox Presbyterian warrior who taught that all theology must be based on scriptural fact; he rejected all attempts to reconcile the supernaturalism of Christianity with the naturalism of science. In the summer recess Robertson returned to Canada for mission work in the newly settled areas of southwestern Ontario. In 1868 he enrolled in the more liberal Union Theological Seminary in New York City, and there he expanded his missionary experience by working in a downtown settlement house.

Robertson was ordained into the pastoral charge of Norwich, Ontario, in 1869. He distinguished himself as a forceful preacher, who made the harsh dictates of Calvinism abundantly clear. Basing his exposition on the text 'I will cause you to pass under the rod, and I will bring you into the bond of the covenant,' he pointed out that 'God's design in all his dealings with his people, is to render them obedient in heart and life to the requirements of the covenant.' In uncompromising tones he said that God wished to teach his people the 'lesson of unhesitating submission to his revealed will ... [by]

sending affliction upon them to teach them the way of his law.'[38] Such preaching was harsh, but it was full of certainty. Robertson did not express the doubts about the basic doctrines of orthodox Christianity that other clergymen were raising. There was no question in his mind about what one should believe and what one's responsibilities were. Soon Robertson was receiving calls from other churches. Attracted by the challenge posed by the West, he accepted a call from Knox Church in Winnipeg.

The Presbyterian church was in a confused state in the West, for when Robertson arrived in Winnipeg he discovered that the Knox pulpit had already been filled. Robertson agreed to tour the West and preach at mission stations where no permanent pastor existed. On this first tour Robertson concluded that the primary requirement for successful missionary work in the West was permanent churches and regular worship with a good minister in charge. The major impediment to the church's cause in the West, he pointed out, was 'the sort of men they have here ... Men of small ideas and little zeal. I do hope they may get some vigorous man to take hold in Winnipeg and work up the whole province ... The Church has lost a great deal by not having the right material here.'[39] Robertson began contacting ministers and congregations in Ontario, informing them of the needs and opportunities of Prairie society. This first tour proved to be the foundation of Robertson's work in building the Presbyterian church in the West.

On a second tour, during the summer of 1874, Robertson reached some important conclusions about how to conduct the Western missionary effort. Things were greatly neglected because there was 'no system, no regular laid-down scheme according to which to work.'[40] To develop a system Robertson began acquiring detailed information regarding the social circumstances and economic potential of the West. He understood that an accurate picture of population, land settlement, and crop yields was necessary to carry out an effective missionary strategy. Only then could the church know where to focus its home mission effort and whether a community needed assistance in building a church and providing for a minister. Robertson had an 'insatiable greed for statistics' and he applied some of the methods of the emerging social sciences to aid in the work of the church.[41] While visiting Prairie communities, Robertson mixed preaching and pastoral work with the business of raising funds and collecting statistics. He was becoming a church bureaucrat rather than a missionary seeking souls, and in his own view he was more effective at this more mundane task. Indeed Robertson wondered whether he could be a successful minister of the gospel in the West. 'I do not feel at home here' he confided to his wife. 'Never preached satisfactorily here yet. Nor am I getting much better.'[42] Nevertheless, Robertson received a call to be the minister of Knox Church in Winnipeg in 1874.

Being stationed in Winnipeg, however, did not curtail his missionary activities throughout the Prairies. His attitude towards the cause of Christianity in the new land was one of great hopefulness. 'The next few years,' he reported to the General Assembly of the Presbyterian church 'are to decide largely the religious future of this country. God is calling on us to go in and possess the land.'[43] The formidable challenge of making the West Christian would regenerate Canadians. The Presbyterian church soon realized how valuable Robertson's approach to missionary work was and appointed him superintendent of missions in the Northwest. His duties included the oversight and visitation of all mission stations that were not self-sustaining, the organization of new mission fields, the distribution of home mission funds, as well as the general supervision of the missionary work in Manitoba and the Northwest Territory. He had few illusions about the difficulties in bringing Christianity to Western settlement. While visiting Fort Macleod in 1885, he wrote: 'I never saw a place like this. You only get a very few who believe in anything except money, women and whiskey ... In the Mounted Police Force there is not much religion ... I find barrack life most demoralizing ... What to do I am at a loss ... What the people will do themselves for the support of the Gospel I do not know ... If we had a suitable man I am convinced that he could do good work.'[44] By suitable Robertson meant ministers who had considerable pulpit power and strong Christian character. Finding such ministers proved to be Robertson's greatest challenge.

The missionary enterprise, more than any other church activity, demanded that the question of the essence of Christianity be addressed. This was especially true for those who tried to export Christianity to non-Christians. It was thought that this was also the case for the Canadian West since, according to Robertson, those who had migrated west had broken their 'home association,' and their 'religious instincts [were] becoming enfeebled.' The Christian faith propagated by the Canadian churches, however, could not be simply transplanted to the West. Much that had dominated Presbyterian church life, whether it be doctrine, learned theology, or the special traditions of the denomination, was unsuitable for the conditions of frontier society and the religious needs of the settlers. 'With them,' Robertson reported, 'the office and denomination will avail little.'[45] That which was the product of the social and intellectual concerns of troubled modern society might not thrive in the prairie West. A Christian message stripped of such cultural baggage seemed more appropriate.

Robertson had a keen sense of what exactly the Christian message ought to be in a new society, and he impressed his ardent view on the many ministers he recruited to work in the Prairie mission field.[46] In an address on the topic of sermons he pointed out that the subject matter of Christ's preaching and prayers was not philosophy, physical or social science, history, economics, or politics. Robertson did not counsel ministers to turn their backs on modern knowledge or ignore contemporary concerns. Clergymen should study secular topics, he cautioned, for such investigation had a 'liberalizing' influence and was immensely important for successful pastoral work. But the pulpit was not the place to air one's thoughts on secular matters. A minister 'is to preach Christ and Him Crucified: All his learning is to make plain the way of salvation ... All his scientific & historic lore is to illustrate the truth that is in Jesus.' Robertson noted that in the American pulpit the sermon had become a 'moral essay' and that this was failing since people still wanted the gospel.[47]

Robertson was typical of many dedicated to missions in that he insisted that the missionary effort was dependent upon the holding of certain beliefs as well as a life devoted to religious experience. Reflecting his Presbyterian heritage, Robertson thought that it was impossible for one to be elevated in Christian character unless the vital truths of Christianity were unquestioned. Absolute belief that there was a heaven and hell, the Holy Spirit renewed the soul, Jesus was divine and was crucified for humanity's sinfulness, and that there was a resurrection, was necessary. These Christian doctrines, at best, were only loosely accepted, Robertson admitted. 'The tendency of the age is toward being broad. Men want convenient comfortable creeds. They want them so drawn that they may mean what a man chooses.' This was a dangerous kind of charitable liberalism, for according to Robertson what was truth and what was error was clear and indisputable. The result was that God's ordinances were no longer being fully attended to. 'Do we read the Bible as often as we used to? Do we pray? Do we ask a blessing at the table? Have the services of the sanctuary lost their relish?' This departure from the certainties of traditional evangelical beliefs alarmed Robertson. At stake, in his view, was the fate of the missionary enterprise in the West. It seemed clear that a church that believed in the severity of sinfulness and held that preaching the gospel of Jesus Christ was necessary for salvation would support missions with more vigour than a church which thought that such doctrines were debatable.[48] Robertson sought missionary recruits who would preach salvation and would remain true to the canons of evangelicalism. Without missionaries who were motivated by an overwhelming desire to save the souls of unbelievers, the sense of commitment and urgency which fuelled the missionary effort would wane, in Robertson's estimation.

One of the many young ministers whom Robertson impressed his views upon was the Rev. C.W. Gordon, destined to become the best-selling novelist 'Ralph Connor.' Gordon was born in Glengarry County, Canada West, in 1860. His father was Daniel Gordon, a Presbyterian cleric. After completing a BA at the University of Toronto, Gordon attended Knox College. During his first year, 1885, he heard Superintendent Robertson speak regarding the challenge of the West, and he decided to do his summer mission work there. Robertson took a special interest in the young missionary while he was riding the plains of southern Manitoba.[49] C.W. Gordon's impression of the religious situation in the Prairies was strikingly similar to that of the superintendent's. In the *Knox College Monthly* Gordon reported that 'men's hearts grow harder when for a few years they are without the softening influence of the gospel; and the tone of morality is such that open vice makes no discord.' He observed that worship services were infrequent and consequently the 'impressions made were often lost before they could be deepened.' The battle to establish Christianity in the West would have to be waged single-handedly by the missionary, Gordon concluded, for the settlers were not alarmed by irreligion and seemed uninterested in forming congregations.[50]

Gordon completed his theological training in Edinburgh. The Scottish divines he encountered there were as instrumental as Robertson and the Canadian West in shaping his commitment to missions. During the 1870s and 1880s the balance of theological opinion in Scotland was becoming increasingly liberal. His mentors were A.B. Davidson, Marcus Dodds, Alexander Whyte, and especially Henry Drummond, the author of the influential *Natural Law and the Spiritual World* (1883), which reconciled evolutionary theory to Christianity. They were 'trailblazers of a new attitude' which 'helped to carry at least some Christian graces and convictions into an age of increasing secularity, disorder, and despair.'[51] For Gordon, the great appeal of these teachers was that they blended the traditional with the modern. Their outlook openly acknowledged the results of scientific advance and biblical criticism, but attending to the spiritual needs of individuals remained the cornerstone of a minister's work, in their view. They emphasized the need for salvation and the importance of preaching personal conversion; they had not abandoned their evangelical heritage.[52]

While studying at Edinburgh, Gordon had become deeply troubled by higher criticism, and Whyte gave reassuring advice: 'You are to be a minister, see that you feed your people. Never mind your theological, your scientific, your higher critical problems. Keep them for your study.' Perhaps the most significant fact for Gordon's later career was that Drummond and Whyte had been inspired by Dwight Moody during his campaign in Scotland in 1874. Under the tutelage of Moody, Drummond began a long crusade to persuade young men to follow Christ. His message was similar to Moody's in its appeal to common folk and its lack of harsh, rigid theology. 'He spoke,' Gordon recalled, 'with unaffected simplicity ... and penetrated with an intense and throbbing sympathy. He was not speaking down to them, there was nothing of criticism, no attempt to "convict them of sin."'[53] Gordon seemed most impressed by the requirement for ministers to save souls.

When Gordon returned to Canada in 1890, he was ordained and was appointed missionary to the Banff area, where he carried out religious services with the ranchers, lumbermen, and miners of the foothills. For three years he carried out Robertson's mandate to establish worship services in unchurched areas. In Gordon's services individuals were encouraged to profess their faith in Jesus Christ as Saviour and Lord in order to be received within the church. He frequently preached on the text 'Except ye be converted, and become as little children, ye shall not enter the kingdom of heaven.'[54] This evangelical style reflected the influence of Robertson, the Scottish divines, and indirectly Dwight Moody.[55] In 1894 Gordon accepted a call from St Stephen's Presbyterian Church in the outskirts of Winnipeg. Before taking up responsibilities in this charge, he returned to Scotland to brush up on his reading, which had been neglected while doing missionary work.

During this period Gordon renewed his close association with Superintendent Robertson, who had been struggling to recruit men for the West. Serious difficulties with regard to Robertson's missionary program for the West, however, were developing. There was consid-

erable discontent on the part of missionaries regarding money and
the opportunity for meaningful religious work. Indeed by 1887 dissatisfaction amongst Presbyterian missionaries had become so intense
that they made a formal protest to church authorities. Only some of
the Western missionaries' grievances were met. The Home Mission
Committee agreed that the church would assume responsibility for
travelling expenses to the mission fields but refused to guarantee the
whole salary of the missionary. Grants from the Presbyterian church
were available for the mission fields that were not self-sustaining. In
a manner consistent with the voluntarist tradition, missionaries would
still be dependent on donations from the local congregations. A
missionary's standard of living depended on his ability to draw settlers
and frontier labourers into the church and collect contributions from
them.[56] The collections from mission fields were usually meager, no
matter how effective and devout the missionary was, because financial
conditions in the West were precarious.

Complaints about the lack of adequate financial support enraged
the superintendent. He charged that most theological students were
too worldly since they sought comfortable and wealthy parishes in
Ontario. On the other hand, he acknowledged that there was widespread indifference in the ranks of the church regarding the financial
condition of the missionaries. This neglect was 'doing more harm
than the Higher Criticism,' he thought. The discontent it fostered
weakened the integrity of Western ministers, for they were unable to
carry out their pastoral duties adequately.[57] The Rev. D.G. McQueen,
who was stationed in Edmonton during the 1880s and 1890s, lamented that 'it is really hard work to concentrate on the real work of
the pastor.' He reported that 'things are getting worse & worse every
day the church is kept open, it is a question as to whether it is morally
right to run the concern any deeper into debt.'[58] This precarious situation seemed to undermine the faith of the struggling congregations.
One elder in McQueen's church acknowledged that 'as a congregation we are defunct ... The spiritual life of the people, or congregation
is at a low ebb. We have service and *that is all*.'[59] There was a sense that
the church was failing in its mission to the West. Superintendent
Robertson was finding that the Presbyterian church was unwilling to
meet the challenge of renewing itself by planting Christianity in the
new territory.

The difficulties on the mission fields of the Canadian West were
one of the major motivating factors for C.W. Gordon's decision to

write fiction. The majority of reports he received in 1897 regarding conditions on the home mission fields of the Presbyterian church indicated that there was a general lack of interest in things spiritual, indifference to religious ordinances, and reluctance to attend church.[60] 'My sole purpose,' he explained in *Postscript to Adventure*, 'was to awaken my church in Eastern Canada to the splendour of the mighty religious adventure being attempted by the missionary pioneers in Canada beyond the Great Lakes.'[61] Indeed it was the positive response he received from other clergymen after his first fictional sketches were published that encouraged him to continue writing. James Macdonald, the editor of the *Westminster*, solicited opinions from leading Presbyterians such as J.G. Shearer, who thought that the 'tales would do more good to Home Mission work than all the reports and sermons of the whole year.' In encouraging tones Macdonald told Gordon that in his fictional sketches he had 'struck something and my injunction is to strike hard.'[62]

'Ralph Connor's' early novels were set in the Western mission fields that Gordon had become familiar with during his missionary service in the foothills region. The plot of these early novels, especially *Black Rock*, *The Sky Pilot*, and *The Prospector*, basically followed the same outline. A missionary hero, usually a dedicated and earnest college graduate from the East, is faced with tremendous odds in bringing Christianity to the rugged frontier. The men, in particular, posed a great challenge for they had been divorced from the uplifting influences of church, community, and family. For them irreligion was 'alive, cheerful, attractive, indeed fascinating.' There was an 'utter indifference' and 'audacious disregard' for religion in the frontier environment. The lumber and mining camps depicted in Connor fiction were places in which the liquor trade and all its accompanying vices ruled.

Connor's characterization of the missionary conveyed the same image as the portrait of missionaries in late-Victorian historical and autobiographical literature. The missionary was confronted by the greatest hardships and challenges but was able to overcome them and successfully evangelize because of his tremendous faith and unwavering dedication. For example, despite the many hardships of missionary life on the prairie, everything from poor diet, arduous treks, isolation, the threat of Indian attack, the climate, and epidemic disease, McDougall's biographer portrayed him as being steadfast in his belief in God and the missionary enterprise of the Methodist church. McDougall's own correspondence from the 1850s and 1860s suggests the same. From Rossville House he wrote, 'most of the time a homeless wanderer amongst savage tribes, exposed to the vicissitudes of Indian life, more than once escaping a special interposition of Providence.'[63]

In trying to reach the hardened and indifferent of the frontier, Connor's missionary heroes preached the gospel of redemption. They were not concerned about the advances in biblical criticism or science that seemed to be distracting many others from appreciating the simplicity and power of the gospel. For example, in *The Sky Pilot*, the missionary hero's first sermon in the foothills mission field was interrupted by a critic who charged that the biblical story of the miracle of the loaves of bread and fish simply was not natural. The Sky Pilot was unable to debate the questions regarding the existence of miracles raised by the sceptic. He admitted that 'there are a great many things I don't understand' and instead emphasized the 'great Personality' of Christ. Attention was drawn away from theology, metaphysics, and difficult doctrinal questions and diverted towards an active faith. In Connor novels the missionary heroes set forth the Gospels in a simple form. The central biblical stories, such as those of the prodigal son, the garden of Gethsemane, and the arrest of Christ, were 'dressed in modern and western garb.'[64] Precisely how the biblical stories were recited is never conveyed, for Connor never dwelt on the content of the sermons. The telling of the gospel story was important, for that alone, according to Connor, was able to redeem fallen souls from the 'devil's arm's.'

Connor's Westerners responded to straightforward appeals for conversion and the presentation of biblical truths in a plain style. Indeed, in *Black Rock* it was the missionary's account of his own conversion which had an impact. He read the biblical account of the Christmas story to the men at the Christmas eve celebrations in the lumber camp and then explained that after a long period of indifference he heard the story again and its impact was powerful and immediate. 'It came over me like great waves, it was He that should save men from their sins. Save! Save! The waves kept beating upon my ears, and before I knew I had called out, Oh can He save me?' This was the moment that he decided to devote his life to Christ and missionary work. Old Nelson, 'the hardest, savagest, toughest sinner in the camp,' was moved by this plain account. At the first communion service at Black Rock he persuaded many to sign the communion roll by leading a prayer: 'Father we're all gone away, we have spent all, we are poor, we are tired of it all, we want to feel different, to be different; we want to come back.' Then, while on his knees, Old Nelson expounded on the theme of Christ's sacrifice for all. 'Jesus came to save us from our sins, and He said if we came he wouldn't cast us out, no matter how bad we were, if only we came to Him.'[65] This was a Christianity stripped of everything but the essential saving gospel. Ultimately, the newly converted in Connor stories always become champions of moral reform and social uplift. The frontier communities become models of respectability; they were church-going and dedicated to temperance.

These early novels reflected Canadians' hopes regarding the prairie West. The frontier environment was presented as a force which renewed and purified Christianity. Those elements of the Christian apology that had been developed to meet the challenge posed by modern thought and urban-industrial problems seemed unnecessary. Connor's missionary heroes did not compromise the evangelical message; the vital fundamentals were stressed. There was a degree of environmental determinism in this; but Connor was careful to stress that the frontier was not exclusively responsible for this purified Christianity. It was the encounter between the open society of the West and the established truths of Christianity introduced by the missionaries which was responsible. When the missionary established worship services in a frontier community, 'the Old and the New, the East and the West, the reverential Past and iconoclastic Present were jumbling themselves together.'[66] It was hoped that the renewed gospel preached in the West, which was untainted by the secularizing influence of modern doubt and material success, would reform the struggling churches of Canadian society by providing them with a plain message to win back those who were drifting away from Christian worship.

This possibility was the concluding motif of *Black Rock*. One of the men touched by the simple gospel stories of the Western missionary was Graeme, a member of a devout Ontario family who sought adventure in the West to escape the confining influence of his father's orthodox religion. He observed how the hardened men of the lumber and mining camps were converted to Christianity. When he returned to his hometown, he spoke enthusiastically about the power of the gospel. He explained that in the West Christianity was not subscription to creeds and doctrines but instead simply faith that 'God is at the back of a man who wants to get done with the bad.' This explanation quelled the doubts of the modern sceptics in the Ontario community.[67] The impression Connor created was that the evangelical gospel that was produced in the West not only made the frontier Christian but also had the potential to revitalize religious faith and the church in the East.

The early criticism of the romantic view of the West in the Connor novels came from other Western missionaries. Their harsh experiences and disillusionment made it difficult for them to regard the West as the source for a religious revival for Canada. One particularly severe critic was the Rev. Robert Milliken, a Methodist itinerant preacher who was attracted to the West by James Woodsworth. Milliken's first mission station was Oak Lake, Manitoba, a sparsely settled community where there were only four families enrolled in the Methodist church. He recalled that he was completely unprepared for the task of building a church and imparting Christian faith. 'I had no experience in organization of church work. I had never preached, never taken a real public service ... I stood on that vast expanse of prairie with dismay ... and despair.' According to Milliken, the West depicted in Connor novels was completely different from that experienced by the missionaries. He stressed the loneliness and the lack of opportunity for nurturing deeper religious faith. It was impossible to keep up one's reading of theological and devotional literature and there was no time for meditation. Most of the missionary's time was occupied visiting new settlements and establishing a semblance of religious worship. 'All things considered,' Milliken wrote, 'it is not to be wondered at that a great many of us yielded to the line of least resistance and let that vital part of the ministerial equipment go.' There was no reference to the emergence of a vital Christian faith or record of making Western communities Christian in Milliken's account. He left the impression that religion was being weakened on the western frontier.[68]

For many earnest young men in the East, however, Connor's rousing stories of missionary adventure seemed to have the desired effect. A literary fan who wrote to Gordon after reading *Black Rock* thanked him 'for its loyalty to the Master's power in one's life' and confessed that it was his 'wish and prayer' that 'you may long exemplify and hold forth such an ideal.' This correspondent encouraged Gordon further by telling him that he had been moved 'to pray and ... to fight' in the manner of the missionary hero in the novel.[69]

C.W. Gordon returned to the theme of missions on the Western frontier in *The Prospector* (1904). The tone of this novel, however, was less romantic than the first novels. Gordon was still writing to appeal to Canadians for support of the missionary enterprise. But he did so by recounting actual conditions, basing his characters more directly on the leading figures in the Presbyterian church in the West, especially Superintendent Robertson, and describing church policy and activity. He included excerpts from documents such as home mission reports and missionary correspondence in order to create a more realistic setting.

In The *Prospector* the missionary hero was confronted by indifference. A sense of the inability of the evangelical message to make an impact permeates this novel. The evangelical style was too emotional and unsophisticated for the residents of the civilized fort. Many were 'contemptuously critical' of evangelism; they found such preaching 'alienating.' Even in the less civilized frontier setting of the lumber camps the missionary hero relies on measures other than preaching the Word of God. A social centre offering intellectual interest and physical recreation is constructed to create a 'clean and wholesome atmosphere.'[70] The opportunities for planting a vibrant Christian faith that was not compromised by the dictates of civilization seemed to be fast disappearing in the West. In both mission stations described in the novel preaching the saving gospel and reciting biblical stories were no longer sufficient to win converts or create a Christian community. The missionary's appeals for regeneration fell on deaf ears, and he was forced to be involved with social projects. *The Prospector*, therefore, signalled the Rev. Gordon's awareness of the passing of the heroic or evangelical age in Canadian missions. The idea that the West would regenerate the church across Canada was abandoned. The early Connor novels, *Black Rock* and *The Sky Pilot,* were among the last expressions of hopeful confidence in the West's ability to rejuvenate religious faith.

The note of disenchantment that was beginning to characterize Canadians' attitude towards missions was sounded by Alexander Sutherland in his historical accounts of Methodism in Canada. Overall, his selection and interpretation of evidence was progressive. How Methodism developed from a disorganized and sparse system of itinerancy to a well-established institution through the efforts of heroic missionaries was emphasized in *Methodism in Canada*. The impression Sutherland created was that the history of the Methodist church was

one of continuous growth and increasing influence. There were hints
of unease, however, in his references to present conditions. He noted
that Methodism's success in the past had rested on its ability to reach
the masses. 'Till you press the believers to expect full salvation *now*,' he
explained, 'you must not look for any revival.' It seemed that the
religious doctrines and institutions of Methodism which promoted
conversion, however, were no longer being heeded by ministers or
congregations, A 'paralysis of worldliness ... had fallen upon the
Church.'[71] According to Sutherland, the prospect for further progress
or growth was dimming for the Methodist church was losing touch
with its evangelical heritage.

Sutherland reworked *Methodism in Canada* to suit the purposes of
the church's Young People's Forward Movement, mission study
classes, and Sunday school. The most important change in *The Methodist Church and Missions* (1906) was that he extended the coverage of
Methodist missions in the Canadian West to include the period following the completion of the Canadian Pacific Railway. This altered
his perspective. He became even more concerned about the state of
Methodism. For Sutherland, the West still represented the best hope
for the creation of the Kingdom of God in Canada; but problems were
developing making this ultimate objective increasingly unlikely. Many
people settling in the West were 'very ignorant of Scripture truths,'
making the task of planting the Christian gospel exceedingly difficult.
Furthermore, he observed that 'even now ... a tidal wave of materialism
flings its spray over town and country, and should it gather full
strength it may submerge all ... righteousness.' For Canadian churchmen the promise of the West, its regenerative influence, was disappearing. Moreover, Sutherland feared that the missionary imperative
was fading in the church. To conclude his history of Methodist missions he thought it was necessary to outline the 'great truths related
to the missionary enterprise.' Christian missions should not be considered in the category of experiments, expedients, or voluntary benevolence. The purpose of the church was evangelization. Indeed the
strength of any church was best measured by its missionary spirit
and enterprise, Sutherland claimed. 'The non-missionary church de-
cays and dies, and the missionary church lives and grows.'[72] If confidence in the Word of God as saving gospel declined, then so would
the missionary effort and then the Christian church. Exactly this,
however, was occurring, Sutherland feared. So powerful were the
forces of secularization that within less than a generation the hope for

the revival of the Canadian churches through the example of a purified Christianity on the mission fields was disappearing.

Something had happened 'to chill the ardour' of missionary enthusiasm. Confidence in Christian missions was waning. Often missionary
reports betrayed more frustration than fulfilment. The expectation of
quick, relatively easy triumph had been too romantic; but there was
so little missionary advance that serious questioning emerged.[73]
Whether in the home missions of the Canadian West or the foreign
missions overseas, there was less emphasis on conversion to Christianity. Instead long-term evangelization emerged as the new missionary objective; there was little sense of urgency. The changing nature
of missions reflected the growing lack of confidence in the truth of
Christianity. The idea of development of doctrine and the realization
that the interpretation of the Word of God was not final meant that it
was difficult to discern what was Christian truth and what was myth
or merely the product of Western civilization. This doubt created a
crisis of confidence with respect to what to preach in the mission
fields. Although the superiority of Christianity was still assumed,
greater tolerance for non-Christian religions emerged. Moreover, rather
than being a force that clarified the essentials of Christianity, the
missionary endeavour only became more confused or entangled with
secular culture. The more secular missionary impulse of the late
nineteenth century was a form of escape for those unsure about the
legitimacy of the traditional missionary task of proselytizing Christianity and disillusioned about the fact that so few advances in evangelization were being made.

5

Stemming the Tide
of Secularization,
1890–1914

To suggest that the churches in Victorian Canada were somehow a failure would be terribly inaccurate. They were the central voluntary institution, along with their mortal enemy the tavern, in Canadian society. Sometime in the late nineteenth century their position began to falter as they faced a more open and competitive situation. By the 1890s churchmen had become conscious of the fact that Canadian society was increasingly pluralistic and secular. There were organized and competitive sports, recreational sports such as cycling, amusement parks, Mechanics' Institutes, trade unions, social clubs, political organizations, libraries, theatre, and music-halls, which could assume some of the functions that the church and religion traditionally held.[1] Moreover, these institutions and activities competed directly with religion and the churches for the attention of the masses.

Furthermore, industrialization meant that a growing number of people had more disposable income through a regular weekly wage to spend on consumer goods and recreational or leisure activities.[2] Perhaps the best symbol of Canada's greater material wealth and this maturing consumer culture was the emergence of Timothy Eaton's retail enterprise as a full-fledged department store. Eaton's store in Toronto was forever expanding the variety of products it displayed for sale and the number of its departments, such as a huge sporting goods section. The store was also more than a place to shop. Many services and forms of entertainment were made available, so that people could pass their time within the confines of his 'cathedral of consumerism.' And in recognition of the existence of a national market, the catalogue and mail-order service was introduced. Joy Santink has suggested that the Eaton's catalogue became much more than what it was intended to be. It was referred to as a 'want book' or 'prairie Bible.' By the late nineteenth century shopping was becoming a way of life and a means to enjoying recreation and leisure, not merely a commercial transaction for subsistence purposes.[3] As one contemporary social commentator remarked, 'the department store tends to replace the church. It marches to the religion of the cash desk ... and fashion ... [People] go there to pass the hours as they used to go to church.'[4]

A major problem facing the clergy, therefore, was what must the Christian message and mission be in this more secular consumer-oriented culture in order for it to remain vibrant and alive in Canadian society. This was a difficult task for the ethos of consumerism was clearly at odds with a great deal of the Christian religion. Consumer culture lauded the values of material well-being, immediate gratification, the pursuit of pleasure, and self-fulfilment.[5] Some clergymen sought to make the Christian message more relevant to the concerns of the day through the social gospel, while others sought to make it more entertaining and accessible. It was difficult to resist pressure to make Christianity a commodity that would guarantee some form of recreation or entertainment, satisfaction or contentment, or social and material improvement so that it would have some currency in a consumer society.

One way in which the clergy attempted to deal with the increased competition they faced was to harness many of the new leisure activities directly to the church. The modern church housed many functions, such as Sunday schools, temperance activities, and missionary societies; but it also hosted literary and debating clubs and sponsored many leisure activities, including organized sports and games. Adjacent to many sanctuaries not only were there Sunday school rooms, but facilities for social and political gatherings, and in the basement a hall or gymnasium for recreation or entertainment. The clergy hoped that the various clubs, organizations, and activities sponsored by the churches would produce a large number of communicants. Like the modern store, churches housed many specialized departments, each designed to attract people looking for specific services, whether it be for their spiritual well-being, their physical culture, their education, social contacts, or the satisfaction of their curiosity about the world. The churches were not a place for worship only. Numerous other activities were carried out within their sacred walls. They were opening their doors to the competition.

For the clergy the rise of the multi-faceted institutional church meant that much of their effort was consumed by a complex array of administrative duties. One pastor complained that he was seriously hampered by the multiplicity of the non-religious duties he was obligated to carry out. Meeting with official boards, doing missionary and relief-related work, raising funds, gathering support for social causes, and being present at a congregation's numerous social functions made it difficult to remain a shepherd of the flock. William Cochrane frequently complained in his diary that the heavy burden of church business gave him little time for spiritual growth and pastoral duties. He wondered if attending meetings and writing reports was the 'right kind of work for a Gospel minister,' and towards the end of his career, he concluded that his work was 'getting as much secular as religious.'[6] Church leaders were keenly aware of the danger of the possibility that the secular functions of the church would displace its essential role as a place of worship. After describing and approving of the many sporting and social activities taking place in most churches, William Withrow cautioned that 'a Church is not an Academy, it is not a Club, and it certainly is not a Variety Show ... The more institutional it is, the more spiritual it needs to be ... The more of the so-called secular work the Church is doing, the greater the need for spiritual preaching in the pulpit.'[7] Nevertheless, the complex bureaucratic structure that developed along with the increasing number of functions carried out by the church seemed to be necessary for the churches to compete in society.

Some observers were struck by the secular atmosphere of many churches. Although they still appeared as divine or sacred places from the outside, the impression one received indoors was different.[8] When the religious columnist for the *Week* entered Sherbourne Street Methodist Church in Toronto, he was impressed that 'the church is an auditorium, not a temple.' The design of the pulpit and the pews was like that of the theatre. He did not feel that he was in a Holy place.[9] The church columnist for Toronto *Saturday Night* penned much sharper criticism of the secular appearance of large urban churches in his series on preachers and preaching in Toronto. While attending Metropolitan Methodist Church, he wrote that 'the church, with its warm, reddish interior furniture, is more of the hall than the cathedral

... the place behind the pulpit, with its glass windows and fragile casement, looks like an ordinary business office ... in almost any store or warehouse.'[10] There did not seem to be much that impressed these two observers that they were in the house of God.

Similar conclusions were being drawn about the atmosphere and physical surroundings at old Methodist camp-meeting grounds. During the 1860s the Grimsby camp-meeting grounds were open for one or two weeks, and the sole purpose of the gathering was the salvation of souls. According to Harriet Youmans's historical account of the early years, 'there sometimes seemed to be a hallowed influence about the place which was felt as soon as the door was entered, and many remarkable conversions took place there.' Before the campmeeting there was much prayer and preparation among the preachers and people of the various circuits, and they arrived 'full of holy expectation.' The atmosphere was earnest, emotional, and spiritual. A host of improvements were begun in the 1870s to make Grimsby more comfortable and enjoyable. Grimsby Park became a summer resort open for three months during the year. The tents were replaced by elegant cottages, and the natural setting was tamed with the construction of parks, winding walks, and ponds. It boasted every facility for 'innocent and healthy enjoyment and sport,' such as athletic grounds, bicycles, boat-houses, and tennis courts. At the Temple concerts, lectures, and other forms of entertainment were staged.[11] People arrived there, not with the expectation of any significant religious experience, but to have a holiday or enjoy a retreat away from the rigours of urban life. 'It has become a necessity of modern life,' one Methodist wrote while describing the modern Grimsby Park, 'that the o'er-strung bow shall be unbent, that men in business take a brief holiday from toil, that ladies and children find respite from the exactions of society and school.'[12] Grimsby Park was a perfect example of the attempt by churches to make sure that modern leisure activity somehow remained in a religious setting.

Grimsby Park had not completely abandoned its religious roots. Indeed one of the motivations of the board of directors for converting it into a resort was to make it possible for Methodists to attend a summer retreat without endangering their spiritual health. Provisions were made for numerous religious and moral influences. Grimsby Park was on the tour of many of the great late-Victorian preachers, and there were frequent concerts of sacred music featuring notable choirs and musicians. For those who wished, Bible study classes were available. Worship and devotion, however, were not the primary activities at the park. The primary motive in maintaining the facility no longer seemed to be providing for religious experience. In the emerging leisure and consumer society of turn-of-the-century Canada the pressure to make religion something that was marketable to the respectable middle classes was overwhelming. At Grimsby Park the religious heritage of the camp-meeting had all but disappeared in the rush to make the site a popular resort.

By the late nineteenth century clergymen were attempting to embrace various leisure activities as a way to maintain a following. For example, they advocated sporting activities by espousing muscular Christianity, a reading of the gospel which attached piety to physical fitness. As William Cochrane explained, 'the healthy action of the body tends to the healthy action of the mind, and is intimately related to manliness and morals.'[13] Through physical training, especially on the athletic field or in sporting games, the necessary qualities to dedicate oneself to the service of the Lord, such as effort, courage, loyalty, discipline, and endurance, were somehow developed. Muscular Christianity was always justified by referring to the New Testament passage in Corinthians: 'Know ye not that your bodies are the temples of the Holy Spirit? Glorify God, therefore, in your body.' But muscular Christianity was a perfect example of the lengths to which clergymen went to come to terms with the changing values of society. No doubt this was a popular gospel; but it was also a gospel that was secular in its implications. As the missionary heroes in the Ralph Connor novels indicate, manliness not godliness seemed to be the Christian standard. By espousing such a material conception of Christianity, the clergy were admitting that sports and athletics were of primary importance.[14] Contrary to their puritanical image, most clergy not only tolerated but also promoted different amusements and entertainment, such as lectures, concerts, and sports, provided these activities were carried out in a manner consistent with a Christian conscience.[15] Only in this way, it was thought, could the church remain at the centre of people's expanding leisure activity.

C.W. Gordon seemed to be particularly aware of the necessity of churches competing with secular culture. In 1913, his publisher, George H. Doran, approached him about granting the dramatic rights for *The Sky Pilot*. His response was enthusiastic, but it was mixed with concern since the stage was such an immoral institution in his view. 'The theatre as it is now conducted,' Gordon wrote, 'is an injury to the spiritual and moral sense of the people, because the whole atmosphere is anti-spiritual. But this is because the Church has neglected her opportunity as on so many other departments, and allowed the world to get control.' Gordon agreed to let his books be dramatized and hoped that his work might aid the churches in taking hold of the stage to improve it. He was convinced that in the right hands and with the right dramatic material, the stage could become 'a powerful agency for moral and spiritual instruction and inspiration.'[16]

One of the reasons compelling clergymen to compete with the secular more directly was the growing evidence that church attendance and membership were declining. Church leaders in Canada paid close attention to statistics because they provided a basis for the appraisal of efforts towards the evangelization of Canadian society. There was a constant accounting which sought to measure the strength of the church. The annual reports of the Methodist and Presbyterian churches were statistical compendiums. Both institutions had special committees charged with assessing the growth of church membership and the numbers of churches, ministers, Sunday school teachers, and scholars. It was expected that the number of church members and adherents would continually rise in proportion to the Canadian population. Furthermore, the Methodist and Presbyterian churches had been accustomed to steady growth, and they viewed their progress as a clear sign of God's favour regarding their message and methods as well as the piety of their flock. The idea of continual progress or growth was an integral part of each denomination's sense of its history.[17]

According to concerned clergy, the most troubling trend and the most tangible evidence indicating that Canadian society was becoming more secular and that the churches were in difficulty was the decline in sabbath observance. In Canada there was sabbath observance legislation in each province, with the exception of Quebec. Restriction of Sunday activity was probably the most extensive in Ontario. Its 1845 legislation made it unlawful for any person 'to hold, convene, or attend any public political meeting or to tipple or to revel or to brawl or use profane language in the public street or open air.' Further clauses prohibited hunting, fishing, organized games, and public recreation. Servile labour, excepting works of mercy or necessity, was also prohibited. Similar pre-Confederation legislation existed in Nova Scotia and New Brunswick. In British Columbia, Sunday legislation outlawed hunting and the operation of any establishment for public entertainment. In the Prairie jurisdictions the game laws made hunting and shooting unlawful.[18]

Indeed churchgoing remained a necessary ritual in the estimation of many Protestant clergy for it was one of the few rites which could distinguish the faithful. As John Bossy has explained, holiness meant separation, and attending church on Sunday was one of the few rites of separation available to Protestants since other rites of separation had been downplayed by the fathers of the Reformation.[19] The sabbath was regarded by Protestant clergymen as a day for churchgoing, not for relaxation or amusement; it was not to be simply a day of rest. We 'must keep prominent the idea of worship,' Bishop Carman proclaimed.[20] Attendance at church was considered a means of protection against the forces of materialism. As D.J. Macdonnell explained, 'man is a spirit with Godward and heavenward aspirations, which are too often checked and chilled by the atmosphere in which he lives.' People needed time for prayer and 'an opportunity to gather in thoughts and hold communion with God.' This was not possible 'amid the disintegrating forces which are at work in daily life.' The institution of the sabbath, Macdonnell concluded, was necessary for any spiritual fellowship or growth.[21] To an extent, church leaders were positing a golden age of religiosity in their view of sabbath observance. Both the Methodist and Presbyterian churches had established committees on sabbath observance which were charged with collecting evidence of sabbath desecration, inculcating respect for Sunday worship, and pressing for better government legislation. For the churches, then, the continuation of Sunday observance was a sign that the Christian religion was still publicly recognized, and declining observance of the sabbath was the most troubling indication of both the church's failure and the secularization of society.

Neither the extensive legislation nor the church's efforts at moral suasion was adequate to protect Sunday as a holy day against the demands of urban society and the requirements of an industrialized economy. The Christian sabbath in Canada was in decline by the end of the nineteenth century. Since the mid-1880s results from religious surveys had been discouraging. The Presbyterian church's Committee on the State of Religion and then the Committee on Church Life and Work both submitted reports to the General Assembly suggesting that evangelization was not what it should be. The church seemed to be having little success in attracting new members into full commun-

TABLE 1
Church Membership

	Methodists	Presbyterians	Total
(a) Professed belief	916,886	842,531	1,759,417
(b) No. of communicants (church members)	269,910	226,228	495,838
Church members as % of denominational pop'n (Ratio of b to a)	(29.4)	(26.8)	(28.2)
(c) No. of Sunday school scholars	226,568	147,062	373,630
Churchgoers as % of denominational pop'n (Ratio of b+c to a)	(54.1)	(44.3)	(49.4)

Source: *Fourth Census of Canada* (1901), vol. 4, Table 19, 361–3

ion. 'We do not need to beckon to one another to come and help,' the committee declared. 'There has been altogether too little strain on the nets.'[22]

The most important and scientific of these surveys was the Dominion census of 1901, which collected statistics on church membership. The results indicated that the percentage of Methodist and Presbyterians who were committed church members was strikingly low (see table 1). Fewer of those professing Presbyterian affiliation were church members than those professing to be Methodists, and the gap widened when Sunday school scholars were computed. Perhaps it was the comparatively poor figure for churchgoers among the Presbyterians which accounted for the greater attention paid to the question of sabbath observance by Presbyterian church leaders. William Cochrane's warning from the 1870s that the church was 'fatally' deceiving itself about its actual condition if it assumed that growing numbers meant inner strength was now very difficult to dispute.

What was most alarming was that Sundays were becoming days of recreation. Indeed, in urban industrial society Sunday was the only day that workers could set aside for leisure, and in response to this weekly time pattern many entrepreneurs established sporting and recreational activities that were designed for mass participation and large numbers of spectators. The churches had to compete with an organized and well-financed leisure industry that was offering many entertaining pastimes on Sundays.[23] Increasingly the sabbath was a day on which newspapers were read, excursions were operated, sports were played, theatre, circuses, and concerts were held, and fraternal society picnics took place. Also canals, railways, and urban streetcars ran in order to get the urban masses to these activities.[24] If these activities did not attract people away from Sunday worship, they forced many workers to labour on the sabbath, leaving them no opportunity to attend church. 'The spirit of modern greed,' stated one Presbyterian clergyman, 'regards the week as too short, and would secularize the Sabbath. The clamouring for the Sunday newspaper and the Sunday streetcar are simply indications of the intense and feverish spirit of worldliness which characterizes our times.'[25] This worldly spirit indicated a breakdown in the social consensus about Sundays. Any semblance of an ecclesiastical monopoly on Sunday was being challenged in urban Canada.

The contagion of worldliness had also affected family worship, considered as important as Sunday worship in the Protestant scheme of things. Indeed, in the earlier part of the nineteenth century, before the rise of Sunday schools and regular church services, family devotion was in many cases the most important form of worship and source of religious knowledge.[26] The surveys carried out by the Presbyterian church's Committee on Church Life and Work indicated that the practice of daily family worship was waning. The Presbytery of Lunenburg-Shelburne observed that 'as regards family worship, it is a sad and lamentable fact, that in the majority of congregations reporting, it is observed in comparatively few families.' The report from the Presbytery of Paris, Ontario, was typical: 'We have to lament the indifference of our people to the power and influence that flow from, and the hallowing associations that cluster round, the family altar.' The committee concluded that 'to a large extent the family altar is in ruins.' The reasons cited for the decline of family worship were that many parents assumed that the Sunday school looked after the religious instruction of the young, but also that families were becoming too involved in worldly activities. They were no longer willing to devote time to regular prayer, Bible study, and religious training. The impact of this decline in family worship was clear: the number of young people joining the church was declining.[27] But much more than this was at stake in the decline of the Christian home. The centre of Protestant family devotion was Bible reading or study. The decline of this practice was yet another factor in the weakening position of the Bible in Canadian life. Without family worship there would not be daily recognition of 'God's presence, goodness, and grace.' Devout families were essential to the church. Indeed, it was widely believed that, along with the church, the family was the foundation of the moral and social order. In the estimation of the clergy one of society's most important religious institutions was becoming more secular in its daily routine.[28]

The issue that was largely responsible for the creation of an organized Sabbatarian movement was the operation of street railways on Sunday. This service provided people with better access to all sorts of secular amusements. According to the Presbyterian church, the Sunday streetcar was 'a mighty engine for the dishonour of the Lord, the demoralization of the land, and the spiritual ruin of those employed in connection with it.'[29] The threat of the Sunday streetcar galvanized the Lord's Day movement in Canada. Prior to 1895 the forces seeking to protect the sabbath were scattered and there was little communication between the groups located in different urban centres. At a convention held in Toronto in early 1895 leading Sabbatarians agreed to form the Ontario Alliance for Better Observance of the Sabbath Day. The Rev. J.G. Shearer, a Presbyterian minister known for his superior organizational skills, toured the province to broaden the base of the burgeoning organization and then travelled across Canada to form similar organizations in other provinces. Most of his recruiting was done within the churches. A national, broadly interdenominational Lord's Day Alliance of Canada was formed. Shearer was appointed general secretary of the alliance and editor of its official organ, the *Lord's Day Advocate*. He considered the Sunday streetcar as merely the first of a never-ending parade of secularizing forces and therefore realized that the battle against the Sunday car would have to be won as the first step in stemming the tide of secularization.[30] By 1900 the alliance claimed that it consisted of seventy local branches throughout Canada, but it is doubtful that this growth reflected real strength. The Lord's Day Alliance had virtually lost the battle against Sunday streetcars for they were operating in Toronto, Hamilton, Ottawa, St

Catharines, Berlin, Niagara Falls, and Windsor, Ontario, and inter-urban lines were also running.[31]

The Sabbatarian movement was thrown into a deeper sense of crisis when a series of court decisions in the early 1900s ruled that Lord's Day legislation enacted by the provinces after Confederation was *ultra vires*. In the case of Ontario this meant that the 1845 legislation could remain standing; but recent legislation prohibiting Sunday excursions and the operation of electric street railways was unconstitutional. The Privy Council's decision, however, would have the greatest impact on Manitoba and the Northwest Territories, where all the Lord's Day legislation had been passed since Confederation. The *Lord's Day Advocate* pointed out that the way for 'most serious' encroachments upon the integrity and sanctity of the Lord's Day had been opened. C.W. Gordon was especially alarmed about the prospect of an open Sunday in the West. He explained in a letter to J.G. Shearer that the pull of materialism was very great in the West; and therefore constant 'spiritual recall' was necessary to bring the eternal into view. 'If we are able to save our Sabbath,' Gordon suggested, 'we have saved so much else in addition, our morality, our business, our integrity, our homes, our faith; if we lose our Sabbath, we can keep nothing else long.'[32] The alliance was convinced that the uncertain status of Lord's Day legislation meant that the forces of secularization had the advantage. It was noted that the streetcar interests were pressing for licences to operate on Sunday. More alarming was the aggressive campaign underway in numerous Ontario communities to publish Sunday newspapers. The Lord's Day Alliance developed a siege mentality as it feared that without protective legislation the Christian Sunday would be destroyed.[33] What seemed clear was that federal legislation was required.

In seeking national legislation for the protection of the Lord's Day, clergymen advanced secular arguments over religious ones. At the 1904 Ontario convention of the Lord's Day Alliance the Rev. Principal Caven, reflecting voluntarist principles, explained: 'We seek no legislation to compel men to worship or to perform any sacred duty. God cannot be honored by any service except when it springs from the heart.'[34] The sacred purpose of Sunday was not emphasized by clergymen in public forums. General health and well-being was stressed, and the Lord's Day Alliance joined lobbying forces with the Trades and Labour Congress and other secular organizations which had little interest in making Sunday a day for worshipping.[35] The argu-

ment of divine authority was no longer convincing enough for the
maintenance of the sabbath as a holy day just as the Word of God
seemed no longer compelling enough to attract people to worship in
church. This quest to protect the Christian sabbath through legislation
demonstrated that the church was in a weak position as a social
institution and moral authority. To combat the increasingly powerful
forces of secularization the Protestant churches could not stand alone;
the assistance of the state was crucial. For even a semblance of a
Christian sabbath more comprehensive restrictive legislation on secular
activity was required.

A bill for the better observance of the Lord's Day, substantially
drafted by the alliance, was tabled in the 1906 session of parliament.
In presenting the legislation, the minister of justice, Charles Fitzpatrick,
outlined its general principles and objectives. He insisted that it must
not be inferred that Lord's Day legislation was 'intended to regulate
or in any way affect the question of the religious observance of the
Sabbath.' The legislation was 'really intended to provide a day of rest
for all.' Fitzpatrick hoped that public regard for sabbath observance
would increase; but he recognized that a culture of consumerism and
the pursuit of leisure was emerging for he pointed out that 'among all
classes Sunday is becoming more and more an accepted period for
expeditions of some sort in pursuit of pleasure.' To discourage this,
the business of amusement, organized recreation, and excursions was
prohibited. Forms of entertainment where no money changed hands
were not restricted.[36]

The passage of Lord's Day legislation was not a victory for the
churches or religion. It was an accommodation by those advocating a
Christian Sunday to the needs and demands of a society that was
becoming increasingly secular. Public officials simply could not enforce religious observance. During the House of Commons debates
Fitzpatrick stated that it was 'desirable to abstain from placing an
individual in the position of being obliged to choose between his
honest religious convictions and his personal gain.' There were just
as many concessions to secular interests as there were to sacred ones
in the legislation.[37] The quest for a legislated sabbath, on the part of
the clergy, represented an attempt to maintain traditional patterns
of churchgoing in a society in which recreational activities and consumer values were successfully competing with Christian worship on
Sunday. What was disturbing to the churches was that there was
little public outcry against incidents of sabbath breaking. Despite the

federal legislation it seemed that the battle against secularization of the Lord's Day was being slowly lost, and the church's ability to rally people to the defence of a Christian Sunday was waning.

Many clergymen had concluded that the only way to survive in this more secular society was to make Christianity more appealing by making it more secular in both form and content. This change was most apparent in sermon style. Traditional expository preaching, in which the strict format of elucidation of text, application of text, and final exhortation was followed and the purpose of the sermon was always a discussion of the meaning of Scripture, was in decline. Sermons were becoming less doctrinal and more narrative in character. The Moody style of preaching was having an immense impact in Canada. His sermons were anecdotal. They featured bits of biography and graphic stories from everyday life instead of 'dry argument and the accumulated texts.' Whenever Moody did refer to Scripture or retold biblical events, he did so in a fashion that made the characters and stories more contemporary. As one Canadian clergyman remarked, a preacher who was influenced by the Moody style 'took a text, but speedily wandered away from it.' Clarence Mackinnon's first sermons preached at Westchester Station in Nova Scotia were failing to hold the attention of the small congregation, until he attempted an experiment. According to his memoir:

> I stepped to the side of the little pulpit and began to describe Cain and Abel building their altars, and began at the same time rather timidly to act the scene. To my surprise the people were actually looking and listening. The next Sunday I tried a whole sermon after that pictorial style ... Henceforth I laboured to secure interesting and if possible vivid material. Conventional authorities would doubtless have had much to frown upon, grotesque illustrations and unwarranted humour, but the course had been set to be followed through for many years.[38]

The clergy understood that they were competing with newspapers, novels, theatre, and film for public attention, and many concluded, despite charges of sensationalism and sentimentality, that they had to preach entertaining sermons with mass appeal in order to reach an increasingly secular culture. That there was a visual element in Mackinnon's more sensational style was consistent with the broader shift in popular culture from reliance on print and the verbal medium to more visual forms of expression, such as photography, image-laden newspapers, magazines, advertising, and film.[39]

One Canadian clergyman who adopted the narrative style in the fullest possible manner was C.W. Gordon. He found traditional forms of preaching and Bible study to be ponderous and uninspiring. He recalled: 'In going through Philippians and the Epistles one was made to think of the class-room and its methods in a way that tasked one lest some point should be forgotten.'[40] The early Connor novels, which in essence were secular sermons, captured the imagination of the reading public. In his memoirs, Gordon advanced two reasons for the popularity of his writing. One was that the stories depicted 'an authentic picture of the great and wonderful new country in Western Canada, rich in color and alive with movement.' Secondly, he considered the religious motif in his novels to be 'a very influential cause' of their popularity. Christianity was set forth 'in its true light as a synonym for all that is virile, straight honorable withal tender and gentle in true men and women.' He was suggesting that his novels were examples of sentimental as well as muscular Christianity. Fiction with a religious foundation, Gordon explained, 'startled that vast host of religious folk who up to this time had regarded novel reading as a doubtful indulgence for Christian people.'[41]

No doubt, many readers would have taken the evangelical condemnation of novel reading very seriously. H.T. Crossley constantly warned that the great majority of novels were harmful because they destroyed reverence for the Bible, inculcated false ideas about life, and were often 'sceptical and anti-religious in their tendencies, or misrepresent the religion of Jesus Christ.'[42] Indeed the Rev. Alexander Sutherland received complaints about the books that his Board of Missions was sending to children who had collected money for mission enterprises. It was charged that the novels were 'not calculated to increase spirituality and intensify loyalty to Methodism.' One novel was particularly objectionable because the young Christian protagonists in the story dance and play cards, activities that were outlawed in the Methodist church's code of discipline.[43]

Curiously few commentators have followed Gordon in his religious explanation. Most critics have dismissed the Christianity in Connor novels as being oversimplified, and therefore do not consider it worthy of serious attention.[44] This harsh analysis ignores the fact that the early Connor novels were part of a rich genre of religious fiction in North America.[45] Clergymen who wrote popular religious fiction insisted that adopting the dramatic fictional format was consistent with biblical Christianity. One of the first Canadian clergymen to write fiction was the Rev. John Carroll. In the preface to his fictional account of early Canadian Methodism he was defensive about breaking the Puritan taboo against the ungodly novel. 'To those who overlook the dramatic character of the books of Job, Ecclesiastes, and Solomon's Song, the similitudes of the prophets, the parables of Jesus, and the highly figurative and hyperbolic character of the great part of Holy Scripture ... and yet pounce upon a brother for giving a dramatic or tale-like character to veritable Methodist history,' he declared, 'I have nothing whatever to say.'[46] Another author of religious fiction, the Rev. William Withrow, made it clear that his purpose was primarily devotional. 'The religious lessons' in his stories were 'designed to lead readers to a fuller consecration of all their powers and faculties to the glory of God.'[47]

Gordon's first fictional sketch, which he wrote for the Christmas issue of the *Westminster Magazine*, introduced the prodigal son theme that dominated much of his early fiction. This sketch was too lengthy for the purposes of the magazine, and so with the encouragement of its editor, James MacDonald, Gordon expanded it into his first novel, *Black Rock*. The Connor canon, therefore, opened with a fictional depiction of a common religious odyssey – from childlike belief to doubt, unbelief, and despair, then awakening, and finally a life devoted to Christianity – which must have struck a responsive chord with many readers. The impact the Christian message had upon the lives of the major characters was the central feature of religious fiction. Early Connor fiction not only featured the exploits of heroic missionaries but also contained many dramatic deathbed and conversion scenes. For literary critics these scenes were the least satisfactory aspects of the Connor novels.[48] But to dismiss this aspect of Gordon's writing ignores those elements of the novels that were central to popular religious literature and of great appeal to many readers at the turn of the century. Indeed Gordon's literary fan mail contained many letters that described how uplifting the religious themes in the novels were. For example, one woman indicated that *The Sky Pilot* and *Black Rock* had been an 'inspiration to better and stronger Christian living.' She explained: 'The type of Christianity your heroes present is so simple direct and practical, almost devoid of doctrine, but leaving no section of life unsanctified, that I believe it must influence many lives for good.'[49]

For many, religious novels provided solace. They were optimistic and reassuring in an age of tremendous spiritual anxiety and doubt about Christianity. Attention was drawn away from difficult theological questions and troubling discussions of the role of the church in modern society, and it was diverted towards a simple and active faith. The main concern of religious novelists, like Gordon, was to present a reassuring and inspirational Christian message in fictional form. Presenting Christianity in a concrete manner was considered the best way to establish faith by many clergymen. Only in this way could Christ be seen to be 'alive ... moving among us ... touching our lives.'[50] Christianity had become too much a matter of intellectual understanding as opposed to a simple matter of the heart or faith, according to Gordon. The 'husks that the churches too often' offered in the 'shape of elaborate services and eloquent discourses' were removed from the spiritual needs of many people. The result was a drift away from the churches and worship. This indifference convinced Gordon that there had to be a return to the 'simplicity and rugged grandeur of the faith.'[51]

In the early Connor novels important religious questions, such as the presence of a loving God and individual mortality, were made real and tangible. The novels could be read as dramatic narrative sermons on universal Christian themes. *Black Rock* can be considered a sermon in fictional guise on the possibility of redemption for all believers; *The Sky Pilot*, a highly sentimental sermon on the difficult theme of divine purpose in human suffering and pain; and *The Man from Glengarry*, a dramatic sermon on the necessity of forgiveness. Gordon's stories had a specific didactic purpose. The central section of *The Sky Pilot* was reprinted in 1899 and 1904 as a short story under the title *Gwen: An Idyll of the Canyon*. The dedication of this clearly devotional volume read: 'To All Who Question the Why of Human Pain.' This story featured Gordon's parable of the canyon flowers on the prairie, which illustrated that under God's guidance 'rest and peace and joy' will emerge from the most stormy, dark, and bleak conditions. The idea for this pastoral sermon occurred to Gordon while he was addressing a congregation of children on the topic 'the good that pain can do for us.' In his memoirs he stated that of the many letters he had received, he 'cherish[ed] the canyon letters the most. They bring me the love and gratitude of those whose canyons of pain have been brightened with the flowers that bloom only in the canyon.' What was important to Gordon was not that he had written a good story, but that he had written an effective sermon that reached many. By writing novels, Gordon did not think he was abandoning the Christian ministry; instead he thought he was expanding it.[52]

To reach the home in which there was less inclination to read the Bible, Gordon wrote devotional literature that in essence made the Gospels much like the popular fiction of the day. *The Angel and the Star* (1908) was a popularized account of the news of Christ's birth. The outlines of the biblical account of Christ's coming appear in the story, but the emphasis was on a pathos-filled drama in which the witnessing of Christ's arrival helps a sceptical shepherd cope with the tragic death of his baby. In this story Scripture was transformed into entertaining fiction. *The Angel and the Star* contained direct quotations from the Bible, but the emphasis was on drama, spectacle, and sentiment.

Such embellishment of the Gospels was even more obvious in *The Recall of Love* (1910) and *The Dawn by Galilee* (1910). These stories centred on the disciple Peter's denial that he knew Christ when questioned during Christ's trial. Gordon filled in a great deal of detail that was not present in the gospel accounts. He speculated about events in order to convey, in concrete and dramatic terms, the idea of forgiveness:

> Where Peter met the risen Lord first none of us know. There is an exquisite reserve now and then appearing in the story of Jesus Christ, but none more exquisite than this that draws the curtain over the meeting of the Master and the man who failed Him in the hour of His need. They met somewhere alone. They had their talk out together. I do not know what Peter did. I like to think of him with his face in the dust and his arms around those wounded feet. I like to think of the passion of self-reproach and the agony of shame and tears that broke his heart as he confessed his sin to his Lord. But I like more to think of the kingly word of grace that lifted the sinner up and said to him, 'Be at peace; it is all forgiven.' I like to think of Christ that day who would not lay it up against this man that he had been so base. For behind Peter I come creeping, hoping for forgiveness.[53]

Clearly Gordon had taken great liberties with the Bible in order to reach an audience that perhaps was no longer responding to strict scriptural explication and needed its Bible study dressed up in fictional garb.

To an extent, Gordon's biblical fiction reflected the impact of biblical criticism on Canadian cultural life. It had been considered sacrile-

gious to tamper with the Word of God; but modern scholarship revealed that the Bible could be revised or improved. There could be
embellishment of the central biblical stories or events. In response to
the growing concern that many people found the Bible dull, all sorts
of dramatic effects and embellishment were 'added to make biblical
stories appealing for a more secular audience. Moreover, as the Bible
was rendered a difficult book by critical insights, many tried to rediscover the simplicity and power of the Gospels in religious fiction.
They were compelled to turn to religious fiction for inspiration, edification, and devotional reading. One of Gordon's Presbyterian colleagues from Nova Scotia was convinced that *The Angel and the Star*
told the story of Christ in a manner that 'would reach a class to which
the ordinary life of Christ does not appeal.'[54]

The adoption of fiction by the clergy indicated that secular methods
had to be used for sacred ends. Rarely did the Connor novels dwell
on the content of the sermons; rather, the telling of the gospel story
was part of the action. Also, important religious concepts, such as the
nature of sinfulness, were made insignificant and superficial. Sin was
never a matter of innate depravity; rather, it was associated with
immoral behaviour and was regarded as a troublesome product of an
unchristian environment. The drunkenness, profanity, and violence
associated with the antagonists in Connor novels were the product of
the frontier, not fundamental alienation from God. By contrast, a
religious life was associated with proper morality, idealism, and heroic
action, not an ever-deepening faith and piety. Piety was equated with
the sentimental ethic of virtue and service. This romanticized view of
sin was disturbing to some clergy. One critic responded to this sentimental Christianity in popular religious fiction by pointing out that
while it was 'a great blessing' when the 'deep, touching tenderness
and forgiveness of God' is conveyed to readers, 'there is so often the
danger of making us lose the horror of sin and thinking of the loving
God as a mere goodnatured indulgent father, to whom sin is not
exceedingly sinful, whose chief thought is to make his child stop
crying and be happy.'[55]

The secular landscape was crowding out the religious content in
the Connor novels following *The Man from Glengarry*. Christianity was
increasingly on the periphery. According to Edward McCourt, *The
Doctor* (1906) was met with severe criticism because 'there was growing impatience on the part of critics and the reading public with
sermons in the guise of fiction.'[56] This transformation in Gordon's

writing to a more secular novel became most clear in his 1909 social gospel novel, *The Foreigner*. This story was set in a cosmopolitan urban community. One missionary explained his role: 'I am not sent here to proselytize. My church is not in that business. We are doing business, but we are in the business of making good citizens.'[57] Moral and social issues consumed the missionary's attention, while matters of theology and faith as well as spiritual concerns were secondary. The missionary rarely preached. Evangelical Christianity as the rallying message for personal salvation was in decline as a major motif in the Connor novel.

Reading popular religious fiction was a devotional act. Connor novels might have been read for edification or contemplation, but this activity was part of private not public worship. In a middle-class society consumed by concerns about respectability people were often reluctant to discuss religion or demonstrate their piety openly. Reading novels was evidence of religion being relegated to the private sphere. Moreover, the rise of the popular religious novel indicated the emergence of religion as a consumer or mass entertainment product.[58]

Whereas the statistics on church attendance were particularly alarming for the Presbyterian church, the statistics on church growth seemed to be especially distressing to the Methodists. Protracted discussion appeared in the columns of the *Christian Guardian* on the question Is Methodism declining? The debate was touched off in 1898 by a submission to the *Christian Guardian* by a concerned layman who was distressed by the marked slowdown in the rate of increase in membership that had been experienced by the Methodist church since the early 1890s. Between 1888 and 1892 there was an increase of 36,399 Methodist church members. Over the next four years an additional 27,584 people joined the church, and between 1896 and 1900, a period of significant population growth, there were only 19,584 new Methodist members.[59] A great variety of opinions were expressed in this debate, but the majority of contributors leaned in the direction of a pessimistic analysis. Generally it was admitted that spiritual life within the church was weak and that some form of renewal was required. The major dispute was whether this renewal should come through preaching traditional evangelical theology or by moving in a more liberal direction and becoming more active in society.[60]

The new generation of clergy thought a bold new direction in message and mission was required to renew Methodism. The Rev.

Samuel Dwight Chown, who was destined to become a leader in increasing the Methodist church's awareness of social and economic problems, was particularly conscious of breaking away from the evangelical heritage. S.D. Chown was born in 1853 in Kingston, Canada West. The major influences in his early life were the Wesleyan Methodist church and the Canadian militia. His father was Sunday school superintendent at the Sydenham Street Methodist Church and president of the local Temperance Reformation Society. At age sixteen, Chown enlisted in the local militia and graduated from the Military School in Kingston. He attained the rank of sergeant and was given command of the guard at Fort Henry when the Fenian raids were anticipated.

Chown's early ministry was dominated by revival meetings. He exhorted his congregations to make immediate and wholehearted decisions for Christ. Any remarks about social problems were couched in a strong sense of personal sinfulness and were limited to the liquor question. Indeed, prohibition campaigns became an integral part of Chown's early ministry. In recalling the 1880s, he wrote in his memoirs that 'after various revival meetings, in order to consolidate our gains, it was our custom in those days to summon the people together for the signing of the pledge against strong drink. I found great advantage in this.'[61]

Involvement in the prohibition movement quickly led Chown to the recognition of many other abuses, especially political corruption and economic oppression. By the late 1880s Chown began to move beyond the evangelical approach. Like others influenced by liberal theology Chown thought that ministers should become more prophetlike and 'preach upon themes which recognize the faith of the Lord's Prayer, the Sermon on the Mount, the Golden Rule, and the epitome of it all which Paul gives: Bear ye one another's burden and so fulfill the law of Christ.'[62] The Bible and the life and teaching of Christ remained Chown's primary inspiration. The influence of economists and social critics and the example of settlement houses and labour churches as well as the works of idealist philosophers were secondary in the formation of Chown's social conception of Christianity. When he began to preach a social gospel, Chown stressed that he did 'not propose to join hands with Edward Bellamy, Annie Besant, and others and declare that sin and misery are the remarkable results of social circumstances and that poverty, ignorance, and class distinctions consequently are at the root of all crimes and wretchedness afloat.' He cautioned against the idea that charity or brotherly love was the solution for society's troubles. Any quest for social regeneration without the love of God as the primary inspiration, in his view, would remain an unfulfilled dream.[63] To this extent, Chown remained attached to his evangelical heritage. The primary source of Chown's advocacy of the social gospel was his understanding of Christianity, not economics or social theory. Perhaps this was why Chown was destined to explore the implications of social Christianity within the Methodist church while other 'regenerators,' most notably J.S. Woodsworth, left the church.

Conditions in urban society encouraged Chown to advance beyond evangelical Protestantism. In 1895 he was transferred to Carlton Street Methodist Church, a large Toronto pastorate. There he fell under the influence of the Rev. James Henderson, one of the boldest thinkers in Canadian Protestantism, who had been preaching that Jesus was dedicated to overthrowing tyranny and injustice in this world and was the greatest socialist who ever lived.[64] Chown was deeply disturbed by the condition of the urban church. At a spiritual conference of Toronto West district clergymen he pointed out that the church was failing to reach 'the labouring or poorer classes.' The artisan class had abandoned the church in favour of the labour organization. Workingmen placed their hopes in unions for assistance in their struggles and had turned to writers such as Karl Marx and Henry George for salvation, instead of the Gospels. This demonstrated the need for ministers 'to socialize' their preaching, Chown argued. It seemed that only in this way could the demands of an increasingly secular society be met.

In advocating the social gospel, Chown emphasized that its strength was that it was not theological. In the final judgment, he argued, there will be no word about theology or belief in doctrine; instead, demanding ethical questions will be posed. Christianity existed before any system of doctrine was formulated, and it was based solely on the person of Christ. The social gospel, Chown reasoned, was a return to this original Christianity.[65] Chown's position left Christianity on a very shaky foundation – the life of Christ about which very little was known.

This position was significantly different from the response of the evangelical generation of clergy to the social gospel. In one of the first extended studies on the question of Christianity and the problem of urban industrial society, *The Kingdom of God and the Problems of Today*,

Alexander Sutherland opposed many of the tenets of the social gospel on the grounds that they represented a dangerously materialistic understanding of Christianity. The social gospel, he thought, had a weak theological foundation. It was the product of 'erratic developments of modern theology.' Sutherland was troubled with the tendency of the social gospel to equate socialism with Christianity. According to his reading of Scripture, Christ neither advocated any particular program of social reform nor espoused a certain political system. To suggest otherwise, he claimed, 'puts Jesus Christ on a par with the *doctrinaire* reformers who have appeared from time to time and reduces the Kingdom of God to the level of Plato's "Republic" and More's "Utopia."' Christ was not like any other theorist or social activist for his teachings and example were timeless and universal. Advocacy of a specific social program diminished Christianity, for it robbed it of its unique spiritual or sacred qualities, according to Sutherland. This criticism was not merely an expression of the central tension between a Christianity of worship or contemplation and one of action and service. Sutherland was speaking for most nineteenth-century evangelicals when he stressed that the church should be what Jesus had intended – bread for the hungry, clothing for the naked, protection for the friendless, a refuge for the oppressed, and above all a place where common brotherhood is forged and in which God is acknowledged as the Father of all. The danger of the social gospel, in Sutherland's estimation, was that it based religion on the secular ethic of material contentment in the world.[66]

Nevertheless, Chown was anxious to ground the social gospel in Christian tradition. He insisted that the social gospel was a resurrection of Wesleyan Methodism and that the Canadian Methodist church had buried this more vital half of its founder's legacy. 'We have kept his sermons of doctrine, but we have neglected his example as the guide to life. The present generation of Methodists seem to have forgotten the social sympathies of John Wesley.'[67] Chown was aware that Wesley applied Christianity to the whole of life, not just inward spirituality. Wesley gave advice in sermons and addresses concerning stewardship, use of time, temperance, the conduct of business, leisure, and money. The Methodist idea of Christian Perfection had been transformed by Chown from an evangelical doctrine applied to individuals to a reform blueprint to be applied to society.

In 1902 Chown was appointed secretary of the Committee on Sociological Questions and named general secretary of the Department of Temperance and Moral Reform. This department quickly became one of the most powerful and influential bodies within the Methodist church. When Chown began to devise social gospel policies for the Methodist church, he equated social questions with religious ones and advanced a secular concept of the Christian ministry. The study of sociology was necessary, he argued, for the training of the modern minister. A minister's training should not be limited to learning how to write sermons on religious topics. He must know how to explain and apply the Sermon on the Mount. Ministers were true to their calling only if they were men of affairs, and promoters of social justice and action. Chown counselled ministers to become social workers within the church. Unwittingly, he was encouraging the secularization of the church's mission. This concept of a ministry involved in secular affairs, Chown thought, would attract more candidates to the calling.[68] By 1910 Chown was advocating an almost completely secular notion of Christianity. He thought that 'the circle of historic theology' would be completed 'by inserting the arc of sociology.'[69] This reasoning reflected Chown's understanding of the concept of progressive revelation. What was striking was that Chown viewed sociology as the culmination of the development of doctrine. The most advanced understanding of Christianity, therefore, was concerned with contemporary society, not the supernatural or the transcendent. Chown's idea of progressive revelation reflected the modernists' faith in science and humanity's ability to build the Kingdom of God. Indeed God was barely noticeable in Chown's social gospel.

By Chown's own estimation his view of the Christian faith had radically changed. He announced that he no longer thought that attendance at prayer or class meetings was an unfailing sign of religious life and evidence of Christian character. The evangelical emphasis on personal repentance was not sufficient. Instead Chown suggested that ministers 'must hold our people up to the standards of the Judgement Day, feeding the hungry, clothing the naked, visiting the sick.' Good works replaced faith as the primary sign of religious life. According to Chown, evidence of Christian devotion should be measured by dedication to humanity, recognition of Christian social and industrial obligations, and the church's desire to be the healing agent of the world's problems.[70] Chown envisioned a modern religious revival that was quite different from an evangelical one. 'Its manifestations will not be the same,' he wrote. 'It may not be so open to observation, but will be proportionately deeper, and more ethical in purpose and spirit. The preaching that shall produce it may not be nearly so dramatic as that of the past, and therefore the results will not be so sensationally and superficially striking.'[71] This view repudiated one of the central features of nineteenth-century revivalism; there was nothing outstanding, transcendent, or supernatural. There was no expectation of obvious or sudden change that might distinguish the redeemed or the sacred from the secular.

Chown was also keenly aware of the changing role of the church in modern Canadian society. 'Twenty five years ago,' he explained, 'most people inside and outside the Church would have defined it to themselves as an organization which exists to provide opportunities of public worship.' But now 'the Church is held to account by all enlightened people as at least the inspiration, if not the organization for the satisfaction of all human needs, and the building up of the whole of human life.'[72] Chown was pointing out precisely how secular understanding of religion was becoming. Christianity was viewed as a foundation for the material goals of society. The values of a consumer culture were clearly dominating people's expectations, for they were looking more towards material well-being than to spiritual fulfilment.

Chown and the Methodist church went much further in exploring the implications of the social gospel than their Presbyterian counterparts. As Brian Fraser has convincingly demonstrated, the leaders in articulating and implementing social policies in the Presbyterian church believed that the social order could only be shaped by 'the spirit of Christ' if 'individual consciences were revived and reformed by the evangelical witness of the church.'[73] George Pidgeon, the convener of the Board of Social Service and Evangelism, was deeply committed to social reform. He was convinced that the clergy should be instrumental in solving social and moral problems through preaching the Word of God and taking a direct and active role. In one of his most frequently repeated sermons he argued that the social gospel was an insufficient form of Christianity because it substituted 'morality and benevolence' for 'the personal contact of the soul with God.' He charged that many incorrectly believed that they could 'earn eternal life by fulfilling temporal obligations.' Crusades for temperance, welfare, and social justice, he thought, were necessary; but they were not religious movements since they 'neither saved souls nor glorified Christ.'[74]

The Methodist and Presbyterian churches had instituted an impressive bureaucratic structure dedicated to defining and implementing a progressive social gospel.[75] These churches also undertook sophisticated social science research to acquire a precise knowledge of actual social conditions. The most ambitious foray into social science was the series of social surveys sponsored by the Board of Temperance and Moral Reform of the Methodist church and the Board of Social Service and Evangelism of the Presbyterian church. The director of these surveys was W.A. Riddell, a Presbyterian minister who had also been trained in sociology and economics. Indeed he was a perfect example of a minister turned social scientist. The purpose of the surveys was to investigate why the churches were failing to lead in the 'rehabilitation of the country.'[76] In Riddell's view the whole social reform effort was dependent on a vibrant church. Behind the Methodist and Presbyterian churches' sponsorship of the social surveys there was an enthusiasm for social regeneration and concern about secularization.

In those surveys that investigated religious conditions the results were disheartening. The most extensive survey of religious conditions was undertaken in the city of London, Ontario. This survey clearly revealed that the Christian religion was losing its hold. Statistics indicated that enrolment in Sunday school decreased 'alarmingly' once children reached the age of twelve. As a part of the survey the Presbyterian church's Committee on Religious Education sent a questionnaire on biblical knowledge to London-area schools. Among the twenty questions included were the following: 'Where was Jesus born?'; 'What man sentenced Jesus?'; 'In what book is the Sermon on the Mount?'; 'Why is Easter kept?'; 'What happened at Pentecost?'; 'What is the Golden Rule?'; and 'Name one Apostle.' On average less than half of the questions were answered correctly. This poor result was accounted for by the Sunday schools' failure to give Bible instruction and the fact that an 'alarmingly small' proportion of churchgoing families gathered together for prayer and Bible reading. Also the survey noted a disturbing trend in church membership. While well-to-do citizens were reported to be 'active in religious work, a growing percentage of the skilled and unskilled labor classes were inactive.'[77] The remainder of the surveys did not report on religious conditions or church life. These social surveys, although sponsored by the churches and inspired by the ideology of the social gospel, clearly indicated how quickly the church became irrelevant when it made itself into an institution for social reform. What was most important about these surveys was that they demonstrated that none of the new measures to strengthen the church's position in Canadian society was very effective.

The much-heralded revival of religious faith and renewed vibrancy and relevance for the churches that was to come with the social gospel was not occurring. The social gospel may have given the churches a prominent voice in the social reform movements of the early twentieth century, but it did not create regular churchgoers. As a result of the social surveys it was hard to avoid the conclusion that the churches seemed to be without purpose or meaning and were out of touch with the community. In the late 1890s it had been possible for the advocates of modern Christianity to argue that the Methodist church's position had never been stronger, but after a short decade of social gospel activity it was clear that Methodism was in decline.

The failure of the social gospel to bring about significant renewal forced S.D. Chown to begin to question his commitment to sociology as the pinnacle of Christianity. What Chown feared was that much of the 'religious sentiment ... in the air' was not related to 'really distinctive Christian conviction in the heart.' Social action did little to foster belief in the supernatural aspects of Christianity or to promote a yearning for prayer and worship. There was no question, Chown proclaimed in his stirring General Conference Address of 1912, that an increasingly large proportion of people 'live outside the sphere of the preacher's influence' and are alienated from the church. Earnest ministers, he observed, have been 'painfully and not without some perplexity aware that the truths of scripture ... are now dull and their thrust ineffectual.' Chown became critical of modern trends in Christian thought which had turned people's attention 'from the deity to the personal worth of Christ, from the value of the death to the moral supremacy of the teaching of Christ, from the supernatural to the natural, from the authority of the Bible to the authority of Christian consciousness.' He wondered if this was not responsible for weakening the sense of personal responsibility, an essential motive in leading people to accept Christ for salvation.[78] Chown, however, was quick to insist that he did not want 'to controvert' the social gospel he had been advocating.

Disillusionment about the declining importance of religion and the church in Canada was setting in by the end of the first decade of the twentieth century. It was clear that the new departures undertaken by the churches – church-sponsored leisure activities, more entertaining preaching, the use of popular media to convey the Word of

God, a social gospel, and sabbath campaigns – were unable to stem the tide of secularization. The Presbyterian church's complaints regarding falling church attendance, the lack of worship at home, and the low number of candidates for the ministry became more frequent.[79] The new principal of Knox College, the Rev. Alfred Gandier, questioned whether the church had been moving in the correct direction. 'In this work ... I need to pray daily to be kept from growing hard and cynical. There is so much in all our Churches utterly out of harmony with the spirit of Jesus.'[80] In one of George Pidgeon's frequently repeated sermons during the months before the outbreak of the First World War, he suggested that the church of the day was lacking in holiness. Without criticizing the social orientation of the Board of Social Service and Evangelism, he mentioned that the Presbyterian church was in need of spirituality and more familiarity with the unseen. Devotion to noble causes was not sufficient for true religious progress.[81] Both clergymen and concerned laity were beginning to express doubts about whether modern Christianity was strengthening the church and individual faith. A questioning of liberal theology, albeit tentative and informal, was part of the intellectual atmosphere of pre-war Canadian society.[82]

Indeed there was little evidence there was a rejuvenation of Christianity in Canadian society during the first decade of the twentieth century, and it was in this atmosphere of being unable to stem the tide of secularization that the long pre-war church union discussions took place. The challenge that many clergymen thought was confronting them was whether or not Canada would remain a Christian nation. Not only were the churches struggling against the inroads of secularization and competing in an evermore consumer-oriented society, but they were faced with the tremendous task of attempting to Christianize the growing number of immigrants who did not share the same religious heritage as the Protestant mainstream. The evangelical churches in Canada had been long cooperating with each other in temperance crusades and other moral reform activity and more recently in urban revivalism as a means to combat the powerful forces of social vice, religious apathy, and secularization. In 1902 serious negotiations began between the Methodist, Presbyterian, and Congregational churches to formalize this cooperative action into one church.[83]

The idea of church union – essentially an expression of liberal Christianity – was firmly tied to the optimistic assumptions that still dominated church life. Denominationalism and church doctrines, according to the tenets of liberal religious thought, were considered the product of history and civilization, not of God or the Bible. They were not necessarily the embodiments of essential and enduring Christian truths; on the contrary, it was thought they were barriers to the building of the Kingdom of God. The great hope was that a united Protestant church would be free of the doctrines that obstructed faith. The act of union would strip away everything that was not vital. Furthermore, it would be efficient in its mission work and more effective in Christianizing the social order by bringing about moral and social reforms such as temperance and Sunday observance. A national church would ensure that Canada was a Christian society.[84] On one level the church union movement was consistent with the tenets of liberal theology, and as Marguerite Van Die has argued it can be considered an advance of both Methodism and Presbyterianism. Indeed it was entirely consistent with the decline of distinct denominational identities based on rigid orthodox doctrines and the emergence of modern evangelicalism that had characterized recent developments in both churches. Church union had roots deep in the theological and historical developments that were underway in the 1870s.[85]

But much of the urgency behind the church union movement was a response to a growing atmosphere of alarm about the prospect of Christianity remaining central to Canadian life. Complicating the negotiations and only heightening the sense of unease that pervaded the churches and the union discussions was the fact that the evangelical consensus that was clearly strained as early as the 1880s was now breaking down. Within the Methodist and Baptist churches there were highly contentious and protracted heresy trials in 1909, in which the lines between the modern approach to the Bible and a conservative or fundamentalist point of view were clearly drawn. Within Presbyterianism there was growing division over church union itself. The opponents' concern was partially rooted in a more conservative concern about the liberal and social gospel thrust of the church union movement.[86] At the very time the Protestant churches in Canada were faced with perhaps the most serious challenges they had encountered in their history – not so much from the world of theology and ideas, but rather from the social order – they were becoming seriously divided and weakened from within. After a generation of accommodation with secular forces the churches had lost confidence in their message and mission, the very thing that was necessary if they were to withstand the increasing pressure of secularization. This troubled situation, in which a weakened church, uncertain about its doctrine and mission, had to confront a number of challenges that undermined its role and authority in Canadian society, was not the result of an abrupt break from the past; rather, it was the culmination of a long process of religious beliefs and institutions being adapted to social, cultural, and intellectual change.

While church union negotiations were staggering forward, the realization was also gradually dawning that a quest for Christian renewal through accommodation with secular society was itself hastening the tide of secularization. As the trend of secularization forced clergymen to reconsider the accommodations being made with modern society, there was serious questioning whether the church's broadened mission and more liberal discipline were having the desired effect. The modernization of Christianity was not leading to a revival of faith in terms of either inspiring people to stronger and more certain belief or encouraging them to a more consecrated life and greater commitment to the church. As a result, the optimistic assumptions behind the spirit of accommodation, liberal theology, and the social gospel had to be questioned. The outbreak of the First World War and the horrific consequences of that struggle would sharply focus this critique.

6

Battling with the Great War

The Great War proved to be a disillusioning and painful event for the Protestant churches in Canada. There was much brave rhetoric about the war providing the opportunity for Christianizing the social order and bringing about the Kingdom of God. The progressive assumptions behind liberal Christianity persisted, especially at the home front. In particular, beliefs in God's immanence and the perfectability of human society through the application of Christian ethical principles remained. The war seemed to be a catalyst for the refinement of a thriving social gospel. Confidence endured among Methodist and Presbyterian leaders that the war experience would promote the redemption of Canadian society. The awful carnage and destruction unleashed by the war forced critical reassessment of many of the doctrines or beliefs that had dominated thinking since the late nineteenth century. The war had made apparent the dangers in identifying Christianity too closely with secular society, and it forced Christians to confront the fact of human sinfulness once again. Why such a tragedy was occurring was a perplexing and ever-present question for many. Although there was some serious re-evaluation by certain church leaders and theologians who remained in Canada during the First World War, it came in the most trenchant form from those ministers who served as soldiers or chaplains overseas at the battlefront. A common observation made by those who had served overseas was that 'over here and over there are two different worlds.'[1] At the front it was increasingly difficult to find any evidence of the evolution of the Kingdom of God. Christianity could not be easily associated with the thought and actions of human civilization. A Christianity which focused on personal suffering, sacrifice, and the hope of eternal life was more meaningful. Those at the front were thrown back to a fundamental concern for individual salvation as opposed to the more secular concerns of moral and social reform.

Not only did the war challenge the tenets of liberal Christianity, it also confirmed clergymen's growing concern about the decline of the church's influence and the drift away from religion. The comradeship between soldier and chaplain permitted a growing revelation and understanding of the religious confusions of the young men, something that had previously been difficult. What the chaplains overseas discovered was that the soldiers had little understanding of Christianity and scant regard for the church. Moreover, the war itself made belief in Christianity extraordinarily difficult. Indifference to religion and rebellion against religious institutions became more widespread as the war dragged on. Attitudes became hardened, increasingly sceptical, and embittered. Chaplains were so distressed by the impact of the war that they were convinced 'the Church would come out of the struggle weaker as an institution.'[2] Somehow, it was thought, the church would have to recover its sacred purpose and define a more realistic theology that appreciated the potential of evil and existence of sinfulness. But during the war clergymen struggled to offer a believable explanation of the cataclysm and provide comfort for the bereaved and confused. The haunting question that they struggled to answer and that became the topic of many sermons both at the front and in the churches at home was how could such sacrifices in human life be allowed by a loving, merciful God? What possibly could the divine purpose be in such carnage? These were pressing issues, for the very existence of God and therefore the truth of Christianity were being brought into question by the war in a much more profound and challenging manner than they had been by the doubts raised during the late nineteenth century by moral concern, science, critical inquiry, and comparative religion.

The churches in Canada enthusiastically supported the war at its outbreak. By the middle of September 1914 S.D. Chown, now the superintendent of the Methodist church, was entreating Methodists to answer the will of God and enlist. Christianity itself was deemed at stake and Chown committed the Methodist church to doing everything possible to raise volunteers.[3] An Army and Navy Board was established to make sure that Methodism fulfilled the national duty by making a just sacrifice. Similarly the Rev. W.T. Herridge, the moderator of the Presbyterian church, told the General Assembly in October 1914 that the war was part of a larger battle in which the forces of righteousness were combatting evil and injustice. The church, he announced, must join in the cause of war unreservedly. Questions regarding whether involvement in warfare was Christian or not were dismissed by Herridge as being presumptuous as it was impossible for humanity to understand the deeper purpose of God.[4] In the *Canadian Baptist* one minister suggested that serving Christ was the essence of the soldier's oath. The militant attitude of many Baptists was probably best captured by the popular and powerful T.T. Shields of Jarvis Street Baptist Church in Toronto. He explained to his congregation that the war was not a matter of defeating Germany, but rather of casting out the devil that dominated German society. 'The devils of autocracy and predacious militarism, and all their vile progeny must be cast out,' he proclaimed.[5]

These calls to arms had a commanding effect upon ministers and theological students. Canada's universities, including the theological colleges, were fertile grounds for recruitment.[6] As one student surveying the wartime mood at Victoria College in Toronto wrote, 'the only real religion lay in the operation of the idea of self-sacrifice.'[7] For example, F.G. Brown, a probationer from Nova Scotia, 'felt it in accordance with Divine Will that I proceed to France as a private and combatant.' Because his brother had been killed at the Somme, it was 'the imperative call of Duty ... that I must do a bit to help complete the noble task he had laid his life down for.'[8] In the early stages of the war, at the home front, the war was characterized in romantic and chivalrous terms. In the autumn of 1916 the Western Universities Battalion was being formed. The chaplain, the Rev. Dr E.H. Oliver, who was the principal of Presbyterian College at the University of Saskatchewan, declared, 'What a spectacle we now behold in Western Canada. Once again Athens goes forth to Marathon. The Muses march with Mars. The Universities have become militant ... Today we are fighting for civilization, we are fighting for the Christ.'[9] In the minds of many leading churchmen the war was a religious crusade. No statement better indicated the degree to which Christianity was being identified with the fighting than S.D. Chown's bold declaration: 'Khaki has become a sacred colour.'[10]

Wartime idealism went far beyond the belief that the battle was a divine crusade. The war was also thought to be redemptive. It was thought that the spirit of sacrifice which it demanded would reform Canadian society. Both Methodists and Presbyterians were confident that a new brotherhood, economic and social justice, and a rekindling of faith would result. Indeed the wartime success of prohibition and the Union government were regarded by many clergymen as clear signs that Canadian society was moving closer to becoming a Kingdom of God. It was confirmation that the terrible sacrifices wrought by the war were indeed worthwhile. For many, such clear signs of progress amidst the great cataclysm were a signal that God was still present in the affairs of the world; and, moreover, that he cared for his Christian flock. This identification of the cause of Christianity with the war and the changes in society it fostered is well known in the case of Methodism; it was nearly as strongly held within the Presbyterian church. During the national debate on conscription, the Rev. G.C. Pidgeon sermonized that to be indifferent was to be traitorous to God as well as the Canadian war effort. W.T. Herridge, stressed that war provided an opportunity for the application of Christian principles to the whole conduct of life. He looked forward to the end of the drink traffic, the eradication of poverty, and improvement in industrial relations. There could be 'no sharp dividing line, in the present crisis ... between the sacred and the secular.'[11] The war seemed to have conquered the churches in Canada, despite the concern they demonstrated about militarism in society before the Great War.[12]

Commitment to the war effort, therefore, did not sidetrack the cause of social Christianity. Indeed, some clergymen made the naïve claim that the bloody battle in Flanders' fields paled beside the fight for social justice in Canada. 'The guns of the enemy are merciful in comparison to the evils by which the manhood of our nation is sapped of its virtue and virility and degraded to the dust of the earth,' Herridge told the General Assembly meeting in the fall of 1914. 'The death of the soldier in the trenches is easy and honourable beside the prolonged torture and hopeless disgrace of the evils permitted in the midst of our Christian civilization.'[13] Such thinking could only be sustained as long as it was held that the sacrifices made at the front were somehow noble and uplifting, a sentiment that was persistent, at least publicly, at the home front. News of the reality of war did not quell the expectation that the Christian social order was imminent. Emphasis on social salvation persisted throughout the war on the home front.

The social gospel's enduring influence did not prevent the war from raising serious questions regarding modern theology. In the early months of the war Chown pressed his doubts regarding social Christianity a little further. Recent events caused him to wonder whether Methodism had been on the correct course. 'The essential thing for our Church to-day to remember is that the Christian life is God inspired and God centred. We have been to a large extent losing the idea, and it has been an immense loss ... we have been making man, not God the great centre of our spiritual universe. We have been hoping for salvation through education, through training, through decision of the human will, through social sympathy. But all this is inadequate.' Chown called upon the commonplaces of earlier Methodism, which he defined as 'regeneration consciously experienced and testified to by the spirit of God,' to be revived and made imperative in the mission of the church.[14] At the annual conference of the Theological Alumni Association of Victoria University held in the autumn of 1916 Charles R. Cragg, a young Methodist theologian and church historian, echoed Chown's concern. He objected to the current emphasis on Christ's humanity as opposed to his divinity. The appeal being made by Methodist ministers was on the practical side of Christianity, to duty and sacrifice instead of salvation. 'Is not the lack of enthusiasm and religious fervour today due to our failure in preaching the true conception of sin?' Cragg asked. 'We need a new note as to the place and power of the cross of Jesus Christ.' Since the beginning of the war, Cragg claimed, there had been a call for evangelical Christianity.[15] A similar note was sounded by Baptist ministers throughout the war. Many columnists in the *Canadian Baptist* worried that the church would not be able to provide any moral support or spiritual guidance to the returned soldier unless 'we ourselves get a new realization of the presence of God and of the power of His Grace. For a long time we have been drifting into a kind of scepticism as to the reality of the power of grace to renew the soul. We still talk of the value of religious life, but we have been drifting perilously near a creed in which there is neither place for repentance nor renewal.'[16]

A critique of the social gospel based on an appreciation of the realities and spiritual needs of wartime was emerging. In the *Christian Guardian* a particularly forthright letter appeared from a minister stationed in Ashmount, Alberta. 'It is clearly false and unsatisfactory,' the Rev. J.E. Collins wrote, 'to proclaim Jesus Christ as an excellent ideal merely. No doubt the pursuit of moral excellence is part of salvation, but man's life has been dislocated by sin ... prior to any pursuit of moral excellence there must be deliverance from the spell and domination of sin. Jesus Christ is the great means of deliverance. He must be preached ... as the Redeemer.' To strike at the root of the present spiritual unrest and touch the beginnings of regeneration, a preacher had to 'emphatically declare' Jesus Christ as the means of reconciliation between sin-stricken humanity and God. Collins insisted upon a return to the evangelical doctrine of the necessity of atonement for sin. Preaching this doctrine, however, was 'a lost art in Canadian Methodism.' Surely, this defiant minister argued, the war ought to encourage Methodism to change its current superficial conception of sin.[17]

This challenge to Methodism's optimistic faith in Christian Perfection and commitment to social salvation was not taken up by church officials at the home front. The Army and Navy Board, a branch of the Department of Social Service and Evangelism, was charged with issuing a report on the questions raised by the war to the 1918 General Conference. The report, entitled 'The Church, the War, and Patriotism,' did not address any of the substantial spiritual questions or theological issues raised by the war. Instead it dealt with social questions. Positions on the issue of conscientious objectors, reform of capitalism and the industrial system, and making the ideals of justice, mercy, and brotherhood supreme in international affairs were extensively outlined. The commonplaces of the social gospel were reiterated: 'Methodism was born in revolt against sin and social extravagance and corruption ... To it the ideal of the Christian life was simply love made perfect.'[18] Faith in progressive development through the application of Christian moral and social principles remained intact. The Methodist church could not face the difficult and dismal implications of the war without sacrificing much of its perfectionist doctrine. It seemed that Methodism could not provide an understanding of the war without shattering its theological foundation.

By contrast, the Presbyterian Church of Canada undertook a major reassessment of its doctrine and teachings. The General Assembly set up a Commission on the War and the Spiritual Life of the Church. Leading theologians from Presbyterian colleges in Canada were members of this commission, and they were each responsible for a different aspect of how the war was influencing Christian faith. They recognized that it had become extremely difficult for people to believe in Christianity. It was becoming apparent that the Christian faith needed to be explained in a new light. J.W. Falconer tried to come to grips with the profound disillusionment that Christians were struggling with:

> The war has uncovered the hideous features of evil. By its entail of calamity it has confirmed the Scripture, 'Sin when it is finished, bringeth forth death.' We had been flattering ourselves upon the progress of the world ... We were priding ourselves on our refinement, our ability, our humanism, thinking that culture was winning its way towards a human perfectability ... Even the Church had begun to forget that this is an evil world, where the children of the Heavenly Father cannot go on their way unmolested.

Falconer thought that the war had 'cleared the air'; it had allowed people to see the character of sin clearly once again.[19] The Rev. Professor T.B. Kilpatrick concurred with Falconer's assessment. 'There has not been a thorough-going diagnosis of the moral hurt of mankind,' he wrote. 'Palliatives and remedies have been applied; and the heart of the disease has not been reached.' The Christian church had to deal with the fact of sin's power 'to degrade and corrupt and destroy the whole moral nurture.'[20] Without sacrificing their commitment to Christian-based social reform and their belief in the possibly of a better world resulting from the war, both Falconer and Kilpatrick concluded that the reality of sinfulness had to be incorporated into the preaching of the Christian gospel.[21]

This task was considered an urgent one. Faith was strained to the breaking point, Kilpatrick warned. The first article of the Christian faith, 'I believe in God the Father Almighty,' was being questioned. How could God be omnipotent and loving if the war was allowed to drag on? Why were the innocent allowed to suffer? Only the crucifixion and resurrection of Christ could assure people of the gospel of redeeming love. By the atonement, the tragedy of human sin had been 'judged once for all' and 'broken for ever more.' The mission of the church in wartime, therefore, was preaching the Cross. 'Any other Gospel is no Gospel, a mere imagination of man, vapid, flaccid, useless,' Kilpatrick concluded. According to Professor J.M. Shaw of the Presbyterian College in Montreal, God's design in this terrible strife had to be interpreted in ways that would relieve the growing confusion and perplexity. It was necessary to explain the doctrine of 'redemptive suffering' through the example of Christ's suffering in the garden and on the cross. Shaw wrote: 'For there in the suffering of Christ, even unto death, we see, not man only, but God Himself suffering with and for a sinful world. There we see God, not as a mere spectator or onlooker, dwelling apart from all our agony and passion, in unconcerned repose, but as Himself, the chief sufferer, in the struggle for the redemption of men and nations, suffering even to the sacrifice and death of His Son.'[22] This was not a return to orthodox Calvinist theology and its image of a harsh, exacting and remote God; but the Christ of Calvary was again being recognized. Moreover, this approach sought to lead humans closer to God, instead of bringing God closer to humanity. The Calvinist heritage of Presbyterianism, most notably the strong sense of sin and faith in the Providence of God, made warfare somewhat understandable – even in Christian terms. Presbyterians were able to consider what the war meant without having the foundations of their religious beliefs brought into complete question.

Preaching in Presbyterian pulpits changed as a result of the war. According to one member of the Commission on the War and the Spiritual Life of the Church, the most significant development was the renewed interest in the hope of immortality. For example, the Rev. G.C. Pidgeon reassured the members of Toronto's Bloor Street Presbyterian congregation that their hardship and suffering and that of the soldiers overseas were being shared by God. Pidgeon confronted the tragedies of life in his sermons and explained that they were part of God's plan. He tried to show that the death of a soldier on the battlefield and the grief that this caused those at home were comparable to the agony of Christ's crucifixion and the sorrow it brought to his mother. As Christ's crucifixion was part of a larger purpose and ultimately a demonstration of God's love, so too were the sacrifices of wartime.[23]

A similar transformation was evident in the preaching in the Baptist church. It was well understood that a gospel for wartime had to be defined for too many people were 'going blindly through this period of world strife and sacrifice.' According to the Rev. A.T. MacNeill of Woodstock College, this confusion was shared by many ministers, who discovered that their theology failed to meet the questions which arose because of the war. He pointed out that the 'easy and complacent' outlook of the pre-war era was utterly inadequate to provide an understanding of the staggering losses, the suffering, and the anguish of war, and as a result ministers were at a loss to know what to preach. In trying to define a preachable gospel for wartime, MacNeill suggested that a Christian understanding of sacrifice was essential. In other words, for there to be any appreciation of why God was allowing the war to take such a heavy toll, the Christian meaning of the sacrifices that were being made had to be grasped. The sacrifices gave meaning to the war. 'I believe,' MacNeill explained, 'that the measure of the sacrifice will give to us the measure of the sins and the iniquities, the wrongs and the oppression, the evils and injustices that this struggle is destined we believe to remedy.'[24] Despite the recognition that pre-war preaching was too optimistic and had failed to recognize the presence of human sinfulness, this wartime preaching was still rooted in a fundamentally optimistic outlook. The idea of sacrifice being a precondition for the triumph of a greater good, especially as it was demonstrated through Christ's suffering on the cross and his resurrection, seemed to be the only message that was able to preserve people's faith in God and Christianity. Indeed emphasizing the idea that redemption would ultimately result from the horrific sacrifices of war was, in many cases, the only message that saved many people from utter despair.

An even more radical reorientation in religious thinking was made by ministers and theology students who served overseas. Those who saw military action at the front as combatants, chaplains, members of the Canadian Army Medical Corps, or as YMCA workers were faced with reconciling the senseless deaths with their religious convictions and idealism. They were forced to reconsider their faith in a fashion that those who remained at the home front were not. Near the close of the war a Methodist chaplain, writing from a dugout somewhere in France, summed up the perspective of those who went overseas. 'Our experiences over here are epochal and have done for us what no Conference, no College, no Congregation could do ... The men at home can never understand the soldier. The people at home can never understand what the war has meant to the soldier.'[25]

Where the perspective of those at the front most obviously diverged the most from those at home was in their understanding of the true nature of the war. Belief that the Great War was a noble Christian crusade was quickly shattered in the disillusionment of the battlefield. The war was not a theatre where the forces of Christianity and righteousness would vanquish the enemy, and it could not easily be viewed in terms of the religious ideals that both the Methodist and Presbyterian churches of Canada had so confidently espoused. Clergymen overseas quickly developed a realistic, even cynical, view of the war which contrasted sharply with the naïve innocence of those at home. They refused to camouflage the war in idealistic terms and found it difficult to maintain any faith in the war's moral purpose. E.H. Oliver wrote that the war was 'hideous in its cruel costliness' and explained that poison gas and the casualties suffered at Ypres in the spring of 1915 'were the first rude shock to awaken us to the more serious dimensions of the struggle.' The lessons in idealism taught in cultural studies at universities no longer applied, he concluded.[26] H.E. Thomas, a Methodist minister from New Brunswick who served as a chaplain at Bramshott Camp, seeking to correct the romantic view entertained by the church at home, wrote of 'the hollowness of any victory which means nothing more than a supremacy of military genius.' No longer could military victory be regarded as a sign of spiritual superiority. It was clear to Thomas that 'this war will save England from many things, but to imagine that by it the Empire will be saved with an intelligent Christian Salvation, with a Salvation that gave a purity of heart and life, is utter folly.'[27] Thomas was indicating that war and military life demanded much that ran counter to the principles of Christianity.

This stark realism directly contradicted what was being preached in the pulpits, at conferences, and at the recruiting drives in Canada, and it caused tremendous conflict between ministers overseas and the official policy of the Methodist and Presbyterian churches. One Presbyterian chaplain explained that war was not conducive to clear thinking and 'doubtless the church like other organizations, has been blinded by the stupid complacencies of war-time.'[28] Another chaplain, E.E. Graham, a Methodist minister from Nova Scotia, became furious at the sanitized version of the war being presented by the Methodist church's Army and Navy Board in its reprinting of extracts from chaplains' correspondence. He accused the board of erring on the sentimental side and being 'false to actual conditions here.' For the Methodist church to identify 'that which is Caesar's with that which is God's' disturbed him deeply. To Graham the notion that the war was a Christian crusade was 'all tommy-rot.' The fighting was too well known by the soldiers, he defiantly concluded, 'to presume to identify it with the cause of Jesus.'[29] The apparent inability of church leaders at home to grasp what the war entailed was a source of great frustration for clergymen overseas. As well, this conflict about the true nature of the war became the basis of the polarization of moral and religious viewpoints between ministers overseas and the church in Canada.

The deepening gulf between experience on the war front and the domestic front was highlighted by evidence of 'deplorable moral conditions.' In both Methodism and Presbyterianism moral character was considered evidence of piety. Alcohol, card-playing, and dancing were frowned upon and extramarital sex and the 'social disease' were considered to be morally reprehensible. Indeed the Methodist church was so alarmed by reports of the incidence of venereal disease that S.D. Chown went on a special mission overseas to investigate actual conditions and make recommendations regarding what the church could do to strengthen the soldiers' moral fibre.[30] But at the front the church's strict puritanical morality was being questioned by soldier and chaplain alike. Chaplains were forced to shake off certain ethical commandments of evangelical Protestantism because they feared losing the support of the soldiers. A.D. Robb, a Methodist minister from Hamilton, was the chaplain of the 100th Battalion CEF. In a troubled mood he wrote that the 'furor' in Methodist circles over the fact that Canadian soldiers were playing cards caused 'all sorts of ridicule and jeering among the officers and men.' According to Robb, the issue of moral standards was having a detrimental effect, and he encouraged the church to drop its puritanical outlook and adopt a more tolerant understanding of the soldiers predicament. 'I do greatly fear,' he warned, 'that this sort of thing will find many men alienated from our beloved Methodism. The Church must be big enough to contain those soldiers or we will lose them from our beloved flock.' He was well aware that many of the soldiers who engaged in 'immorality' were the same men who were responsible for what might be considered acts of real courage, such as risking one's life to pull an injured combatant out of the line of fire. Any clear sense about good and evil was muddied by the nature of warfare. This ambiguity about morality was forcing Robb to reconsider the importance Methodism had placed on adherence to a code of rules and moral values as a barometer of piety and religious conviction. Concerned about how this broader understanding would be regarded by Methodists in Canada, Robb pleaded, 'Don't put me down for a heretic or a degenerate – or a backslider – or a disloyal member – I am not.'[31]

Making things even more complicated was the fact that veneration of morality was inappropriate and sometimes meaningless for conditions at the front. Clear ideas of what was noble and heroic simply could not be sustained. As one chaplain painfully discovered, distinguished actions that were the result of the highest motives could easily end up in sheer slaughter. T.C. Colwell decided that the only way to clear a dressing station for the incoming wounded was to move those whose injuries had already been cared for. Under heavy bombardment Colwell got a party of wounded men started off. Suddenly he heard a shell. It made a direct hit on the wounded men he had gathered. As Colwell explained to the senior chaplain of the division, 'I was humbled, perhaps, if I had been more careful or not so hasty in getting them off the poor fellows might have been spared.'[32] Events were compelling those at the front to appreciate a world in which there could be no certainty about morality or righteousness. Soldiers and chaplains were more likely to be struck by the irony of engaging in war and slaughter in order to sustain Christian civilization than those who did not have to confront the reality of war directly.

The problem of immorality, however, seemed to have a significant effect on the religious thinking of some chaplains. H.E. Thomas confessed that the moral conditions at Bramshott Camp were 'making an Evangelist of me where I never [was] one before.'[33] To provide alternatives to what they regarded as behaviour and conditions which threatened moral character and devotion to Christianity, chaplains, in cooperation with the YMCA, organized sports, entertainment, and reading rooms.[34] Improving social conditions overseas as a means to protect the Kingdom of God proved futile, however, since the environment in the camps and trenches was too coarse and brutal for social salvation to be effective. As Major George Fallis, a leading Methodist chaplain, observed, 'redemption of character' was stressed instead.[35] Chaplains were thrown back to a more fundamental concern for individual salvation as opposed to the more secular moral and social reform position that had been so influential in Canada. They realized the best way to maintain what they considered to be the soldiers' moral fibre and religiosity was to foster a personal relationship with God.[36] George Kilpatrick, a Presbyterian chaplain who served with the 42nd Battalion of the Royal Highlanders of Canada, observed that the experience of war had only served to reveal in new and wonderful ways God's power to save men. 'On the battlefront it has been seen daily as men in the grip of pain ... felt the need of power greater than their own and fell back on God.'[37] Greater commitment to one's personal relationship with a transcendent, powerful,

yet merciful God was sought as the source of inspiration and conviction.

This concern over moral conditions, therefore, was secondary to
the more important task and much greater challenge of explaining
the purpose and suffering of the war. The gospel had to be expli-
cated so that it would stand the test of battle. Combatants and chaplains
alike, however, testified that the war severely tested their Christian
faith.[38] Holding to any beliefs, whether they were strictly religious
ones, such as certainty of the presence of love of God, or more el-
emental ones, such as confidence in the goodness of humanity, was
exceedingly difficult. During the course of the war attitudes became
only more hardened and sceptical, if not outrightly contemptuous,
since it appeared that God was not going to stop the war. It was this
crumbling of faith in the presence of God that had the greatest impact
on the religious thinking overseas.

An impressive variety of worship services were organized by
chaplains to combat doubt and despair. First, there was the compulsory
church parade. This service began with a hymn led by the regimental
band and followed by the prayer of general confession and the Lord's
Prayer. Then came a scripture lesson, the sermon, and more hymns.
The church parade was concluded with the national anthem and the
blessings. There was also a Holy Communion service on Sunday
mornings, and whenever possible, chaplains held Bible study classes,
a Sunday evening service, nightly prayer meetings, and a mid-week
service. These voluntary services were informal and short, and were
often conducted in primitive circumstances. They were held in farm-
houses, squares, barns, billets, cellars, gun-pots, dugouts, and wherever
else men would could be safely gathered.[39] At these services worship
usually included Bible reading, prayer, hymns of devotion and intercession, and a brief talk in which the Christian message was delivered.

Christian worship seemed to appeal to soldiers particularly just
before their battalions went to the front line or entered combat. A
Presbyterian chaplain, the Rev. J.S. Miller, reported that 'many men
have learned the need of God in the nerve destroying ground of
steady trench warfare.'[40] Major Fallis recounted one incident when he
was approached by a soldier, in the moments before having to advance
to the battle scene, who asked if the Lord's Supper could be adminis-
tered 'as we may never come out alive.'[41] While passing the communion elements to soldiers at the battlefront, the Methodist chaplain of the Second Canadian Division heard 'the murmuring of the

men engaged in earnest prayer to God asking for deliverance from sin and for strength to face the great struggle.'[42] Communion services also attracted soldiers after battle. The sacrament of the Lord's Supper was regarded as a protection and a thanksgiving.

There was some debate among chaplains about the impact of their services. Was the peril of combat making the soldier more open to the Christian message? Were the evangelistic services bringing about a revival of faith? Chaplains' 'Reports of Activities' gave a good indication of the results of their religious services. At the Seaforth Camp in England, where Captain E. Chambers was a Methodist chaplain, there were always between two and three thousand men. Chambers reported that on the average only about twenty-five or thirty men attended his Bible classes. Attendance at the lighter and more inspirational mid-week services was higher, ranging from two hundred to two hundred and fifty. The best indicator of the hold religion had upon the men, Chambers thought, was the number who took Holy Communion after the parade services. For the summer of 1918 Chambers reported the following figures: on 21 July, 96 men stayed for the sacrament; on 28 July there were 112; on 4 August, 175 men took Holy Communion; and on 18 August, 70 soldiers joined in the Lord's Supper. After most communion services Chambers reported that he was 'encouraged' by the response, but occasionally he noted that 'not nearly enough for a camp of this kind' attended.[43]

Others were sceptical of the significance of attendance at worship services. Another Methodist chaplain also stationed at the Seaforth Segregation Camp, A.C. Farrel, concluded that there was not 'any great evangelization of deep religious desire such as it was said the war was producing.' He complained that there was indifference, if not resistance, to religious services unless they were 'baited or camouflaged with some special attraction.'[44] While at Bramshott Camp, Major Kilpatrick complained that despite his hope that the men would become more receptive to religion, they were 'turning their backs on the higher call.' He was discouraged about doing Christian work at the front.[45] Soldiers readily admitted that they attended religious services to escape chores or to be entertained.[46]

As the war dragged on, however, many chaplains noticed that an ever-growing number refused to partake in the Lord's Supper at the front. They were becoming superstitious, fearing that communion was a preparation for death.[47] Away from the battlefield, reports indicated that a need for communion was not as strong. In the training camps and on the lines of communication, 'where things were more normal,' there was an 'indifference painfully evident' towards attending communion service.[48] Generally, habits of prayer, worship, and Sunday observance declined as the feelings of bitterness and outrage became more intense.

Methodist and Baptist religious services had an old-fashioned revivalistic tone. The emphasis was on 'deciding for Christ.' After prayer, one Methodist chaplain wrote, 'I gave a short address, urging the men to accept Christ as their Saviour from Sin, and as the only refuge when the men were facing danger and death. The men were greatly moved, and when asked to decide for Christ hands went up all over the large audience. There must have been at least one hundred decisions for Christ.'[49] At the dugout services during the battles of Vimy Ridge, the Somme, and Passchendaele, T.C. Colwell discovered that there was a great need for emphasis on the vital fundamentals. He acknowledged that before 'we were forgetting the real truths of the Gospel but the war called us back to a realization of its great truths: "Faith in God," "The Need for Redemption," and the "Redemptive Work of Christ."'[50] It was as though the Methodist chaplains were retreating to their rural saddlebag heritage in the rustic surroundings and harsh conditions of the camps and trenches. Captain W.A. Cameron of Bloor Street Baptist Church toured the Canadian camps in England in 1917 and 1918, and the character of this tour was much like that of a nineteenth-century revivalist travelling from one town to another encouraging great numbers to make a personal decision for Christ. According to reports, the gospel Cameron proclaimed to the soldiers was 'essentially evangelistic, and sin, the Cross, and salvation were, as ever, central facts in his message.' He challenged the men to accept the leadership of Christ. Although, at Cameron's insistence, there was no statistical accounting of the number of men who signed the cards indicating they had made a decision for Christ, the eyewitness accounts suggested that Cameron made a powerful impression at the numerous YMCA camps he visited. The officers at Witley Camp, for instance, reported that hundreds of their men were 'spiritually helped.'[51]

George Pidgeon's sermons at the front were reminiscent of the evangelical era in Presbyterian preaching when the necessity of conversion was presented in urgent tones. He went overseas under the auspices of the Canadian YMCA. After visiting the camps in England, he was placed in charge of the religious work in the 2nd Division of the

Canadian Corps in France for a five month period in the summer of 1918. His sermons focused on repentance, sacrifice, and salvation. The central message of the Christian gospel, that humanity was sinful and in need of a saviour, was constantly emphasized. Pidgeon pressed the soldiers in a revival-meeting fashion to repent immediately. 'Settle with it – now – while it is open to settlement. If you will give your life to God, He will assume responsibility for your past: That is what Christ died for – to make such a thing possible.' The idea of atonement – that through sacrifice comes life – permeated Pidgeon's message to the soldiers. This was not explained in doctrinal terms, however, but rather in terms of the soldiers' experience. By going to the front, Pidgeon reassured the men, you have laid your 'lives unreservedly on the altar, in order that others might live and the world be saved.' The rough wooden crosses lining the fields of France and Flanders, therefore, were symbols of Calvary. Those who had been killed or wounded had 'caught something of the spirit of the Master.' Before the war, Pidgeon claimed, people had been striving to find a Christianity without the cross. 'Now they see that this is the distinctness of Christianity and the only way for the world's salvation.' Attention was being drawn back to what was distinctive about Christianity: the vicarious suffering experienced by the innocent for the guilty.[52]

It is impossible to know how the soldiers responded to this evangelical preaching. There was an element of glorification in Pidgeon's sermons which might have been resented. The idea of redemptive death or that sacrifice was necessary for redemption was stressed, and this might have been construed as an attempt to give positive meaning to what struck many combatants as sheer slaughter. Moreover, what the chaplains emphasized about the cross and what the soldiers saw in the image of the cross might have been different. Perhaps the image of Jesus Christ being crucified on the cross was a powerful and meaningful one for the soldiers because it depicted the passion of self-sacrifice and suffering.[53]

There were important differences between the religious awareness and understanding of the soldiers and that of the church and chaplains. One of the reasons for the more traditional evangelical emphasis in the chaplains' preaching was that the men were almost constantly in the shadow of death. The chaplains believed that only a Christian message that gave assurance of personal salvation could provide a glimpse of a caring and merciful God, or any sort of answer, solace, and hope, to the spiritually troubled soldiers. The possibility of individual salvation and life everlasting that the clergy at the front so confidently proclaimed, however, was made dependent on evangelical theology. Soldiers were told that their immortality rested upon their confession of sinfulness and acceptance of Christ as the Redeemer. The question of some form of immortality was uppermost in the minds of soldiers. The flyleaf of one soldier's prayer book contained the following: 'General Sir A.W. Currie to the Canadian Troops: – To those who fall I say, You will not die, but step into immortality.'[54] This faith in soldiers' personal salvation certainly reflected a belief in the supernatural and may have indicated a return to more traditional Christianity; but it was not a revival of evangelical orthodoxy. In the chaplains' estimation the Christian faith of the soldiers was 'without form or definiteness.'[55] According to George Kilpatrick, the men did not know precisely what their faith was; and yet they were 'reaching and groping for ... a coherent interpretation of their inner experience.' Confronting the soldiers, however, were creeds, confessions, and articles of the Christian faith which seemed meaningless, especially when they were faced with the grim realities of the battlefield. Even the 'venerable and loved Apostles Creed' became mere recitation without conviction after the first two sentences, Kilpatrick pointed out. Soldiers wholeheartedly repeated, 'I believe in God the Father – and in Jesus Christ, the only Son, our Lord'; but the Virgin Birth, the descent to hell, and phrases such as 'the Communion of Saints' struck the men as being unbelievable. When the church espoused these words it was not pronouncing truths which gripped the men.[56] As another chaplain explained in the Christian Guardian, complex theology and the fine points of denominational doctrine and ritual were 'rent into shreds and whirled away by the hurricane of the shells and the storm of this most frightful war.'[57]

There was little hint of judgment or insistence that only regenerate soldiers would go to heaven in the soldiers' understanding. To soldiers, the dead 'were not a people apart, but a sort of elder brotherhood to which at any moment one may be transferred.'[58] It was on these most important questions of death and immortality that the churches struggled to find satisfactory answers or a preachable gospel and that their teachings seemed to be at odds with the popular beliefs of the soldiers. If the church had been able to find a preachable gospel to explain the suffering and losses of the war, then perhaps it would have been more successful in reaching the troubled soldiers at the front and mourning families at home. The extent to which the soldiers did believe in the supernatural, therefore, was not necessarily a reflection of their acceptance of church doctrines. A certain amount of the religious sentiment at the front developed separate from the teaching of the chaplains and outside the churches.[59] This was not a completely new departure, for in pre-war Canadian society there was a great deal of religious thought that was not grounded in the doctrines or teachings of the churches.[60]

There was further debate as to whether the ideals and values of the soldiers could be considered religious. One informal survey that inspired much commentary was based on the interviews a Baptist chaplain held with many of the returned soldiers who spent four or five days in Quebec City before travelling further west. Few of the soldiers expressed belief in any particular creed, and they did not express their religious beliefs in biblical language. Moreover, many claimed to hold no religion. The chaplain at Quebec City, however, insisted that 'the majority carry in their conduct religious truths of primary significance. ... these soldiers show their spiritual convictions in their course of action.' This rosy interpretation of the returned soldiers' religion was disputed in the columns of the *Canadian Baptist*. One contributor, who was being more realistic, pointed out that possessing a Christian character and Christian conduct was not tantamount to being a Christian. Such a notion of Christianity, he stressed, differed radically from the Bible, which insisted on salvation or the new birth as being essential. The fact that many soldiers claimed they had no faith could not be ignored or simply dismissed as being typical of the returned soldiers' silence. It was probably more accurate, according to this critic, to paint the returned soldiers as being 'unbelievers' instead of saints.[61]

A major stumbling block that inhibited soldiers' willingness to accept Christianity was a personal sense of being degraded and undeserving. One Methodist probationer who endured this sense of unworthiness in a particularly acute fashion was Pierre van Paassen. He felt that he and his comrades had 'crawled through a ditch of mire and filth' as 'little by little we learned the whole modern techniques of serial murder. In less than three months, we were deemed sufficiently expert in assassination, theft and arson to be sent over to France.'[62] Dealing with the soldiers' disillusionment proved to be one of the most difficult tasks for ministers overseas.

There was a widespread opinion that the chaplains had failed to reach the average soldier. A Methodist probationer from the British Columbia Conference, G.H. Hamilton, who was a private attached to the 11th Canadian Field Ambulance and who was applying to become a chaplain himself, revealed to the Rev. T.A. Moore that many enlisted men felt 'the most useless man out here is the chaplain.' One reason for this, he thought, was that chaplains were hampered by being a 'link in the military chain.'[63] In a way chaplains were in their own no-man's-land. As officers, they were isolated, and specific military conventions had to be observed before a soldier could have an interview. For many, the spiritual effectiveness of religious services was destroyed by the necessity of military discipline and routine. Compulsory church parades, in particular, were the target of much hostility, for the men 'strongly resented being made to fall in a parade and go to listen to the padre and officers singing "Fight the Good Fight" and a sermon they scorned.'[64]

Chaplains were rarely given any credit for developing a Christian understanding of the realities of the war or for assisting the battle-scarred men in dealing with the horrors of the fighting. There was sharp criticism of the efforts of the chaplains in an open letter in the *Christian Guardian* signed by an anonymous private. Although the correspondent admitted that some chaplains were doing 'helpful work,' he charged that 'others are doing positive harm by their disregard of the bitter feelings that are generated in the hearts of the boys who enlisted to do their bit.' Some Methodist probationers, he claimed, were not going to return to their studies for the ministry because neither the chaplains nor the churches had attended to the 'deep trouble' they were having with their temptations, thoughts and actions.[65]

After the war Methodist soldiers complained bitterly about the church's response to their spiritual needs. C.T. Watterson, a private in the Canadian Army Medical Corps, had been at Wesley College in Winnipeg before enlisting. After the armistice of 11 November 1918, but before returning to Canada, Watterson wrote a letter to the Army and Navy Board on the behalf of other Methodist soldiers. He angrily criticized the church for its war policy and activities. 'We as a church advised our youth to join the army. In that organization their spiritual and moral ideals have suffered a great change. Not anywhere in my three years of army life have I heard of or come into contact with, a great spiritual or moral leader ... there was no note of leadership in the church that found an echo in the heart.' In dismissing the chaplains' attempts to reach the soldier as 'deplorable,' he warned that 'many have done with the Church.'[66] No doubt some of this anger and disillusionment was a part of the more widespread sense of injustice that was responsible for the outbreak of violence in the months after the armistice.[67]

Some men's suffering and sense of guilt for the destruction and murder unleashed in battle was so intense that for them the Christian message was ineffective and empty. To these men the Methodist church no longer seemed to have the spiritual resources or theology to make sense of the world they lived in. After returning to Toronto, Pierre van Paassen remembered he had drifted aimlessly through the streets 'like a man in a daze.' The thought of returning to theological studies at Victoria College, which had so greatly excited him before he was pressured against his will to enlist, occasionally crossed his mind, but the idea filled him 'with an inexpressible contempt.' The life of a clergyman seemed too confining. There was a further reason for van Paassen's rejection of the ministry. Shortly after being discharged, he encountered the dean of theology at Victoria College, who assured him that everything was ready for him to pick up from where he had left off and said it would be an honour to have him studying for the ministry. When this prospect was seriously presented, van Paassen was shocked, almost horrified. 'An honour? An honour to take back an apostate. How can one like me – whose hands were stained with blood – ever approach the Lord's Table?'[68]

The extent of the disenchantment with the Methodist church by those ministers and probationers who served in the Canadian Expeditionary Force was significant. Of the 426 who went overseas, 39 'resigned from the ministry' on returning to Canada. More alarming was the fact that another 113 clergy and theology students were never heard from by the Methodist church after they were demobilized.[69] They did not return to college to complete their theology degrees, apply for a station, or submit an official resignation. Connection with the Methodist ministry was completely severed. Precisely why many of these veteran ministers and probationers left the church is impossible to know. No doubt, some were physically incapacitated, and perhaps others were told they would not receive a station. However, the discontent with the Methodist church at the front indicated that many either felt too unworthy or were rebelling against the church.

Because of the difference in perspective between the domestic and battle fronts, the chaplains were convinced that their work was not

complete until they had interpreted the war and its lessons for those
who had endured it to the churches at home. Near the end of the war
the director of chaplain services appointed a committee representing
all the Protestant churches and charged it with preparing a message
from the chaplains of the overseas military forces. Representing the
Methodist church was Lieutenant Colonel Fallis and Major L.W. Moffit,
and representing the Presbyterian church was Captain H.A. Kent,
Lieutenant Colonel E.H. Oliver, and Lieutenant Colonel G. Kilpatrick.
These chaplains were instructed to submit a questionnaire to the
chaplains from their church and draw up a report based on the responses. Then all the representatives were to gather and formulate a
document giving 'expression to the great common convictions regarding Church work and Christian Service that the war has led us to
form.'[70]

The nature of the questionnaire, of course, biased the content of the
chaplains' message. It canvassed the chaplains on the religious faith
of the soldiers, the effectiveness of the churches in dealing with the
spiritual problems raised at the front, and on what reforms the
churches at home should undertake. What was striking about the
questions was their negative thrust. The first read: 'Does our Church
appear to you in a measure to have failed to win and hold men?'
Subsequent questions asked if there had been a neglect of instruction
in the fundamentals of Christianity and what the soldiers considered
to be the chief sources of ineffectiveness in the church and the ministry.
The questions themselves assumed difficulties, failure, and the loss of
men from the church.

Only the responses from the Presbyterian chaplains are extant.
They confirmed the committee's worst fears that religion and especially
the Christian church were held in low esteem by the men. There was
near unanimity that the churches had failed to win and hold the men
at the front. Many chaplains concluded that the churches were not
providing any leadership. They had failed to provide an understanding of their function or mission, define a commanding vision of the
Kingdom of God, or impress upon those at the front the necessity of
regular worship, public profession of faith in Christ, and the practice
of private devotion.[71] E.H. Oliver was particularly harsh in his assessment. The men had not been told of the spiritual aim of the struggle,
he charged, and the church had left them bewildered about the moral
government of a world where such a catastrophe might occur. Finally,
the church had failed to stress the futility of the war. This, Oliver

pointed out, struck many soldiers as an inexcusable shortcoming. The response to the questionnaire indicated that there was profound disillusionment in the ranks of the Presbyterian ministers who had served overseas; but, in contrast to the Methodist church's experience, there was no exodus of ministers and theological students from the Presbyterian church. Perhaps the difficulties which war brought to Christianity were felt more deeply and aroused more anger amongst Methodists because theirs was a faith based on the idea of human perfectability; whereas Presbyterians may have been somewhat better prepared for the grim reality of the war because of their stronger sense of sin and faith in divine Providence.

What was most 'appalling' to the chaplains was the widespread ignorance of Christianity that they discovered at the front. The men were in the dark concerning the vital truths of religion. According to one report, 'there is in some quarters an amazing ignorance of the Bible itself, and nowhere does there seem to be reliable acquaintance with the creed of the Church ... confusion is rife regarding the meaning of Conversion, the necessity of Atonement by the death of Christ ... All kinds of vague and often ludicrous theories of eschatology abound.' Another reported that the meaning and purpose of the sacrament of Holy Communion was not clear even though it had been repeated constantly throughout the war. In surveying the soldiers, the chaplains were forced to acknowledge that what they had been preaching at the front did not get through. The chaplains' survey also suggested that the churches' failure at the front was rooted in the pre-war period. Most of the men, the chaplains found, had some relation with the Presbyterian church, but it was not vital or personal in nature. Instead it was sentimental, domestic, or conventional. The men stated that they had found Sunday school 'dull and monotonous' and that they dreaded the critical debates of Bible class. E.H. Oliver recounted that 'in my hospital experience I never had a soldier designate a definite passage of Scripture as his favorite portion. Our men are at a loss to express themselves in a religious way. Even the Christian soldier can scarcely tell you what it means to be a Christian beyond "trusting" in Christ and saying your prayers.' Little was known besides a few hymns and the Lord's Prayer, and the Bible was an unknown book. It seemed clear to Oliver that the church and Sunday school were failing to impart a clear understanding of Christianity. 'We must revive the educational side of Church work,' he concluded; 'our preaching must become less topical and casual and more expository and systematically instructional.' The sense of dismay expressed by the chaplains indicated that they understood that the lack of strong and clear Christian faith among the soldiers was the result of the failure of the churches to indoctrinate Christian beliefs and knowledge and insist on religious experience. This failure was not merely a wartime phenomenon; it was rooted in the accommodations the churches had made with the modern thought and social trends of the Victorian era.

A common response to the questionnaire was that the churches should return to the essentials. The fact that they had been ignoring the essential truths of Christianity was thought to be a major reason for people drifting away. Some responses indicated that many felt there were too many meetings, societies, and clubs in the churches. Said one disgruntled soldier, 'If you are out for pleasure, have it. If you want to worship God, don't mix it.' Instead of giving the people 'a weak, flabby "be good and you'll be happy and when you die you will go to Heaven"' sort of sermon, clergymen should be impressing upon people that Christianity means loyalty to God even at the greatest sacrifice. The church would recover its purpose only when it remembered that the first word of the Gospel was 'REPENT.' The thoughts of the Presbyterian chaplains were aptly summarized by Captain W. Christie's concluding comment: 'The Church must remain a Church, and dare not develop into a Social Club ... The dignity, orderliness, and spirituality of Christian worship must be maintained. It must have a clear evangel for war-worn and sin-stricken mankind.'

In assessing these responses, the overseas chaplains argued that 'we have but poorly used the available resources of Divine Power ... It is our little faith, our lack of consecration and of loyalty that stands arraigned.' That the 'great verities of the Christian Faith' had to be clearly espoused was the central recommendation put forth in 'A Message from the Chaplains of the Overseas Military Forces of Canada to the Churches at Home.' It was stressed that the 'supreme duty' of the church was 'the preaching of the Cross' and the 'uplifting of Jesus Christ,' and that refusal to do so left the church 'without power to fulfill her mission.' In order to halt the drift away from the church, however, the chaplains cautioned that these fundamentals had to be expressed in a manner and with a language that met with the soldiers' demand for 'reality' in worship. Many old creeds and prayers could no longer meet 'the soul's true longing.' Basic Christian conceptions of humanity, Providence, prayers, salvation, Christ, and God, the chaplains agreed, required 'a fresh presentation in the Church's teaching.' War had made the soldiers intolerant of the 'disguise,' 'make belief,' and 'unreal utterances' that much of Christianity had been lost in. As the *Canadian Baptist* argued, 'all the returned soldiers want is that, instead of drapery there shall be real religion, instead of ritual a message, instead of a social club a church of God, instead of a nice little essay, a worth-while sermon.'[72]

In a similar vein some ministers, after having gone to the front, became troubled by their church's commitment to progressive social reform. A notable example of this was S.D. Chown. Just prior to the war Chown had expressed some reservations about the social gospel. The war pushed him further along in his reconsideration. His three-month tour of the military hospitals and trenches in 1917 seemed to be the turning point.[73] He remarked that he was 'learning much ... from the boys at the front.' Upon returning, Chown revealed that he was overcome by a perplexing sense of doubt and was finding it difficult to see where the hand or love of God was. 'Our faith,' he proclaimed, 'has been trembling if not crumbling and our philosophy has not been adequate to our need.' In another wartime sermon he questioned the insistence by 'broader Churchmen' that Methodism further develop a program of social activity and economic and political reform. This struck him as 'extravagant.' 'A more evangelical conception' of the Christian message, 'without any well defined strategy of constructive social activities,' now seemed more suitable.[74]

This outlook marked the beginnings of a serious questioning of the modern emphasis on social salvation. War had made apparent the inadequacy and outright sentimentality of much of the liberalism which had dominated thinking in Presbyterian and Methodist circles. The real presence of evil in human nature and Christian civilization was made clear. It seemed no longer possible to trust in progress and look exclusively to human nature or history as a means to under-standing and reaching God. Salvation would not be brought about by some evolutionary process; there had to be fundamental redemption of the human personality. Although the war did not produce a religious revival, it did lead to a renewal of interest in theology. Returned Methodist probationers pressured theological colleges for greater concentration on the Bible and more instruction of theology in the curriculum.[75] The quest for a deeper theological understanding of the Word of God and Jesus Christ in the postwar era had its roots in the bloodied soil of the battlefields.

The enthusiasm for the war and the optimistic belief that it would create a more Christian society came to be regarded as tragic and maddening mistakes by the war's end. The idea that the Great War could be a force for regeneration had proved to be a hopeless doctrine. Revulsion against warfare forced church leaders into a defensive position. After the war the Rev. C.H. Huestis, a former Methodist minister who had become secretary of the Lord's Day Alliance, sent out a questionnaire to citizens of Alberta asking them about their attitudes to the church. There was strong criticism of church policy towards the war. Many believed that the churches had failed to utter one word of rebuke.[76] There seemed to be nothing distinctive or Christian about the churches' teachings throughout the war. Some clergymen agreed with this criticism. One of the causes of the church's failure, G.C. Pidgeon admitted, 'has been her own inability to rise above national prejudices and the national viewpoint. This is one of the discouraging things in modern religious life. The church followed the nation and often constituted herself the expounder and apologist for the nation's policies.' The Christian churches stood convicted since they had been either silent or had only protested in subdued tones against the sinful tendencies in all societies that had made the war inevitable.[77] Clearly the identification of the Christian gospel with the interests of secular society and the nation had seriously undermined the church's spiritual and moral authority. Chown sermonized in a repentant fashion that to glorify war again would be like 'painting roses on the lid of hell.'[78]

The problems that the Great War brought to the Canadian churches were intractable ones. Both at home and overseas the churches struggled to maintain a following. There had been signs of dissatisfaction and a drifting away from the church before the war. This subtle and gradual withdrawal from worship and religion had been accelerated by the war. What was clear by war's end was that a new theology or a new religious language to express the insights gained by the war had to be developed.

7

The 1920s:
An Era of Drift

In the aftermath of the Great War, Methodist and Presbyterian clergymen quickly resumed their quest for church union. The difficult questions raised by the war, in a sense, were forgotten as attention was turned to the great promise for renewal that was attached to union. After a long struggle church union was finally achieved in 1925 and was regarded as a sign of the ongoing progress of Protestant Christianity within Canadian society. Denominationalism had been criticized for being a great barrier to effective church work, and the leaders of the church union movement thought that Christianity would be strengthened throughout Canadian society as a result of this unprecedented ecumenical action. In the first issue of the *New Outlook* E.H. Oliver celebrated the accomplishment of union by announcing, 'Canada is our parish. It is ... the vision of Dominion wide service that inspires the new union ... There will not be a hamlet or rural community in the whole land where the United Church will not serve.'[1]

The achievement of church union overshadowed both the disenchantment of many clergymen and the struggle to develop a Christian theology for the postwar world. Defeat, confusion, and despair characterized the mood of many churchmen throughout most of the 1920s. It was thought that religion's sway over the lives of Canadians was continuing to decline and that the church would not be able to play a role as the spiritual leader or moral and intellectual guide for postwar society. There was concern that the Protestant religion was becoming a lifeless convention, no longer a supreme and vital force. The Rev.

John Maclean, the chief archivist of the Methodist Church of Canada and librarian of Wesley College in Winnipeg, was convinced that Methodism was a passing phenomenon in Canada. He expressed the undercurrent of pessimism held by many clergymen to a Winnipeg congregation. 'The Church,' he said, 'is in trouble. There is an unsettled condition of affairs ... some are drifting from the faith of their fathers. There seems to be a lack of spiritual energy and ... want of spiritual vision and real fellowship with God and the Church seems to be passing through a period of unrest and depression.'[2]

In the estimation of many clergy this sense of disillusionment and drift was something much more serious than what had existed previously. The churches were failing to understand or interpret the age; they were failing in their prophetic mission. The war had raised the question of God's character and role in history as well as his very existence in the most urgent way, and the churches did not seem to have any answers. In a survey of religious life in Canada after the war S.D. Chown noted that people were wondering whether God should be trusted in the future or 'revered and obeyed as a righteous and loving Governor of mankind' since such a 'terrible cataclysm of destruction' had been allowed to happen. He observed that 'in many minds the war shook with the violence of a moral and intellectual earthquake the foundations of Christian faith. It shattered many structures of belief in which devout people found refuge from the storms of life ... In deep perplexity, many silently drifted into a sheer atheism which denied the very existence of the Almighty.'[3]

It was hoped that the spiritual and moral resources the churches had dedicated to the war effort would be rededicated to the purposes of the Kingdom of God in Canada. There was a pressing need for spiritual regeneration; Christianity had to regain its lost initiative. This was the dominant theme of Pidgeon's postwar sermons. 'We need a creative period in the church's thought; no generation can ever be renewed spiritually unless its thinking is captured. We need a creative period in action – the actual changing of human beings by the grace of God in a new scale both in numbers and in quality. This can be attained only by a new incoming of the spirit of God. All upward movements of the past have sprung from a rediscovery of God – a rediscovery of God in His relation to human life.' According to Pidgeon, the key to this desperately needed religious revival rested in the example of the soldiers' willingness to make sacrifices for their beliefs. A similar kind of sacrifice had to be made in the postwar world so that the churches could restore their prominence in Canadian society.[4]

The insights gained at the front about regenerating the church and making the Christian message more vital and widespread, however, were not pressed by the chaplains once they returned to Canada. There were many reasons for this. One was that the churches were not particularly open to the returning ordained chaplains and soldiers. Veterans had difficulty enough finding a parish let alone influencing the conferences or assemblies of the churches. Postwar circumstances were so intolerable for many returned Methodists that they sent an open letter of protest to the *Christian Guardian*. They expressed their dissatisfaction regarding the absence of stations, poor financial remuneration, and the fact that chaplaincy service overseas was not regarded as part of training for the ministry.[5]

Even those who did find their way back into the upper echelons of the Methodist or Presbyterian church did not press the issue. For most veterans memories of the war experience were too uncomfortable and the perspective still too short to communicate what had been learned at the front. Many simply wanted to forget. E.H. Oliver had been one of the most militant about applying what had been learned at the front to reform the church; but shortly after being demobilized he confessed that he did 'not want to talk about the war ... I am fed up on the whole subject and the whole experience. I want to escape that utter depression of soul that overwhelms me when I think of Ypres and Passchendaele, the hell of Lens, the mad ruin that stretches from Vimy and Arras to Cambrai and Valenciennes. The sheer havoc and appalling desolation of it all haunts me.'[6] Those who had been overseas were more comfortable concentrating on church union because the experience of interdenominational cooperation at the front was something they could draw upon that had positive, forward-looking, and progressive implications.

One minister who did try to push his church into thinking about some of the broader theological insights gained from the war experience was S.D. Chown. His three-month tour overseas was relatively brief, and perhaps the war's disturbing reality was not so psychologically troubling for him. Whatever the case, he was able to advance the ideas that had been stirred while at the front to a more forceful conclusion. He criticized the Methodist church for its inability to make the crucial distinction between evangelism and social service. 'There is a profound difference,' he pointed out, 'between Christian character and the ideals that are influenced by Christianity. This distinction was being lost in the Conferences of the Methodist Church of Canada.' Chown admitted that 'I myself may be held largely responsible.' Christian social idealism did inspire a humanitarian motive which contributed to an improved society; but this failed 'to impart the greater gift of divine life.'[7] In reassessing his previous progressive outlook, Chown concluded that 'although we cannot forget the Good Samaritan, we must save the Prodigal Son.' He advocated the promotion of deeper theological understanding of God and the worship of the risen Christ, instead of the more liberal concept of Christianity which venerated a clear moral conscience and which focused its teachings on creating Christ-like behaviour in all social relationships. Historically the church had grown by preaching and practising Christian evangelism, Chown argued. It was time to return to that 'simple faith' as the best means for the struggling Methodist church to renew itself.[8]

This critique of Canadian Methodism did not cause great excitement or much commentary. The Methodist church had become too dependent on the possibility of creating a Christian social order to accommodate itself easily to the more pessimistic notions of humanity and society implicit in the adoption of a more evangelical Christianity. In advocating this position, Chown was conscious of expressing ideas 'within the category of experience not often referred to.'

One area where there was some response to the demands of the war-hardened was in the curriculum of the theological colleges. Students who returned with their faith intact looked for theological training that was positive or affirmative in character. At Methodist colleges returned probationers sought greater concentration on the Bible, more emphasis on religious education, and less attention to critical evaluation.[9] Presbyterian educational institutions, such as Westminster Hall in British Columbia, reported that as a result of the war there was a modification of the curriculum towards more emphasis on the basics of Christianity. There was a decided movement at Pine Hill in Halifax in favour of greater attention to religious education in response to the demands of theology students who had served overseas. In 1921 the Presbyterian church conducted a survey of its educational institutions. The recommendations suggested that the English Bible should be given a larger place in the curriculum and stressed that less emphasis should be placed on critical studies, while more should be placed on 'the true value of the body of truth contained within the record.'[10] The advances made by biblical criticism were not being rejected; but it was thought that the approach to Scriptures should be more reassuring.

Despite these efforts to reform theological curricula the churches continued to have great difficulty in attracting men to the ministry. This became a recurrent subject for editorial commentary in the *Christian Guardian, Presbyterian Witness*, and *Canadian Baptist* throughout the early 1920s. Because of the large number of probationers who never returned to college after being demobilized, the Methodist church felt a particularly acute sense of crisis. Enrolment in theology never reached pre-war levels.[11] In a series of articles in the *Christian Guardian* on college student unrest, concern was expressed over the 'distrust of the organization of the church' found on the campuses. Students went to the Bible 'to get facts for themselves' instead of relying upon the Methodist church and its theologians and ministry.[12]

In the 1921 report on Presbyterian colleges it was acknowledged that other faculties, such as engineering, medicine, law, science, and agriculture had growing numbers of students, while theology did not. Moreover a survey was taken of students in the arts asking them if they intended to enter theological studies, and the results were most discouraging. At Westminster Hall in Vancouver and Robertson College in Edmonton approximately only 2 per cent of the students in arts stated that they would enter the Faculty of Theology. These figures were a little more encouraging – around 7 per cent – at the University of Saskatchewan, Presbyterian College in Manitoba, and Queen's University. At Knox College and Pine Hill over 10 per cent of the students in arts expressed an intention to enter theology, while at McGill over 17 per cent indicated an interest in theology. According to the report the war had an indirect impact on these results.[13] 'We may be suffering at the present time from a moral reaction following the war. We had entertained high hopes and thought in our foolishness that the heroism and sacrifice displayed by soldiers on the battlefield and by other folks at home would be diverted to the service of the Christian Church when the war was over. Instead ... people are more frank in their disregard of Christian principles.' A more fundamental reason for the refusal of the young to respond to the call of the church, the report suggested, was that the ministry was becoming an unattractive calling. It was viewed as being unrewarding, isolating, and impoverishing.

There was no easy remedy for this ongoing problem of attracting recruits for the ministry. Church leaders reasoned that one solution might be the consolidation of educational facilities with church union. The theological colleges had poor financial support and therefore inadequate staff and facilities. In part, this situation was caused by the duplication of resources and institutions, and it was one of the obvious crippling by-products of interdenominational rivalry. By attaching so much hope to the concept of church union as a means to overcome these problems, church leaders were overlooking fundamental reasons for the apathetic response to the church's calling.

Discussion of church union had been set aside in 1915 for the duration of the war, although it was almost universally advocated by chaplains at the front as a partial solution to their demands for a Christianity that was clear about the essentials and free of doctrinal complexity. Negotiations were resumed in the early 1920s. Carrying the mantle of church union in the postwar period were S.D. Chown, T.A. Moore, G. Pidgeon, E.H. Oliver, and C.W. Gordon, who had been involved in moral and social reform and had been deeply influenced by liberal Christianity and a maturing Canadian nationalism. The postwar union movement was carried out in an atmosphere of great 'urgency.' There was an underlying fear that if union failed, then the cause of Protestant Christianity in Canada would be seriously jeopardized. S.D. Chown warned that 'if the major Churches of Protestantism cannot unite, the battle which is going on now so definitely for the religious control of our country, will be lost within the next few years.'[14] And Principal Walter Murray of the University of Saskatchewan, a leading force in the Presbyterian church, wrote that if union did not 'go through we will find the rural congregations in the west break up and become almost secular congregations and the whole country will drift back to an indifference of religion that will leave its mark for generations.'[15] At stake in church union was the religious life of Canadian society. Union was considered to be a necessary measure to stem the tide of secularization. It was for this reason that supporters of organic union within the Presbyterian church proceeded in an uncompromising way even at the serious cost of dividing the church.[16] Church union, therefore, was not the product of a religious revival; instead, it was carried out in an atmosphere of weakness and decline, and it was regarded as an opportunity for a new beginning. The United church's first General Council called for 'the re-consecration of spiritual life, re-visualization of the task of the church, the re-dedication of the entire membership to God.' Attention now had to be turned away from organizational matters and redirected to the most important religious or spiritual concerns.[17]

In the end, church union did not rectify the underlying problems that were confronting the churches. The United church was soon faced with a shortage of clergymen.[18] The decline in candidates for the ministry went to the heart of the churches' problems in postwar Canadian society and could not be easily solved by structural or organizational reform. A Special Committee on Recruits for the Ministry was appointed by the United church's Board of Education in the summer of 1926 to determine why the problem persisted. The committee sent a confidential questionnaire to students and professors at theological colleges. It was designed 'to elicit expression of any discontent which may exist with the course of training, its effectiveness, vitality, and variety.' The assumption was that the theological curriculum was largely responsible for college men deciding against the ministry.

This notion was rejected by the respondents. Neither intellectual nor spiritual freedom was restrained in theological college, they claimed. As for the suggestion that the theology program's standards be lowered to attract more candidates, the respondents countered that 'suitable men are not deterred by the high standards but have been repelled by an idea that it was not sufficiently high.' If flawed, the curriculum at theological colleges was not challenging enough. Drastic changes in the course requirements for ministerial training would not affect the supply of candidates; the problem lay elsewhere. The respondents indicated that the outstanding factor accounting for the low number of students in theology was that the vocation of a clergyman was not considered to be a fulfilling one. Students thought that being a minister could be inhibiting because 'church opinion' would certainly exclude one from engaging in 'certain activities of life.' Respondents from the West complained that the prospect of financial hardship was a deterring factor. Finally, according to many, the ministry no longer provided opportunities for social or intellectual leadership in the community.[19] These answers suggested that in terms of status, whether it be social, intellectual, or financial, the station of the clergyman was falling in Canadian society.

The committee concluded that the main reason for the declining number of recruits for the ministry was 'fundamentally spiritual, and hence the remedy for the situation must be spiritual.' There was a lack of strong religious conviction on the part of the restless and intellectually rebellious young. To stop the turning away from theology at college the committee called for more adequate provisions for 'quickening and sustaining vital religious experience in college life during the critical transition from unquestioning enthusiasm of childhood to the more reflective and informed direction of mature life.' The committee also concluded that secularization of life in the home denied the young a primary Christian influence. A return to family worship and prayer was considered an essential part of the solution to persuading the young to answer the sacred call. And, finally, the committee called for an infusion of spirituality in the church. 'The whole Church needs a fresh vision of the need of the age ... when the fires of devotion burn brightly upon the altars of the church we shall hear less and less about the difficulty of securing men for the Church's ministry.'[20] Decline in the status of the ministry and trouble in attracting recruits were dramatic signs of a deeper and more widespread religious depression.

Further evidence of a deep spiritual malaise became apparent as a result of a survey carried out by the Committee of Church Life and Work of the Manitoba Conference in 1926. Most of the pastors who responded complained about the significant amount of religious indifference that they encountered. Many pointed out that church members attended worship services only occasionally and that for them religion was only a 'side-line.' Those ministers that could report regular churchgoing and a full church on Sundays were equally despondent. The Rev. R.E. Spence of Killarney observed that 'religion seems to be so stereotyped instead of the free, spontaneous expression of life bubbling over with joy in the service of one's great Saviour.' The Rev. David Howarth from the small rural parish of Harding, Manitoba, could report that his church was always full; but he did not take comfort in this apparently strong indication of religious commitment. 'In spite of this fine quality,' he wrote, 'I feel that *my people are not deeply religious*; even the intimate experience of the Quarterly Communion seems to pass off and so few feel the sacred tenderness and covenant of it ... *My people as a whole are not praying.* There are few family altars in the Charge and few to take part in family prayer. They live so little in His Presence. The prayer in secret is very seldom I am afraid.'[21]

Much more difficult than identifying this lack of piety was accounting for the indifference to religion and worship that seemed to be so widespread and deeply rooted. According to Howarth, *'the clutch of the material'* was responsible. 'The average man or woman,' he explained, 'will brush aside the deep appeal of their own hearts for the thing they can grasp and hold for their physical pleasure as a new car, a new machine, a new farm, more and larger crops. A few thoughts for God each week and the vast bulk of its time for pursuit of material things.' The direct result of this consumerism, he noted, was that his parishioners had less time and resources to support the church and its various moral and social reform programs and its missionary endeavours. Howarth had perceptively recognized that the consumer ethos had largely replaced spiritual concerns in postwar Canada.

Indeed, the 1920s have been regarded as the period in which the long-developing consumer culture in Canada matured. The majority of families in Canada had become consumers rather than producers. As Veronica Strong-Boag has recently demonstrated, a wide variety of items ranging from automobiles to a vast array of personal goods and services were consumed by Canadians eager to attain the good life. The new technology for the modern home, particularly indoor plumbing and electricity, led to a wide variety of new consumer items being placed on the market. Household appliances such as stoves, washing machines, refrigerators, and vacuum cleaners and home entertainment items, especially radios and phonographs, were eagerly purchased. If families had not saved a sufficient amount of money, they could now apply for consumer credit or buy in instalments in order to purchase major items. Encouraging this consumerism was a modern advertising industry that aimed to manipulate people through the powerful suggestion that purchasing a certain item somehow would be fulfilling and lead to a better life. Dire consequences in terms of personal well-being and social status were suggested if an item was not purchased.[22] The emergence of consumer culture was central to the secularization of Canadian life, for the path to a sense of well-being was now clearly defined in material terms rather than spiritual or ethical ones. As T.J. Jackson Lears has argued in relation to American society, the culture of consumption signalled a shift in dominant values from salvation in the next world to material well-being in this world.[23]

Despite the rampant materialism that so many clergymen had identified as the great challenge facing the churches, the United Church of Canada's first moderator, George Pidgeon, was hopeful regarding the impact the new church would have upon the future of religion in

Canada. In a sermon that he delivered across Canada as part of the moderator's tour, he claimed that the spiritual renewal that would ultimately result from union would overcome what had become the most troubling development in Canadian church history. The three uniting churches, he pointed out, had dedicated their efforts to social and missionary activity. Sermons were delivered and books written on the social teachings of Jesus Christ, exclusively. 'This,' Pidgeon asserted, 'was the most beneficent error in the history of interpretation ... Christ was no mere social reformer.' His mission was deeper than improving human institutions and social conditions; it was to transform the nature of individuals and link them with God. If the United church was to be successful, it had to turn its attention away from the 'external and practical' matters of social betterment, for 'social service is not religion.'[24] An effective ministry could not compete with secular activity; rather, it had to be clear about its own sacred realm. One of the professors at Emmanuel College, the United church's newly created theological college, echoed Pidgeon's position by rejecting the idea that the church should seek relevance or make accommodation with the transitory interests of secular society. Alfred Gandier proclaimed, 'Let the minister and the Church aim to be strong in their own special field of *worship* and *Christian fellowship* – a realm where other things cannot compete and for which the deepest elements in human nature cry out.'[25] There was deep concern that the United church, like its antecedents, was too secular in its understanding of its mission to Canadian society.

The great difficulty in redirecting church life, however, was that the United church lacked a statement of theology suitable for the age. United church doctrine did not deal with the serious questions which the war experience posed for liberal theology or with the profound sense of disillusionment with Christianity that the postwar generation was struggling with. As one of the leading proponents of union concluded, 'there is no attempt in the *Basis of Union* to introduce anything new and startling.' For the most part the doctrinal basis of union merely outlined the historic creeds of the Protestant tradition. It was not a vital statement of the living common faith of the new church.[26] Indeed the document read much like a series of compromises designed to avoid any conflict or controversy. Contradictory concepts, such as the Calvinist view of divine sovereignty and the Methodist or Arminian view of human liberty, were merely stated side by side without any attempt to reconcile them in a new Christian understanding. Church leaders seemed to abdicate the responsibility of outlining a 'nobler form of Christianity' that had been expected to come with union. The doctrinal platform of the United church was something which few disbelieved in any serious manner, but which few believed with any firm conviction.

Some commentators pointed out that neither personal evangelism nor social redemption successfully met the spiritual needs of the age. In the first issue of the *New Outlook*, the Rev. T.A. Moore suggested that these two cornerstones of the church's message were now bankrupt. Personal evangelism had become identified with a bold appeal to emotionalism, without any regard for intellectual or moral content. It was discredited by 'unabashed commercialism and financial exploitation.' On the other hand, social redemption work by the church was threatened by the rise of the professional social worker. In the face of the growing specialization of knowledge and complexity of modern life, churchmen regarded the work of social engineers as being beyond the scope of the church. The movement for social service was being divorced from organized religion. Moore was very perceptive in concluding that this meant the 'loss of the religious incentive in redemption, and the loss of the ethical outlook for the Church.'[27] Many Canadian Protestants had held what appeared to be two opposing viewpoints, personal and social Christianity, in an uneasy tandem. It was becoming difficult to hold on to either one of these doctrines. The position of liberal evangelism, which sought a balance between personal and social Christianity, was crumbling. It was becoming harder to hold a middle position as the conservative and progressive wings of the church became divided on religious questions and theology, instead of matters of social reform.

This theological vacuum highlighted the United church's dilemma in the 1920s, and confusion and controversy reigned about its task and message. What the renewed message and mission of the United church ought to be proved extremely difficult to work out in the 1920s. The fundamentalist-modernist controversy and the growing indifference to the church that characterized this era only made church leaders realize that clarifying Christianity's central doctrines was an essential task. In the United church the dispute that raged between fundamentalists and modernists in the United States and in Baptist circles in Canada did not dominate sermons or the pages of its publications. The roots of the fundamentalist-modernist disputes rested in the late nineteenth century, and the outcome of the various heresy trials in Canada before the First World War suggested that Methodist and Presbyterian church leaders were determined to avoid controversy by seeking consensus.[28] They seemed committed to making their churches moderately progressive and liberal in spirit. A further reason why the United church was relatively unscathed by the controversy was that many of the most conservative elements in Presbyterianism did not join the union; they remained within the Presbyterian church.[29]

Nevertheless, the United church was subject to the fundamentalists' critique. There were church members who held fundamentalist beliefs, and they expressed concern with respect to the modernism found in the United church. The fundamentalists' insistence on unquestioning belief in the inerrancy and literal truth of the Bible, the Virgin birth, Christ's miraculous works, the atonement, and the bodily resurrection clashed with certain elements of the church's liberalism. Those of fundamentalist persuasion were alarmed that under the present leadership there would be no Christianity remaining in the United church. The 'most advanced Methodist views' published in the *New Outlook* were singled out for attack. The dreaded descent to complete denial of the resurrection, then agnosticism and a conviction that there was no deity, and finally atheism seemed to be an unavoidable one, according to some critics.[30]

One of Pidgeon's correspondents concluded that the United church had gone so far in the direction of 'skeptical liberalism' that it was now time to protest. J.R. Dobson of Montreal wrote, 'I do think that with some of our leaders in the United Church of Canada, a profession of agnosticism is regarded as a primal condition for canonization as a modern saint.' He explained that 'certain men today are giving up – everything ... miracles are ruled out; our Lord is reduced until he becomes merely a leader and an example; no Virgin Birth – no empty tomb, no sacrifice for sin on the Cross, and God Himself spoken of as the soul of the Universe and oftentimes as "It" the force behind External things [sic].' Recognizing that there was 'a danger also in cold self-satisfied unloving orthodoxy,' Dobson argued that 'the time has come as never before perhaps in the history of our churches, to formulate a statement of beliefs.' Vagueness in the doctrines of the United church was a major reason, this conservative-minded layman thought, for the decline the church was suffering. Certainty had to be reestablished in order to stop the drift away from belief in the essentials of Christianity.[31]

The fundamentalists' critique troubled United church leaders. Even the more conservative, such as Pidgeon, found the attack disturbing. He warned that the United church's already vulnerable unity of organization and spirit was being threatened by the zealous intolerance expressed by those who identified the true church and Christianity with certain statements of belief and forms of thought. Fundamentalists wanted to oust from the church all those who were not in agreement with their particular view of the gospel and theory of inspiration. They were intolerant and exclusive. It seemed as though they sought to drive Christians out of Christianity, he charged. This was a challenge to the United church's desire to be an open and inclusive church.[32] On the other hand, 'the very success which the appeal of the Fundamentalists, Pentecostals et al. are having' indicated to Pidgeon that these people could not be alienated or excluded from the United church without seriously jeopardizing the objective of becoming a national institution.[33] The flourishing of so many Bible colleges in the 1920s, especially on the Prairies, was a source of real concern to United church ministers, for they realized that these institutions were responding to a growing constituency who sought a more literal understanding of the Bible, a strict moralism, and evangelical preaching, which stressed the importance of sinfulness and a emotional conversion experience.

Since many United church clergy wanted the church to be modern, while still proclaiming essentials of the Christian faith, their response to the fundamentalist-modernist controversy was equivocal. Fault was found with both points of view. J.M. Shaw, who taught at Presbyterian College in Montreal, charged that fundamentalists were shifting the emphasis of the Christian faith from loyalty to Christ to a belief in certain 'doctrines' about Christ and his work. Such devotion to doctrine was considered inadequate since doctrinal formulations, according to the modern understanding, were merely the reflection of the particular thoughts and circumstances of an age. Reiterating one of the central conclusions of liberal Christianity, Shaw pointed out that doctrine was transitory and was in constant need of revision and restatement with advancing thought and knowledge. One's faith was made too vulnerable when it was based on absolute insistence on certain non-essential doctrines of Christianity. A fundamentalist's faith was in danger of becoming a fragile shell of empty doctrine in the tide of increasing knowledge and social change.[34] Fundamentalists' insistence on unquestioning belief in certain doctrines was viewed as a stumbling-block in the way of people's acceptance of the Christian gospel.

On the other hand, the church's leaders were also alarmed by certain elements of modernism. Modernists were too willing to ignore 'the spiritual' in an overly 'humanistic' outlook. They did 'doubt' what was absolutely essential to Christianity: belief in the divinity of the Holy Spirit and the saving power of the Cross. These two articles of faith were thought to be so vital to Christianity that when they were denied or merely called into question 'the whole edifice of the Christian faith would be threatened with collapse.' Such thinking was considered tantamount to 'modern heresy.' Church leaders were sympathetic to the fundamentalist position to the extent that it defended the gospel against the negative onslaught of secularized thinking. The Rev. J.R.P. Sclater, a close friend of Pidgeon's, admitted that he understood and concurred with the fundamentalists' fear as they watched 'the essentials of Christianity falter in the wake of modern knowledge.'[35] Despite this criticism most United church leaders remained sympathetic to the modern liberal spirit.

The fundamentalist-modernist controversy forced the United church to define what it thought was basic to the Christian faith. Many clergymen in the United church focused on the meaning of the Cross as the central article of Christianity.[36] The foundation of a 'standing or falling' church was whether or not there existed faith that Jesus was the son of God, incarnate, who came into the world to save humanity. What was fundamental, therefore, was belief in God and loyalty to the crucified and resurrected Christ.[37] Reflecting the United church's quest to be an inclusive religious community, Pidgeon suggested that 'if a man believes clearly in the living, all-powerful Redeemer, and has a personal experience of this saving grace, we can afford to give him considerable liberty in his thinking along other lines. I am inclined to think that this is the New Testament standard.'[38] In attempting to hold a broad middle ground, the United church hoped to quell the fundamentalist-modernist dispute.

Some realized, however, that the church could not merely straddle both the fundamentalist and modern viewpoints. In one sermon Pidgeon announced that the 'need' of the United Church of Canada was 'a fresh experience of God and a new interpretation of His Gospel in the terms of our own life and in relation to our own sins and needs.' In this statement Pidgeon simply suggested that there was a need for a renewed statement of theology suitable to the times. He did not define what this ought to be, except to acknowledge that the concept of sin should be included.[39] The United church was unclear about its doctrine, and this was a significant indication of a persistent 'theological depression.'

The fundamentalist-modernist controversy was not nearly so restrained in the Baptist church.[40] The bitter disputes over certain editorials in the *Canadian Baptist* and faculty appointments at McMaster University and Brandon College that erupted in the 1920s, largely at the instigation of the militant and uncompromising fundamentalist T.T. Shields, split the Baptists, at least publicly, into two clearly defined camps. But many within the Baptist church were as confused and uncertain as those in the United church. Just how uncertain many Baptists were is best demonstrated by the chancellor of McMaster University, H.P. Whidden. During the disputes in the 1920s Whidden was determined not to give into Shields's demands that no one with modernist religious sympathies be allowed to teach at Baptist institutions. He was absolutely committed to the traditional Baptist principle of complete religious liberty. But during the height of the controversy Whidden agonized over the number of graduates who had abandoned the ministry. He worried that exposure to modernist ideas at university weakened faith, and as a result Baptist ministers were unable to maintain their religious beliefs when confronted by doubt or opposition. Basically, Whidden was concerned that perhaps a whole generation had 'lost their bearings.'[41] The fundamentalist-modernist controversy was not a sign of theological clarity or certainty; but rather a sign of yet another denomination with a strong evangelical background experiencing a theological malaise, an inability to find a gospel suitable for the postwar world. As George Rawlyk has concluded, the 'rigidities' of the struggle 'stifled and distorted the Christian gospel and channeled religious thought back over well-worn paths, thus discouraging the truly daring, the venturesome, and those who might have spoken with prophetic voices and revitalized insight.'[42]

One United church minister who dedicated much of his time throughout the late 1920s and the 1930s to defining a renewed theology was the learned Richard Roberts. His concern about the decline of religion in modern society caused him to become one of the most trenchant critics of contemporary Protestantism. Roberts thought that the church's 'confusion about its business in the world' and, moreover, its uncertain gospel paralysed it when confronted with a theological

controversy such as the one between fundamentalists and modernists. There was no unifying gospel in the United church which ce-
mented a strong and assured fellowship able to withstand the tide of
advancing and widespread secularization.[43]

Roberts was born in Wales in 1876. In his first year as a preacher,
around the turn of the century, he was involved in the religious
revival led by the Forward Movement in the seaports and coalfields
of Wales. In 1900 he was called to Willesden Green, London, and
there he began his career as an urban minister. The Great War undermined Roberts's confidence in the strength of religion in modern
society. His pacifism led to his resignation from the ministry at Crouch
Hill Presbyterian Church. In a letter to church officials he argued that
for a Christian church to adopt a militaristic attitude was tantamount
to denying Christ. In his final sermon to the congregation he announced that the church had abandoned the way of Christ. 'We see,'
he pointed out, 'the Church itself riven, broken, shattered by the war.
We perceive how the national bond has everywhere proved stronger
than the Christian bond, and in the midst of this welter the Church
stands, impotent and speechless.' No longer did Roberts talk in confident tones of the coming religious revival. He was now convinced of
the failure of the church and realized that the world was a long way
from accepting the Christian imperative of conversion and living
according to the demands of the Sermon on the Mount.[44] Roberts's
activities throughout the war, in Britain and the United States, focused on a pacifist organization of Christian clergymen and laity,
the Fellowship of Reconciliation. The central objectives of the FOR
were to bear witness against war and militarism and to work against
compulsory military recruitment. This commitment to the FOR reflected Roberts's belief in a Christian-based social activism, which, for
him, had been ignited in the Welsh coalfields, where Kier Hardie, the
inspirational leader of the labour movement, had worked alongside
the religious revivalists.

In 1923 Roberts accepted a call from the American Presbyterian
Church in Montreal and arrived in Canada during the campaign for
church union. He enthusiastically supported it, thinking like many
others that its achievement was a hopeful sign for the future of the
church. Most of Roberts's energies were still involved with developing
the idea of Christian pacifism.[45] Hints that he found the years in
Montreal isolating appeared in a colleague's letter commending him
for his decision to accept the call to Sherbourne Street United Church

in Toronto. 'I am sure,' the Rev. A.E. Kerr wrote, 'that you will find more congenial atmosphere than there was in Montreal. You will enjoy the closer friendship with men like Sclater and Pidgeon ... And besides you will be able to exert an influence in the formation of public opinion in Toronto which you never could in Montreal because of the predominantly French character.'[46] In calling Roberts, Sherbourne Street had made a decision for a 'great preacher' who emphasized the theological aspects of the ministry.

When Roberts transferred to the Sherbourne Street United Church, it was experiencing many of the problems typical of downtown urban churches. The strongest supporters did not reside in the immediate vicinity. Sherbourne's weak position in its surrounding community of immigrants and transient labourers was the source of great difficulty and even controversy for Roberts and his ministry. Roberts encountered some pressure from his congregation to improve the pastoral side of his ministry in order to assist Sherbourne in its fight against declining attendance and falling membership and donations. There was a debate about whether the church needed a minister who would give more attention to gathering and fostering a congregation by systematic pastoral work or one who excelled as a preacher. Many believed that a minister's pastoral contacts with a congregation were crucial to the strength of a church in the community. The ties that bound pastor and people had to be personal, it was thought, if the church and ministry were to stand the corrosive impact of urban conditions. This controversy caused Roberts to speculate on the problems of the modern urban ministry. He suggested that 'systematic pastoral work' could be carried out in a rural parish but was impossible for clergy working in an urban setting. There were simply too many demands placed on the urban minister.[47]

In the end Sherbourne parishioners agreed that the problems facing their church were not the result of the scholarly nature of Roberts's ministry. They agreed with Roberts that 'counter-attractions' were a major factor accounting for religious decline in urban centres. In a letter to Roberts one prominent church member summarized the social trends of the 1920s which were drawing people away from the church. Sir Edward Kemp wrote:

The cinema or picture show, the automobile, the radio and jazz, as well as other things, have all had an effect on home life, drawing young people particularly away by themselves for entertainment ... some seat-

holders, during summer and autumn months have homes distant from
the City altogether. There is, it is said, a somewhat changed attitude of
people regarding church attendance brought about by these and other
reasons, and in contrast with the past, with some exceptions, is not now
considered a social centre in the sense that it formerly was.[48]

The parish atmosphere that Roberts worked in, therefore, was one
under significant secularizing pressure. Indeed the secular atmosphere
of the 1920s had also permeated the home, formerly a centre of religious instruction and devotion in many families.[49]

By the mid-1920s Roberts had become quite concerned about the
drift away from religion and the church. In a key sermon from his
Montreal years Roberts warned that it had to be recognized that
'religion has become a pale and anaemic counterfeit of itself, a dull
thing of rules and prescriptions, of ceremony and formula, of medio-
cre hopes and middling performances, the sanction of a standardized
morality and the temple of an incrusted faith.' Religion had declined
into a round of observances that did not retain even a memory of its
previous intensity.[50] Indifference was victorious. In the late 1920s,
Roberts wrote in his weekly column in the *New Outlook*, 'The Quiet
Hour,' that 'the urge to worship has in our time suffered an ominous
arrest. Some of us still feel in a vague way the need to worship; but
we no longer feel the inevitability of it. Worship does not command
us.' Any worship that did exist, he suggested, was becoming secularized. It no longer sounded the notes of thanksgiving, penitence, ado-
ration, supplication, or intercession. Moreover, the key to worship,
praise, was lacking. Modern people, Roberts lamented, had forgotten
how to praise.[51]

Although Roberts was aware that there were many social and intellectual forces contributing to the decline of religion, he was also
convinced that the church and theologians were responsible too.
Commenting on recent events in Canada in a book he published in
1926, Roberts pointed out that ecclesiastical reform was an inadequate
means to bring about a resurgence of religion. It should be 'as plain as
daylight,' he wrote, that none of the church's programs, or 'new era
movements,' or 'efficiency devices' was going to help in the crucial
matter of bringing people to God. In pursuing such measures, the
United church indicated that it was 'chiefly marking time.' The United
church could only be successful, Roberts argued, if it discovered the

Word of God and learned how to utter it. If not, he warned, it 'will remain in its present state of unrest.'[52]

The reason for the lack of clarity in the United church's understanding of the Word of God and uncertainty about its role in society began to dominate Roberts's thinking and writing. In 1927 he delivered a series of lectures entitled 'The Scope of Theology' to the students of Emmanuel College. The lectures were not published, and, as a result, they are extremely valuable in understanding Roberts's thinking since he spoke freely and 'dealt more boldly with the great themes than he would have cared to do with a wider public.'[53] Roberts argued that there was confusion about God, and this meant there was no clear focus for worship or theology. 'The ultimate problem of religion lies with the nature of God,' Roberts stated, 'and most candid minds allow that they have no very satisfactory account to give of it.' Roberts defined this quandary in religious thinking as being between the traditional view of a transcendent God and modern one of an immanent God. There was a logical contradiction involved in these ideas. They could not be reconciled, Roberts declared, for 'immanence implies in some sense the identity of man with God, while transcendence implies that He is a Real Other.' The irreconcilability of these two notions was made apparent by the fundamentalists' war against the doctrine of evolution. 'An Act of Incarnation,' Roberts stated, 'can by no means be dressed up as a process of Evolution.' What was really at issue, according to Roberts, in the fundamentalist-modernist controversy were competing conceptions of God. He explained:

> Creation implies a 'transcendent' God, Evolution an 'immanent' God. Creation requires a God standing outside the universe, having brought it into being by his own *fiat*, and operating upon it from without in perfect freedom according to his own will. It may be true that evolution does not logically imply immanence; but there is no doubt that the two ideas make good company in the mind. And to most minds, evolution certainly does suggest a God *within* the universe, involved in and therefore limited by its processes, and somehow fulfilling Himself in its development.[54]

In stating that these two conceptions of God, and thus fundamentalism and modernism, were not reconcilable, Roberts was rejecting the dominant liberal notion that some accommodation was workable and essential. This stood him in contrast to other United church clergymen. To Roberts the United church's approach to the fundamentalist-modernist controversy was feeble. The liberal position was crumbling because it was in a middle position that was very difficult to maintain in the postwar debates about religion.[55]

A way out of the paralysing theological dilemma did not yet seem to exist. 'For the moment,' Roberts declared in a remarkably clear and candid statement, since 'it seems impossible to construct a single theology that shall do full justice to the implications of both immanence and transcendence, the only alternative open to those who desire to preserve the full values of both is to consent to a provisional dualism.' Moreover, either position by itself was inadequate, according to Roberts. Transcendence alone led to a much too distant God; and immanence alone led to a tyranny of contemporary concerns. This was the position Roberts was reluctantly forced to accept until a new synthesis emerged. Roberts, therefore, was not much further ahead than his colleagues in the United church in dealing with the crippling theological problems of the postwar era. His final position was no different than that of ministers who confronted the dilemma with the approach that the church had to be both fundamental and modern. Nevertheless, his analysis dissected the theological vacuum, sense of spiritual drift, and religious decline that Protestant clergymen were struggling with during the 1920s. To an extent, Roberts considered the modernist-fundamentalist controversy to be irrelevant. 'It is immaterial,' he wrote, 'whether the story of the Crucifixion is even a correct record.' What was important was that people found the story of the crucifixion to be 'self-authenticating and ultimate.' The event at issue, he suggested, had 'become symbolic of a permanent crisis and conflict in human life.'[56]

What was clear in Roberts's 'The Scope of Theology' was his argument that the optimistic liberalism of the late nineteenth century no longer suited the more sceptical and realistic mood of the postwar era. Liberalism's 'superstitious surrender to the Spencerian Doctrine of fate's progress' meant that sin was viewed as being no more than an 'infantile disease' which would be outgrown in the course of continuous evolution. Sin had not been a fashionable topic, and even the pulpit had been 'shy of it.' Any theological breakthrough that had been made since the war had 'knocked the bottom out of the pleasant mood.' Indeed, the editor of the *New Outlook* was recommending that ministers should 'remind an age of soft sentimentalism that the universe is grim and has at its heart a God capable of grim devotion.'[57] Like others somehow touched by the war, Roberts charged that sin could not be neglected in the light of the 'persistent human sense of moral accountability with its sequels in such universal emotions as remorse, penitence, contrition, and self-loathing.' Any renewed understanding of God had to include a rediscovery of the 'basis of fact upon which the sense of sin rests.'[58] Roberts's commentary suggested that he was despairing about human nature. Anticipating the neo-orthodox critique of liberalism, he argued that the flaw with liberal theology rested in its overestimation of human nature.

Clearly the United church was in need of a theology to deal with the realities of the postwar period. The new insights of crisis theology that had been developed by European theologians over the decade had not been absorbed. It was not until the late 1920s that the work and thought of the leading proponents of crisis theology were noticed in the United church. In 1928 Barth's ground-breaking work *Der Wort Gottes und Die Theologie* was translated into English by the American theologian Walter Horton.

Within the United Church of Canada the leading forum for theological discussion was the *Canadian Journal of Religious Thought*. Though published in Toronto between 1924 and 1932 as an interdenominational enterprise, it was clearly dominated by United church ministers as they contributed the most articles and held the greatest number of positions on the editorial board. The opening editorial commented that as a result of the war there was greater 'endeavour to get a deeper understanding of the Christian faith ... The dominant interest in many religious quarters today is the search for reality, the conviction that life is not to be measured in terms of things done, but in terms of man's participation in the eternal life. Consequently men are seeking the content of their faith; and doctrine in no narrow sense of that term, is coming to its own again.'[59]

The initial response to Barth was cursory and cautious. In the March/April 1929 issue of the journal, John Line, an ordained minister and professor of philosophy at Victoria College, reviewed the translation of Barth. In a fashion that was typical of the uncertainty of Canadian clergy at this time there was neither advocacy of Barth's attack on theological liberalism nor commentary on his stark view of a transcendent God who 'stands toward our world in radical antimony and polarity, in perpetual tension with it.' For the most part, Line quoted passages of Barth in translation and simply noted, 'Barth is a fascinating and disturbing writer; his paradoxes fall like sledge hammers on our conventional and complacent habits of thought ... no one interested in the Church and its problems should be content to remain ignorant of it.'[60] An assessment of Barth's thought by D.L. Ritchie of United Theological College in Montreal, then studying in Europe, was instrumental in giving Canadian churchmen a better understanding of Barth's significance. Ritchie proclaimed that Barthianism was a revolt. It was a 'stand against all tendencies to lose the Christian religion in thin humanisms, to submerge theology in facile psychologisms, and to make God the product of this creation rather than the Author and Saviour of it.' Ritchie recognized that Barthianism challenged the liberalism so dominant in the United church.[61]

There was little further commentary on Barth in United church circles. For example, in the pages of the *Canadian Journal of Religious Thought* the liberal faith in the goodness and perfectability of humans remained strong; whereas the idea of human sinfulness and need for redemption, typical of the more conservative outlook of the neo-orthodox, was rarely expressed. The journal's considerable emphasis on biblical criticism and the social gospel reflected the liberal heritage of most United church ministers. There was scant evidence of the reorientation in theology that the *Canadian Journal of Religious Thought* heralded in its first editorial.

That the United church was avoiding the challenges posed by the more 'realistic' theology emerging in the 1920s was suggested by a leading critic of the church union movement and liberal theology in Canada, the Presbyterian Walter Bryden. He was born on a farm near Galt, Ontario. After matriculating from Galt Grammar School in 1901, he went to the University of Toronto, graduating in honours philosophy and psychology in 1906. Then he completed an MA in psychology in 1907. After that, he entered Knox College to prepare for the ministry and was ordained in 1909. Bryden did 'spade work' for the church in Lethbridge, Alberta, and Melford, Saskatchewan, but returned to Ontario when he received a call from Woodville in 1918. It was from here that he launched his criticisms on the Protestant mainstream in Canada.

His decision to remain in the Presbyterian church was an early indication of his disillusionment with the progressive orientation in liberal Protestantism. He was disturbed that during a time when Reformed churches in Europe were 'discovering their own foundation-springs' of sixteenth-century Reformation theology, church union leaders had 'ignored the necessity for a definite doctrinal understanding or attitude in regard to those vital interests which essentially concern a church.' Bryden thought that United church clergymen 'were too much under the dominance of the prevailing popular temper and outlook of the later nineteenth century and earlier twentieth century; a period in which indulgent human sensibilities were the governing factors in man's religious thought.'[62]

With church union there were many vacancies in the upper echelons of the seriously weakened Presbyterian church; and so Bryden was asked to lecture on church history at Knox College. In 1927 the General Assembly elected him to the chairs of church history and the philosophy of religion at Knox. It was in his lectures that Bryden advanced his challenge to the liberal establishment of Canadian Protestantism. In his exploration of the implications of Barthian thought Bryden made clear the vast difference between the current thinking in the United church and that of theologians touched by the realization of humanity's inadequacies and society's failures. Like his mentor, Bryden easily penetrated the weakness of modern liberal religious thought. In the hands of the liberal-modernists the contemporary challenge of the Word of God, he argued, rested in nothing more than in its ethical imperatives as they applied to individual lives and social conditions. 'We look in vain,' Bryden observed, 'for that strange awe before the miracle of the Incarnate Christ.' He sought a renewed appreciation of the supernatural in Christianity since, in his estimation, the concept of the Holy Ghost had been 'terribly impoverished.' God had come to be little more than an impersonal creative principle.[63] In their enthusiasm to demonstrate progression towards the Kingdom of God, United church leaders had abandoned what was fundamental to Protestantism, in Bryden's view. United church ministers who had noticed the inadequacy of liberal theology had done so largely because of their disillusionment with the absence of a much-needed spiritual revival in Canada, not because they had developed a sense of impending crisis when considering the prospects of modern society. They still believed that their society was continuing on the path of progress.

Church union had been regarded as a means to consolidate the resources and energy of Protestantism in Canada. But denominational competition had clearly not been the major cause of trouble for the Methodist and Presbyterian churches. Their difficulties could not be overcome by better organization and use of resources because they were not primarily the result of institutional factors which could easily be reformed. Decline in church attendance, continuing problems of the rural church, difficulty in attracting recruits for the ministry, falling support for missionary activity, the lack of vitality or clarity in the church's message and sense of its mission, and the disintegration of the dominant liberal theology of the church – all were signs of a broader religious depression. Indeed, clergymen were increasingly convinced that the problems they faced were spiritual ones. In 1928 Pidgeon wrote to Clarence Mackinnon of Pine Hill College, 'There seems to be a sense of spiritual need through the Church deeper than anything I have ever seen.'[64] By the late 1920s, a mood of discouragement and futility set in among clergymen. They felt they were no longer successful in drawing people to church or winning them to the spirit of Christianity.

8

'Why No Revival?'

The most troubling and persistent question that Protestant ministers confronted during the interwar years was Why no revival? It became the refrain of many churchmen by the late 1920s. Theological controversy, disillusionment with social service, and growing evidence that the churches were not holding their congregations led to a renewed emphasis by church leaders on evangelism. Calls for an evangelical revival became more urgent with the dawning of the Great Depression as the already depressed church was thrust into even more serious problems by the economic crisis. Furthermore, the social dislocation of the 'Dirty Thirties' seemed to many to be a symptom of the already marked religious decline and its attendant moral confusion. No matter what their denominational heritage, religious outlook, or theological background, clergymen agreed that a religious revival was necessary in Canada.

It was in this desperate atmosphere that a revival-like movement swept across Canada in late 1932 and most of 1933. During the bleakest period of the depression the Oxford Group movement inspired what appeared to be renewed commitment to religion throughout Canada. The movement was enthusiastically endorsed and joined by many clergymen who regarded it as the revival they had been waiting for. But rather than fulfilling hopes for significant religious revival, the Oxford Group movement, in the final analysis, merely served as evidence that the evangelical tradition in Canada was in a state of decay and that the church's spiritual message and program was unable to meet the needs of its followers in a fresh, creative, or effective way. The 'religious revival' of the 1930s confirmed the depressed state of the United church; there was little spiritual recovery. Indeed, the success of the Oxford Group movement demonstrated the extent to which the consumer ethos of self-fulfilment in this world had penetrated religious values and institutions in Protestant Canada.

Those clergymen assessing the religious situation in Protestant Canada during the late 1920s and early 1930s attributed the weakness of the Christian church and religious faith to the decline of evangelism and religious revivalism. G.C. Pidgeon became increasingly alarmed by the tenuous hold Christianity had upon the Canadian people. The pulpit, he thought, had given up passionate pleading for souls and had weakened itself.[1] S.D. Chown echoed this sentiment in one of his last pieces of writing. He lamented that it was unusual to hear preachers proclaiming the gospel of salvation and calling for complete dedication of one's life to God. No longer was there an emphasis upon the experience of an immediate and vividly conscious personal conversion. To its great detriment the church's attention had been diverted away from evangelism.[2] Recalling things as they were during the Welsh revival of the early 1900s, Roberts wrote, 'What stands out most conspicuously in my mind is that not a single Sunday evening passed that men and women were not converted to God. They were authentic conversions, provoked by no sensationalism, a worked-up emotionalism, but by straight competent preaching ... with converting power.'[3]

Along with Pidgeon and Chown, Roberts argued that the decline of evangelical preaching was responsible for the church's present weakness. 'The most characteristic symptom of religious decadence,' Roberts wrote, 'is that the preaching of the Word of God recedes from its vital centre into a wilderness of miscellaneous and tepid pulpiteering.' For preaching to be effective and meaningful it had to be 'evangelistic.' People had to be constantly moved to a new direction and a new beginning in Christian life.[4] By 1930 the existence of religious depression in Canada was clearly recognized, and there was consensus among clergymen that the church had to return to its evangelical roots for the Protestant religion to become vital once again. To Pidgeon this task was very urgent for he thought that Canadian society was in serious danger of becoming completely removed from its religious heritage. In outlining the necessity of a religious revival, Pidgeon drew upon his own religious experiences while growing up in the lumber community of New Richmond, New Brunswick, and the powerful influence of Principal MacVicar of Presbyterian College in Montreal, who was uncompromising in stressing evangelicalism as the cornerstone of the church. He referred to the formative period of Canadian religious history, when, as he noted, the spirit of revivalism dominated and there were spontaneous outbreaks of spiritual energy which led thousands into vital union with Christ. Religious faith in Canada, according to Pidgeon, had been planted in revivalism and evangelical doctrine. This was what churches had to recapture and foster if they were to remain an integral part of the Canadian social fabric.[5]

During the late 1920s there was renewed interest in evangelism on the part of the church bureaucracy. Even the traditionally socially conscious Board of Evangelism and Social Service of the United church was concentrating more of its efforts on programs of evangelization.[6] The secretary of the board, the Rev. D.N. McLachlan, a pastor since 1904 and a social activist in the Presbyterian church, wrote that evangelism now had to be regarded as the centre of church life, not as something 'special' or 'sporadic.'[7] The Board of Evangelism and Social Service developed a program, largely organizational in nature, to promote evangelism. It recommended that the United church appoint specially trained evangelical workers and outstanding preachers. As well, it encouraged the organization of conferences, so that new methods to bring about the evangelization of church members could be explained to ministers and lay workers. The board also suggested that the church organize prayer groups and Bible studies with an evangelical orientation and start visitation programs by the trained evangelists to every congregation.[8]

United church clergymen thought it was time to create a revival. The fact that an increasing proportion of the church's effort was concentrated on trying to create or organize a revival of evangelical religion was testimony to how desperate things were becoming. There were, however, fundamental obstacles in the way of a successful revival. Chown, in particular, was keenly aware of the forces working against a religious revival in Canada. The reasons evangelism had little appeal in modern society were outlined by Chown in *Some Causes of the Decline of the Earlier Typical Evangelism*. This 1930 pamphlet completed Chown's reassessment of the church's emphasis on the social gospel, which he had begun before the Great War. He recalled that in the late nineteenth century people still strongly believed in the immediate presence of God and in life after death. The minister, therefore, had a relatively easy task in making the character of sin, the atoning sacrifice of Christ, the redeeming power of God, and the guidance of the Holy Spirit alive. He was assisted in this by the fact that many believed in the efficacy of prayer and conceived the results of sinfulness in a 'tragic and vividly terrible form.' As well, the Bible was considered to be the Word of God. Its doctrines and command-ments were accompanied with the force of 'Thus saith the Lord.'

Such beliefs had faded, according to Chown. Religious beliefs and practices had been radically altered by the rise of science and modern social and psychological thinking. Faith in the fact of Christ's death as the means to redress human guilt and individual sinfulness had been replaced by an emphasis on Christ's moral teaching. The urgency of repentance and conversion disappeared as a result. The supreme and final authority of biblical revelation had been seriously questioned. Even those who remained faithful were painfully aware, in Chown's view, that portions of Scripture, which in a former day were considered the Living Word, were now dull, suspect, and ineffective. Also van-ishing was belief in prayer as a means of communicating with God. Instead, Chown pointed out, an unsatisfying conception of prayer's psychological utility was taking over. This denial of the efficacy of prayer left the evangelical effort shorn of its 'greatest incentive to action and its essential means of success.'

From the perspective of the troubled church life and the declining religious faith of 1930 it seemed to Chown that accommodation with modernism had seriously undermined the appeal of the biblical Word and the strength of the bond between the individual and God. 'It must be conceded,' Chown wrote in a dejected tone, 'that the last twenty-five years have witnessed a remarkable commingling of agencies which have diluted the strength of the earlier evangelical message.' The result, Chown wrote, was that people no longer vener-ated the divine. 'A veil' had been 'drawn over the face of God' as the 'human ethos' took precedence. In a sense Chown was rejecting his own personal religious odyssey from the late 1890s to the Great War – the liberal age in Canadian religious history – and was looking back to the certainty of the earlier days of his ministry when he stressed personal evangelism and reliance on Scripture. His critique reflected the conservative mood in religious thinking which had been growing since the war but did not become current until around 1930 in United church circles.[9] This analysis made it clear that the prospect for the revival that church leaders in Canada were calling for was a remote one.

Richard Roberts forwarded other reasons to explain why the possibility of a religious revival was unlikely in postwar Canada. He contrasted the experience of his generation, those who had matured prior to the outbreak of the Great War, with that of those who matured during the war and the postwar period. The inheritance of the prewar generation, according to Roberts, was a 'serene faith' in the ultimate goodness of things, the meaningfulness of life, and in the 'unshadowed love' of God. Before the war, Roberts claimed, unpleasant things in the world did not blot out faith in God. As a result the horror of war, the disastrous inequity of the peace, and the anxiety of the depression could be faced by the pre-war generation 'without forfeiting the belief that beyond this evil there is an unchangeable good.' Such abiding faith, Roberts thought, was difficult for the war and postwar generations, 'who have seen nothing but the cruel, dreadful, inhuman muddle of these years.' This disillusioned and pessimistic youth, Roberts warned, would resist any evangelical effort.[10]

In a way, Canadian clergymen's insistence that a revival was essential was somewhat surprising, for revivalism had fallen into serious disrepute during the twentieth century. Indeed, revivalism had failed as a method to reach the new and ever-expanding urban population and to halt secularization. Revivals had become increasingly emotional in their appeal and sensationalist in their methods as the quest for an outbreak of religious enthusiasm became more difficult. To get results at any cost, high-pressure tactics were employed. Clergymen had become outrightly harsh in their assessment of contemporary revivalism. For example, in a series of lectures to the students at Emmanuel College Roberts denounced the methods of current mass evangelism. In particular, he expressed contempt for the hectic publicity that preceded the 'revival show' and for the working up of mob excitement through tactics such as the singing of hymns in a style little removed from jazz. 'The last thing Jesus Christ desired,' Roberts declared, 'was that men should be stampeded into the Kingdom of God.'[11] Much of what had been entailed in revivals was now the subject of disdain and outright opposition. Many believed that the high-pressure, flamboyant tactics used by professional revivalists to 'get results' had undermined the reputation of evangelical revivalism in North American society.[12]

The call for an evangelical revival was not just a nostalgic yearning for a return to a past golden age of religious enthusiasm. It was the promise of a religious movement that made 'each individual's spiritual condition before God' its chief concern that struck clergymen as the required solution for the religious indifference and theological confusion of the postwar years.[13] What was sought was a new understanding of what evangelism meant. Roberts tried to provide this in his paper entitled 'Normal Evangelism,' in which he placed evangelical doctrine in the context of the current struggle to come to grips with the war and the failed peace. Echoing the view of other ministers and theologians who had pondered the meaning of the Great War, Roberts defined evangelical doctrine in realistic and stark terms. 'War is the bitter fruit, the nemesis of public sin: and public sin is the grim addition sum of personal sin. We are all under judgement in these times, and there is none guiltless, no, not one.' Human redemption came about in a 'crisis of personal experience' which accompanied a realization of one's sinful spiritual condition, and only God could provide the assurance of forgiveness and salvation.[14] The legacy of the war had profoundly influenced Roberts's understanding of what evangelism involved. The strong emphasis upon human sinfulness and how it was manifest in society was an interpretation of the gospel that was suitable for the troubled postwar world. Such reiteration of the evangelical message, Roberts hoped, might lead the pessimistic, the aimless, and the spiritually troubled back to Christianity. The First World War and its aftermath were clearly of central importance in the transition to a more conservative outlook that was taking hold in Canadian Protestantism during the late 1920s.

The Great Depression only intensified the call for a religious revival. One woman, a devoted follower of Pidgeon's radio ministry, wrote in 1933, 'Most of us are suffering very bad times, as the people elsewhere and we feel the need of a deeply sincere religious revival ... So please help us – We are praying for guidance and long for knowledge of how to find it.'[15] The quest to bring about an evangelical revival became more pronounced, and the wave of conservative religious thinking became more definite and prominent in the 1930s.

It was not uncommon for Canadian clergymen to suggest that the hardships of the 1930s were the result of the wrath of God. From his pulpit at Bloor Street United Church, Pidgeon asked his congregation, 'Do you think it is pure coincidence that drought destroyed the productiveness of our richest lands at the same time that depression struck the human world? Was not the hand of God in it ...?' During the 1920s many did not believe that their prosperity was God's gift; they had 'shut God out.' The result, Pidgeon contended, was social dislocation and economic hardship. Human sinfulness had brought on the depression. It was just punishment for the secularized ethics of the age.[16] This view was not put forth solely by conservatives with a strong sense of sin. Roberts was also convinced that 'events are exact overtures from God.' He suggested to his congregation that if God 'was to come among us today, he would have no other word than this: Return ye children of mine, for he would see our loot of swift gold, our frenzied pleasure seeking ... our contempt of public worship, and the sheer materialism of our hopes and desires, and beneath it all our indifference to the values of the spirit.'[17] Rampant consumerism, which indicated a clear revolt against religious values to most clergymen, was thought to be responsible for the economic and social disaster of the 1930s. Canadian society was exposed as being spiritually hollow.

The Great Depression was conceived of as a fundamentally moral and religious problem instead of an economic one by these clergymen. The solution, therefore, had to be a religious one – a revival. Roberts concluded that God was calling on humanity to 'come back to the old forgotten ways, to old forgotten altars, to old rejected sanctities, to ways of simplicity and purity and piety.' Pidgeon went even further, insisting that accompanying every social or economic reform, there 'must be the humbling of the individual before God, prayer for his forgiveness, and the acceptance of the authority.' In essence, Pidgeon was arguing that there could not be a recovery without repentance and a deepened conviction of Christian faith on the part of individuals. External or structural change was not sufficient; there had to be a spiritual revival.

This Providential view of the cause and remedy of the depression was not confined to religious leaders or to those who were unaware of the intricacies of economics and untrained in the social sciences. Speaking at the Empire Club of Canada in Toronto during the winter of 1933, Professor Gilbert E. Jackson of the Department of Political Economy at the University of Toronto stated, 'The root causes of the depression lie in no fault of the economic mechanism by which we live, but in ourselves. The mechanism is not a bad mechanism but we have shown ourselves not good enough to work it ... Not till we recognize this shall we succeed in making this mechanism function properly. Perhaps – and here I tread upon the threshold of theology – perhaps the depression ought to last, until we recognize that it is due to the faults in ourselves.' Furthermore, at a conference of the Social Service Council of Canada Jackson likened contemporary society to the 'prodigal son.' Resources, he charged, had been squandered by a 'get-rich-quick attitude.' He concluded that religious and moral factors as well as economic ones were responsible for the depression. Consequently, he claimed that the church had a crucial role to play in leading Canada out of the depression. And this from an economist who had been actively engaged in statistical studies of the business cycle and unemployment in Canada.[18]

It seemed clear that the prospect for a great spiritual revival had never been more promising. To this end, a Joint Committee for the Evangelization of Canadian Life, consisting of clergymen from the United church, along with some from the Presbyterian, Anglican, and Baptist churches, was formed in the fall of 1932. Indeed, the Baptist church had enjoyed a season of revivalistic activity in the early months of 1932. In helping to organize evangelistic activity for the Baptist Convention of Ontario and Quebec, A.L. McCrimmon, the ex-chancellor of McMaster University who was nearing the end of his career, emphasized that the time was ripe for evangelism. 'The world is a very sick world,' he wrote in the *Canadian Baptist*; 'the religious world is confused by the babel of cult tongues; the church is not characterized by evangelistic fervour as it should be.' He stressed that the economic impasse had demonstrated that there must be things beyond the material for people to have faith in. 'There is a growing recognition that the supreme need in this time of testing is a return to God.' In response to the widespread contemporary criticism of evangelism McCrimmon argued that 'sane evangelism guards against spasmodic emotionalism, pseudo-conversion, extravagant sensationalism, and questionable psychological methods.'[19] Evangelism, understood to be the 'art and science of soul-winning,' was considered to be essential for renewed understanding of the gospel and the continuation of church life. To bring about a revival the Baptist church appointed special evangelists to lead the soul-winning campaigns in various centres. Throughout the months of February and March successful evangelistic activity was reported in Montreal, Ottawa, and throughout southwestern Ontario, in particular.[20] The Baptist hierarchy hoped to continue this religious enthusiasm through the program being arranged by the Joint Committee on the Evangelization of Canadian Life.

All members of the organizing committee agreed that 'when men consciously or unconsciously in the darkness are groping for a way out, is a time when, recognizing their own impotence, our people are ready to turn to a Greater than themselves for leadership and salvation.'[21] This admission revealed the extent to which the tenets of liberal Christianity had been undermined. The Great War and the Great Depression were perplexing and confusing, and they made it extremely difficult to believe in the human potential to bring about either social or personal regeneration. Faith in God or complete despair about the human condition seemed to be the only alternatives for many struggling to make sense out of their destiny.

The committee started to organize an interdenominational campaign of repentance and prayer. Plans were made for a special call to prayer to take place during the Lenten period of 1933 and for a simultaneous effort on the part of all Protestant churches for the evangelization of Canadian life during the following autumn. To meet the 'spiritual thirst' of the times it was suggested that the doctrines of traditional evangelism be stressed. Literature discussing the sovereignty of God and the meaning of Christ's atonement and resurrection was recommended by the committee to serve as a basis for the proposed campaign's message and for the Bible study groups which would prepare the way for the planned revival.

These plans for engineering a renewed commitment to evangelism were interrupted by an enthusiastic reception given to the Oxford Group movement's first Canadian crusade, which opened in Montreal in October 1932. This evangelical movement concentrated on changing lives and was led by the charismatic Frank Buchman, who billed himself as a 'lecturer in personal evangelism.'

Buchman, born in Pennsburg, Pennsylvania, in 1878, had been influenced by the pietistic Keswick Convention movement which combined personal evangelism with a deep concern for holiness and missions. Social issues were eschewed, and if any social concern was demonstrated by this pietistic movement it was in the form of a moral purity crusade. In the United States, while employed by the YMCA, he became a leading figure in the Student Volunteer Movement, a conservative-minded missionary organization dedicated to the 'evangelization of the world in this generation.' Buchman travelled extensively

with John R. Mott, the influential spokesman of this crusade to convert the world. From Mott, Buchman learned a great deal about the
techniques of evangelization, and in 1922 he launched his own evangelical program. Buchman's stated purpose was to create 'a movement
within the Church for the awakening of personal religion.' His crusade
began as a student movement with the first study group being held in
Christ College at Oxford University. By the late 1920s the Oxford
Group movement was reaching the broader public, especially in urban
and suburban communities in the United States, England, Holland,
and parts of Germany.

News of the 'stir' which the Oxford Group movement was making
in Montreal quickly spread. One Montreal minister wrote to Pidgeon
that he was impressed by the spiritual nature of the Oxford Group's
work. 'The basis of the movement,' he observed, 'is religion as a
personal experience, with the idea of sharing and witnessing. That is
New Testament doctrine and thoroughly sound. You need have no
misgiving about the movement, it is certainly of God.' Assured by
this account that this was a religious movement, Pidgeon dropped
his organizational tasks with the Joint Committee on the Evangelization of Canadian Life and hurried to Montreal. There he discovered
congregations that were 'stirred deeply.'[22]

From Montreal Pidgeon followed the movement to Ottawa, so that
he could observe it firsthand. The Oxford Group's draw in Ottawa
was impressive. At the opening general meeting approximately nineteen hundred people showed up in the elegant ballroom of the Chateau
Laurier Hotel. The next day, Sunday, members of the Oxford Group
team spoke in churches throughout Ottawa outlining the movement's
message of 'Life Changing.' On Monday, 7 November, Buchman and
his team met with Prime Minister R.B. Bennett and the federal cabinet
and with prominent Ottawa businessmen. Throughout that week the
Oxford Group held evening testimonials, where members of the team
and local Ottawa people told how their lives had been changed by
their commitment to the four Oxford Group principles of 'Absolute
Honesty, Absolute Purity, Absolute Love, and Unselfishness.' Attendance at the meetings remained high during the course of the week.
The *Ottawa Citizen* reported around two thousand people at each
gathering and, furthermore, claimed that on each occasion there were
'first time hearers.'[23] While in Ottawa, Buchman also trained local
converts in the ways of the Oxford Group, so that the 'life changing'
could be continued after the team moved on.

Pidgeon was excited. To a colleague he wrote that the movement's 'appeal is for personal relations with God and it has had excellent results ... Many lives have been completely changed ... I am hoping that it will solve many of the problems which are distressing us.'[24] In his view the Oxford Group movement was managing to achieve what those who had been advocating an evangelical revival since the late 1920s had sought. It seemed to be the religious revival that Canadian clergymen had been desperately calling for. Since the Oxford Group revival was having successful results and Buchman had announced his plans to visit Canada's major cities, the Joint Committee on the Evangelization of Canadian Life postponed its revival program.

The Oxford Group movement initially attracted much favourable comment. Ministers and newspapers alike agreed that the movement was meeting the needs of the times. To the Rev. D. MacLennan of Emmanuel United Church in Montreal the movement was infusing the moribund church with much needed spirituality.[25] The *Ottawa Citizen* proclaimed that the movement's emphasis on personal religion was the key to the way out of the depression. 'Reliance on material methods has apparently failed,' the *Citizen* editorialized; 'people are awakening as never before to the need of putting first thing first. It is being made clear that the way out begins at home, with the individual – Many of us are learning the way by the testimony of the Oxford Group.'[26] The Oxford Group's reliance upon individual 'life changing' under the guidance of the golden rule was the last resort for those who had abandoned faith in the economy, business, and politics.

Analysis of the religious characteristics of the crusade was initiated by the *Montreal Witness*, the evangelical Protestant newspaper. The *Witness* likened the Oxford Group movement to traditional Methodism. It was most impressed by the fact that Oxford Group meetings resembled Methodist class meetings. Also similar to Methodism, according to the paper, was the movement's growth by 'contagion' and its lay theology. 'It has no officers, no finances, no roll of membership, no order of service, no preaching. The great truths of Evangelical Christianity are taken for granted, there is no written creed or separate professional ministry.' Despite the modern methods and surroundings, one Presbyterian contributor to the *Witness*, the Rev. G.H. Donald of the Church of St Andrew and St Paul in Montreal, was struck by the Oxford Group's tradition-bound emphasis on personal evangelism. 'Their phraseology is different,' he commented.

'We speak of conversion, consecration, communion, they of change, surrender, sharing. The words are different, the meanings the same. Not so dignified as the old way, perhaps, but more suited to the age.' Such use of the vernacular was not regarded by this commentator as an indication that the Oxford Group movement was offering a diluted Christian message or a bland form of piety; but rather it was defining the gospel in a vibrant and readily understandable manner. The *Montreal Witness* became a convert to the Oxford Group, and under the stewardship of F.E. Dougall it became the official organ of the movement.[27] Such an unquestioning reception of the Buchman movement reflected the conservative mood in some Canadian religious circles.

After the campaign in Ottawa the Oxford Group moved on to Toronto, where it was greeted by thousands at the King Edward Hotel. The pattern of Oxford Group activity was similar in each city it visited. The initial meeting took place in a large ballroom or conference room of a hotel. These public gatherings tended to attract members of wealthier churches, businessmen, professionals, and community leaders. Oxford Group team members were formally dressed. They were 'dinner-jacket evangelists.' The meetings were showy but to the point. Testimonies of personal conversion were the highlight. There were no traditional religious preliminaries, such as prayers, hymn singing, or Scripture reading. Team members of the Oxford Group gave accounts of their spiritual change. They told of their former aimlessness and selfishness, their defeats in life's endeavours, and their dissatisfaction with things before coming into contact with the Oxford Group. Each person testifying elaborated on how he or she was led to a 'life change.' Mention was made of one's decision to confess past sins and to surrender to the fellowship of the movement. Then the testimony was concluded by an account of that changed life which was being guided by the principles of honesty, purity, unselfishness, and love. The accounts glowed with a sense of fulfilment and righteousness.[28] These testimonies were repeated for a number of nights in order to gain a following. They were only the preliminary stage, however.

The crucial phase of the movement's program took place in smaller, more intimate surroundings. Once contact was made at the large gatherings with people who desired a 'life change,' house-parties were organized. Attendance was by invitation only, and wherever possible the parties were held in a country hotel or inn. In essence, the 'house-party' was a retreat. The purpose was to guide potential new converts into fellowship with the movement. There was a set daily routine at the house-parties. The day began with a 'quiet time' for penitent contemplation and 'listening' for God's guidance. Between 9:30 A.M. and 10:30 A.M. group instruction in the Oxford Group's central ideas and methods was given. The central part of the program occurred throughout the afternoon. Activity focused on 'sharing.' The house-party, which usually consisted of about two hundred people, was divided into smaller groups. In this setting the usual procedure was for an experienced member to reiterate, in franker terms than at the public meetings, the story of his or her conversion. Then attention was turned towards the guests. They were invited to recount the story of their lives. In order to encourage acknowledgment of sinfulness the life changers exhorted the prospective converts to speak of their feelings of unhappiness and frustration. The life changer would then suggest that such feelings were the result of personal sinfulness and that escape from this condition rested in dedication of one's life to absolute honesty, purity, love, and unselfishness. Usually, confessions followed. According to one observer, this was the critical moment. Once candidates made a confession and expressed repentance, they were then led forward to a decision to make an absolute surrender to the movement's four absolutes.[29] After this life-changing experience close contact between each new convert and a life changer was continued. During this stage the conversion experience was discussed with the new members so that they could formulate their own testimony and then continue on by guiding others to a life change.

The Oxford Group movement's program seemed evangelistic and was clearly reminiscent of the campaigns of Crossley and Hunter and other late-Victorian evangelists. It sought to arouse in each individual a conviction of sinfulness, recognition of one's reliance upon God's grace, an obligation to change oneself, the assurance that a changed life could be maintained by following God's guidance, and the promise to share one's 'life change' experience with others. The central premise of the movement was that the world was replete with sinners and therefore in need of spiritual regeneration. Buchman and followers of the movement insisted that only a religious revival could save society from collapse, and such a revival could only be accomplished through the changed lives of individuals.

This formula proved successful across Canada. After the first gathering in Toronto the Star's headline read, 'Thousands Surge Hotel to

Meeting for Sinners.' Many clergymen invited members of the Oxford Group to speak at their churches. That Sunday the movement's
message of 'life changing' and 'sharing' was heard from forty-seven
pulpits. The *Globe's* reporter observed, 'I have never seen such
churchgoing in Toronto.'[30] Interest remained high throughout the
Oxford Group's ten-day stay in Toronto, according to the newspapers. At the final meeting Buchman encouraged the Toronto converts
to carry on the movement after the team had departed. While Buchman
moved on to Hamilton for a three-day campaign, a Toronto-based
team immediately began to organize groups throughout Toronto and
to spread the movement's message to other Ontario communities. At
the movement's height of activity there were more than thirty Oxford
groups in Toronto, and many of these had organized similar groups
throughout Ontario in Oshawa, London, St Catharines, Woodstock,
Brantford, Kitchener, Galt, St Thomas, Orillia, Port Hope, and
Kingston.[31] Much of the movement's growth and vigour, therefore,
was the result of local initiative and commitment. The dimensions of
the movement went beyond the appeal of colourful oratory and charismatic leadership.

The Oxford Group movement's emphasis on 'life changing' provided an answer to the desperate search for renewed direction in the
dismal and chaotic life of the 1930s. For those with a strong sense of
personal responsibility, commitment to the movement's straightforward moral principles was one way to end the sense of drift and
despair that seemed to be taking over. Some suggested that it was the
Oxford Group movement that had pulled them out of the depression.
Indeed, one woman wrote to Pidgeon telling him of her experience
after having been dismissed from her job at the Children's Aid Society.
'It was just then that I got hold of the Oxford Group.' She confessed
that 'I realized that I had brought so much pride and superiority to
my work here and been so critical that I had ruined my own good
work by my personal attitudes.' This woman attributed her loss of
work to her own personal shortcomings or sinfulness, not to poor
economic conditions or a lack of funds in the Children's Aid Society.
After she was changed by her commitment to the movement's principles of love, purity, honesty, and unselfishness, she got her job
back.[32] In this case betterment in one's lot was attributed to improvement in religious conviction and especially moral attitudes, not to a
change in economic or social factors. The movement's popularity
during the depression is good evidence that 'the Canadian people ...

had too much discipline, too much individualism, too much nine-teenth-century grit, or too little political sophistication to fight back in protest against a whole economic and social system.'[33] Its insistence on 'life changing' as the means to eradicate larger social problems allowed people the luxury to think that they were aiding in the renewal of society without having to support or even contemplate more substantial reform which would alter the social structure.

In Toronto the Oxford Group movement encountered its first serious criticism. An editorial in the *New Outlook* fuelled the controversy. W.B. Creighton exclaimed that Oxford Group meetings were 'the most unblushing piece of exhibitionism we had ever seen.' To support this view Creighton published articles by 'informed people' who had observed the movement firsthand. The most damning assessment of the movement was put forward by a psychiatrist, who wrote: 'Extremes are nearly always dangerous, and when the Oxford Group spend so much of their time reviewing every trivial divergence from one's best endeavour and regarding such divergences as "sin," and insist on "sharing it" with other members, a psychiatrist would feel that a pathological degree of introspection had been reached which might have harmful effects on the personality.'[34]

Response to this assault was fast and furious. 'A Protest' was submitted to the *New Outlook* by Pidgeon and six other clergymen. They cautioned that the movement did not attempt to be inclusive of all elements of Christianity, but rather gave a special message for a particular need. What enraged the protesters was that the *New Outlook* was blinded by its opposition to 'methods and forms of presentation' to the most important fact of the movement's results. 'Lives in great numbers are being "changed," often with dramatic suddenness; in other cases fears and doubt and anxiety are being replaced by peace and rejoicing confidence; and many defeated and discouraged workers, including ministers, have become "life changers," in whose hands the Gospel is once more "the power of God unto salvation."'[35]

The Oxford Group movement was becoming an extremely divisive force within the United church. The *New Outlook*'s criticism of the movement led to severe criticism of the church's leadership. One sympathizer of the movement informed Pidgeon that editorials such as the one on the Oxford Group had 'killed the *New Outlook* in our town.' He went on to suggest that Pidgeon should investigate the number of subscribers to the *New Outlook*, speculating that there would be a big falling off due to its controversial content.[36] And indeed this was the case. In 1931 subscriptions fell by 1,615 to 28,306. This decline levelled off in 1932: there were only 739 fewer subscribers. But in 1933 and 1934 the drop in subscriptions was dramatic: in 1933 the number fell 3,567 to 24,000, or by about 13 per cent, and in 1934 the decline was even greater – another 5,600. The total number of subscribers at the end of 1934 was merely 18,400, a drop of 35 per cent since the beginning of 1931. No doubt some of this decline can be attributed to reduction in personal income, but the dramatic rise in cancellations in 1933 and 1934, during the aftermath of the Oxford Group controversy, suggests considerable dissatisfaction with the paper's opposition to the movement. Some attributed the paper's opposition to the movement to the 'extreme modernism, disbelief in the Bible, doubts concerning the deity of Christ, and rejection of the necessity of conversion which they detected in its pages.'[37] The Oxford Group's presence in Canada served as a catalyst for the expression of more basic and enduring tensions within Canadian Protestantism.

In the pages of the *Canadian Baptist* the analysis of the spiritual qualities of the movement was largely positive. On the one hand, commentators acknowledged that the movement only stressed certain aspects of the Christian gospel; but, on the other hand, they agreed that the movement had identified certain fundamental truths of Christianity that had been ignored. The Rev. E.E. Bingham wrote two articles arguing that the Oxford Group principles of 'guidance' and 'sharing' were central to a Christian life and entirely consistent with the Gospels.[38] In the end, Baptist ministers insisted that the only criterion by which the movement should be judged was its fruits. One minister, the Rev. F.H. Wentworth of Simcoe, Ontario, submitted a moving testimony of the movement's impact on his spiritual life. 'Prayer was becoming a very hurried and disconnected experience in my life. The Bible was fast becoming a text book for sermons and a study book for Sunday School lessons. I was fast losing the personal messages it had for my own soul.' After attending the Oxford Group crusade in the King Edward Hotel in Toronto, Wentworth confessed that he made 'a new and complete surrender to Christ.' As a result, Wentworth admitted that he 'had no heart to criticize the Oxford group. It would be too much like dissecting lovely flowers, as a botanist; then asking the sick patient to accept the analysis instead of the bouquet fresh from the hands of God.'[39] Whatever misgivings that arose were buried as the spiritual results of the movement were realized.

Despite persistent controversy the Oxford Group movement was enthusiastically welcomed in every city it visited. After the Hamilton campaign Buchman and the International Team toured the United States. Then, at the end of March, they returned to Canada. In Vancouver eight thousand people attended the first meeting. On the second day Oxford Group members spoke at over sixty Vancouver-area churches during the Sunday services. Supportive ministers argued that the movement was turning around the declining vitality of worship in Vancouver churches. A minister who was not initially supportive of the movement was forced to conclude, 'There has been a noticeable raising of the spiritual temperature of this community. I notice it in my own congregation ... in pastoral visitation doors are readily opened into the spiritual heart of things that were previously very hard to unlock.' The movement's emphasis on the 'quiet hour' and the notion of 'guidance' seemed to have inspired a renewed commitment to prayer, and the intimacy of the house-party was restoring fellowship.[40]

From the 'triumphant' Vancouver campaign the Oxford Group moved on to Edmonton and Calgary. According to the *Edmonton Journal*, citizens turned out *en masse* to hear the revivalists. The meeting place was overflowing. At each meeting the Oxford Group was met by Alberta Premier Brownlee. He informed the crowds that he had been profoundly impressed by the 'extraordinary spirit of happiness and inspiration radiating' from the movement. In suggesting why the movement was so popular in depression-riddled Alberta, Brownlee announced that the 'Group had fully demonstrated the superior joy of true Christian living and indicated the possibility of solving the world's ills by a crusade of life changing.' On the Sunday of the movement's crusade in Edmonton ten thousand people crowded into twenty churches to hear testimonies emphasizing the necessity of 'getting rid of sin.'[41] From Edmonton Buchman sent a delegation to Lethbridge, while he travelled to Calgary, where the movement was also greeted enthusiastically.

In Saskatchewan there was a strong tradition of socially conscious Protestantism, and the Oxford Group movement was not met in an unquestioning manner. The reporter for the *Regina Leader-Post* wondered whether the movement was a 'fad' or of 'deep religious influence' and whether it marked a rebirth of Christianity or the seeds of its death. As well, he asked if the leaders of the movement were Christian geniuses or victims of a pathological sense of sin.[42] But even in Regina, where the reception was relatively cool, the Oxford Group made a significant impact. Its 'whirlwind quick-fire campaign to change lives and quell sin' was launched from an overcrowded hotel ballroom and three churches to an audience of over three thousand. The fruits of the three-day campaign were clear throughout. Dozens of Regina citizens made public testimonials. Answering Pidgeon's inquiry concerning the impact of the movement in various communities, the Rev. W.E. McNiven of Regina expressed his amazement at how people 'love to discuss religious experience, and to study portions of Scripture for hours on end when not long ago an address on a spiritual theme would have bored them to death. But they have changed.'[43]

In Winnipeg the movement met with the greatest amount of initial resistance. At Knox United Church eighteen hundred people attended the service to hear an Oxford Group member talk about the movement. But they went away 'distinctly disappointed.' Throughout the three-day campaign attendance at Oxford Group meetings continually declined.[44] After Winnipeg Buchman concluded the Canadian tour. The climax was another grand house-party, this time held in the Chateau Frontenac in Quebec City, where six hundred prominent Canadians who had been changed were present.

The movement did not falter immediately after the Oxford Group left Canada. The *Montreal Witness* reported that there were frequent open meetings for public witness along the lines of the Oxford Group on Vancouver Island. In typical 'house-party' fashion they were held in recreational surroundings. As late as October Edmontonians were still gathering in large hotels to hear each other give witness to the change in their lives. In November a prominent Edmonton minister, the Rev. A.C. Farrell, wired the *Montreal Witness* that interest was constantly growing, providing evidence that the Oxford Group movement had enduring qualities. Ministers from other centres were also impressed by what appeared to be the movement's ability to sustain itself. The Rev. J.W. Milne of Ottawa reported that people were 'standing firm with no sign of backsliding' in their commitment to the movement. Throughout 1933 a growing number of Oxford groups were organized in the Ottawa area, and lives were being 'constantly changed' at the numerous meetings. As late as the fall of 1933 the Toronto-based team was organizing groups throughout Ontario, and a Calgary group was leading 'a great spiritual revival' in Medicine Hat and Redcliff.[45]

The debate over the spiritual qualities of the movement followed it to every Canadian community. The movement's success caused serious discussion within the United Church of Canada. C.E. Silcox, who had been working on a study of church union in Canada, worried that the controversy surrounding the Oxford Group would wreck union.[46] Much of the division surrounding the movement was manifest in terms of social class, for Buchman openly sought the support of the wealthy and influential. The Oxford Group's methods and message were directed to the 'up and ins.' A profile of one of the Toronto-based Oxford Groups shows that the movement attracted the middle and upper classes or professionals and white-collar workers. The team that went to Oshawa was composed of thirty-one teachers, a psychiatrist, four corporation presidents, three general managers of companies, seven salesmen, six stenographers, one engineer, an auditor, two doctors, an architect, a lawyer, and a retired army major.[47] The ostentatious and partylike nature of the meetings caused feelings of bitterness and disdain. One outraged but concerned citizen wrote to the *Toronto Globe*: 'Religion in a ballroom, clothed in tuxedo coats and evening gowns, accompanied by bursts of laughter it is startling ... it is a mockery. It may be religion, but it certainly is not Christianity; one is glad to read that there was no reading of the Scriptures or prayer as no doubt it would have been entirely out of place in such a group.'[48] Critics suggested that the movement appealed to the comfortable classes since the social implications of Christianity were not stressed. Buchman's attitude towards the plight of the unemployed was callous and simple-minded in the extreme. He informed a reporter for the *Regina Leader-Post* that the solution for Canada's unemployment crisis was to 'put the unemployed to work for Christ. Teach them that when their lives are adjusted god will provide.'[49] The ethics of capital-labour relations and the existence of poverty were neither pursued nor questioned.

The parlour confessions seemed to be used by certain people to deal with their guilt feelings as they observed the terrible impact of the depression. The overwhelming concentration on public confession made the movement dangerously close to a psychological cult, in the opinion of D.L. Ritchie, the dean of United Church College in Montreal.[50] Indeed, the Oxford Group movement appeared to be one expression of a significant and worrying transformation in the nature and role of religion in Canada. Theology was becoming psychology; sin was being regarded as sickness or moral improbity; and religious gatherings were developing the function of 'therapeutic communities.'[51] The Christian faith, as it was being presented by the Oxford Group, was being reduced to a simple panacea for the ills or psychological needs of individuals. The transformation that was required did not involve a profound conversion. What was demanded by the movement was a mere tinkering with one's personality and lifestyle.

The movement had become so controversial that the United church commissioned an official evaluation. A Committee of Thirty was formed. Reflecting the divided and confused reaction of church members to the movement, the committee was unable to formulate a clear and definite position. On the positive side, the appraisal concluded that the movement 'seems to make God near at hand, demonstrably and actively interested in the security and happiness of individuals. It restores a vivid sense of direct contact with the supernatural power and reproduces some of the phenomena of our evangelical revival.'[52] The notions that humans were sinners, that they could be changed, and that confession was a prerequisite to change, all stressed by the Oxford Group movement, were approved by the committee. On the matter of the movement's social conscience the committee's judgment was harsh. It claimed that there was little evidence of appreciation of the 'interdependence of social and individual salvation.' Indeed, the committee charged the movement with 'a policy of neutrality toward the terrible social evils, which drag man down to war, to crime, to poverty, and to despair.' Fellowship in the movement was thought to be a means of escape from the full liability of Christian discipleship.

The most troubling aspect of the Oxford Group movement, according to the appraisal, was that basic Christian doctrines in regard to God, Christ, and salvation were avoided. The committee attributed the 'silence' to the desire of the movement to 'escape from divisive and difficult features of Christianity.' This assessment suggested that even the basics of evangelical doctrine could no longer unite Canadian Protestants into solid fellowship. These basics had become too controversial for those subscribing to the tenets of social Christianity and too difficult to believe in for those who had a 'modern' outlook. A revival devoid of explicitly Christian doctrine seemed to have better prospects for success. Ernest Thomas assailed the movement because 'not one feature associated with mass evangelism is here. There is no sermon, no address, no exhortation, no gospel, hymns or singing of any kind except in rare occasions. There is not a word about the "plan of salvation" or the need of forgiveness, no reference to sin as bringing penalty or to escape from it through the Atoning death of Christ.'[53]

Richard Roberts denied that the Oxford Group movement was an evangelical revival at all. He did not think it met society's call for a realistic appraisal of humanity's sinful nature. Not only did the movement lack a sense of social sin, but more seriously, it had a very weak grasp of individual sin. The idea of personal sin was constantly in the air at the meetings, Roberts observed; 'but,' he argued, 'their understanding of the nature of sin was singularly naïve and un-analyzed. It seemed no more than the sum of peccadilloes. I failed to see real evidence of the formidable character which the New Testament gives to sin.' Accounts of Oxford Group house-parties suggest that the confession of sinfulness was usually trivial. Most of the testimonials did not include any more heinous sin than overindulgence in cigarettes and alcohol, riding in fast cars, insincerity in conversation, self-consciousness, minor examples of selfish behaviour, or, at worst, entertaining sexual fantasies. The difficult attempt to deal with human sinfulness in Christian terms was not made. Furthermore, commitment to absolute honesty, purity, love, and unselfishness did not necessarily involve deeper commitment to Christ or a turning to God. Instead, it indicated a surrender to better moral standards. The process of conversion or 'life changing' was neither profound nor demanding. Roberts noted that a reference to God or Jesus at Oxford Group meetings was just that – a reference – without any commentary on the atoning sacrifice of Christ or the redeeming power of God. Whether the movement had anything to do with the traditions of evangelism or even the basic notions of Christianity became the central issue for Roberts. In the end, he concluded that the Oxford Group movement was not a religious revival. Notoriously few permanent spiritual results remained, he claimed.[54]

On balance, appraisal of the movement was negative. The Committee of Thirty concluded that there was little of enduring value to the church or religion in the methods or ideas of the movement. 'No Evangelistic programme can permanently be sustaining unless it rests on a sound basis of thought about God – shallow theologies do not produce spiritual change.' Clergymen who supported the movement seemed to have overlooked their statements regarding what was essential for Christianity and what kind of revival and theology were necessary for the postwar age. Consideration for the Christian faith had been swept aside by uncritical enthusiasm for what was thought to be the long-awaited revival. The appeal of the Oxford Group movement indicated that Canadian Protestants were capable of responding to renewal in moral and psychological terms. A religious awakening seemed to be much more difficult. The veneer of piety that surrounded the movement only masked or obscured its obsession with individual well-being. This form of 'therapeutic mind cure' was central to the emergence of a consumer consciousness and at the heart of the shift in Protestant values from a spiritual emphasis on salvation to a secular emphasis on self-fulfilment.[55]

Despite the evidence of ongoing activity, interest surrounding the Oxford Group movement was beginning to wane by the summer of 1933. Although new Oxford groups were still being formed, other groups created out of the enthusiasm of the life changing experience were quietly disbanding. Circulation of the movement's official Canadian organ, the *Montreal Witness*, was dropping drastically from 32,000 at the end of 1932 to 17,000 by the end of 1934. Supporters of the movement were convinced that its decline was the result of a lack of good organization, well-trained leaders, and adequate theological background. Pidgeon thought this was the United church's fault since it had refused to recognize or cooperate with the movement. The revival, he claimed, would not be able to sustain itself without the resources of the church. The reasons for the movement's faltering, however, went beyond these factors. The Oxford Group's limited purpose in large part accounted for the demise of enthusiasm. After one's life had been changed, apart from spreading the life-changing experience to others, there was little to do or look forward to.

Nevertheless, clergymen recommended that the churches try 'to harness' the Oxford Group movement's 'energy, to show that we are not dependent on strangers and pilgrims for the further carrying on of the work of evangelism.' The most ambitious attempt to capture the spiritual quickening engendered by the Oxford Group was undertaken by the Joint Committee on the Evangelization of Canadian Life. Plans for a Lenten-period revival program for the following spring were revived during the fall of 1933.[56] In the committee's program the scriptural basis of the assurance of God's forgiveness and redeeming power, Christ's suffering for humanity, and the more general notion of human redemption were emphasized. Also contrary to the Buchman movement were the discouragement of public confession and the highlighting of devotional prayer. This church-inspired evangelical program sought to overcome 'the blind obedience to social pressure and wayward individualism' and the inadequate thinking about God which had troubled church leaders about the Oxford Group movement.[57] This church-led attempt to discipline and sustain the spiritual quickening touched off by the Oxford Group movement failed. Ministers reported little enthusiasm. There was not a significant outpouring of renewed commitment to Christianity and there was no noticeable improvement in church attendance. To an extent, the United church was too late, for many had already received what they considered to be the evangelical message and had experienced a personal conversion.

The failure of the theologically enriched evangelical program of the joint committee, however, was further evidence of the depth of the Canadian religious depression. The most effective spiritual revival of the 1930s embraced no more than what was involved in 'Moral Rearmament,' the name by which Buchman's movement came to be known in the latter 1930s. When churchgoers were presented with a call for repentance which was delivered in the context of Scripture and more sophisticated evangelical theology, they did not respond with the enthusiasm they did for the more sensational and secular-oriented Oxford Group movement. In the summer of 1934 the Board of Evangelism and Social Service concluded that any church-sponsored program of evangelization had to 'conquer the intellectual habit that excludes the knowledge of God.'[58] The soil for Christian evangelism was drying up in Canadian society. This was what church leaders had argued prior to the outbreak of enthusiasm surrounding the Oxford Group movement. In the end, the experience of 1932-3 did not change this assessment.

There remained an urgent cry for a new interpretation of spiritual life and Christian obligation. Clergymen were left with the question Why no revival? The Oxford Group movement's success was superficial because, like many other twentieth-century revivals in North America, it 'had no fresh insights to offer to meet the deeper currents and problems' of the age.[59] Indeed, the success of the Oxford Group movement and the fact that it was uncritically endorsed by many prominent clergymen indicated the degree to which religion had been transformed into a secular value system largely concerned with material comfort and psychological contentment.

9

Stumbling towards a Theological Reformulation

The disruption that the Great Depression brought to church life and religious thinking in Canada was as troubling as the damage it brought to the economy and social order and the change it forced upon the political agenda. Declining revenues had a devastating effect. Many home mission fields were abandoned, and the extent of unemployment and poverty in the cities made church-sponsored urban mission work inadequate. The United church was particularly hard hit because of its considerable stake in the drought-devastated and destitute Prairies. J.W. Grant has pointed out that there was just enough funds to keep the United church's 'existing machinery from breaking down.'[1] Doing any kind of church work had become disheartening, for the church and its ministry had the difficult task of meeting the spiritual, and in many cases the material, needs of those who were suffering. This was not a time for innovations in pastoral, missionary, or educational work. Church life was bleak. United church ministers desperately tried to hold on to what their Methodist and Presbyterian predecessors had achieved.

Despite the dreary atmosphere of Canadian society and church life during the 1930s, religious thinking was not stagnant. The optimistic assumption that Canada was a progressive society on the path to realizing the Kingdom of God was confronted by a gloomier reality. During the depression religious thought itself was caught up in the prevailing mood of disillusion and despair. The persistence of economic depression and social unrest as well as the threatening international situation forced Canadian theologians to reassess their notions of Christianity, humanity, and society. This forced the church to reconsider its task and message. Some of the bolder theologians in the church attempted to steer the church in a new direction, away from the perfectionism of the old social gospel and traditional personal evangelism and towards a starker, more realistic theology of crisis. They thought that the optimism with respect to religion and the church in Canadian society was inappropriate and that the secular nature of Canadian society must be recognized. They wanted the church to confront society with radical Christian teachings, instead of seeking to make accommodation with secular society in the hope of somehow conquering and remaking it. Although these theologians were clear about the realities that confronted the churches and realized that a theology of crisis was more suitable for the postwar industrial age, the United Church of Canada remained hesitant about grasping any new insight or understanding. In the end, a defeated church, uncertain about its message, mission, and future, floundered. It held tenaciously to the perfectionist liberal notions that were rooted in the optimism of the late-Victorian period.

Like most institutions during the 1930s the United Church of Canada was forced to retrench. The total of contributions for all purposes declined by 33 per cent, from the 1929 high of $16.8 million to a 1935 low of $11.2 million. The decrease in money received for missionary and maintenance purposes was even more pronounced, reflecting the declining interest in missionary activity which was already apparent in the 1920s. Questioning about the value of foreign missionary activity was increasingly common in the postwar years. Financial support was becoming more difficult to raise. The Inter-Church Forward Movement of the 1920s – essentially an interdenominational, lay-sponsored fund-raising campaign for missions – was the last of the great campaigns. Enthusiasm on the college campuses was also waning and this was most evident from the declining support for the Student Volunteer Movement for Foreign Missions. There was also questioning from the mission fields and churches about the nature of foreign missionary activity. The intense nationalism of the postwar years led to sharper criticism of the cultural imperialism that accompanied much of the missionary effort. As Alvyn Austin has concluded in his study of Canadian missionaries in the China inland mission, 'by the end of the decade with the coming of the Depression foreign missions were in disarray, beleaguered from within and without, understaffed and underpaid, their buildings overseas falling into disrepair or irretrievably secularized.'[2] From a 1928 high of $2.89 million, contributions had fallen by 45 per cent to $1.57 million in 1935.[3]

Overall, the United church was operating on a much smaller budget, and it incurred a heavy debt of $1.7 million. This slump in financial support seriously affected the church's work. The drastic decline in revenues forced the United church to consider closing many of its operations and significantly reducing staff. The economy measures most assiduously followed were those reducing the number and salaries of church officials. The departments of Home Missions, Christian Education, Evangelism and Social Service, and Literature and Education were especially affected. But such measures saved only a modest sum of money and had only a marginal impact on church finances.[4]

Much of the burden of financial hardship was carried by the clergymen as they were forced to accept cuts in their salaries. Congregations in destitute areas could not support their ministers, and as church revenues decreased, the denominational maintenance fund could no longer provide adequate support when a congregation was unable to do so. Salaries became one of the most problematic issues within the United church during the 1930s. The lot of the ministry had become unrewarding for many pastors. Ministers from rural districts, but especially from drought-stricken areas of the Prairies and communities of acute unemployment, suffered the greatest deterioration in salary and living standards. The most discouraged in these areas left their field and frequently quit the ministry. A shortage of ministers existed in the three Prairie conferences, the Bay of Quinte Conference, and the Northern Ontario area. Many of the surplus ministers from the Toronto, British Columbia, and Maritime conferences were unwilling to serve in the hard-hit areas.[5] After his 1931 tour of Canada as moderator of the United church, E.H. Oliver concluded that many of the best people would abandon the ministry. He encouraged the clergy to 'stay on the job. The United Church of Canada will stand behind you. We don't give you luxuries. We won't even give you the minimum. We will see you don't starve. We will see you are here to break the bread of life to all the people on the prairies.'[6]

As a result, the United church was forced to close some of its pastoral charges and home mission fields in the 1930s. In 1928 there were 3,117 pastoral charges and home mission fields organized by the United church. By 1935 there were 2,884, a drop of 233. Nearly three-quarters of the closings occurred in the Prairie conferences. In Manitoba there were 43 fewer charges and fields, in Saskatchewan 58, and in Alberta 63. The decline in home mission fields was most dramatic. Between 1925 and 1928 424 new home mission fields were opened. In 1933, there were only 4 new fields created.[7] This indicated a serious lowering of the church's vigour along the whole frontier. It was the most visible sign of the church's retrenchment.

The United church's problems in the 1930s could not be solely attributed to the economic depression. To confirm that the church was suffering something more serious than the effects of economic depression, the Committee on Finances developed a comparative study of 'religious and economic trends' based on United Church of Canada and Dominion Bureau of Statistics data. In comparing church income with national income during the 1930s, the committee discovered that the former had declined much further and for a longer period of time than the latter. After 1933, while national income was recovering, church income continued to fall until 1935 and then only recovered marginally. More alarming was the discovery that givings for missionary and maintenance purposes continually declined throughout the period 1931–6. (See table 2.) To explain why church contributions continued to decline, while national income was recovering and the cost of living index remained relatively stable, non-economic factors had to be considered, according to the Committee on Finance.[8]

The Committee on Finance recognized that higher taxation, personal indebtedness, the necessity of assisting others, and a general feeling of insecurity made people less willing to pay tithes; but it concluded that other factors also contributed. It was suggested that the extension of social services by the state had the effect of decreasing people's sense of personal responsibility for charitable and philanthropic enterprises. This, the committee argued, directly affected contributions to the church's missionary work and maintenance program. On a more theoretical level the committee wondered if the notion that science and the state should do all that was required for effective social services, adequate medical service, and education was raising in people's minds the question whether the church should have any active role in such sectors of society.[9] The result, church leaders feared, was that members were less willing to support church enterprises. There were also, the committee reasoned, religious reasons for the church's present difficulties. Understanding of the requirements of 'Christian discipleship' and loyalty to the church and its undertak-

TABLE 2

Decline in National and Church Income

	National income est. by DBS	Cost of living	Total receipts from pastoral charges (all purposes)	Receipts (missionary and maintenance)
1931	100	100	100	100
1932	85.98	96.7	86.82	77.88
1933	79.05	86.5	81.11	71.25
1934	90.87	87.7	78.96	66.44
1935	97.91	88.3	78.72	65.19
1936	102	90.2	80.25	64.85
1937	108		80.18	62.73

Source: *Reports of Proceedings, Eighth General Council* (1938)

ings were in decline. 'The feeling of obligation to Christ has grown dim.' The theological foundation for the Christian missionary adventure had been shaken. Canadian society had a 'lowered spiritual tone.'[10]

For relief of the church's financial situation the committee advocated a deepening of spiritual life and the development of a convincing missionary apologetic. Recommendations to reform church organizations, develop better methods of missionary enterprise, and improve the ways to raise and spend money were considered secondary. The Committee on Finance's data and conclusions suggested that in the 1930s the United church was experiencing the continuation of the religious depression which emerged in the 1920s.

For many pastors, much more troubling than falling salaries and the church's declining fortunes was the privation and suffering that so many individuals, families, and communities endured. Clergymen took a personal interest in members of their congregations. For example, George Pidgeon arranged to have money and provisions sent to families in desperate need, and he wrote letters to prominent Toronto employers seeking jobs.[11] Manses were turned into 'clearing houses' or 'stores' for the distribution of clothing and other essential supplies. Some pastors made significant personal sacrifices in their 'relief ministry.' If no alternative source of relief was available, ministers bought food for starving families out of their own pockets and advanced money to farmers in order to forestall foreclosures. Many did this when their own savings were seriously depleted. The Rev. W.H. Colter of Mortlach, Saskatchewan, revealed the desperate situation he faced in his parish. 'I've had to feed 4 families myself, and I am receiving $50 a month towards my salary from Islington, Ontario. Up to the 1st of July I have received from the pastoral charge, $325. My south point used to pay $540. This year it has paid $7.50.'[12] Charitable activity occupied much of the church's efforts during the 1930s. A National Emergency Relief Committee was organized. Through this central committee carloads of food and clothing were sent from relatively unscathed congregations to those in desolate areas.[13]

All United church clergymen had to confront the reality of suffering in this time of crisis. What kind of theological understanding or religious message they could offer to sustain Christian faith in such circumstances was for them a new and difficult problem. Only a gospel of hope could overcome the barren sense of discouragement and abandonment that was being experienced by many. During a tour of Assiniboia and Weyburn presbyteries in Saskatchewan, one clergyman noticed that at well-attended church meetings 'the people seemed hungry for some word that would bring light and comfort'; and so he attempted 'to bring people a message that would revive or confirm their faith in the providence of God and strengthen their courage.'[14] E.H. Oliver concluded that the church's religious services were especially needed for 'only the things that the Church stands for can enable men to carry on ... The usual methods will not suffice and ordinary sacrifice is not enough.'[15] The depression was an unprecedented 'crisis,' and the solution in the view of these and many other commentators had to be spiritual. In stark contrast to Europe, where theologians such as Karl Barth and Paul Tillich had been advancing a theology of crisis based on the idea that society was in decay and liberalism in theology was inadequate, a theology which had unquestioning faith in progress and confidence in the coming of the earthly Kingdom still dominated Canadian Protestantism. This left Canadian churchmen intellectually and spiritually unprepared for the destitution and social unrest of the 1930s.

What encouraged reorientation in Canadian Protestant thinking towards a more conservative outlook which took into account the reality of sinfulness and human tragedy was not the reading of theology but the observation of deterioration in Canadian society. Events of the 1930s made many of the tenets of liberal Protestantism difficult to believe. Faith in human ability to bring about the Kingdom of God and the belief in progress were especially vulnerable. The terrible social dislocation and suffering of the depression, the growing awareness of the weakness of the church, and the recent inability to foster a religious revival promoted reassessment.

Nowhere was this sense of crisis more acutely felt than in the Prairie West. For E.H. Oliver, who had been engaged in numerous progressive reforms and the writing of Prairie history throughout the 1920s, the unthinkable had occurred. Oliver's enthusiasm for Prairie society was shattered by what he saw during his tour of the drought-stricken area of Saskatchewan in 1931. After the Great War, when Oliver had tried to convey what it had been like at the front to the people on the Prairies, he had suggested that they picture, 'if it was possible, the choicest wheat fields of our modern plains churned into yawning gravel pits, streaked with long rows of zigzag, gleaming, chalk trenches with an occasional tree trunk standing, twisted and bent and smashed.'[16] Such a wasteland, however, was what Oliver encountered in Saskatchewan during the summer of 1931. Images of the First World War were recalled by Oliver, for the ruination of that war was the only thing within his experience that he could refer to which was similar to the wind-whipped, sun-scorched, desert-like 'Garden of Saskatchewan':

> It left me weak and sore afraid, as though I had turned the corner of our street, eager and expectant to catch a glimpse of home and found it wrecked by a bomb or burned to the ground. 'An enemy hath done this,' was the thought that leaped into my mind, as though the devastating hand of a malignant spirit had waved a wand over the great Prairie to spread desolation and drought and death. If there were added to the scene a battered house here and there and an occasional trench it would be like the desolation of the western front.[17]

What disturbed him was that, like war, the drought and economic depression were destroying the human spirit. The landscape of abandoned towns, ruined farms, and unused grain elevators reminded people of failure, things gone wrong, and destroyed dreams. In Oliver's view the Prairie West had become a 'desperate Western Front.'

This disintegration of Prairie society profoundly upset Oliver's thinking. In a 1932 rewriting of *The Winning of the Frontier* into a missionary tract for the Board of Home Missions and Women's Missionary Society, a note of pessimism entered into the historical perspective. Oliver's faith in the progress of religion and the church, and in the West as an inspiration for this, was undermined. Oliver's thinking was developing in a radical new direction. His interest had been largely concentrated on improving church mission work and education as a means of extending the Protestant faith throughout Canada. Indeed, his historical writing was designed, in part, for evangelization. He had sought to strengthen the church in Canada by reaching a fuller understanding of the surrounding society. For instance, his sense of the emergence of a new historical frontier, the urban and immigrant West, led him to encourage the United church to set up missions to Europeans in crowded downtown areas.[18] Oliver had utilized his vast historical knowledge to help extend 'His Dominion to every community of Canadian people.' Now, strongly influenced by what he saw of the depression, Oliver turned his attention to establishing a proper appreciation of the relationship between people and God. He had come to the disturbing realization that God had become misunderstood, and worse, shut out by many; and so, instead of analysing historical trends to help the church face the depression, he looked to the Bible. The solution to the depression, for Oliver, was a 'return to God.'[19]

Oliver revealed his new biblical interpretation in lectures entitled 'Sharing in the Bible,' which he gave in 1933 to the students at St Andrew's College. By turning his historical skills to the content of the synoptic Gospels, the Pauline writings, the Acts of the Apostles, and the Gospel of John, Oliver developed what he thought was a new gospel for society in depression. The prevailing notions of God were wanting, in his estimation. Liberalism's 'God of Humanism' was an 'extremely subjective philosophy ... implanting in men the thought that they could manage by themselves.' In this view God had become 'a myth begotten by human fancy,' and as a result impotent and certainly unable to 'meet the needs of people in dire suffering.' The more recent 'God of Pessimism,' that of Barth, was equally inadequate. An image of an omnipotent, but distant and stern, God, Oliver asserted, could not meet people's need for a caring and accessible God.

He put forth a different emphasis. 'The whole New Testament,' he wrote, 'is suffused with the thought of a God not of transcendence only, not wholly removed or alien to the world, not immanent only, but though transcendent also sharing, and though sharing also over-ruling to bless and redeem.' Through the life of Jesus Christ and his disciples as revealed in the New Testament, God showed himself to be an 'objective reality,' but 'intimately personal and constantly active in the redemptive purpose to win his children by sharing.' To Oliver, God was a being of 'utter benevolence' and 'watchful providence,' and he thought that only this understanding could be a basis for continued faith in Christianity.[20] Instead of stressing what humanity could accomplish, Oliver was focusing on what God would provide in the creation of 'His Dominion.' The liberal position was being abandoned for a more conservative, God-oriented one. In another work written during the depression, *Tracts for Difficult Times*, Oliver questioned the efficacy of the social gospel. 'Has Rauschenbusch,' he wondered, 'given us a complete and final answer to his question, What to do? Is his Christian socialism adequate for the political, economic, social, ecclesiastical and religious spheres of modern life?'[21]

The commentary in 'Sharing in the Bible,' especially the critique of liberal theology, lacked originality. But implicit in this later work of Oliver's were some of the central concepts of neo-orthodoxy.[22] Most striking in Oliver's lectures was the emphasis on Scripture. The Bible, although now understood to be mediated by human language and the circumstances of biblical times, was the source of revelation and the highest authority, not contemporary social ethics that had been recently venerated in United church circles. Oliver also realized that the key to a strong church and a vibrant Christian faith was not in understanding and controlling social surroundings, but in knowing God. Furthermore, in *The Winning of the Frontier* Oliver presented the contemporary church as being a product of the environment and its social surroundings, but throughout 'Sharing in the Bible' he showed that there should be a fellowship between the modern church and the primitive one and between the present ministry and that of Jesus. The standards of Christ's teachings and of Paul's messages to the first Christian churches, not the ones of contemporary society, had to be followed. God had a purpose in the depression, Oliver thought, and that was to make better men and women, a better order of society and primarily 'a more Christ-like Church.' Oliver realized that the world was a secularized place where God's will was not necessarily at work. The contemporary church had to stand against the world. The reorientation in religious thought was not well advanced by Oliver in his biblical study, but nevertheless the depression had launched him, as well as other clergymen, onto a quest for a renewed understanding of Christianity and a more realistic picture of Canadian society and the church's role within it.

Members of the United church were seriously divided over the church's social responsibility and Christianity's social message. Questions of social and economic reform disrupted the United church in the highly charged political atmosphere of the depression. The conflict between exponents of personal and social Christianity erupted again in a dramatic fashion. Some of the controversy was touched off by the Oxford Group movement's escapist position on social problems. Bitterness, however, emerged as some of the United Church of Canada's prominent ministers became involved in the development of a radical critique of Canadian society and the formation of a democratic socialist political party.[23]

The debate about the proper role of the church in improving Canadian society reached a climax in the summer of 1933. John Line of the Board on Evangelism and Social Service presented a report to the Toronto Conference on the church's responsibility in the economic field. The report proclaimed: 'it is our belief that the application of the principles of Jesus to economic conditions would mean the end of the capitalist system.' Echoing the Methodist church's 1918 radical pronouncement, the report called for the 'socialization' of banks, natural resources, and transportation as well as other services and industries. This advocacy of the use of the state and structural change for Canadian society was accompanied by a call for more moderate reforms, such as old age pensions, unemployment insurance, and other forms of social welfare.[24] At the Montreal-Ottawa Conference a similar report was being tabled by layman Eugene Forsey and a recently dismissed professor of Christian ethics at United Theological College in Montreal, King Gordon.[25] There was an air of urgency in the presentation of these proposals to United church conferences. Elsewhere Line had written that the challenge confronting the church was whether social and economic improvement would come by secular or spiritual means. If the church failed to be on the vanguard of reform, Line feared, it would become even less relevant in the eyes of Canadians.[26]

Reflecting a deeply split church, these socialist proposals were carried by only a narrow margin of 121 to 97 at the Toronto Conference. The opponents of the report refused to rest. Immediately after the vote was announced, George Pidgeon rose and submitted an official dissent to the adoption of the report signed by 55 clergymen. The dissenters charged that the report was replete with 'generalizations on debateable issues and with proposals the implications of which few of us understand are unworthy of a Church which accepts full responsibility for its utterances and their consequences.'[27] This dissent touched off a long and heated battle which sounded much like the charges and countercharges made by contending political parties disputing the shortcomings of capitalism and socialism. So acrimonious was this debate that it spilled over into a more public forum. Pidgeon and other clergymen placed a statement of protest against the action of the Toronto Conference in the *Toronto Globe* the morning following the debate.

Whereas exponents of the revived social gospel thought that their social advocacy was profoundly Christian, others considered it to be leading the church dangerously close to becoming a secular institution. C.E. Silcox became alarmed by the remedies for the depression being put forth by the United church's social gospel wing. The Toronto Conference resolutions 'postulated the further *idolatry* of the State,' he thought. The appeal was to coercive collective or state action instead of Christianity. There was a danger, according to Silcox, of 'supplanting true religion with mere patriotism.'[28]

Even Richard Roberts, considered a progressive, who was personally committed to working people and the cause of social democracy, decided to oppose this latest expression of the social gospel. He maintained that it was a 'monstrous illusion' to think that Christianity is concerned only with the individual soul and reminded the students at Emmanuel College 'the ideal of a Christian social order is as inherent in the Gospel as is the ideal of the Christlike man.' The problem with the social conscience in the United church, Roberts warned, was that often it could not be restrained from advocating a specific economic program or supporting a political party. In effect, Roberts charged, the Toronto Conference had sanctioned the complete program of the burgeoning League for Social Reconstruction. It was dangerous, he argued, to attribute panaceas for economic problems to Jesus Christ or to encourage the church to give a blessing to a particular scheme of social change or political reform. Doing so made the church too much of the world. 'As preachers,' Roberts lectured, 'we do not qualify for authoritative judgments on matters of economic or political science.' He thought that the church had been discredited by failure to recognize these limits. In the final analysis Roberts was severe in his appraisal of the social gospel movement. 'We waved the red flag in the pulpit. We proclaimed the conditions that should be created, we demanded them; and yet all the time we knew no sure sense of direction or the faintest notion where the big business should begin.'[29] Silcox concurred with this verdict when he wrote that the social gospel's idealism was 'untempered with sufficient knowledge of the rough human material which had to be built into the utopian edifice.'[30]

There was concern that this most recent expression of social activism might cause serious trouble for the United Church of Canada. The *Toronto Telegram* wondered whether the Toronto Conference's action would 'shake the allegiance of its members,'[31] and Silcox noted in his *New Outlook* article that resentment was building up in the church. Indeed, one correspondent wrote to Pidgeon commending the stand he took against 'the intrusion of economics and politics into church life.' Revealing his anger and bitter disillusionment, this Toronto businessman asserted, 'It is not the problem of economics but the problem of sin that is the concern of the church.' If ministers were making their pulpits a forum for discussing politics and economics, he concluded, then 'they have no gospel to preach.'[32] With this final point certain church leaders agreed. Deeply troubled, Roberts lectured that the social gospel had 'filled our horizon ... rather too completely because ... our faith in the validity of our Gospel for the individual has been shaken.'[33] Roberts was admitting that the social gospel had become an unfortunate but easy substitute for the more difficult aspects of Christianity.

Most frustrating to some United church leaders was that there was something hollow about the recent battle between the advocates of a social gospel and its opponents. In the renewed debate over the best means to realize the Kingdom of God neither the supporters of the social gospel nor of traditional evangelicalism were willing to compromise. Both desperately held on to their past positions; and yet according to one keen follower of religious thought, both of these points of view were impossibly perfectionist as they were rooted in the optimistic Victorian age. 'The church has been too much under the blight of superficial optimism and sentimentalism. It has been infected with that particularly vicious kind of sentimentalism which is content to proclaim ideals without provision for those ideals to be carried out in action.'[34]

Critics of the absolutism of the social gospel and personal evangelism were still unable to put forth an alternative theology. Roberts still could not define the new theology he sensed was necessary, except to suggest that it would somehow synthesize personal evangelicalism with 'an equally strong stress on social action.' In his 1933 lectures at Emmanuel College he could give little theological direction to what he regarded as the 'spiritually confused' and 'drifting' church. Roberts seemed to be waiting for a new theological movement to coalesce.[35] The failure to forge a new consensus to meet the crisis of the depression underlined the persistence of a theological depression within the United Church of Canada.

As long as the United church was under the spell of these two perfectionist views, its prospects were not good. Silcox pointed out in his article on the future of the church that 'when half the church is shouting "Forward to Utopia" (which probably never will exist) and the rest are shouting "Back to the good old times" (which never did exist) the Church suffers.' He insisted that this 'period of disintegration of doctrine cannot go on forever.' No church, he argued, 'can make any great impact on the social life of our day until it knows exactly where it stands and why.' The search for a preachable gospel to meet the suffering and sense of crisis experienced by Canadians was becoming a desperate one. Silcox was telling United church leaders that determination of the underlying problems of faith and a realistic but Christian view of society could not be postponed much longer.

Exactly this, however, was being undertaken by a commission that had been appointed by the United church. At the 1932 General Council meeting the Board of Evangelism and Social Service was instructed to set up a commission to ascertain what the Christian standards were which should govern the social order, to discover how far current practice was consistent with these Christian principles, and to inquire into the ways by which these principles might be applied to existing conditions. Recognizing clergymen's limitations in social and economic matters, the board was instructed to appoint lay people expert in the fields of industry, finance, and statecraft as well as United church ministers. Sir Robert Falconer was named chairman of the Commission on Christianizing the Social Order. Others on the commission included prominent Toronto businessman and investment broker A.E. Ames and W.E. Rundle, the president of National Trust. Reform-minded politicians Newton Rowell and E.C. Drury, local Toronto politician and socialist Jimmy Simpson, and cooperative movement activist W.C. Good were also appointed. From the University of Toronto's Department of Political Economy the economists E.J. Urwick and Irene Biss along with Harry Cassidy, a leading expert in the field of social welfare, agreed to sit on the commission. The clergymen on the commission included Richard Roberts, church treasurer Robert Laird, D.M. Solandt from the staff of the *New Outlook*, J.J. Coulter and Ernest Thomas of the Board of Evangelism and Social Services, and the pastors H.W. Avison and William Ames. From Victoria College the principal, Walter T. Brown, the Rev. John Line, professor of philosophy, and New Testament theologian John Dow were also on the commission. The Commission on the Christian Social Order was directed to present a statement to the General Council at its meeting in September 1934.

The commission's starting point was to establish the Christian principles that should govern the social order. To do this, a group of biblical scholars was asked to explore Christian social teaching within the Scriptures. Sir Robert Falconer reported on the Catholic Epistles and Hebrews. John Dow, who represented the Presbyterian tradition in Emmanuel College's New Testament department, wrote on the Gospels. J. Hugh Michael, the professor of the New Testament at Emmanuel who had a Methodist background, studied the teaching of Saint Paul. The Old Testament was surveyed by W.R. Taylor of United College in Montreal. The foundation upon which the commission based its recommendations for the church's role in Christianizing modern Canadian society, therefore, was biblical.

The paramount theme in these studies was that there was no scriptural basis for the church's involvement in the political and economic areas and only a limited one for the social area. In his analysis of Jesus' life as it was presented in the Gospels, Dow noted that Christ's ministry flourished during a time of social unrest, poverty, and political turmoil. But in a fashion that directly contradicted what the social gospelers had concluded about Jesus' ministry, Dow argued that although it was difficult to avoid entanglement, 'Jesus kept himself completely outside.' Jesus' compassion for the multitude arose from the fact that 'they were as sheep without a shepherd, souls derelict for lack of religious leadership.' To explain how Christ resisted becoming a political and material Messiah in these conditions Dow suggested that it was his 'terrific conviction' that 'Man's first need is God.' Christ addressed his ministry to the religious order, not the social order. 'Repentance' and 'the right relationship with God' were Christ's primary concerns, Dow concluded.[36] Professor J. Hugh Michael's reading of the social teachings of Saint Paul corroborated Dow's view. Michael noted that in his letters to the Corinthians, Paul feared that 'the Christian movement might run off into a movement of social emancipation.' If this occurred, it would mean the end of Christianity as it was preached by Jesus.[37] Both these commentators, along with Sir Robert Falconer in his paper, suggested that the church's role in creating a Christian social order had to be largely a spiritual one, instead of one of social advocacy.

Their commentary, however, did not imply that there was no social message or objective in Christianity. These biblical scholars suggested that any assessment of government, business, and industry had to be based on human welfare, but according to their understanding this meant spiritual well-being, not material interest. On these grounds Dow thought that 'the law of supply and demand, the symptom of pitiless competition, the load of grinding interest, the tyranny of the employer who is law unto himself and of the trade union that challenges the authority of the state' were unchristian and should be condemned. But a Christian social order, Dow warned, could not be attained 'mechanically.' Neither the mathematic division of wealth and opportunity nor the adjustment of the laws of society could ultimately secure human welfare. Moreover, Jesus Christ offered the standard of 'love' and 'service' for creating the Christian social order. Beyond preaching these 'wide principles,' Dow concluded, the church and its ministry should not venture.[38] By insisting that the United church be guided by Christ's example as it appeared in Scripture, these scholars were prodding the church to be more radical, but radical in a strictly Christian way. They were suggesting that the church pull back from its involvement in politics and economic reform. It was this understanding of the early Christian church's historic role that guided the commission. There was widespread consensus that in approaching the secular world and its problems, the church had to put forth 'the fundamental teaching of Christianity, going back to the Old Testament prophets, Jesus, and his disciples.'[39]

By the fall of 1933 the Board of Evangelism and Social Service decided that the undertaking of the Commission on Christianizing the Social Order was of such magnitude and importance that the judgment and participation of the church as a whole were required. Auxiliary groups from across Canada were organized to study 'from their own angle' the issues being examined by the commission. The board directed these groups to forward their considerations to the executive of the commission, so that all opinions within the church could be examined and a consensus could be obtained.

The question which produced a significant amount of study and consultation was the one which dealt with the nature of the existing economic order. Discussions were based on the report on the industrial system, 'Modern Industry,' submitted by the economists E.J. Urwick and Irene Biss. Their report concluded that profit-making permeated economic activity in Canada. 'Rival combines' increasingly controlled the economic order, and competition was becoming 'fiercer and more deadly.' In this economy and social order of 'huge impersonal corporations' human values were neglected. Greater disparity of opportunity, income and welfare was the outcome.[40] This analysis of the Canadian situation was in line with others advanced during the depression, especially in the pages of the *Canadian Forum* and discussions of the League for Social Reconstruction.

Of particular concern to the United church was the view that the monopoly of power which accompanied combination of industry robbed individuals and institutions of the means to alleviate social injustices. Attempts to stabilize competition or control industry were futile, Urwick and Biss suggested, since concentration of industrial enterprise was not solely 'a result of purposed combination of capital' but also 'a natural result of the machine processes themselves.' Little could be done, therefore, to combat the worst abuses of the industrial system. For the church to say, 'Let us change profit-seeking into service, competition into cooperation, free enterprise into well-directed effort' was meaningless, in Urwick and Biss's view.[41] The Christian ethic seemed powerless in modern society. In this analysis of the church's task in building a Christian social order, utopian platitudes about creating industrial cooperation and goodwill, typical of a bygone, optimistic era, had been replaced by a more realistic evaluation of the causes of economic distress and the actuality of the church's power. At the beginning of 'Modern Industry,' a quotation from Reinhold Niebuhr's *Moral Man and Immoral Society* appeared. Urwick and Biss's outlook was similar to his, as they thought essentially Christian people and institutions were being overwhelmed by an unchristian industrial order.

The commission was led by this bleak estimation of existing conditions in Canada. In the final report, *Christianizing the Social Order*, Canadian society was portrayed as being marked by recurrent and widespread depression, replete with insecurity and dependency, flawed by inequitable distribution of income, and endangered by social unrest.[42] The commission, however, was less concerned with the economic order than with the ethical character of that order, and it judged the present arrangement to be 'materialistic' in values and aims. In the opinion of the commission it was the unchristian attitudes towards wealth and property and the complacent acceptance of them that were the major factors behind the intolerable social conditions in Canada. 'Against a civilization thus debased,' the commission proclaimed, 'the Church must set herself in uncompromising opposition.'[43] Ministers and church members were urged by the commission to study the existing order in the light of Christian standards, and to arouse Christian conscience when injustice and intolerable conditions were discovered. But, the commission cautioned, this had to be done in a manner that kept the church 'independent of any political organization.' Indeed, the commission did not respond to the General Council's directive that it 'define the particular measures which must form the first steps toward a social order in keeping with the mind of Christ,' for it argued that the 'specific task of the Church in the process of reform is to be the light rather than the engineer of the City of God, to point directions and reveal goals rather than elaborate programmes of successive changes.'[44] There was no declaration of specific social or economic policies that the United church should adopt and champion in *Christianizing the Social Order*. How Canadian society could be moved closer to the Kingdom of God on earth was considered too difficult a question by most members of the commission for any confident advocacy of a particular reform or political position. The problem with specific political and economic platforms for the church was that they were not essentially Christian in their inspiration, frame of reference, or objectives.[45]

Although some of the commission's hesitation to be more explicit on political and economic issues might be attributed to the divisions within the United church, it also signified an important transformation in understanding of the church's social teachings. *Christianizing the*

Social Order was one indication of liberal Protestantism's decline. The argument from human progress, a hallmark of liberalism, did not appear in the commission's assessment. Confidence in the advance of the earthly Kingdom was gone. It was banished from the consideration of the commission by the troubling events of the depression. There was a new mood in theological circles that attempted to confront all the facts of life candidly, no matter how troubling. In the case of the commission this meant a more 'realistic' awareness of the serious and difficult problems in the economic and social order and, more importantly, of the church's limited power and ability to effect change along Christian lines in Canadian society. The commission contended that the church's message should be less utopian. The identification of the coming of the Kingdom of God with improvement in civilization, a cornerstone of liberal faith and the social gospel, was not possible. The members of the commission had faced the most disheartening of facts: a realization that Canadian society was an unchristian one.

This awareness of how starkly different existing society and Christian values were made liberal theology's advocacy of accommodation with society by the church a position that was no longer tenable. Now the church had to stand against the social milieu, so that it could remain distinctively Christian. It was recognized that in its advocacy of specific economic programs or political platforms, the United church was becoming too adjusted to the world. It gave it the appearance of being a secular institution, for such a stance was not radically Christian enough. Only if the church was biblical in its approach to social issues, as the Commission on Christianizing the Social Order had outlined, could the Christian witness continue to be manifest in a Canadian society that seemed determined to leave behind Christianity.

In an attempt to define an enlightened approach to evangelism the Board of Evangelism and Social Service came to conclusions similar to those of *Christianizing the Social Order*. A cross-section of the United church ministry, representing the evangelical, liberal, and social gospel traditions, the missionary interest, the publishing house, rural and urban parishes, and each conference of the church, was involved in the board's Commission on Evangelism. The membership included George Pidgeon, Richard Roberts, E.H. Oliver, Ernest Thomas, Hugh Dobson, and James Endicott. Their report contended that 'in a startling degree the civilization that has enshrined our Christian religion is now menaced by deep-seated and almost universal sins.' In particular, the board pointed to the approval and glorification of material riches as the standard of human worth and the retention of privilege and power at the expense of the common good. These were considered 'sins of personal attitude' but also 'sins fostered and protected by institutions designed to foster, protect and satisfy evil desires.' For these corporate as well as personal sins to be 'dethroned,' the committee recognized that only a 'radically Christian' outlook would suffice.[46]

Richard Roberts was a member of both the Committee on Evangelism and the Committee on Christianizing the Social Order, and he clarified this renewed understanding. Merging the evangelical concern with sinfulness with the objective of realizing a Christian social order, Roberts claimed that repentance had 'to spring from penitence for *personal complicity* in *collective sin.*' He explained: 'We have lived in and accepted the advantages of a social order which has involved, for others, poverty, malnutrition, overcrowding, exploitation ... This is our sin. To call us to repentance for permitting this state of things is the immediate and prophetic ministry of the Church.' The ministry of the church had to be 'more radical' than the mere 'protest and indignation' and 'vague and confused socialist doctrine' of the social gospel. For the church's social conscience to be effective, Roberts thought, it had to be as 'radical' as the evangelical emphasis, 'going down to the roots of social wrong in human sin and to the roots of the remedy in divine grace.'[47] Society was no longer regarded as a progressive or redeeming force. There was recognition that it was not simply personal sinfulness that was the force drawing people away from God, but also the more powerful and elusive one of secularization.

Perhaps the most striking thing which emerged from the depression was the sense of urgency concerning the future of Protestantism in Canada. The Joint Committee on the Evangelization of Canadian Life proclaimed, 'Former Christian standards by which men lived and built up a worthy civilization are disappearing and we have nothing to take their place. It is time to raise the alarm.'[48] Instead of viewing evangelism as a means to create the Kingdom of God, clergymen now viewed it as a last resort in fending off secularization. Just how vulnerable Protestantism and the church had become in Canada was made clear to Richard Roberts during his term as moderator of the United church between 1934 and 1936. Another campaign for the evangelism of Canadian life had been organized. Although it attracted great interest and high attendance, there was disappointment and frustration with its message, for it focused on the outmoded method of witnessing. Roberts harshly judged that the program was 'the last kick of a decayed Moodyism' and lacked the Word of God. Commenting on this latest effort to evangelize Canadian society and the campaign's lack of vital theology, Roberts dejectedly wrote, 'I am obsessed by the fear that the campaign may lead us more deeply into the doldrums than we are ... I very earnestly hope for the best. But I'm scared.'[49]

In his farewell address as moderator Roberts reiterated what he had been arguing with greater and greater clarity since the mid-1920s. For the United church to win back an increasingly secularized society to faith in Christianity it had to be clear and outspoken on what it believed to be the meaning and responsibilities entailed in Christ's teachings. What was essential, unique, and enduring about Christianity had to be emphasized. Accommodation with the secular values and interests of society was perilous, Roberts understood, for often the result was a secularization of the faith. A moratorium for liberal Christianity was advanced by another United church clergyman:

> It may be too much to say that Liberalism is dead, but it is certainly discredited as an effective evangel. If the Christian religion is anything at all, it is not a top-dressing of culture, but a fundamental transformation of human nature, a declaration that, without what Jesus Christ offers, men 'perish' ... If the church is at bay, it is not because she has no gospel, but because she has whittled out of it every disquieting and warning element and has preached a 'God of love.'[50]

Despite the theological insights developed during the depression the United church still seemed theologically timid and unsure. Its official response to *Christianizing the Social Order* was meek. The General Council merely recommended that the statement be sent to presbyteries and congregations for study, and unfortunately regarded it in a limited fashion, as merely 'a statement of the Christian attitude and approach to the economic question.' There was no acknowledgment of the renewed emphasis on a biblically based theology or of the more radically Christian definition of the church's task in society.[51] This reluctance to give positive endorsement to the theology of crisis indicated the depth of the theological depression in the United church. Basically, insights gained from the Great War and the Great Depression, which would have aided a spiritually struggling United church in defining a preachable gospel for the age, were relegated to the dust-heap. The more optimistic liberal evangelism and social gospel still endured, and in the end the church members and the clergy, despite some reservations, seemed more willing to respond positively to the banal ethics and hollow theology offered by the Oxford Group movement. Accommodation to the secular values of consumer culture seemed to take precedence over the call to espouse a radical Christianity that challenged these dominant social mores.

Believing in the Providence of God, clergymen interpreted the depression as a test of faith for Canadian society. Precisely this made the 1930s such a disheartening time in the United Church of Canada, for the persistence of the depression, the ongoing inability of the church to foster a religious revival and formulate a statement of Christian theology, and the sense that Canadian society was becoming an unchristian one all suggested failure.

Conclusion

Methodist, Presbyterian, and Baptist clergymen had become aware by the 1870s that the forces of secularization were undermining the authority of the Christian religion and the role of the church in Canadian society. Some changes indicating secularization were obvious ones, such as the shift from church to state control of education and social welfare. Other developments, such as the withdrawal of the church as the social centre and moral authority in the community and the decline of the pulpit as a source and medium of knowledge, were more subtle. Generally, Canadians relied less and less upon religious explanations or references to the supernatural for an understanding of events and their surroundings. Instead they were looking to natural or scientific explanations. For many, science became the foundation for the realization of their hopes and dreams.[1] Also, as Canadian society emerged from its pioneer beginnings, the difficult quest for subsistence was eased, and people enjoyed much more security, wealth, and leisure time. The result was the emergence of a consumer culture that directly challenged Christianity's central other-worldly orientation. In a society in which the principle of religious liberty had been established by the 1840s, therefore, the Canadian churches were confronted by different values and institutions which had powerful secular foundations. Exactly how these various social and intellectual forces undermined belief in the supernatural or miraculous and contributed to a more secular society is difficult to discern.[2]

Another important factor in the secularization of Canadian society has been the manner in which the churches and clergy have responded. In confronting secularization, religious institutions have two options: they can modify Christianity in accordance with social, intellectual, and cultural demands; or, ignoring contemporary trends, they can entrench themselves and continue to preach historic Christianity. The clergy of the Methodist, Presbyterian, and Baptist churches in Canada, for the most part, pursued the course of accommodation. They sought renewal through preaching a gospel that they considered to be relevant to the social, intellectual, and cultural concerns of the day. This quest for relevance only resulted in a compromising of Christianity's supernatural orientation and the church's sacred mission.

According to many clergymen, the changing atmosphere of Victorian society required a different religious understanding. What distressed the clergy was that religious doubt seemed to be widespread and was based on the feeling that traditional Christian teachings were somehow irrelevant or unsuitable for modern society. Throughout the late nineteenth century there was a great deal of debate about the cardinal doctrines of Christianity, including whether the Bible was the inspired Word of God. The churches and clergy were losing their authority as guardians of morality and truth. By the 1890s Christianity was refashioned into a religion that accepted the discoveries of science and principles of historical inquiry.

One of the most far-reaching implications of this renewed understanding of Christianity was the emphasis placed on moral standards and ethical values. Jesus was interpreted in historical terms rather than miraculous or spiritual ones. This more secular emphasis meant that attention was paid to Christ's moral example and social teachings, not the atonement or resurrection. God was no longer understood to be outside history and beyond human comprehension. Clearly some of the mystery surrounding Christianity had been compromised for the purpose of providing greater assurance of the truth of Christianity. This accommodation seemed necessary in a more secular society which was experiencing difficulty in accepting many of the spiritual and doctrinal aspects of the Christian faith. By minimizing the miraculous and supernatural while emphasizing morality and social reform, clergymen hoped to maintain religion's strong presence in Canadian society. The evangelical churches had modified their historic traditions and certain aspects of evangelicalism and had adopted a vague, less vivid, less active conception of the supernatural. Ironically, this more secular understanding of Christianity was thought to be necessary to combat the advance of materialism, turn around the progress of doubt and unbelief, and provide a foundation for a revival of religion.

The modernization of Christianity did not bring about a renewal of Christianity in terms of inspiring people to stronger religious beliefs or greater commitment to the church. Liberal theology proved to be shaky ground, and opposition to it emerged, based on the fear that Christianity was being seriously compromised by secular considerations. As the drift away from religious faith continued during the late-Victorian period, many clergymen argued, without rejecting the liberal spirit's moral vision or social concern, that preaching personal salvation had to remain their primary mission. Religious movements outside the churches as well as evangelistic preachers within the churches sought to revive a more traditional personal Christianity that stressed the importance of conversion and the promise of salvation. The process of secularization fostered religious revivals which involved those who were desperately trying to preserve Christianity's other-worldly and evangelical heritage. Despite the outbreak of revivalistic activity in the late-Victorian era, evangelization was becoming increasingly difficult as Canadians became more urbanized, better educated, and prosperous. To meet the demands of this more secular audience, the message of the modern revivalists was shorn of a sense of awe for the supernatural, and the path from sinfulness to salvation was laid out in gentle or lenient terms. The techniques employed did not disrupt concerns about respectability and conformed to the standards of popular culture or mass entertainment. Many of the more challenging aspects of evangelicalism were placed into the background as modern revivalists made religion a commodity that was broadly appealing in modern society.

To ensure continued growth the churches were compelled to look to new fields. Missionaries were attracted to places where the prospect of building strong religious faith and institutions seemed more feasible. In the foreign mission fields contact with other religions undermined confidence in the absolute superiority of Christianity. Most disturbing was the realization that other religions shared with Christianity certain beliefs concerning ultimate spiritual and moral questions. Also, as the difficulties in planting Christianity in other societies became increasingly apparent, medical and educational work was emphasized instead of proselytizing.

Many thought that the only hope for the rejuvenation of Protestantism in Canada rested in the establishment of a Christian faith that was not compromised by the demands of secular society, one that was stripped down to its essential form. This purified Christianity, it was thought, could take root and flourish in the relatively unsettled West and serve as an inspiration for the troubled Methodist and Presbyterian churches. This promise was not fulfilled; the appeal of a simplified evangelical faith was often met with indifference in the mission fields. Missionaries tended to preach on moral issues and focus their attention on social projects. Missions, therefore, were also under secularizing pressure; they did not rejuvenate the struggling churches. If anything, they merely directed attention away from the considerable challenge of secularization and created a false impression of religious vitality.

The strategy of trying to maintain religion and the church as leading forces in Canadian society by identifying Christianity with the secular order seemed to reach new heights in the first decade of the twentieth century. By then the churches were faced with the full force of modern Canada's pluralistic character. Not only did the churches have to face the challenge of massive immigration, but also the realities of a more prosperous urban industrial society in which people had both the time and the money to pursue numerous recreational activities and purchase an ever-growing variety of consumer items. Religion and the churches had to compete more vigorously for attention and support.

Clergymen persisted in trying to make Christianity relevant by emphasizing social reform and applying the principles of the social gospel to industry, capital, and the political system. Also the clergy attempted to preach the gospel in a fashion that appealed to a mass audience by adopting a more secular narrative preaching style, adapting the Christian message to contemporary values and trends, as well as using popular media, such as the novel. Religion was being repackaged to meet people's craving for respectable entertainment. By 1910, however, there was a rising chorus of church leaders commenting on falling church attendance, low numbers of candidates for the ministry, and the lack of family worship. Clergymen concluded that despite all their efforts to preach a more appealing gospel, a growing number of Canadians were living outside the influence of the church. The clergy had to turn to the state in order to protect Sunday from being a day that was completely secularized.

The questioning of this strategy of seeking religious revival and church renewal through social relevance was sharply focused by the

reality of the Great War. Many of the optimistic beliefs that characterized liberal Christianity had to be reassessed. The war demonstrated in dramatic fashion that Christianity could not be identified with
the interests of society, so that the association of Christianity with
moral and social reform was undermined. There was a retreat from
progress-oriented social Christianity, and the clergy, especially those
who served at the front, were thrown back to a more evangelical
concern for repentance and personal salvation.

Furthermore the chaplains discovered that young men had little
knowledge of the basic tenets of Christianity – its rites, Scripture, and
traditions – and were indifferent to the church. What the chaplains
encountered in the close quarters of army camp life was not outright
disbelief or atheism, but what Jeffrey Cox has termed 'diffusive
Christianity.' Like many Canadians of the early twentieth century the
young men held a general belief in God, thought that the Bible was a
worthwhile book for moral guidance, approved of the church's role
in the rites of passage, and venerated the image of a loving and
suffering Christ. There was little reference in these beliefs to the
supernatural.[3] The fact that churches had been ignoring the essential
spiritual truths of Christianity in favour of pursuing social action or
making religion somehow more acceptable to the dictates of popular
culture was thought to be responsible for the weakened character of
Christian belief and commitment. The chaplains were convinced that
the churches were failing to reach those touched by the war and
recommended a return to a Christianity that concentrated on the
meaning of the Cross.

There seemed to be a significant difference between the pre-war
and postwar generations in Canadian society. Prior to the Great War
there was an optimistic faith in the human ability to reform society
so that the realization of the Kingdom of God was closer. This hopefulness endured, as many of the pre-war generation were able to face
the horror of war, the disappointments of the 1920s, and the destitution of the Great Depression without completely abandoning their
belief that beyond such tragedies there was certain progress and that
God was still present. Such abiding faith was difficult for the war and
postwar generations, since they had developed a discouraging sense
of the destructive and immoral forces in society. Those willing to
confront the reality of war had great difficulty in sustaining confidence
in the human capacity to build a Christian society. They sought a new
understanding of Christianity, one that dealt with the reality of sin-

fulness and the historic Christian doctrine of redemptive suffering. Utopian dreams about the certain establishment of Christian moral and social principles in Canadian society were not easily entertained by those touched by the war.

The Methodist and Presbyterian clergy were not prepared to deal with the postwar mood of disillusionment. Despite the achievement of church union, there was little to be optimistic about. People were not attending worship services and were seriously questioning the existence of God. The United Church of Canada was born into a period of theological depression in which there was little vision or vitality. The new church lacked a statement of faith suitable for the age. A new synthesis had not emerged; and so the church drifted, suffering a loss of overall coherence and direction. Clergymen had difficulty finding their way to a clearer understanding of Christianity and deeper resources for evangelization. These difficulties could not be easily overcome. The improved organization and utilization of resources that resulted from union did not meet the church's deeply rooted spiritual and theological problems.

During the 1920s, George Pidgeon, while moderator of the United Church of Canada, declared that the church's role was 'marginal ... in many aspects of modern life.'[4] Clergymen recognized that a consumer consciousness was now dictating the values and concerns of many Canadians. The maturing of a consumer culture in Canada – which had its roots deep in the nineteenth century – was central to the secularization of society, for it involved a fundamental transformation of values. In order to attain a sense of well-being, people were focusing on material comfort or prosperity in this world instead of salvation in the next. Insightful clergymen understood that the growth of consumer culture was the most substantial reason for the increasingly marginal position of religion and the church in modern society.

The clearest evidence of the postwar spiritual depression was the increasingly urgent call for a religious revival. This quest to recapture the evangelical heritage struck many as the required solution for the religious indifference and theological confusion of the period. Many clergy understood, however, that after years of accommodating religion with modernism and diluting the supernatural elements of Christianity, recovering the spiritual vitality of a previous age would be extremely difficult. Just how desperate some clergy had become was indicated by the fact that they embraced the Oxford Group movement as the long-awaited revival. This movement lacked a strong

Christian theology, or even Christian or biblical point of reference, and it stressed the importance of moral uplift rather than a conversion to Christianity that resulted from a profound understanding of sinfulness or experience of religious faith. But this shallow, indeed hollow, religious content was overlooked. The fact that the Oxford Group movement was embraced by so many clergy and churchgoers demonstrated how secular ethics had penetrated religious beliefs in Canadian society, for the movement stressed little more than psychological well-being as its central doctrine. The appeal of the Oxford Group movement indicated that Canadians had difficulty responding to a challenging religious message. The peril of identifying Christianity too closely with secular concerns was now tragically apparent. There was a growing mood of defeatism in the churches.

It was during the Great Depression that Methodist and Presbyterian clergymen in Canada were finally forced to work out a Christian theology equipped to deal with the reality of an unchristian society. There was a sense that the world was a secular place where the sacred had been thrust to the periphery and God's will was not necessarily at work. Liberal Christianity's advocacy of accommodation with society seemed no longer tenable. Some perceptive clergymen had concluded that the strategy of accommodating Christianity to modern political, social, and intellectual trends was a serious mistake because these secular forces were overwhelming Christianity. The strategy of accommodation did not make society more Christian; rather, it secularized religion and the church. It now seemed imperative that the church stand against secular society in uncompromising opposition, for only in this way could a distinctive Christian religion be maintained. Unfortunately, this bold new understanding was not easily accepted. The theology of crisis did not become the harbinger of a revitalized church; rather, it was largely ignored in the councils of the churches.

Nevertheless, the optimistic assumption that Canada, under the inspiration of its churches, was on the path to realizing the Kingdom of God lay in ruins. It was clear that Christianity either strongly believed or practised or experienced was rare. The church seemed to be in dramatic retreat as a social institution and as a moral and intellectual leader. Religious thinking in Canada was increasingly based on the most disheartening of conclusions: secularization was proceeding and there was little that could be done to stem its tide.

Not all denominations or churches in Canada pursued accommodation with secular forces as the means to preserve the role of religion and the church. Adhering to a more distinctive and historic Christianity was thought to be a more effective way to maintain a vibrant religious outlook and discipline in society. A major issue facing Canadian historians is whether those denominations that were committed to an other-worldly orientation and eschewed accommodation with the secular managed to balance the objectives of religious integrity and social influence more effectively than the liberal modernist mainstream within the Methodist, Presbyterian, and Baptist churches.[5]

Whatever the case, an understanding of the difficulties the clergy had in defining a gospel and mission that would be responded to in a secular society, but would not compromise what was essential to Christianity, reveals that Canadian religious history cannot be written as a story of progress. Instead, a major theme has been the dilemma confronting the clergy in preaching a gospel that somehow appealed to a secular society. Seeking accommodation with a secular society has only risked secularizing the Christian gospel and mission. There always was the danger of making Christianity relevant to the point that the Church had nothing that was mysterious or challenging to communicate, and this was a danger that many Canadian clergy wrestled with throughout their ministries. To resist accommodation with society, however, has risked making the church and religion even more remote; maintaining historic Christianity has meant losing social and intellectual contact with the dominant secular culture. This dilemma, balancing the central objectives of religious integrity and social influence as the process of secularization has proceeded, has constantly confronted the clergy.

Notes

The following abbreviations are used throughout the notes:

ANB   Methodist Church, Army and Navy Board Papers
AO   Archives of Ontario
AV   *Acta Victoriana*
CB   *Canadian Baptist*
ChG   *Christian Guardian*
CHR   *Canadian Historical Review*
CJRT   *Canadian Journal of Religious Thought*
CMM   *Canadian Methodist Magazine*
CMQ   *Canadian Methodist Quarterly*
CMR   *Canadian Methodist Review*
DCB   *Dictionary of Canadian Biography*
KCM   *Knox College Monthly and Presbyterian Magazine*
LDA   *Lord's Day Advocate*
NAC   National Archives of Canada
NO   *New Outlook*
PR   *Presbyterian Review*
PW   *Presbyterian Witness*
QUL   Queen's University Library
SN   *Saturday Night*
UCA   United Church Archives
UM   Department of Archives and Special Collections, University of Manitoba

INTRODUCTION

1 Egerton Ryerson, *First Lessons in Christian Morals: Canadian Families and Schools* (Toronto: Copp Clark 1871), 69

2 E.H. Dewart, 'Christianity and Skepticism: An Essay on Current Infidelity,' in *Living Epistles; or, Christ's Witness to the World* (Toronto: Christian Guardian Office 1878), 231–44

3 Goldwin French, 'The Evangelical Creed in Canada,' in W.L. Morton, ed., *The Shield of Achilles: Aspects of Canada in the Victorian Age* (Toronto: McClelland and Stewart 1968), 15–35

4 Ramsay Cook, *The Regenerators: Social Criticism in Late Victorian Canada* (Toronto: University of Toronto Press 1985), 26–36

5 Dewart, 'Christianity and Skepticism,' 226–31. Recently a strong case has been advanced claiming that clergymen – 'the guardians of belief' – have 'paved the road to unbelief.' See James Turner, *Without God without Creed: The Origins of Unbelief in America* (Baltimore: Johns Hopkins University Press 1985), xiii

6 Owen Chadwick, *The Secularization of the European Mind* (Cambridge: Cambridge University Press 1975), 16–17

7 A.D. Gilbert, *The Making of Post-Christian Britain: A History of the Secularization of Modern Society* (London: Longman 1978), 6; Bryan Wilson, *Religion in a Secular Society: A Sociological Comment* (London: C.A. Watts & Co. 1966), xi–xiii

8 This is the approach taken by Michael Gauvreau, *The Evangelical Century: College and Creed in English Canada from the Great Revival to the Great Depression* (Montreal and Kingston: McGill-Queen's University Press 1991). Throughout this study Gauvreau attacks the secularization thesis by arguing that the evangelical creed persisted in the minds of theologians and clergymen-professors throughout the nineteenth century. This argument says much about nineteenth-century intellectual life in Canada but little about the complex social and cultural problem of secularization.

9 The fruitfulness of this approach is apparent in George Rawlyk's work on Henry Alline and his role in shaping a Maritime evangelical tradition. See especially George Rawlyk, *Ravished by the Spirit: Religious Revivals, Baptists, and Henry Alline* (Kingston and Montreal: McGill-Queen's University Press 1984).

10 Quoted in James G. Greenlee, *Sir Robert Falconer: A Biography* (Toronto: University of Toronto Press 1988), 100

11 C.W. Hawkins, 'The Law of Revivals,' in *Sermons on the Christian Life* (Toronto: William Briggs 1880), 58

12 Burkhard Kiesekamp, 'Community and Faith: The Intellectual and

Ideological Bases of the Church Union Movement in Victorian Canada'
(PHD diss., University of Toronto, 1974); N.K. Clifford, 'His Dominion:
A Vision in Crisis,' *Studies in Religion 2*, no. 4 (1973), 315–26

13 The Baptists believed that the question of baptism distinguished them
from other evangelical churches. They held steadfastly to the belief that
baptismal immersion for adult believers was the only practice that was
consistent with biblical teaching and that the other churches, which
practised the baptism of infants, were clearly undermining Christ's
example and teaching. There were many pamphlets written by Baptist
ministers and laypersons throughout the nineteenth century defending
the church's insistence on adult immersion and arguing that this was the
issue that set the Baptist church apart. This sense of separateness or
independence persisted into the twentieth century. See, for example,
Calvin Goodspeed, *The Peculiar Principles of the Baptists* (Toronto: Dudley
and Burns 1878) and H.H. Bingham, 'Have Baptists Still a Distinctive
Message for Modern Times?' *CB*, 7 March 1919.

14 Most of the recent work on the Baptists has focused on Baptist higher
education. See George Rawlyk, ed., *Canadian Baptists and Christian Higher
Education* (Kingston and Montreal: McGill-Queen's University Press
1988); and Charles M. Johnston, *McMaster University, Volume 1: The
Toronto Years* (Toronto: University of Toronto Press 1976). A more broad-
ranging study of the Baptist experience, although limited to the
Maritimes, is George Rawlyk, *Champions of Truth: Fundamentalism,
Modernism, and the Maritime Baptists* (Montreal and Kingston: McGill-
Queen's University Press 1990).

15 Frank Epp, *Mennonites in Canada 1776–1920: The History of a Separate
People* (Toronto: Macmillan 1974); Frank Epp, *Mennonites in Canada
1920–1940: The Struggle for Survival* (Toronto: Macmillan 1982); William
Kaplan, *State and Salvation: The Jehovah's Witnesses and Their Fight for
Civil Rights* (Toronto: University of Toronto Press 1989).

16 Agnes Machar, *Faithful unto Death: A Memorial of John Anderson, Late
Janitor of Queen's College, Kingston, C.W.* (Kingston: James Creighton 1859)
and Nathanael Burwash, *Memorials of the Life of Edward and Lydia Ann
Jackson* (Toronto: S. Rose Methodist Bookroom 1876) provide sketches of
such devotional lives.

17 For a discussion of domestic religion in American society, see Colleen
McDannell, *The Christian Home in Victorian America, 1840–1900*
(Bloomington: Indiana University Press 1986).

18 S. Budd, *Varieties of Unbelief: Atheists and Agnostics in English Society,
1850–1950* (London: Heinemann 1977)

19 Cook, *The Regenerators*, passim

20 A. Sutherland, 'The Methodist Church in Relation to Missions,' in
    Centennial of Canadian Methodism (Toronto: William Briggs 1891), 254.
    For the Providential sense of their history among the Baptists, see John
    Mockett Cramp, *The Centenary of the Baptists in Nova Scotia: A Discourse*
    (Halifax: Christian Messenger Office 1860).
21 Thomas Webster, *History of the Methodist Episcopal Church in Canada*
    (Hamilton: Canada Christian Advocate Office 1870), 158, 201
22 There were numerous denominational histories of the Canadian
    churches which were written in this progressive tradition and published
    after 1860. For example, George F. Playter, *History of Methodism in Canada*
    (Toronto: Christian Guardian Office 1862); John Carroll, *Case and His
    Cotemporaries; or, The Canadian Itinerants' Memorial: Constituting a
    Biographical History of Methodism in Canada*, 5 vols. (Toronto: Methodist
    Conference Office 1867–77); T.W. Smith, *History of the Methodist Church of
    Eastern British America*, 2 vols. (Halifax: S.F. Huestis, 1877–90); I.E. Bill,
    *Fifty Years with the Baptist Ministers and Churches of the Maritime Provinces
    of Canada* (St John: Barnes & Co. 1880); William Gregg, *History of the
    Presbyterian Church in the Dominion of Canada from the Earliest Time to 1834*
    (Toronto: Presbyterian Printing and Publishing Co. 1885); Edward
    Manning Saunders, *History of the Baptists of the Maritime Provinces*
    (Halifax: Burgoyne Press 1902); and A. Shortt and A.G. Doughty, eds.,
    Canada and Its Provinces, Vol. XI: Missions (Toronto: Glasgow, Brook &
    Co. 1914).
23 E.H. Dewart, 'The Methodist Church of Canada, 1873–1883,' in *Centennial
    of Canadian Methodism*, 135–40. The impression of Methodist progress
    was made clearer in other essays in this volume. See George H. Cornish,
    'Statistical Record of the Progress of Methodism in Canada during the
    First One Hundred Years of Its History,' 321–39; and W.W. Withrow,
    'Methodist Literature and Methodist Sunday-Schools,' 273–95.
24 William Withrow, *Religious Progress in the Nineteenth Century* (Toronto:
    Bradley Garretson 1900), 6. This lengthy volume, which focused on
    missions, denominational growth, advances in religious thought, and
    practical religious activity in the community, was designed 'to utterly
    disprove' the 'astounding assumptions' of Goldwin Smith's 'The
    Prospect of a Moral Interregnum,' *Canadian Monthly and National Review*,
    Dec. 1879.
25 For a broader discussion of the progressive or whiggish bias in late
    Victorian Canadian writing see Carl Berger, *The Sense of Power: Studies in
    the Ideas of Canadian Imperialism 1867–1914* (Toronto: University of
    Toronto Press 1970), 109–115. M. Brook Taylor's *Promoters, Patriots, and*

Partisans: Historiography in Nineteenth-Century English Canada (Toronto: University of Toronto Press 1989) lacks discussion of the numerous church histories.

26 J.W. Grant, *The Church in the Canadian Era: The First Century of Confederation* (Toronto: Ryerson 1972), 227

27 Alexander Sutherland, *Methodism in Canada: Its Work and Its Story* (Toronto: Methodist Mission Rooms 1904); C.W. Gordon, *The Life of James Robertson: Missionary Superintendent in Western Canada* (Toronto: Westminster 1908); James Woodsworth, *Thirty Years in the Canadian North-West* (Toronto: McClelland 1917)

28 See Oliver's comments on Sutherland's book in E.H. Oliver, *His Dominion of Canada* (Toronto: Board of Home Missions of the United Church of Canada 1932), 164–5.

29 For a full assessment of Clark's career, see H.H. Hiller, *Society and Change: S.D. Clark and the Development of Canadian Sociology* (Toronto: University of Toronto Press 1982).

30 S.D. Clark, *Church and Sect in Canada* (Toronto: University of Toronto Press 1948), 338–42, 366, 431

31 H.H. Walsh, 'Canada and the Church: A Job for Historians,' *Queen's Quarterly* 61 (Spring 1954), 71–9

32 There are good summaries of the debate in W.W. Bowden, *Church History in the Age of Science: Historiographical Patterns in the United States 1876–1918* (Chapel Hill: University of North Carolina Press 1971), 229–37; and Jerald C. Brauer, 'Changing Perspectives on Religion in America,' in *Reinterpretation in American Church History* (Chicago: University of Chicago Press 1968), 19–23.

33 For an assessment of the genesis of the national school, see N.K. Clifford, 'Religion and the Development of Canadian Society: An Historiographical Analysis,' *Church History* 38 (Winter 1969), 520–2. There are many works in this 'national school.' For example, H.H. Walsh, *The Christian Church in Canada* (Toronto: Ryerson 1956); J.W. Grant, ed., *The Churches and the Canadian Experience* (Toronto: Ryerson 1963); J.W. Grant, 'The Church and Canada's Self Awareness,' *Canadian Journal of Theology*, July 1967; and N.G. Smith, 'Nationalism in the Canadian Churches,' *Canadian Historical Association Report*, 1966.

34 Grant, *The Church in the Canadian Era*, 216–17. In the postscript to the second edition of this book, published in 1988, Grant is not nearly so optimistic.

35 John S. Moir, *Enduring Witness: A History of the Presbyterian Church in Canada* (Hamilton: The Presbyterian Church in Canada 1974), xi

36 R. Allen, *The Social Passion: Religion and Social Reform in Canada, 1914–1928* (Toronto: University of Toronto Press 1973). Other historians making the same case include W.H. Magney, 'The Methodist Church and the National Gospel, 1884–1914,' *Bulletin*, no. 20, 3–95; and G.N. Emery, 'The Origins of Canadian Methodist Involvement in the Social Gospel Movement 1890–1914,' *Bulletin*, no. 26, 104–19.

37 Carl Berger, *Science, God, and Nature in Victorian Canada* (Toronto: University of Toronto Press 1983); Doug Owram, *The Government Generation: Canadian Intellectuals and the State* (Toronto: University of Toronto Press 1986); Christopher Armstrong and H.V. Nelles, *The Revenge of the Methodist Bicycle Company: Sunday Streetcars and Municipal Reform in Toronto, 1888–1897* (Toronto: Peter Martin Associates 1977)

38 A.B. McKillop, *A Disciplined Intelligence: Critical Inquiry and Canadian Thought in the Victorian Age* (Montreal: McGill-Queen's University Press 1979); William Westfall, *Two Worlds: The Protestant Culture of Nineteenth-Century Ontario* (Kingston and Montreal: McGill-Queen's University Press 1989); Cook, *The Regenerators*

39 J.W. Grant, *A Profusion of Spires: Religion in Nineteenth-Century Ontario* (Toronto: University of Toronto Press 1988), 195–9, 229

40 Rawlyk, ed., *Canadian Baptists and Christian Higher Education*, 36–9; Rawlyk, *Champions of Truth*, 36–7

41 This debate is analysed by A.B. McKillop, 'Culture, Intellect, and Context: Recent Writing on the Cultural and Intellectual History of Ontario,' *Journal of Canadian Studies* 24, no. 3 (Fall 1989), 19–24; Chad Reimer, 'Review: Religion and Culture in Nineteenth-Century English Canada,' *Journal of Canadian Studies* 25, no. 1 (Spring 1990), 192–203; and Doug Owram, 'Writing about Ideas,' in J. Schultz, ed., *Writing about Canada: A Handbook for Modern Canadian History* (Scarborough, Ont.: Prentice Hall 1990), 62–4. John Webster Grant explores some of the major issues in the revised edition of *The Church in the Canadian Era* (Burlington: Welch Publishing Co. 1988), 240–2. The boldest challenge to the secularization thesis comes from Gauvreau, *The Evangelical Century*, 4–7, passim. See also M. Gauvreau, 'Beyond the Half–Way House: Evangelism and the Shaping of English Canadian Culture,' *Acadiensis* 20, no. 2 (Spring 1991), 158–77.

42 M. Van Die, *An Evangelical Mind: Nathanael Burwash and the Methodist Tradition in Canada* (Kingston and Montreal: McGill-Queen's University Press 1989), 7–12, 186–96

43 Ruth Compton Brouwer, *New Women for God: Canadian Presbyterian*

Women and India Missions, 1876–1914 (Toronto: University of Toronto Press 1990), 53–91

44 Mariana Valverde, *The Age of Light, Soap and Water: Moral Reform in English Canada, 1885–1925* (Toronto: McClelland and Stewart 1991), 132–3

45 Gauvreau, *The Evangelical Century*, 3–12, 181–5, 218–22, 287–90

46 Richard Carwardine, *Trans-Atlantic Revivalism: Popular Evangelicalism in Britain and America, 1790–1865* (Westport: Greenwood Press 1978). For a superb study of the emergence of a more secular world-view in the eighteenth century, see David Spadafora, *The Idea of Progress in Eighteenth-Century Britain* (New Haven: Yale University Press 1990).

47 G.R. Cragg, *The Church in the Age of Reason* (New York: Penguin Books 1960), 141

48 Carroll, *Case and His Contemporaries*, 1: 182

49 Quoted in Playter, *History of Methodism in Canada*, 208

50 There is a superb discussion of religious diversity based on ethnic background and church affiliation in Grant, *A Profusion of Spires*, 20–35.

51 Jones H. Farmer, ed., *E.W. Dadson, B.A., D.D.: The Man and His Message* (Toronto: William Briggs 1902), 137

52 William Westfall, 'Order and Experience: Patterns of Religious Metaphor in Early Nineteenth-Century Upper Canada,' *Journal of Canadian Studies* 20, no. 1 (Spring 1985), 5–24

53 J.S. Moir, *The Church in the British Era: From the British Conquest to Confederation* (Toronto: McGraw-Hill 1972), passim

54 Egerton Ryerson, *Canadian Methodism: Its Epochs and Characteristics* (Toronto: William Briggs 1882), 138–9

55 D.A. MacGregor, 'The Inspired Estimate of Orthodoxy,' in *Memoir of Daniel Arthur MacGregor, Late Principal of Toronto Baptist College* (Toronto: Alumni Association of the Toronto Baptist College 1891), 169

56 H. Butterfield, *The Whig Interpretation of History* (New York: W.W. Norton 1965), 38

57 Chadwick, *Secularization*, 27–32

58 This section draws on Egerton Ryerson, *First Lessons in Christian Morals*, iii–iv, passim; J. George Hodgins, ed., 'The Story of My Life" by the Late Rev. Egerton Ryerson* (Toronto: William Briggs 1893), 423–32; Alison Prentice, *The School Promoters: Education and Social Class in Mid-Nineteenth Century Upper Canada* (Toronto: McClelland and Stewart 1977), 128–9; Susan Houston and Alison Prentice, *Schooling and Scholars in Nineteenth-Century Ontario* (Toronto: University of Toronto Press 1988), 248, 278; and Bruce Curtis, *Building the Educational State: Canada West, 1836–1871* (London, Ont.: The Althouse Press 1988), 110–11, 246–52.

59 R.D. Gidney and W.P.J. Millar, *Inventing Secondary Education: The Rise of the High School in Nineteenth-Century Ontario* (Montreal and Kingston: McGill-Queen's University Press 1990), 31, 90–3

60 William Westfall, *Two Worlds*, 109–11, 123–5. The best general study of the period is J.M.S. Careless, *The Union of the Canadas: The Growth of Canadian Institutions, 1841–1857* (Toronto: McClelland and Stewart 1967).

61 Rosalind Williams, *Dream Worlds: Mass Consumption in Late Nineteenth Century France* (Berkley: University of California Press 1982), 4–9. The consumer revolution is far less familiar than the industrial revolution, even though they are 'two facets of a single upheaval that decisively altered the material basis of human life.' The consumer revolution or emergence of a consumer culture awaits study by Canadian historians. For Britain, see Neil McKendrick, John Brewer, and J.H. Plumb, *The Birth of a Consumer Society: The Commercialization of Eighteenth Century England* (London: Europa 1982).

62 See the chapter entitled 'The Promise of Canadian Life' in David Gagan, *Hopeful Travellers: Families, Land, and Social Change in Mid-Victorian Peel County, Canada West* (Toronto: University of Toronto Press 1981). A consumer ethic of self–fulfilment through material gain can be seen most clearly in the affluent elite. A marvelous example is the prominent Toronto lawyer Larratt Smith. See Mary Larratt Smith, *Young Mr. Smith in Upper Canada* (Toronto: University of Toronto Press 1980). See also W.R. Graham, *Greenbank: Country Matters in Nineteenth Century Ontario* (Peterborough, Ont.: Broadview Press 1988), a superb study of the activities and mores of four rural families.

63 See William Case, cited in Westfall, *Two Worlds*, 79

64 This concept of secularization is also central to Jeffrey Cox, *The English Churches in a Secular Society Lambeth, 1870–1930* (New York: Oxford University Press 1982). At the conclusion of his survey of the Presbyterian Church in Canada, John Moir writes: 'a century of secularization has eroded the influence of the church in community and national life so that today there are many effective rivals to the church for public attention' (*Enduring Witness*, 263).

1 CLERGYMEN AND THE PROBLEM OF RELIGIOUS DOUBT

1 Goldwin French, 'The Evangelical Creed in Canada,' in W.L. Morton, ed., *The Shield of Achilles* (Toronto: McClelland and Stewart 1968). The strong evangelical strain in Canadian Presbyterianism, in part, can be attributed to the dominance of the more evangelical Free church as opposed to the

moderate Old Kirk. On the emergence of the Free church in Canada after the Great Disruption of 1843, see Richard Vaudry, *The Free Church in Victorian Canada, 1844–1861* (Waterloo, Ont.: Wilfrid Laurier University Press 1989).

2 John G. Marshall, *The True Plan and Means for Obtaining Religious Revivals* (Halifax: William McNab 1876), 5

3 UCA, Thomas Webster Papers, 'My Memoirs: A Story of Early Pioneer Life in Canada West' (1871), 61–2

4 George Young, *Manitoba Memories: Leaves from My Life in the Prairie Province, 1868–1884* (Toronto: William Briggs 1897), 14–15

5 G.O. Huestis, *A Manual of Methodism: Being Outlines of Its History, Doctrines and Discipline* (Toronto: William Briggs 1885), 138–9

6 E. Pilcher, 'The Confession of Sin,' in B.F. Austin, ed., *The Methodist Episcopal Church Pulpit: A Volume of Sermons by Members of the Niagara, Ontario and Bay of Quinte Conference* (Toronto: William Briggs 1879), 98

7 Young, *Manitoba Memories*, 17

8 This point is emphasized in Egerton Ryerson, *Canadian Methodism: Its Epochs and Characteristics* (Toronto: William Briggs 1882), 110–12.

9 J.E. Sanderson, *The First Century of Methodism in Canada, Vol. II: 1840–1883* (Toronto: William Briggs 1910), 133

10 Marshall, *The True Plan and Means for Obtaining Revivals*, 3

11 Ryerson, *Canadian Methodism*, 80

12 UCA, Albert Carman Papers, box 25, file 138, 'Address to Matilda Division No. 22 Sons of Temperance,' 7 Feb. 1857

13 Carman Papers, General Correspondence, Albert Carman to Phillip Carman, 23 Sept. – 2 Oct. 1858

14 Carman Papers, box 26, file 151, 'The Covenant,' 9 Oct. 1858

15 UCA, William Case Papers, box 1, 'Journal'

16 AO, MS 409, William Cochrane Papers, Diary, 7 June 1859. For the details of Cochrane's life, see R.N. Grant, *Life of Rev. William Cochrane, D.D.* (Toronto: William Briggs 1899); and for a briefer account, David B. Marshall, 'The Rev. William Cochrane,' *DCB* 12: 201–3.

17 T.A. Higgins, *The Life of John Mockett Cramp, D.D., 1796–1881* (Montreal: W. Drysdale & Co. 1887), 56. This entry was from 26 August 1831. For biographical detail, see Barry Moody, 'John Mockett Cramp,' *DCB* 11:209–10.

18 M. Van Die, *An Evangelical Mind: Nathanael Burwash and the Methodist Tradition in Canada, 1839–1918* (Kingston and Montreal: McGill-Queen's University Press 1989), 20–35

19 *Memoir of Daniel Arthur MacGregor, Late Principal of Toronto Baptist College*

(Toronto: Alumni Association of the Toronto Baptist College 1891), 24

20 UCA, Nathanael Burwash Papers, box 1, 'Reminiscences of My Life,' n.d., 1–8

21 N. Burwash, *History of Victoria College* (Toronto: Ryerson 1927), 180–1; C.B. Sissons, *A History of Victoria University* (Toronto: University of Toronto Press 1952), 97–8. Colleges were fertile ground for revival activity. See Jones H. Farmer, ed., *E.W. Dadson: The Man and His Message* (Toronto: William Briggs 1902), 19–25, for an account of revivals at the Baptist Canadian Literary Institute at Woodstock in the 1860s. For revivals at Acadia College, see Barry Moody, 'Breadth of Vision, Breadth of Mind: The Baptists and Acadia College,' in George Rawlyk, ed., *Canadian Baptists and Christian Higher Education* (Kingston and Montreal: McGill-Queen's University Press 1988), 13–14.

22 John Carroll, *My Boy Life, Presented in a Succession of True Stories* (Toronto: William Briggs 1882), 229

23 Burwash, 'Reminiscences,' 9–10. For a sensitive modern account of Burwash's experience at Victoria College, see Van Die, *An Evangelical Mind*, 48–51.

24 Burwash, 'Reminiscences,' 24–5

25 This important point is explored by Van Die, *An Evangelical Mind*, 30.

26 John Carroll, *Case and His Contemporaries*, (Toronto: Methodist Conference Office 1867–77), 5:234–5

27 On the revival question, see Ryerson, *Canadian Methodism*, 124. In 1854, Egerton Ryerson questioned another central institution of evangelical Methodism, the rule of compulsory attendance at class meetings as a condition for church membership, touching off a long and difficult debate within Canadian Methodism. On this question, see Ryerson's account in J.G. Hodgins, ed., *'The Story of My Life' by the Late Rev. Egerton Ryerson* (Toronto: William Briggs 1883) 470–90.

28 On the changing social values of mid-Victorian Canada, see Alison Prentice, *The School Promoters: Education and Social Class in Mid-Nineteenth Century Upper Canada* (Toronto: McClelland and Stewart 1977); and Susan Houston and Alison Prentice, *Schooling and Scholars in Nineteenth-Century Ontario* (Toronto: University of Toronto Press 1988).

29 UCA, Henry Flesher Bland Papers, Diary, 26–9 Oct. 1859; 4–11 April 1861; 15 July 1861; 4 Oct. 1861 and file 30, 'The Harvest Field,' 19 March 1867. Bland's diary is a superb source for gaining an appreciation of the activities of an evangelical itinerant preacher in mid-nineteenth-century Canada. See also the discussion in William Westfall, *Two Worlds: The Protestant Culture of Nineteenth-Century Ontario* (Kingston and Montreal:

McGill-Queen's University Press 1989), 50–81.

30 UCA, Francis Huston Wallace Papers, box 4, 'Memoirs of the Manse, the Parsonage, and the College,' vol. 1, 70

31 George Rawlyk argues that Calvinist revivalism was flexible enough to include both predestination and universalism. What was most important was the ability for preachers to bring about conversions. See *Ravished by the Spirit: Religious Revivals, Baptists, and Henry Alline* (Kingston and Montreal: McGill-Queen's University Press 1984), 50.

32 Wallace Papers, box 1, 'My First Address Delivered to Papa's Prayer-Meeting, West End Presbyterian Church Toronto, May 30, 1871'

33 Wallace, 'Memoirs,' 71–7

34 Wallace Papers, box 1, 'Acts XVI:31,' Sept. 1871

35 Wallace, 'Memoirs,' 74

36 Charles W. Dewesse, 'Church Covenants and Church Discipline among the Baptists of the Maritime Provinces,' in Barry Moody, ed., *Repent and Believe: The Baptist Experience in Maritime Canada* (Hantsport: Lancelot Press for Acadia Divinity College 1980)

37 J.M. Gibson, 'Now and Then,' in *Canada Presbyterian Church Pulpit, Vol. 1* (Toronto: Westminster Press 1871), 176

38 William Moore, 'Lord I Will Follow Thee Withersoever Thou Goest,' in ibid., 121. For a discussion of these developments within Presbyterianism in the United States, see George M. Marsden, *The Evangelical Mind and the New School Presbyterian Experience* (New Haven: Yale University Press 1970), 46–52.

39 Marshall, *The True Plan and Means for Obtaining Religious Revivals*, 3–4. On Marshall, see C.E. Thomas, 'John George Marshall,' *DCB* 10: 496–7.

40 These events are outlined with extensive quotations from documentary material in *The Last Martyrs of Eromanga: Being a Memoir of the Rev. George N. Gordon and Ellen Catherine Powell, His Wife* (Halifax: McNab & Shaffer 1863), 178–89.

41 William Gregg, *History of the Presbyterian Church in the Dominion of Canada* (Toronto: Presbyterian Printing and Publishing Co. 1885), 19

42 *Week*, 12 April 1895. In *The Evangelical Century: College and Creed in English Canada from the Great Revival to the Great Depression* (Montreal and Kingston: McGill-Queen's University Press 1991), Michael Gauvreau traces the growing emphasis on 'the redemptive side of doctrine' back to Thomas McCulloch at the Pictou Academy in the very early nineteenth century (23).

43 Wallace, 'Memoirs,' 82

44 Egerton Ryerson's resignation from the Methodist Episcopal church

involved these questions. See Hodgins, ed., *The Story of My Life by the Late Rev. Egerton Ryerson, 470 — 89.*

45 On this important mid-Victorian Presbyterian divine, see *Memorials of the Life and Ministry of the Rev. John Machar, D.D. Late Minister of St. Andrew's Church, Kingston* (Toronto: James Campbell & Son 1873).

46 J.F. McCurdy, *Life and Work of D.J. Macdonnell* (Toronto: William Briggs 1897), 24

47 Ibid., 24–34

48 D.J. Macdonnell, *Sermon Delivered at the Opening of St. Andrew's Church, Ottawa, 25th January 1874* (Ottawa 1874), 40–2

49 McCurdy, *Macdonnell*, 48–50

50 There was an extensive pamphlet literature on this question published in Canada, beginning in the late 1860s and extending to the mid–1880s. For a discussion of some this literature, see David Marshall, 'Death Abolished: Changing: Attitudes toward Death in Victorian Canada,' a paper presented to the Canadian Historical Association, Victoria, 1990. See also Geoffrey Rowell, *Hell and the Victorians: A Study of the Nineteenth Century Theological Controversies Concerning Eternal Punishment and Future Life* (Oxford: Clarendon Press 1974).

51 'Rev. D.J. Macdonnell,' *SN*, 24 Dec. 1887

52 No text of the sermon is extant. Accounts appear in the *Toronto Mail*, 12 Oct. 1875, under the headline 'The Hereafter,' and on the same date in the *Globe* under the headline 'Report of the Sermon.' Many of the central documents pertaining to the Macdonnell controversy, including the report of the sermon in question, were collected in the pamphlet *Dissent and Complaint of Mr. David Mitchell, and Others against a Decision of the Presbytery of Toronto in the Matter of Mr. D.J. Macdonnell, D.D.* (Orillia, Ont.: Expositor Book Office 1876).

53 'Report on the Sermon,' in *Dissent and Complaint*, 35–40

54 *Montreal Witness*, 12 Oct. 1875

55 'Mr. Macdonnell's Explanation on Sermon,' in *Dissent and Complaint*, 40–3

56 See the reports in the *PW*, June – July 1876.

57 W.L. Grant and F.H. Hamilton, *Principal Grant* (Toronto: Morang & Co. 1904), 82–3

58 Queen's University Archives, Grant Papers, Grant to Principal Snodgrass, 4 May 1876

59 Grant and Hamilton, *Principal Grant*, 153

60 McCurdy, *Macdonnell*, 98

61 Ibid., 128–9

62 Ibid., 98

63 Analysis of natural theology in Canada appears in Carl Berger, *Science, God, and Nature in Victorian Canada* (Toronto: University of Toronto Press 1983), 31–49, 53–60; and A.B. McKillop, *A Disciplined Intelligence: Critical Inquiry and Canadian Thought in the Victorian Era* (Montreal: McGill-Queen's University Press 1979), 59–91.

64 Owen Chadwick, *The Victorian Church, Part 1* (London: Adam and Charles Black 1973), 4

65 McCurdy, *Macdonnell*, 153

66 Burwash, 'Reminiscences,' chapter 7

67 Ibid., chapter 5

68 Suzanne Zeller, *Inventing Canada: Early Victorian Science and the Idea of a Transcontinental Nation* (Toronto: University of Toronto Press 1987)

69 Alan Smith, 'The Gospel of the Self-Made Man in English Canada, 1850–1914,' *CHR* 59, no. 2 (June 1978), 192

70 The precise relationship between the decline in faith in divine Providence and the rise of science and the idea of the self-made man is impossible to determine. For discussion of this question, see Keith Thomas, *Religion and the Decline of Magic: Studies in Popular Beliefs in Sixteenth and Seventeenth Century England* (London: Weidenfeld & Nicolson 1971), 767–800.

71 D.A. MacGregor, 'Questionings about God's Promises' (1882), in *Memoir*, 185, 193–200. For a more general discussion of the prayer debate, see McKillop, *A Disciplined Intelligence*, 157, 261.

72 Richard Wightman and T.J. Jackson Lears, eds., *The Culture of Consumption: Critical Essays in American History, 1880–1980* (New York: Pantheon Books 1983), xii–xiii

2 THE EMERGENCE OF LIBERAL THEOLOGY: A NEW CERTAINTY?

1 W. Cochrane, 'Sentimental Religion,' in *Warning and Welcome: Sermons Preached in Zion Presbyterian Church in Brantford during 1876* (Toronto: Adam, Stevenson and Co. 1877), 150

2 UCA, E.H. Dewart Biography File, 'How I Went to My First Circuit'

3 E.H. Dewart, *Songs of Life: A Collection of Poems* (Toronto: Dudley & Burns 1869), 115–16

4 E.H. Dewart, 'Robertson of Brighton,' *Methodist Quarterly Review* (New York 1866); reprinted in E.H. Dewart, *Essays for the Times: Studies of Eminent Men and Important Living Questions* (Toronto: William Briggs 1878), 18–19

5 E.H. Dewart, *Living Epistles; or, Christ's Witness to the World* (Toronto:

Christian Guardian Office 1878), iv, 29–33; *ChG*, 17 March 1869

6 E.H. Dewart, 'Scriptural Holiness: The Great Want of the Church and the World,' in *Living Epistles*, 170–7, 191–2

7 The threat of scientific materialism was an underlying theme in the lectures delivered by Presbyterian clergy at McGill University in 1883 and 1884. See *Questions of the Day: Lectures Delivered in David Morrice Hall* (Montreal: William Drysdale & Co. 1885).

8 Dewart, 'Christianity and Skepticism,' in *Living Epistles*, 229–58

9 A.B. McKillop, *A Disciplined Intelligence: Critical Inquiry and Canadian Thought in the Victorian Era* (Montreal: McGill-Queen's University Press 1979), 116–26

10 *PW*, 12 Dec. 1868. See also 'The Darwinian Theory,' 5 Aug. 1871; 'Prof. Tyndall on Prayer,' 17 Aug. 1872; 'Creation versus Evolution,' 1 March 1873; 'Darwinism Assailed,' 19 July 1873; 'God in Natural Law,' 27 Oct.–3 Nov. 1877; and 'Huxley's Metaphysics,' 21 Sept.–5 Oct. 1878

11 James R. Moore, *The Post-Darwinian Controversies: A Study of Protestant Struggle to Come to Terms with Darwin in Great Britain and America, 1870–1900* (Cambridge: Cambridge University Press 1979), 12–40

12 *CMM* 1 (May 1875), 215. Dewart argued the same regarding Draper in an editorial, 'The Conflict between Religion and Science,' *ChG*, 17 Feb. 1875. See also 'Harmony of Science and Religion,' *CMM* 5 (March–April 1877).

13 W. Harrison, 'Science and Religion,' *CMM* 20 (Nov. 1884)

14 Gerald Killan, *David Boyle: From Artisan to Archaeologist* (Toronto: University of Toronto Press 1983), 9–10, 59–61

15 UCA, Nathanael Burwash Papers, box 16, file 444, 'Introductory Lecture on Natural History,' Victoria College, August 1867; Marguerite Van Die, *An Evangelical Mind: Nathanael Burwash and the Methodist Tradition in Canada, 1839–1918* (Kingston and Montreal: McGill-Queen's University Press 1989), 89–113

16 Dewart, 'Christianity and Skepticism,' 262

17 'Christianity and Science,' *ChG*, 6 Oct. 1875

18 Dewart, 'Christianity and Skepticism,' 269–77

19 Ibid., 258–9, 273. For McCosh's influence on Dewart, see McKillop, *A Disciplined Intelligence*, 54, 72, 242.

20 'Evolution from a Christian Point of View,' *PW*, 24 Jan. 1880; 'The Gospel of Evolution,' *PW*, 12 June 1880

21 E.M. Saunders, Preface, *History of the Baptists of the Maritime Provinces*; D.A. MacGregor, 'A Regular Baptist Church,' in *Memoir of Daniel Arthur MacGregor, Late Principal of Toronto Baptist College* (Toronto: Alumni Association of the Toronto Baptist College 1891), 164

22 J.E. Wells, *Life and Labours of Robert Alex Fyfe, D.D., Founder and Many Years Principal of the Canadian Literary Institute* (Toronto: W.J. Gage 1885)

23 Barry Moody, 'Breadth of Vision, Breadth of Mind: The Baptists and Acadia College,' in George Rawlyk, ed., *Canadian Baptists and Christian Higher Education* (Kingston and Montreal: McGill-Queen's University Press 1988), 25–8

24 Rev. D. Ross, 'Let There Be Light,' *Queen's College Journal*, March 1894

25 D.M. Gordon, 'The Spirit of Theological Inquiry,' *PW*, 10 Nov. 1894

26 UCA, F.H. Wallace Papers, 'Memoirs of the Manse, the Parsonage, and the College,' vol. 2, 319

27 S.P. Rose, 'E.H. Dewart,' in L. Pierce, ed., *The Chronicle of a Century, 1829–1929: The Record of One Hundred Years of Progress in the Publishing Concerns of the Methodist, Presbyterian, and Congregational Churches in Canada* (Toronto: Ryerson 1929), 46–56

28 E.H. Dewart, *The Development of Doctrine: Second Annual Lecture before the Theological Union of Victoria College* (Toronto 1879), 16–17, 29, 37–38

29 Ibid., 41

30 Ibid., 7

31 Andrew Drummond and James Bulloch, *The Church in Late Victorian Scotland, 1874–1900* (Edinburgh: Saint Andrew Press 1978)

32 William Caven, *A Vindication of Doctrinal Standards: With Special Reference to the Standards of the Presbyterian Church* (Toronto: James Campbell & Son 1875); William Caven, 'The Church of the Living God – The Pillar and Ground of Truth,' in *Canada Presbyterian Church Pulpit, Vol. 2* (Toronto: Westminster Press 1873), 227

33 J.A. Macdonald, 'Rev. Principal Caven, D.D.' *KCM* 15 (Nov. 1891). Principal Gordon's observations were printed in *the Presbyterian*, 10 Dec. 1904.

34 'Dr. Caven's Sermon,' *KCM* 17 (July 1893)

35 For an account of Burwash's scientific training and ideas, see Burwash Papers, box 1, 'Reminiscences of My Life,' chapter 12 ('Professor of Natural Theology, 1866–1873').

36 Burwash Papers, box 12 file 181, 'All Scripture Is Given by Inspiration of God,' July 1881; N. Burwash, *Bricks and the Bible* (Victoria College 1880), reprinted in *CMM*, Oct. 1886; Van Die, *An Evangelical Mind*, 97

37 Another important Canadian clergymen and biblical scholar who studied in Germany under Harnack was Sir Robert Falconer. This aspect of Falconer's life is superbly detailed in James G. Greenlee, *Sir Robert Falconer: A Biography* (Toronto: University of Toronto Press 1988), 20–104.

38 F.H. Wallace, 'The Principles, Methods, and Results of the Biblical

Theology of the New Testament,' *AV* 19 (Dec. 1895 – Jan. 1896)

39 For more detail, see M. Gauvreau, 'The Taming of History: Reflections on the Canadian Methodist Encounter with Biblical Criticism, 1830–1900,' *CHR*, 65, no. 3 (Sept. 1984).

40 QUL, G. Grant, *How to Read the Bible, No. 2*, Queen's University Sunday Afternoon Addresses (Kingston 1891), 10

41 G.H. Wells, 'The Morality of the Old Testament,' Lecture Delivered in David Morrice Hall, 16 Dec. 1883, in *Questions of the Day*, 147–58

42 E.H. Dewart, 'Moral Teaching of the Old Testament,' in *Essays for the Times*, 124; N. Burwash, 'Guesses at the Riddle of Existence: Book Review,' *CMM* (1897), 275–9

43 'The Position of the Pulpit,' *Week*, 22 Nov. 1889

44 'Dr. Caven's Sermon,' 130

45 E.H. Dewart, 'The Last of the Great Prophets,' in *Essays for the Times*, 136–7

46 A.R. Carman, 'The Gospel of Justice,' *CMQ* 3, no. 3 (July 1891), 286–306. A very similar social gospel point of view was being outlined by E.W. Dadson in his editorials in *Canadian Baptist* throughout the 1880s. See John S. Moir, 'The *Canadian Baptist* and the Social Gospel Movement, 1879–1914,' in J. Zeeman, ed., *The Baptist in Canada: Search for Identity amidst Diversity* (Burlington: G.R. Welch Co. 1980), 149–51.

47 D.J. Macdonnell, *Who May Be Communicants in the Presbyterian Church? Being the Substance of a Sermon Preached in St. Andrew's Church, Toronto, on Sunday 23rd October 1887* (Toronto 1887), 3, 15

3 SALVAGING THE BIBLE AND THE EVANGELICAL TRADITION

1 UCA, A. Carman Papers, 'The Supernatural,' n.d., 16–19

2 William Caven, 'Scriptural Preaching,' *KCM* 7 (Nov. 1887), 14

3 Both the YMCA and the YWCA, interdenominational institutions founded out of evangelical concern, were designed to provide a safe haven with a religious atmosphere for young men and women who had recently arrived in the city and were without a permanent home and therefore subject to the temptation of countless destructive vices. See Diana Pederson, '"Keeping Our Good Girls Good": The YWCA and the Girl Problem, 1870–1930,' *Canadian Women's Studies* 7, no. 4 (Winter 1986).

4 D.H. MacVicar, 'The Value of the Word of God,' n.d., in J.H. MacVicar, *Life and Work of Donald Henry MacVicar* (Toronto: Westminster Press 1904), 269–71

5 For analysis of what the Protestant tradition lost by relying almost solely on the Word, see John Bossy, *Christianity in the West, 1400–1700* (Oxford: Oxford University Press 1985), 97.

6 See Stephen Neill, *The Interpretation of the New Testament, 1861–1986* (Oxford: Oxford University Press 1988), 65–111; and Luther Weigle, 'English Versions since 1611,' in S.L. Greenslade, ed., *The Cambridge History of the Bible: The West from the Reformation to the Present Day* (Cambridge: Cambridge University Press 1963), 371–3.

7 N. Burwash, 'The New Version and Our Theology,' *ChG*, 29 June–3 Aug. 1881

8 UCA, F.H. Wallace Papers, 'Memoirs of the Manse, the Parsonage, and the College,' vol. 1, 155

9 S.P. Rose, 'The Bible and Newer Criticism,' *CMR* 8 (Sept. – Oct. 1895), 405

10 'Dr. Caven's Sermon,' *KCM* 17 (July 1893), 134

11 Carman Papers, box 23, file 3, 'All Scripture Is Given by Inspiration of God,' n.d.; box 24, file 39, 'Address on the Three Main Points of Attack at Present upon Our System of Christian doctrine,' n.d.

12 J.S. Moir, *A History of Biblical Studies in Canada: A Sense of Proportion* (Chico, California: Scholar's Press 1982), 1, 53

13 D. Ross, 'Christ the Great Miracle of Christianity,' in *Questions of the Day: Lectures Delivered in David Morrice Hall, Montreal, in 1883–84* (Montreal: William Drysdale & Co. 1885), 215–16. Ross was the professor of apologetics and New Testament criticism at Queen's University.

14 G.C. Workman, 'Messianic Prophecy,' *CMQ* 2 (Oct. 1890), 430–48, 471–4

15 E.H. Dewart, 'Does Materialism Satisfactorily Account for All Things?' *CMM* 24, no. 2 (Aug. 1886); 'Questionable Tendencies in Current Theological Thought,' in E.H. Dewart, *Essays for the Times: Studies of Eminent Men and Important Living Questions* (Toronto: William Briggs 1878), 71–86

16 E.H. Dewart, *Jesus the Messiah in Prophecy and Fulfillment: A Review and Refutation of the Negative Theory of Messianic Prophecy* (Toronto: William Briggs 1891), 18, 41, 232; 'A Brief Examination of Professor Workman's Teaching and Methods,' *CMQ* 3 (Jan. 1891)

17 Dewart, *Jesus the Messiah*, vii, 22

18 For Dewart's fullest discussion of the virtues and pitfalls of biblical criticism, see E.H. Dewart, *The Bible under Higher Criticism: A Review of Current Evolution Theories about the Old Testament* (Toronto: William Briggs 1900).

19 *ChG*, 22 May 1895

20 Dewart, *The Bible under Higher Criticism*, 37

21 *AV* 14 (Jan. 1892), 16–17

22 G.C. Workman, 'Religious Certainties; or, Things Which Are Not Shaken,' *CMR* 6 (July–Aug. 1894)

23 Wallace Papers, 'Memoirs of the Manse, the Parsonage, and the College,' vol. 1, 186–7; vol 2, 3, 9

24 A. Carman, 'The Church of God and the Education of the People,' *AV* 20 (Sept. 1896)

25 T. Sinclair-Faulkner, 'Theory Divided from Practice: The Introduction of Higher Criticism into Canadian Protestant Seminaries,' *Studies in Religion*, Summer 1981, 328–9; Moir, *A History of Biblical Studies in Canada*, 10–11

26 QUL, John Campbell, *The Perfect Book and the Perfect Father*, Queen's University Sunday Afternoon Addresses (Kingston 1893)

27 Ibid., 10–11

28 QUL, John Campbell, 'Protest against the Decision of the Presbytery of Montreal and Appeal to the Synod of Montreal and Ottawa' (1894), 3, 18–25

29 *PR*, 15 March 1894

30 QUL, G. Grant, *The Old Testament and the Newer Criticism*, Sunday Afternoon Addresses in Convocation Hall (Kingston 1892)

31 G. Grant, 'Does Historical Criticism Do Violence to Special Revelation?' *Queen's Quarterly* 1 (April 1894)

32 On the emergence of fundamentalism in Ontario society, see W. Westfall, *Two Worlds: The Protestant Culture of Nineteenth-Century Ontario* (Kingston and Montreal: McGill-Queen's University Press 1989), 159–85; and J.W. Grant, *A Profusion of Spires: Religion in Nineteenth-Century Ontario* (Toronto: University of Toronto Press 1988), 216–18. On the importance of the Prophetic Bible movement to the emergence of fundamentalism see Ernest R. Sandeen, *The Roots of Fundamentalism: British and American Millenarianism, 1800–1930* (Chicago: University of Chicago Press 1970), 132–61. On the intellectual and social roots of fundamentalism in American culture see George Marsden's indispensable *Fundamentalism and American Culture: The Shaping of Twentieth Century Evangelicalism, 1870–1925* (New York: Oxford University Press 1980).

33 The participants' contributions to the Bible Conferences can be found in *The Second Coming of Our Lord: Being Papers Read at a Conference Held at Niagara, Ont. July 14th to 17th, 1885* (Toronto: Willard Tract Depository 1885). The Denovan quote is on pages 123–4. For a contemporary assessment of Denovan's preaching style see the feature article on him in *SN*, 3 March 1888.

34 QUL, G. Grant, *How to Read the Bible, Nos. 1 and 2*, Queen's University Sunday Afternoon Addresses (Kingston 1891), 3, 10–11

35 W. Shaw, 'Inspiration of Bible Writers,' *CMQ*, April 1889, 127–8; W.D. Armstrong, 'The Christian Ministry and Modern Thought: Higher Criticism,' Address, Knox College Alumni Conference, Jan. 1896

36 Rose, 'The Bible and Newer Criticism,' 339–400

37 There was an extended debate in the columns of *AV* under the headline 'Is the Pulpit Losing Its Power?' 7 (Nov. 1883–Feb. 1884). A similar forum appeared in the *Queen's College Journal* 10 (April 1883). In the denominational press there was also extensive debate and commentary. In *PW*: 'The Ministry of the Age,' 15–22 Aug. 1885; 'The Christian Ministry in Relation to Politics and Public Questions,' 25 May 1889; 'The Work of the Ministry,' 6 Dec. 1890; and 'Public Worship,' 21 Dec. 1895–28 March 1896. In *ChG*: 'Preaching for the Times,' 27 Oct. 1886; 'To Ministers and People,' 17 Feb. 1892; and 'The Sermon Our Business,' 30 Dec. 1896–24 March 1897.

38 Quoted in Jones H. Farmer, ed., *E.W. Dadson, B.A., D.D.: The Man and His Message* (Toronto: William Briggs 1902), 144

39 J. Thompson, 'Doctrinal Preaching,' *KCM* 5 (March 1887)

40 *SN*, 17 March 1888 and 8 Dec. 1888. For an indication of Sheppard's iconoclastic views, see *SN*, 24 Dec. 1887 and 20 June 1891; and the opening chapters of his novel, *Widower Jones: A Faithful History of His 'Loss' and Adventures in Search of a 'Companion.' A Realistic Story of Rural Life* (Toronto: Sheppard Publishing Co. 1888).

41 For background on the Salvation Army in Canada see R.G. Moyles, *The Blood and Fire in Canada: A History of the Salvation Army in the Dominion, 1882–1976* (Toronto: Peter Martin Associates 1977); and the biography of the first editor of the Canadian *War Cry*, Blanche J. Read, *The Life of John Read* (Toronto: Salvation Army Publishing 1901), 31–6, 45–56, 100–2.

42 'Fidelis,' *Red Cross Knights of the Salvation Army* (Toronto: Williamson & Company 1884), 4–5, 25–7, 37–8. For a discussion of Machar's religious thought see Ruth Compton Brouwer, 'The "Between Age" Christianity of Agnes Machar,' *CHR* 65, no. 3 (Sept. 1984).

43 *ChG*, 1 Feb. 1882; 16 April 1884

44 For background on professional revivalism and these revivalists, see W.G. Mcloughlin, *Modern Revivalism: Charles Grandison Finney to Billy Graham* (New York: Ronald Press Co. 1959); and James F. Findlay, *Dwight L. Moody: American Evangelist, 1837–1899* (Chicago: University of Chicago Press 1969).

45 For an account of the crusade in England see John Kent, *Holding the Fort:*

Studies in Victorian Revivalism (London: Epworth Press 1978).

46 NAC, *A Plea for Systematic Evangelistic Work to the Moderator and Members of Assembly and to the Ministers, Office Bearers, and Members of the Canada Presbyterian Church by a Minister* (Montreal: John C. Becket 1874)

47 This account of Moody's contribution to the Christian Convention is drawn from reports in *the Toronto Mail*, 3–5 Dec. 1884.

48 See the accounts of the revival meetings in the *Toronto Evening News*, the *Toronto Mail*, and the *Toronto World*, 3–5 Dec. 1884, and the *Toronto Globe*, 4–6 Dec. 1884.

49 *ChG*, 10 Dec. 1884

50 Robert Boyd, *The Lives and Labors of Moody and Sankey Giving Concise Narrative of the Early Lives, Later Experiences, and Grand Achievements of the Most Successful Evangelists of Modern Times ... with an Introduction by Rev. John Potts* (Toronto: A.H. Hovey 1877), 4–5

51 *ChG*, 20 Oct. 1886

52 *Living Words; or, Sam Jones' Own Book Containing Sermons and Sayings Delivered in Toronto and Elsewhere, with Introduction by Rev. John Potts, D.D.* (Toronto: William Briggs 1886), ii

53 *Sam Jones and Sam Small in Toronto: A Compilation of the Best Sermons Preached by the Rev. Sam Jones and Sam Small at the Great Revival in Toronto* (Toronto: Rose Publishing Co. 1886), vi, 11–12

54 Sam Jones, 'Sermon II, Preached in Carlton Street Methodist Church, on Sabbath Morning, Dec. 12th, 1886,' in *'I'll Say Another Thing!' or, Semons and Lectures Delivered by Rev. Sam Jones during his Second Visit to Toronto, with an Introduction by Rev. E.A. Stafford, Pastor of Metropolitan Church, Toronto* (Toronto: William Briggs 1887)

55 *ChG*, 13 and 20 Oct. 1886

56 UCA, Crossley-Hunter Scrapbook, editorial from *AV*

57 H.T. Crossley, Preface, *Practical Talks on Important Themes to Young Converts, Older Christians and the Un-Converted* (Toronto: William Briggs 1895)

58 Crossley, 'Blundering Comparisons,' in *Practical Talks*, 255; 'The Unpardonable Sin,' in *Practical Talks*, 144

59 UCA, W.H. Hincks Papers, 'My First Eighty Years on Earth,' unpublished memoir, 1930

60 Crossley, 'How to Live a Christian,' in *Practical Talks*, 255; 'Blunders about Faith,' in *Practical Talk*, 246–50

61 Crossley, 'Doubt and Skepticism: Their Causes and Remedies,' in *Practical Talks*, 134–51.

62 According to Susan Tamke, hymns and gospel tunes overlap; but they

had distinct characteristics and uses. 'A true hymn is worship, a sacred song is not. The ultimate objective point contemplated in a hymn is God himself; in a sacred song it is the hearer. A hymn co-ordinates with prayer. A sacred song co-ordinates with exhortation' (Susan Tamke, *Make a Joyful Noise unto the Lord: Hymns as a Reflection of Victorian Social Attitudes* [Athens: Ohio University Press 1979], 36).

63 For analysis of the hymns in the Alline-inspired awakenings see George Rawlyk, ed., *New Light Letters and Spiritual Songs* (Hantsport: Lancelot Press 1983), 14–22, 67–75.

64 See R.P. Hopper, *Old-Time Primitive Methodism in Canada (1829–1884)* (Toronto: William Briggs 1904), 96–8, 206–7.

65 *Methodist Hymn and Tune Book* (Toronto: Methodist Book and Publishing House 1894), viii

66 Duncan Morrison, *The Great Hymns of the Church: Their Origin and Authorship* (Toronto: Hart & Co. 1890), 178, 244–7

67 *Sing Out the Glad News: A Collection of Sacred Songs Used in Evangelistic Work, by the Wright Brothers* (Toronto: William Briggs 1885); *Revival Hymns Selected and Arranged by Rev. J. McD. Kerr for Evangelistic Work* (Toronto: William Briggs 1889); *Gospel Tent Hymns Compiled by Rev. R.C. Horner* (Toronto: William Briggs 1889); John Sweeney et al., eds., *Melodies of Salvation: A Collection of Psalms, Hymns and Spiritual Songs* (Toronto: William Briggs 1900)

68 Sandra Sizer, *Gospel Hymns and Social Religion: The Rhetoric of Nineteenth Century Revivalism* (Philadelphia: Temple University Press 1978), 9

69 H.T. Crossley, *Songs of Salvation As Used by Crossley and Hunter in Evangelistic Meetings and Adapted for the Church, Grace, School, Choir, and Home* (Toronto: William Briggs 1887)

70 *Songs of Salvation*, especially song no. 52, 'Will You Be Saved To-night?' and song no. 83, 'Take Me As I Am.'

71 Ibid., song no. 201, 'I'm Going Home'; song no. 13, 'Hark! There Comes a Whisper'; song no. 105, 'Near the Cross'; song no. 6, 'Christ's Love for Me'; song no. 133, 'Here's a Saviour for the Lost Ones!'; and song no. 117, 'Song of Trust'

72 Crossley–Hunter Scrapbook, *Cobourg Star, London Free Press,* and *Ottawa Citizen,* n.d.

73 Ibid.

74 'Evangelistic Work,' *KCM* 17 (Oct. 1893)

75 Many of the documents surrounding this movement were reprinted in *Divine Worship in Connection with the Presbyterian Church in Canada* (Toronto: Westminster Co. 1900).

76 See the reports from the Kingston, Hamilton, and Winnipeg press in the Crossley-Hunter scrapbook. The statistics from other centres, such as Ottawa, Belleville, Cobourg, Stratford, London, and Port Arthur demonstrate a similar interdenominational appeal. How accurate these statistics are cannot be easily established for both the claims made by revivalists and church membership rolls are notoriously inaccurate.

77 Caven, 'Scriptural Preaching,' 5–7, 17

78 W. Cochrane, 'Sentimental Religion,' in *Warning and Welcome: Sermons Preached in Zion Presbyterian Church, Brantford, during 1876* (Toronto: Adam Stevenson & Co. 1877), 150

79 *SN*, 31 Dec. 1887

80 H.T. Crossley, *A Practical Discussion of the Parlour Dance, the Theatre, the Cards* (Toronto: William Briggs 1895)

81 *PR*, 22 April – 6 May 1886

82 For a discussion of secularization as a cultural phenomenon in which religious beliefs and worship become 'weightless' see T.J. Jackson Lears, *No Place of Grace: Antimodernism and the Transformation of American Culture, 1880–1920* (New York: Pantheon Books 1981), 41–7.

4 THE FALSE PROMISE OF MISSIONS

1 George Bryce, *John Black: The Apostle of the Red River; or, How the Blue Banner Was Unfurled on Manitoba Prairies* (Toronto: William Briggs 1898), v

2 J.W. Grant, *The Church in the Canadian Era* (Toronto: Ryerson 1972), 46–60; J.S. Moir, *Enduring Witness: A History of the Presbyterian Church in Canada* (Hamilton: The Presbyterian Church in Canada 1974), 146–69. For a more general account, see S. Neill, *A History of Christian Missions* (Harmondsworth: Penguin Books 1964), 13–25, 323.

3 *CMM*, July 1880, 92

4 George Patterson, *Missionary Life among the Cannibals: Being the Life of the Rev. John Geddie, D.D.* (Toronto: James Campbell 1882), 41–2

5 James Croil, *The Missionary Problem: Containing a History of Protestant Missions in Some of the Principal Fields of Missionary Enterprise* (Toronto: William Briggs 1883), 13. The same range of attitudes can be found in George Patterson's account of the religions of the world in *The Heathen World; Its Need of the Gospel, and the Church's Obligation to Supply It* (Toronto: William Briggs 1884), passim.

6 John Mockett Cramp to the Rev. R. Sanford, 15 Nov. 1875, quoted in T.A. Higgins, *The Life of John Mockett Cramp* (Montreal: W. Drysdale & Co. 1887), 305–6

7 Of the vast literature in this vein, see, for example, Patterson, *Missionary Life among the Cannibals;* and George Leslie Mackay, *From Far Formosa: The Island, Its People, and Missions* (Toronto: Fleming H. Revell 1896).

8 Patterson, *Missionary Life among the Cannibals,* passim

9 Recent studies have outlined this important transformation in considerable detail. See Alvyn Austin, *Saving China: Canadian Missionaries in the Middle Kingdom, 1888–1959* (Toronto: University of Toronto Press 1986); Ruth Compton Brouwer, *New Women for God: Canadian Presbyterian Women and India Missions, 1876–1914* (Toronto: University of Toronto Press 1990), especially chapters 4 and 6; and A. Hamish Ion, *The Cross and the Rising Sun: The Canadian Protestant Missionary Movement in the Japanese Empire, 1872–1931* (Waterloo, Ont.: Wilfrid Laurier University Press 1990), 4–7, 116–25. For a fascinating contemporary description of this social service missionary work see Mackay, *From Far Formosa.*

10 Brouwer, *New Women for God,* 170

11 NAC, George Grant, 'Our Five Foreign Missions' (1888), 35

12 This point is made by William R. Hutchison, *Errand to the World: American Protestant Thought and Foreign Missions* (Chicago: University of Chicago Press 1987), 91–2.

13 See, for example, *Report of the Carey Centennial Meetings Held in Jarvis Street Baptist Church* (Feb. 1892), 68.

14 George Grant, *The Religions of the World* (London: A. & C. Black 1895), 2

15 Ibid., 77, 120–1

16 Ibid., 28–35, 45

17 Ibid., 5

18 See Katherine Ridout, 'A Woman of Mission: The Religious and Cultural Odyssey of Agnes Wintemute Coates,' *CHR* 71, no. 2 (June 1990) for a superb study of one Canadian missionary who followed this path. See also Ion, *The Cross and the Rising Sun,* 149.

19 Quoted in Charles M. Johnston, *McMaster University, Volume 1: The Toronto Years* (Toronto: University of Toronto Press 1976), 98. This paragraph draws largely from Johnston's fine account.

20 Grant, 'Our Five Foreign Missions,' 35

21 See Austin, *Saving China,* 64–80, for an account of the Boxer Rebellions and their impact on missions.

22 This account is drawn from James A. Slimmon, *The Revival in Honan* (Toronto: College Press 1909); and A.D. Macleod, 'Goforth of China, (1859–1936),' in W.S. Reid, ed., *Called to Witness: Profiles of Canadian Presbyterians* (Hamilton: Committee on History, Presbyterian Church in Canada 1980), 2:81

23 John McDougall, *George Millward McDougall: The Pioneer, Patriot, and*

Missionary (Toronto: William Briggs 1888), 31

24 Doug Owram, *Promise of Eden: The Canadian Expansionist Movement and the Idea of the West, 1856–1900* (Toronto: University of Toronto Press 1979), 214–19

25 UCA, Alexander Sutherland Papers, Sermons 1883–1910, file 12, 'John 1:29,' n.d.; file 13, 'John 5:40,' n.d.; file 13, '1 Cor. 15:6–7, n.d.; file 14, '2 Cor. 4:3–4,' n.d.

26 A. Sutherland, *The Final Outcome of Sin: A Homiletic Monograph* (Toronto: Methodist Book and Publishing House 1886)

27 Sutherland Papers, Sermons, 1883–1910, '2 Cor. 4:3–4'; 'Psalm 119.' See also A. Sutherland, *The Moral Status of Children and Their Relation to Christ and His Church* (Toronto 1876); and A. Sutherland, 'The Attractive Power of the Cross: A Sermon Preached at Chatauqua, July 30, 1882,' *CMM* 16 (Nov. 1882).

28 Sutherland, *The Moral Status of Children and Their Relation to Christ and His Church*, 12–13, 21, 26–8; Neil Semple, 'The Nurture and Admonition of the Lord: Nineteenth Century Canadian Methodism's Response to Childhood,' *Histoire Sociale* 14, no. 27 (May 1981)

29 *Earnest Christianity*, Jan. 1873; Dec. 1873; Jan. 1874

30 On Sutherland's thoughts about *Earnest Christianity* during the final months of publication, see Sutherland Papers, Private Letterbooks, 3 vols., Sutherland to W.H. Withrow, 27 Jan. – 9 Feb. 1876, 12 April 1876.

31 Alexander Sutherland, *A Summer in Prairie Land: Notes of a Tour through the North-West Territory* (Toronto 1881), preface, 70–7, 85–95, 102–3, 122

32 Ibid., 143–4, 150, 170, 194

33 Quoted in J.H. Riddell, *Methodism in the Middle West* (Toronto: Ryerson 1946), 116. A similar sense of optimism and urgency accompanied the Baptist missionary work in the Canadian Northwest. See C.C. McLaurin, *Pioneering in Western Canada: A Story of the Baptists* (Calgary 1939), 50–76; Donald Goertz, 'Alexander Grant: Pastor, Evangelist, Visionary,' in J. Zeman, ed., *Costly Vision: The Baptist Pilgrimage in Canada* (Burlington: Welch 1988).

34 On the challenge of converting the native peoples, see J.W. Grant, *Moon of Wintertime: Missionaries and the Indians of Canada in Encounter since 1534* (Toronto: University of Toronto Press 1984). For an analysis of the attitudes of some of the leading missionaries to Canada's prairie Indians, see Sarah Carter, 'The Missionaries' Indian: The Publications of John McDougall, John McDougall, John Maclean and Egerton Ryerson Young,' *Prairie Forum* 9, no. 1 (1984).

35 Grant, *Moon of Wintertime*, 162

36 Quoted in C.W. Gordon, *The Life of James Robertson: Missionary Superintendent in Western Canada* (Toronto: Westminster Co. 1908), 41–2

37 UCA, A.B. Baird Papers [originals held in the Conference of Manitoba and Northwest Ontario Archives of the United Church of Canada], James Ballantyne to A.B. Baird, 30 Dec. 1880, 7 June 1881, 22 June 1883

38 Sermon by the Rev. James Robertson, preached at Zion Church, Brantford, 15 Jan. 1871, in William Cochrane, ed., *A Quiet and Gentle Life. In Memoriam: Mary Neilson Houstoun Cochrane* (Brantford: Hudson & Sutherland 1871)

39 UCA, James Robertson Papers [originals held in the Conference of Manitoba and Northwest Ontario Archives of the United Church of Canada], Robertson to his wife, 20 Feb. 1874 and 16 March 1874

40 Robertson Papers, Robertson to his wife, 19 June 1874

41 Gordon, *Life of James Robertson*, 128

42 Robertson Papers, Robertson to his wife, 13 April, 15 May, and 16 June 1874

43 Gordon, *Life of James Robertson*, 220

44 Robertson Papers, Robertson to his wife, 11 Nov. 1885

45 James Robertson, 'Report to Board of Home Missions,' *Acts and Proceedings of the Thirteenth General Assembly of the Presbyterian Church in Canada* (1887)

46 Gordon, *Life of James Robertson*, 264–85

47 Robertson Papers, 'On the Topic of Sermons,' Winnipeg, n.d.; 'The Blessedness of Christ,' Address to the St Andrew's Society of Winnipeg, 1874; 'Christ's Presence in Our Business,' 2 Jan. 1876

48 Robertson Papers, Sermons, 'The True and Only Way of Salvation from Sin Is Christ,' n.d.

49 Robertson Papers, Robertson to his wife, 6 May 1885

50 C.W. Gordon, 'Jottings from a Missionary's Diary,' *KCM*, Nov. 1885; 'Mission Work in South Manitoba,' *KCM*, Feb. 1886

51 A.C. Cheyne, *The Transformation of the Kirk: Victorian Scotland's Religious Revolution* (Edinburgh: Saint Andrew Press 1983), 56, 174

52 UM, Charles W. Gordon Papers, box 1, folder 3, 'Reminiscences of Rev. C.W. Gordon, B.A., by a Young Missionary'; box 29, folder 15, 'Henry Drummond'

53 C.W. Gordon, *Postscript to Adventure: The Autobiography of 'Ralph Connor'* (Toronto: McClelland and Stewart 1975), 83–90. For an assessment of Drummond and his mission-revival campaigns see George Adam Smith,

The Life of Henry Drummond (London: Hodder and Stoughton 1899).

54 Gordon, *Postscript to Adventure*, 128

55 For Gordon's estimation of Moody's central importance see Gordon Papers, box 29, folder 15, 'D.L. Moody.'

56 Gordon, *Life of James Robertson*, 279–83

57 Ibid., 270

58 Quoted in E.A. Corbett, *McQueen of Edmonton* (Toronto: Ryerson 1934), 27–34, 50. See also McQueen's correspondence to the Rev. A.B. Baird of Manitoba College, Baird Papers, 7 Sept. 1887, 21 Feb. 1888, and 28 Nov. 1888.

59 Baird Papers, Alex Taylor to Baird, 5 March 1890

60 Gordon Papers, box 8, folder 3, Reports from Mission Fields to C.W. Gordon, Secretary, North-West Missions, Presbyterian Church of Canada, 1897

61 Gordon, *Postscript to Adventure*, 148

62 Gordon Papers, box 32, folder 10, James Macdonald to C.W. Gordon, 9 Feb. 1897

63 McDougall, *George Millward McDougall*, 101, 119

64 Ralph Connor, *The Sky Pilot: A Tale of the Foothills* (Toronto: Westminster Co. 1899), 75

65 Ralph Connor, *Black Rock: A Tale of the Selkirks* (Toronto: Westminster Co. 1898), 16–17, 144–5

66 *The Sky Pilot*, 55

67 *Black Rock*, 279–307

68 UCA, Robert Milliken, 'Jottings from a Methodist Itinerant's Notebook,' n.d.

69 Gordon Papers, box 48, folder 1, unsigned letter to C.W. Gordon, Montreal, 6 June 1899

70 Ralph Connor, *The Prospector: A Tale of the Crow's Nest Pass* (New York: Fleming H. Revell 1904), 278–84, 353–5

71 A. Sutherland, *Methodism in Canada: Its Work and Its Story* (Toronto: Methodist Mission Rooms 1904), 2, 25–6

72 A. Sutherland, *The Methodist Church and Missions in Canada and Newfoundland: A Brief Account of the Methodist Church* (Toronto: Department of Missionary Literature of the Methodist Church, Canada 1906), 234–6, 250–6

73 This applied to all missions. J.W. Grant has shown that missionaries to Canadian native peoples were becoming disillusioned. 'Year after year there were complaints of reversion to traditional practice and of hostility to the missionaries' (*Moon of Wintertime*, 191).

5 STEMMING THE TIDE OF SECULARIZATION, 1890–1914

1 For a study of the vast range of leisure activities Canadians participated
  in see Donald G. Wetherell and Irene Kmet, *Useful Pleasures: The Shaping
  of Leisure in Alberta, 1876–1945* (Regina: Canadian Plains Research Centre
  1990).
2 The question of how far down the social scale this increased wealth
  spread is difficult to resolve. The evidence does not allow for any firm
  conclusions. See David Gagan and Rosemary Gagan, 'Working-Class
  Standards of Living in Late-Victorian Urban Ontario: A Review of the
  Miscellaneous Evidence on the Quality of Material Life,' *Journal of the
  Canadian Historical Association* 1 (1990), 171–93. To suggest that certain
  sectors of Canadian society enjoyed greater disposable income does not
  mean that other sectors did not remain caught in the grinding trap of
  unemployment, ill-health, and poverty. See Terry Cop, *The Anatomy of
  Poverty: The Condition of the Working Class in Montreal, 1897–1929*
  (Toronto: McClelland and Stewart 1974); Michael Piva, *The Condition of
  the Working Class in Toronto, 1900–1921* (Ottawa: University of Ottawa
  Press 1979); and Alan Artibise, *Winnipeg: A Social History of Urban
  Growth, 1874–1914* (Montreal: McGill-Queen's University Press 1975).
3 Joy Santink, *Timothy Eaton and the Rise of His Department Store* (Toronto:
  University of Toronto Press 1990), passim
4 Emile Zola quoted in Michael Miller, *The Bon Marche: Bourgeois Culture
  and the Department Store, 1869–1920* (Princeton: Princeton University
  Press 1981), 177
5 This definition of the consumer ethos is drawn from Richard Wightman
  and T.J. Jackson Lears, eds., *The Culture of Consumption: Critical Essays in
  American History, 1880–1980* (New York: Pantheon Books 1983), xii. These
  authors regard the emergence of consumerism in America as something
  that is antithetical to the religious or spiritual past. Recognizing the
  immense complexity of this cultural transformation, they do not identify
  a period when there was a radical break from the past or a sudden
  emergence of consumerism. This transformation was deeply rooted in
  the nineteenth century and has extended well into the twentieth century.
6 AO, William Cochrane, Diary, Dec. 1892
7 *CMM*, Dec. 1894, 608–9
8 For a superb analysis of Ontario church architecture and how it gave 'the
  sacred a distinctive place in the secular world,' see William Westfall, *Two
  Worlds: The Protestant Culture of Nineteenth-Century Ontario* (Kingston and
  Montreal: McGill-Queen's University Press 1989), 126–58.

9 'Pew and Pulpit I,' *Week* 12, no. 13 (22 Feb. 1895)

10 'At the Metropolitan,' *SN* 1, no. 2 (10 Dec. 1887)

11 Harriet Youmans, *Grimsby Park: Historical and Descriptive with Biographical Accounts* (Toronto: William Briggs 1900), 8, 19–29, 59–65. Another description of the old camp meeting written in a nostalgic tone was A. Sutherland's in *The Methodist Church and Missions in Canada and Newfoundland* (Toronto: Department of Missionary Literature, Methodist Church of Canada 1906), 107–19.

12 'Grimsby Park – Past and Present,' *CMM*, June 1886, 510–11

13 William Cochrane, 'Christian Manliness,' in *The Church and the Commonwealth Discussions and Orations on Questions of the Day, Practical, Biographical, Educational and Doctrinal* (Brantford: Bradley, Garetson & Co. 1887), 251–64. On the intellectual foundations of muscular Christianity see Norman Vance, *The Sinews of the Spirit: The Ideal of Christian Manliness in Victorian Literature and Religious Thought* (Cambridge: Cambridge University Press 1985).

14 On the relation between muscular Christianity and sports in Canada see M. Mott, 'The British Protestant Pioneers and the Establishment of Manly Sports in Manitoba, 1878–1886,' *Canadian Journal of Sport History* 7, no. 3 (Winter 1980); and David Howell and Peter Lindsay, 'Social Gospel and the Young Boy Problem, 1895–1925,' *Canadian Journal of Sport History* 17, no. 1 (May 1986).

15 W. Cochrane, 'Popular Amusements,' in *The Church and the Commonwealth*, 61–9

16 UM, C.W. Gordon papers, box 31, folder 13, Gordon to George H. Doran, 5 May 1913

17 G.H. Cornish, 'Statistical Record of the Progress of Methodism in Canada,' in *Centennial of Canadian Methodism* (Toronto: William Briggs 1891), 331–9; W. Gregg, *Short History of the Presbyterian Church in the Dominion of Canada from the Earliest to the Present Times* (Toronto: Presbyterian Printing 1893), 574ff

18 The provincial legislation is reprinted in *LDA*, July 1906

19 John Bossy, *Christianity and the West* (Oxford: Oxford University Press 1985), 131

20 UCA, Albert Carman Papers, box 24, file 124, 'Sabbath Observance Convention,' n.d.

21 D.J. Macdonnell, 'The Sabbath Day,' *PR*, 13 July 1893

22 'Report of the Committee on the State of Religion,' *Acts and Proceedings of the Eighteenth General Assembly of the Presbyterian Church in Canada* (1892)

23 For a discussion of relationship between the rise of organized sports and

urban industrial society in Canada see Alan Metcalfe, *Canada Learns to Play: The Emergence of Organized Sport, 1807–1914* (Toronto: McClelland and Stewart 1987).

24 'Forms of Sabbath Desecration Prevalent,' *PR*, 15–27 Nov. 1894

25 'The Spirit of the Age,' *KCM* 17, (June 1893)

26 James George, *The Sabbath School of the Fireside* (Kingston: John Creighton 1859), passim

27 'Report of the Committee on Church Life and Work,' *Acts and Proceedings of the Twenty-Second General Assembly of the Presbyterian Church in Canada* (1896); J. Thompson, 'The Home: Woman's Work in the Church,' *KCM* 16, no. 5 (Sept. 1892)

28 Colleen McDannell, *The Christian Home in America, 1840–1900* (Bloomington: Indiana University Press 1986)

29 *Acts and Proceedings of the Fourteenth General Assembly of the Presbyterian Church in Canada* (1888), Appendix no. 14

30 University of Toronto, Thomas Fisher Rare Book Room, Lord's Day Alliance of Canada Papers, Letterbook, J.G. Shearer to A. Scott, 27 June 1900

31 See C. Armstrong and H.V. Nelles, *The Revenge of the Methodist Bicycle Company: Sunday Streetcars and Municipal Reform in Toronto, 1888–1897* (Toronto: Peter Martin Associates 1977) for an account of the defeat of the Sabbatarian forces on the Sunday car question in the city of Toronto.

32 *LDA*, Sept. 1902; Nov. 1903; July 1904

33 For a broader context, see M. Bliss, 'The Protective Impulse: An Approach to the Social History of Oliver Mowat's Ontario,' in D. Swainson, ed., *Oliver Mowat's Ontario* (Toronto: Macmillan 1972).

34 *LDA*, April 1904

35 See *LDA*, March–April 1905 and Dec. 1905 for accounts of the lobbying efforts. The best analysis of the Lord's Day Alliance as a lobby group is S.P. Meen, 'The Battle for the Sabbath: The Sabbatarian Lobby in Canada, 1890–1912' (PHD diss., University of British Columbia, 1979).

36 The final draft of the legislation was reprinted in *LDA*. Feb. 1907. The various points of view regarding the legislation are presented in a documentary collection of the House of Commons debate. See G.N. Emery, 'The Lord's Day Act of 1906 and the Sabbath Observance Question,' in J.M. Bumsted, ed., *Documentary Problems in Canadian History, Vol. 11: Post-Confederation* (Toronto: Holt Rinehart 1969), 23–51.

37 A.M.C. Waterman, 'The Lord's Day in a Secular Society: A Historical Comment on the Canadian Lord's Day Act of 1906,' *Canadian Journal of Theology* 11 vol. XI (1965)

38 Clarence Mackinnon, *Reminiscences* (Toronto: Ryerson 1938), 76–7, 172–3

39 T.J. Jackson Lears, 'From Salvation to Self-Realization: Advertising and the Therapeutic Roots of the Consumer Culture, 1880–1930,' in Wightman and Jackson Lears, eds., *The Culture of Consumption*, 18; Paul Rutherford, *A Victorian Authority: The Daily Press in Late Nineteenth-Century Canada* (Toronto: University of Toronto Press 1982), 118–25, 149–55

40 Gordon Papers, box 1, folder 3, 'Reminiscences of C.W. Gordon' (n.d.), 27

41 C.W. Gordon, *Postscript to Adventure: The Autobiography of Ralph Connor* (Toronto: McClelland and Stewart 1975), 148–50

42 H.T. Crossley, 'Questions about Reading,' in *Practical Talks on Important Themes to Young Converts, Older Christians, and the Unconverted* (Toronto: William Briggs 1895), 86. For an account of the novel's struggle for approval in respectable circles see Carole Gerson, *A Purer Taste: The Writing and Reading of Fiction in English in Nineteenth-Century Canada* (Toronto: University of Toronto Press 1989), 17–35.

43 UCA, Alexander Sutherland Papers, box 10, file 189, Rev. P.M. Moyer to A. Sutherland, 5 July 1907; box 10, file 190, Rev. R. Keefer to A. Sutherland, 14 Oct. 1907; box 10, file 192, W.D. Harrison to A. Sutherland, 12 June 1908

44 F.W. Watt, 'Western Myth: The World of Ralph Connor,' *Canadian Literature* 1, no. 1 1959), 33–5

45 David S. Reynolds, *Faith in Fiction: The Emergence of Religious Literature in America* (Cambridge: Harvard University Press 1981). There were many Canadian examples in this genre, but only those advocating social Christianity have come under close scrutiny. See Mary Vipond, '"Blessed Are the Peacemakers": The Labour Question in Canadian Social Gospel Fiction,' *Journal of Canadian Studies* 3, no. 3 (Aug. 1975).

46 John Carroll, *The School Prophets; or, Father McRorey's Class, and Squire Firstman's Kitchen Fire: A Fiction Founded on Facts* (Toronto: William Briggs 1876), ix

47 W.H. Withrow, Preface, *The King's Messenger: or, Lawrence Temple's Probation: A Story of Canadian Life* (Toronto: Samuel Rose, Methodist Book Room 1879). Withrow's other religious novels were collections of his sketches from the *Canadian Methodist Magazine: Neville Trueman, the Pioneer Preacher: A Tale of the War of 1812* (Toronto: William Briggs, Methodist Book Room 1880); and *Life in a Parsonage; or, Lights and Shadows of the Itinerancy* (Toronto: William Briggs 1886).

48 Edward McCourt, *The Canadian West in Fiction* (Toronto: Ryerson 1949), 29

49 Gordon Papers, box 48, folder 1, Mary Alice Denny to Charles W. Gordon, 30 Nov. 1900

50 R. Connor, *The Dawn by Galilee* (Toronto: Westminster Press 1910), n.p.

51 Gordon, *Postscript to Adventure*, 150

52 Ibid., 148, 151–2. For examples of the letters Gordon referred to, see Gordon Papers, box 48, folder 1, Florence Sherwood Bliss to Charles W. Gordon, 28 Dec. 1901; and folder 2, Emma Boweres to Ralph Connor, 5 Jan. 1902.

53 Connor, *The Dawn by Galilee*, n.p.

54 Gordon Papers, box 48, folder 5, A.W. Monash to Dr Gordon, 11 March 1912

55 J. Paterson Smyth, 'Novel Reading and Religion,' *Canadian Magazine* 33 (May–Oct. 1909)

56 McCourt, *The Canadian West in Fiction*, 19

57 Ralph Connor, *The Foreigner: A Tale of the Saskatchewan* (New York: Fleming H. Revell 1909), 253–5

58 This point is made by Peter Williams, *Popular Religion in America: Symbolic Change and the Modernization Process in Historical Perspective* (Englewood Cliffs: Prentice Hall 1980), 198–9

59 'Is Methodism Declining?' *ChG*, 19 Oct. 1898

60 'Is Methodism Declining in Canada? – A Review of Mr. Robertson's Letter,' *ChG*, 26 Oct. 1898. See also Burwash's celebration of the growth of Methodist institutions (UCA, Nathanael Burwash Papers, box 14, file 382, 'Address on the Development of Methodist Theology and Missions' [1899]). Superintendent Carman disputed Burwash's analysis. See Carman Papers, box 24, file 14, 'Address on the Statistical Growth of Methodism' (1900).

61 Material on Chown's background and early life is from UCA, S.D. Chown Papers, 'Story of My Life,' 1–39. The character of his early preaching can be gleaned from Chown Papers, file 3a, 'Address for Sons of Temperance Prohibition Camp,' Hamilton, 17 Aug. 1892; and file 56, 'Missionary Address,' Jan. 1887.

62 Chown Papers, file 58, 'Ministerial Aims,' Methodist Preachers Meeting, Montreal Conference, Feb. 1887.

63 Chown Papers, file 15a, 'Spiritual Conference – Toronto West District,' 25 Oct. 1898

64 J. Henderson, 'Christian Socialism,' reprinted in Salem Bland, *The Life of James Henderson* (Toronto: McClelland and Stewart 1926), 324–32

65 Chown Papers, file 70, 'Bear Ye One Another's Burdens and So Fulfill the Law of Christ,' n.d.

66 A. Sutherland, *The Kingdom of God and the Problems of Today* (Toronto: William Briggs 1898), 37–8, 50–4, 93–4, 161–8

67 Chown Papers, file 47, 'And the Very God of Peace Shall Sanctify You Wholly,' n.d.

68 Attracting candidates for the ministry was becoming a major problem for the Methodist church. See *ChG*, 18 April 1906; 31 July 1907; 26 May 1909; 13 April 1910; 6 July 1910; 21 Sept. 1910; 8 May 1912; 17 Sept. 1913; 11 March 1914

69 Chown Papers, file 50b, Sociological Course, Lecture 1, 'Importance of the Study of Sociology'

70 Chown Papers, file 34a, 'The Adaptation of the Church to the Needs of Modern Life,' Toronto, 10 Oct. 1911

71 Chown Papers, file 76, 'Ordination Sermon, Bay of Quinte Conference,' Peterborough, 5 June 1904

72 Chown Papers, file 110, 'Jeremiah 20:9,' 10 May 1913

73 Brian Fraser, *The Social Uplifters: Presbyterian Progressives and the Social Gospel in Canada, 1875–1915* (Waterloo, Ont.: Canadian Corporation for Studies in Religion 1988), xiii

74 UCA, George Campbell Pidgeon Papers, vol. 32, file 517, 'Experimental Religion,' frequently preached between 1897 and 1909. See also file 518, 'Building the Holy City,' 20 March 1898; file 522, 'The New Birth,' 5 Jan. 1902; and file 525, 'Spiritual Insight,' 26 Oct. 1902. For Pidgeon's background and pre-war ministry see J.W. Grant, *George Pidgeon* (Toronto: Ryerson 1962).

75 N.K. Clifford, 'His Dominion: A Vision in Crisis,' *Studies in Religion* 2, no. 4 (1973); John Thomas, 'Servants of the Church: Canadian Methodist Deaconess Work, 1890–1926,' *CHR* 65, no. 3 (Sept. 1984); Fraser, *The Social Uplifters*, 90–5, 127–48

76 UCA, *Report on a Rural Survey of the Agricultural, Educational, Social, and Religious Life of Turtle Mountain, Manitoba*, 5–7

77 UCA, *Report on a Limited Survey of Educational, Social, and Industrial Life of the City of London*, 36–50

78 Chown Paper, file 57b, 'The Present Need,' Jan. 1912; file 28b, 'Conference Address,' Winnipeg, 21 May 1912

79 *PW*, 10 Sept. 1910; 10 Dec. 1910; 13 Jan. 1912; 17 Feb. 1912; 14 June 1913; 28 June 1913; 7 March 1914; 28 March 1914

80 UCA, Alfred Gandier Papers, Gandier to his wife, 29 Nov. 1911

81 Pidgeon Papers, file 554, 'The Spirit Filled Life,' first preached 22 Feb. 1914

82 S.E.D. Shortt, *The Search for an Ideal: Six Canadian Intellectuals and Their*

Convictions in an Age of Transition, 1890–1930 (Toronto: University of Toronto Press 1976). See also the articles by Andrew Macphail on religion and the modern church in the *University Magazine* during this period. For a pioneer analysis of the questioning of liberalism in pre-war American society see Henry F. May, *The End of American Innocence: A Study of the First Years of Our Own Time, 1912–1917* (New York: A.A. Knopf 1959).

83 Similar forces – especially the problem of overlapping pastorates and the pressing need for funds to cover the growing expenses of the foreign mission fields, the struggling congregations in the West, and the training of ministers in the colleges – were driving the Regular and Free Will Baptists into union during this period. See George Levy, *The Baptists of the Maritime Provinces, 1753–1946* (Toronto: University of Toronto Press 1946), 267–91; and F.H. Sinnott, 'The Union of the Regular and Free Will Baptists of the Maritimes, 1905 and 1906' in Barry Moody, ed., *Repent and Believe: The Baptist Experience in Maritime Canada* (Hantsport, NS: Lancelot Press 1980), 138–45.

84 For discussions of these aspects of the church union movement see B. Kiesekamp, 'Presbyterian and Methodist Divines: The Case for a National Church in Canada, 1875–1900,' *Studies in Religion* 2, no. 4 (1973); Clifford, 'His Dominion: A Vision in Crisis,' *Studies in Religion* 2, no. 4 (1973); R. Allen, *The Social Passion: Religion and Social Reform in Canada, 1914–28* (Toronto: University of Toronto Press 1973), 250–63; and Mary Vipond, 'Canadian National Consciousness and the Formation of the United Church of Canada,' *Bulletin*, no. 24 (1975). For a historiographical survey see N.K. Clifford, 'The Interpreters of the United Church of Canada,' *Church History* 46 (June 1977).

85 M. Van Die, *An Evangelical Mind: Nathanael Burwash and the Methodist Tradition in Canada, 1839–1918* (Kingston and Montreal: McGill-Queen's University Press 1989), 147–64

86 The Jackson heresy trial, in which Albert Carman led the conservative forces in the Methodist church against modernist teaching, gets full treatment in Margaret Prang, *Newton Wesley Rowell: Ontario Nationalist* (Toronto: University of Toronto Press 1975), 70–87. The dispute about the Rev. I.G. Matthew's teaching at McMaster within the Baptist Convention of Ontario and Quebec is dealt with by Charles Johnston, *McMaster University, Vol. 1: The Toronto Years* (Toronto: University of Toronto Press 1976), 90–113. The nature of Presbyterian non-concurrence is analysed in N.K. Clifford, *The Resistance to Church Union in Canada, 1904–1939* (Vancouver: University of British Columbia Press 1985).

6 BATTLING WITH THE GREAT WAR

1 *ChG*, 28 April 1918
2 UCA, ANB, file 65, 'A Message from the Chaplains of the Overseas Military Forces of Canada to the Churches at Home'; A.M. Gordon, 'A Chaplain at the Front,' *Queen's Quarterly* 17 (Oct. 1919)
3 *ChG*, 16 Sept. 1914
4 *PW*, 17 Oct., 1914
5 'Mobilizing for Active Service – the Soldier's Oath,' *CB*, 24 Sept. 1914; 'To–day, and To–morrow, and the day Following,' *CB*, 1 Oct. 1914
6 This has been demonstrated in the recent university histories. See H. Neatby, *Queen's University, Vol. 1, 1841–1917: 'to strive, to seek, to find, and not to yield'* (Montreal: McGill-Queen's University Press 1978), 291–304; S.B. Frost, *McGill University: For the Advancement of Learning, Vol. II, 1895–1971* (Kingston and Montreal: McGill Queen's University Press 1984), 95–110; C.M. Johnston, *McMaster University, Vol. 1: The Toronto Years* (Toronto: University of Toronto Press 1976), 128–49; M. Hayden *Seeking a Balance: University of Saskatchewan, 1907–1982* (Vancouver: University of British Columbia Press 1983), 78–83; and J.G. Reid, *Mount Allison University, Vol. II: 1914–1963* (Toronto: University of Toronto Press 1984), 3–24.
7 UCA, Alfred Livingston Taylor Papers, Diary, 12 Nov. 1914
8 ANB, file 346, F.G. Brown, 'War Service Record'
9 UCA, E.H. Oliver Papers [originals held in University of Saskatchewan Archives], file 6, Western Universities Battalion, 21 Oct. 1916
10 UCA, S.D. Chown Papers, file 486, 'War Sermon,' 1915
11 J.M. Bliss, 'The Methodist Church and World War I,' *CHR* 44 (Sept. 1968), 213–33; UCA, George Campbell Pidgeon Papers, file 627, 'The Neutral,' 3 June 1917; W.T. Herridge, 'Render unto Caesar's the Things That Are Caesar's and to God the Things That Are God', *PW*, 5 June 1915
12 See Thomas P. Socknat, *Witness against War: Pacifism in Canada, 1900–1945* (Toronto: University of Toronto Press 1987), 11–60, for a full discussion of pre-war anti-militarism and the collapse of this concern in the early stages of the war.
13 *PW*, 17 Oct. 1914
14 Chown Papers, file 101a, 'The Vitality of Religion,' Official Sermon Preached before the General Conference, Ottawa, 28 Sept. 1914
15 *ChG*, 4 Oct. 1916
16 'The Mission of the Church to the Returning Soldiers,' *CB*, 14 June 1917
17 *ChG*, 2 Aug. 1916

18 'The Church, the War, and Patriotism,' *Journal of Proceedings, Tenth General Conference of the Methodist Church of Canada*, Hamilton, 1916

19 UCA, J.W. Falconer, *Religion and the War* (Toronto: Presbyterian Church in Canada 1917), 3

20 UCA, T.B. Kilpatrick, *The War and the Christian Church* (Toronto: Presbyterian Church in Canada 1917), 5

21 For Falconer's thought and activities during World War I, see Greenlee's fascinating chapter in *Sir Robert Falconer: A Biography* (Toronto: University of Toronto Press 1988), 198–241. For background on Kilpatrick and discussion of how the war challenged the assumptions of progressive Presbyterians see Brain Fraser, *The Social Uplifters: Presbyterian Progressives and the Social Gospel in Canada, 1875–1915* (Waterloo, Ont.: Wilfrid Laurier University Press 1988), 155–69.

22 UCA, J.M. Shaw *The War and Divine Providence* (Toronto: Presbyterian Church in Canada 1917), 8

23 Pidgeon Papers, file 583, 'Our Dominion – God's Dominion,' 2 July 1916; file 604, 'I Carry On,' 31 Dec. 1916; file 613, 'Life's Nobler Penalties,' 4 March 1917

24 'The Sacrificial Life in the Light of the Present World Crisis,' *CB*, 9 Nov. 1914; 'Sacrifice in the Life of the Individual and the Community,' *CB*, 7 Dec. 1916

25 ANB, file 16, Captain A.D. Robb to the Rev. T.A. Moore, 25 June 1918

26 E.H. Oliver Papers, file 4, manuscript account of the 196th Western Universities Battalion, n.d.

27 ANB, H.E. Thomas to the Rev. T.A. Moore, 5 Jan. 1916

28 NAC, RG 9, III c15, Chaplaincy Service Papers, vol. 4663, file 'Questionnaire,' Captain J. McCaskill to director of Chaplain Services, 28 Sept. 1918

29 ANB, file 82, E.E. Graham to the Rev. T.A. Moore, 3 Jan. 1918. Graham was referring to what had been reprinted in *First Annual Report of the Army and Navy Board* (Toronto: Methodist Church of Canada 1917).

30 For a detailed discussion of the VD issue and its impact on the social mores of Canadian society see Jay Cassel, *The Secret Plague: Venereal Disease in Canada, 1838–1939* (Toronto: University of Toronto Press 1987), 122–75. For an indication of the Baptists' concern about the moral fibre of the soldiers, see the reports from the Rev. O.C.S. Wallace's overseas tour of the CEF camps in *CB*, 26 Sept.–24 Oct. 1918.

31 ANB, file 165, A.D. Robb to the Rev. T.A. Moore, 20 Nov. 1917

32 Chaplaincy Service Papers, vol. 4625, file C–C–11, T.C. Colwell to Lt Col Woods, 'Report on the Work in Ypres Battle,' 7 Nov. 1917

33 ANB, H.E. Thomas to the Rev. T.A. Moore, 5 Jan. 1916

34 C.W. Bishop, *The Canadian YMCA and the Great War: The Official Record of the Activities of the Canadian YMCA* (Toronto: National Council, Young Men's Christian Association of Canada 1924)

35 ANB, file 235, G.O. Fallis to the Rev. T.A. Moore, 19 May 1917

36 For a fictional depiction of this transformation by a chaplain see Ralph Connor, *The Sky Pilot in No Man's Land* (Toronto: McClelland and Stewart 1919).

37 UCA, G.G.D. Kilpatrick Papers, box 1, G. Kilpatrick to his father, 14 May 1918. For Kilpatrick's war experience, see G. Kilpatrick, 'A Quiver of Arrows,' unpublished autobiography, n.d., 5–8.

38 H.A. Frost, 'Notes from a Chaplain's Diary,' *ChG*, 20 Sept. 1916; T. Fraser, *The Religion of the Soldiers* (Toronto: Presbyterian Church in Canada 1917)

39 Gordon, 'A Chaplain at the Front'

40 Chaplaincy Service Papers, vol. 4663, file 'Questionnaire,' J.S. Miller to director of Chaplain Services

41 G.O. Fallis, 'Leaves from a Chaplain Diary,' *ChG*, 12 July 1916; G.O. Fallis, *A Padre's Pilgrimage* (Toronto: Ryerson 1953), 67–92

42 ANB, file 95, H.W. Burnett to the Rev. T.A. Moore, 27 April 1916; Chaplaincy Service Papers, vol. 4675, File 'Extracts from Chaplains Reports,' Captain A.J. MacDonald, 23 June 1918. In his account of the battle of the Somme, John Keegan noted that there was a significant demand for the Eucharist 'before going in.' See *The Face of Battle* (Harmondsworth: Penguin Books 1976), 241–2.

43 ANB, file 791, 'Report on Activities Month Ending 17 June 1918'; Chambers to the Rev. T.A. Moore, 27 July 1918; 'Report of Work at Segregation Camp, Seaforth,' July, August 1918

44 ANB, file 219, A.C. Farrel to the Rev. T.A. Moore, 25 Dec. 1916

45 Chaplaincy Service Papers, vol. 4629, File C–K–4, Major Kilpatrick to Col Steacy, 4 Jan. 1916

46 G.O. Fallis, 'Leaves from a Chaplain's Diary,' *ChG*, 3 May 1916

47 ANB, file 65, 'A Message from the Chaplains of the Overseas Military Forces of Canada to the Churches at Home'

48 Chaplaincy Service Papers, vol. 4663, File 'Questionnaire,' Major W.F. McConnell, 23 Sept. 1918

49 ANB, file 91, *First Annual Report of the Army and Navy Board* (Toronto: Methodist Church of Canada 1917), 25

50 ANB, file 233, T.C. Colwell to the Rev. T.A. Moore, 28 April 1918

51 See the reports of Cameron's evangelistic campaign in *CB*, 11 Oct. 1917; 20 Dec. 1917; 1 April 1918.

52 Pidgeon Papers, file 648, 'Religious Work in France,' 2 June 1918; file 649,

'Christ and the Lost,' 2 June 1918; file 650, 'Repentance,' 9 June 1918; file 652, 'Christ the Healer,' 16 June 1918; file 655, 'The Law of Sacrifice,' 30 June 1918

53 Alan Wilkinson, *The Church of England and the First World War* (London: Society for the Propagation of Christian Knowledge 1978), 161
54 Ibid., 187
55 Chaplaincy Service Papers, vol. 4665, File 'Questionnaire,' E.H. Oliver to director of Chaplain Services
56 Kilpatrick Papers, box 1, Kilpatrick to his father, 14 May 1918
57 A.E. Lavell, 'The Returning Soldier and the Church,' *ChG*, 24 April 1918
58 *ChG*, 13 Jan. 1916
59 Wilkinson, *The Church of England and the First World War*, 195–6
60 Ramsay Cook, *The Regenerators: Social Criticism in Late Victorian English Canada* (Toronto: University of Toronto Press 1985), passim
61 *CB*, 2 Aug., 23 Aug., and 4 Oct. 1917
62 Pierre van Paassen, *Days of Our Years* (New York: Knopf 1946), 66–8
63 ANB, file 237, G.H. Hamilton to the Rev. T.A. Moore, 12 March 1917
64 W.R. Bird, *Ghosts Have Warm Hands: A Portrait of Men at War* (Toronto: Clarke Irwin 1960), 139
65 *ChG*, 17 July 1918. See also ANB, file 229, T.A. Wilson to the Rev. T.A. Moore, 4 Oct. 1918
66 ANB, file 459, C.T. Watterson to the Rev. T.A. Moore, 30 Dec. 1918
67 Desmond Morton, '"Kicking and Complaining": Demobilization Riots in the Canadian Expeditionary Force, 1918–19' *CHR* 61 (March 1980), 334–60
68 van Paassen, *Days of Our Years*, 91–2
69 David B. Marshall, 'Methodism Embattled: A Reconsideration of the Methodist Church and World War I,' *CHR* 66 (March 1985), 48–64
70 Chaplaincy Service Papers, vol. 4663, file 'Questionnarie,' Office of the Director of Chaplain Services, London, 20 Aug. 1918
71 The following assessment of the responses is drawn from ibid., vol. 4663, file 'Answer to Questionnarie,' Captain J. Foulds, 28 Sept. 1918; Captain J.M. Macgilvray, n.d.; Captain Pringle, 28 Sept. 1918; Major E.H. Oliver, 2 Oct. 1918; Captain W. Christie, 2 Oct. 1918; Captain H.R. Pickup, n.d.; Major J.A. Beattie, 30 Sept. 1918; Captain E.H. Burgess, 29 Sept. 1918; and Captain J.S. McCaskill, 30 Sept. 1918.
72 *CB*, 30 Aug. 1917
73 ANB, file 41, S.D. Chown, 'Report on the Overseas Commission to the Army and Navy Board of the Methodist Church in Canada, 17 May – 13 Aug. 1917'

74 Chown Papers, file 741, 'See That Ye Refuse Not Them That Speaketh,' n.d.; file 1889, 'The Mission of the Church after the War,' n.d.

75 'Recasting Our Theology,' *ChG*, 28 Aug. 1918

76 *ChG*, 21 March 1923

77 Pidgeon Papers, file 788, 'The Spiritual Side of the Forward Movement,' Forward Movement Convention, 5 Oct. 1920; file 666, 'The Moratorium of the Sermon on the Mount,' 13 Oct. 1918

78 Chown Papers, file 616, 'The Abolition of War,' n.d. On the churches' attempts to define a gospel of peace and social justice in the aftermath of the war see Socknat, *Witness against War*, 90–161.

7 THE 1920S: AN ERA OF DRIFT

1 *NO*, 10 June 1925

2 UCA, John Maclean Papers, box 39, file 2d, 'The Claim of the Church on the Young People,' 7 Feb. 1922

3 UCA, S.D. Chown Papers, file 1276, 'The Need of Advancing Religion in a Progressive World,' n.d.

4 UCA, George Campbell Pidgeon Papers, file 788 'The Spiritual Side of the Forward Movement,' 19 Oct. 1919; file 798, 'The Place of the Church in the Nation's Life,' 23 Nov. 1919; file 759, 'The Necessity of Regeneration,' 11 April 1920; file 811, 'Unbelief in Practice,' 1 March 1921

5 *ChG*, 11 June 1921. For a broader discussion of postwar demobilization difficulties see Desmond Morton and Glenn Wright, *Winning the Second Battle: Canadian Veterans and the Return to Civilian Life, 1915-1930* (Toronto: University of Toronto Press 1987).

6 UCA, E.H. Oliver Papers, file 4, historical account, manuscript, no title, n.d.

7 *ChG*, 20 April 1921

8 Chown Papers, file 146b, 'John 12:21, Sir we wish to see Jesus,' 30 Aug. 1923

9 'Recasting Our Theological Curriculum,' *ChG*, 28 Aug. 1918

10 E.H. Oliver Papers, file 104, 'Survey of Educational Institutions under the Auspices of the Presbyterian Church of Canada,' 1921

11 UCA, Methodist Church Committee on Education Papers, box 1, *Annual Report of the Education Society of the Methodist Church*, 1914–23

12 *ChG*, 11 June 1924. See also Earnest Thomas, 'Insurgent Movements in the Church,' *Canadian Forum*, 1 Feb. 1923. For a more general discussion of postwar student culture see the essays by Keith Walden and James Pitsula in Paul Axelrod and John Reid, eds., *Youth, University, and*

Canadian Society: Essays in the Social History of Higher Education (Kingston and Montreal: McGill-Queen's University Press 1989).

13 There were similar discouraging results in the informal studies done at the Baptist institutions of McMaster University and Brandon College. As George Rawlyk points out, Chancellor Whidden was determined to transform McMaster from its Baptist Bible college roots into a more secular-minded modern university. See 'A.L. McCrimmon, H.P. Whidden, T.T. Shields, Christian Education, and McMaster University,' in G. Rawlyk, ed., *Canadian Baptists and Christian Higher Education* (Kingston and Montreal: McGill-Queen's University Press 1988), 52–4, 62.

14 *ChG*, 28 June 1922

15 W.C. Murray to J.A. Calder, 7 Jan. 1924, quoted in David R. Murray and Robert A. Murray, *The Prairie Builder: Walter Murray of Saskatchewan* (Edmonton: NeWest Press 1984), 154. According to W.L. Morton, many farmers were abandoning the churches in favour of the secular utopianism of progressivism or the cooperative movement. See W.L. Morton, *The Progresssive Party in Canada* (Toronto: University of Toronto Press 1950), 9–11; and Ian Macpherson, *Each for All: A History of the Co-operative Movement in English Canada, 1900-1945* (Toronto: Macmilan 1979).

16 N.K. Clifford, *The Resistance to Church Union in Canada* (Vancouver: University of British Columbia Press 1985), 20–5, 43–59, 82–6, 129–41

17 Pidgeon Papers, file 1031, 'Christianity in Action,' 28 Nov. 1926

18 UCA, United Church of Canada, Board of Education Papers, box 7, file 87, 'Memorandum Regarding the Yearly Losses from the Ranks of the Ministry and the Total Numbers Ordained Annually,' 1927; 'Report of the Special Committee on Recruits for the Ministry,' in *Report of Proceedings, Third General Council of the United Church of Canada*, 1928

19 Board of Education Papers, box 7, file 87, 'Report of Special Committee on Recruits for the Ministry to Executive of General Council,' May 1928

20 UCA, United Church of Canada, 3rd General Conference Papers, 'Recruits for the Ministry,' 1928

21 UM, C.W. Gordon Papers, box 25, folder 14. See especially, L.A. Hadfield to C.W. Gordon, 17 May 1926; R. Smalley to C.W. Gordon, 18 May 1926; R.E. Spence to C.W. Gordon, 19 May 1926; and David Howarth to C.W. Gordon 17 May 1926.

22 Veronica Strong-Boag, *The New Day Recalled: Lives of Girls and Women in English Canada, 1919-1939* (Toronto: Copp Clark Pitman 1988), 113–17. For a discussion of the emergence of consumerism in the United States

see Loren Baritz, *The Good Life: The Meaning of Success for the American Middle Class* (New York: Knopff 1989), 76–85.

23 See especially his essay 'From Salvation to Self-Realization: Advertising and the Therapeutic Roots of the Consumer Culture, 1880–1930,' in Richard W. Fox and T.J. Jackson Lears, eds., *The Culture of Consumption: Critical Essays in American History, 1880-1980* (New York: Pantheon Books 1983).

24 Pidgeon Papers, file 996, 'The Spiritual and the Practical in the Church's Life,' June 1926

25 UCA, Alfred Gandier Papers, box 2, file 28, 'Essential Elements in an Effective Ministry,' n.d.

26 A. Gandier, *The Doctrinal Basis of Union and Its Relation to the Historic Creeds*, Ryerson essay, no. 34 (Toronto: Ryerson 1926), 44–5

27 *NO*, 10 June 1925

28 The two classic accounts of the origins and character of the fundamentalist movement are Ernest R. Sandeen, *The Roots of Fundamentalism: British and American Millenarianism* (Chicago: University of Chicago Press 1970) and George M. Marsden, *Fundamentalism and American Culture: The Shaping of Twentieth Century Evangelism* (New York: Oxford University Press 1980).

29 Clifford, *Resistance to Church Union*, 183

30 Pidgeon received a number of letters from both clergy and laypersons which contained a fundamentalist critique. See Pidgeon Papers, file 141, W. Merkle to Pidgeon, 3 March 1926; file 144, E. Wooff to Pidgeon, May 1926; file 148, F.G. St Aubin to Pidgeon, 27 July 1927; file 149, Rev. G. Laughton to Pidgeon, 6 Oct. 1927; and Rev. G. Cochrane to Pidgeon 18 Oct. 1927.

31 Pidgeon Papers, file 140, J.R. Dobson to Pidgeon, 28 Jan. 1926

32 Pidgeon Papers, file 1056, 'The Need of the United Church of Canada,' 4 Dec. 1927

33 Pidgeon Papers, file 150, Pidgeon to the Rev. Principal Clarence Mackinnon, 11 Jan. 1928. A precise statistical picture of fundamentalism in Canada is difficult to establish. The census returns for 1931 suggest that fundamentalist organizations enjoyed significant growth in the 1920s, especially in the West. Between 1921 and 1931 those indicating that they were members of a fundamentalist church doubled in Manitoba from 6,735 to 13,382 and tripled in Saskatchewan from 12,515 to 39,206. In Alberta the fundamentalist following increased from 25,510 to 37,000.

34 J.M Shaw, 'Essentials and Non–Essentials of the Christian Faith,' *NO*, 26 Jan.–23 March 1927

35 J.R.P. Sclater, 'Fundamentalism: What Is It? *NO*, 4 Nov. 1925
36 This becomes most clear in the studies published by United church theologians who taught at Emmanuel College. See, for example, William Creighton Graham, *The Meaning of the Cross* (Toronto: Ryerson 1923); John Dow, *Jesus and the Human Conflict* (London: Hodder and Stoughton 1928); and John Baillie, *The Place of Jesus Christ in Modern Christianity* (New York: Charles Scribner's Sons 1929). These works receive extended analysis in Michael Gauvreau, *The Evangelical Century: College and Creed in English Canada from the Great Revival to the Great Depression* (Montreal and Kingston: McGill-Queen's University Press 1991), 265–83. Gauvreau views these works as evidence of an important theological reformulation in postwar Canada. There is little evidence, however, suggesting that the insights of these leading theologians penetrated to the churches, ministry, or the congregations.
37 See Sclater's series of articles in *NO*: 'Modernism,' 11 Nov. 1925; 'Higher Criticism,' 18 Nov. 1925; 'The Bible as the Written Christ,' 25 Nov. 1925; 'The Bible as the Rule of Faith and Practice,' 23 Dec. 1925; 'The Final Authority,' 6 Jan. 1926.
38 Pidgeon Papers, file 140, Pidgeon to H.T.F. Granger, 22 Feb. 1926
39 Pidgeon Papers, file 1056, 'The Need of the United Church of Canada,' 4 Dec. 1927
40 On the fundamentalist-modernist controversy within the Baptist church during the 1920s see Charles M. Johnston, *McMaster University, Vol. 1: The Toronto Years* (Toronto: University of Toronto Press 1976), 152–7, 170–229; the essays on McMaster University and Brandon College in Rawlyk, ed., *Canadian Baptists and Christian Higher Education*; G.A. Rawlyk, ed., *Champions of Truth: Fundamentalism, Modernism, and the Maritime Baptists* (Montreal and Kingston: McGill-Queen's University Press 1990); and C.A. Russell, 'Thomas Todhunter Shields, Canadian Fundamentalist,' *Ontario History* 70 (1978).
41 This section is drawn from Johnston, *McMaster University*, 188.
42 Rawlyk, ed., *Champions of Truth*, 80
43 R. Roberts, 'On Digging In and Going over the Top,' *NO*, 21 Dec. 1927; R. Roberts, *The New Man and the Divine Society: A Study in Christianity* (New York: Macmillan 1926); R. Roberts, *The Spirit of God and the Faith of Today* (New York: New York: Willett, Clark and Colby 1930)
44 This biographical material is based on UCA, Richard Roberts Papers, biographical typescript, n.d.; R. Roberts, 'Radical Religion, Forty Years Ago,' *CJRT* 1 (1925); and R. Roberts, 'How the Fellowship Began,' *Fellowship: The Journal of the Fellowship of Reconciliation*, Jan. 1943.

45 For this aspect of Roberts's ministry see Thomas P. Socknat, *Witness against War: Pacifism in Canada, 1900-1945* (Toronto: University of Toronto Press 1987), passim.

46 Roberts Papers, file 31, the Rev. A.E. Kerr to Roberts, n.d.

47 Roberts Papers, file 25, 'Statement to the Official Board of Sherbourne Church,' 20 March 1931

48 Roberts Papers, file 44, A.E. Kemp to Roberts, 29 Oct. 1928

49 C.W. Gordon Papers, box 28, folder 10, 'The Canadian Home – Its Environment,' Sermon by C.W. Gordon at St Stephen's, 8 Feb. 1920

50 Roberts Papers, 'Treasure Trove,' n.d.

51 *NO*, 3 April 1929

52 *Roberts, The New Man and the Divine Society*, 169–70

53 Roberts Papers, file 32, 'The Scope of Theology.' Roberts's daughter, Gwen Norman, attributed great importance to these lectures for he was 'more candid' in this forum than he was in his published work.

54 Ibid., 15

55 For the dilemma of liberal Protestantism in the United States see W.R. Hutchison, *The Modernist Impulse in American Protestantism* (Cambridge: Harvard University Press 1976), 257–87.

56 R. Roberts, 'Imago Dei,' *CJRT* 1 (Oct. 1925)

57 *NO*, 24 June 1925

58 'The Scope of Theology,' 18, 48

59 *CJRT* 1, No. 1 (1924), 3

60 J. Line 'Barth and Barthianism,' *CJRT* 6 (March–April 1929), 98–102

61 D.L. Ritchie, 'Barth and Barthianism, *CJRT* 6 (Sept.–Oct. 1929), 317–25. For a Baptist response see J.D. McLachlan, 'Karl Barth and the Barthian Movement,' *CB*, 28 Jan. 1932.

62 W. Bryden, *Why I Am a Presbyterian* (Toronto: Presbyterian Church of Canda 1934), 79–80

63 Ibid. See also Presbyterian Church Archives, Walter Bryden Papers, 'The Presbyterian Concept of the Word of God,' n.d. [circa 1931].

64 Pidgeon Papers, file 150, Pidgeon to Mackinnon, 11 Jan. 1928

8 'WHY NO REVIVAL?'

1 UCA, George Campbell Pidgeon Papers, file 1161, 'Spiritual Descent,' 23 Feb. 1930

2 UCA, S.D. Chown Papers, *Some Causes of the Decline of the Earlier Typical Evangelism* (Toronto: Ryerson 1930)

3 R. Roberts, 'Radical Religion Forty Years Ago,' *CJRT*, April 1925

4 UCA, Richard Roberts Papers, 'Normal Evangelism,' n.d.

5 Pidgeon Papers, file 1151, 'My Quest,' 15 Jan. 1930

6 R. Allen, *The Social Passion: Religion and Social Reform in Canada, 1914-1930* (Toronto: University of Toronto Press 1973), 219–30

7 *NO*, 23 Nov. 1927

8 UCA, Board of Evangelism and Social Services Papers, T.A. Moore, D.N. McLachlan, and W.T. Gunn to the Ministry of the United Church of Canada, 21 Jan. 1926

9 Chown, *Some Causes of the Decline of the Earlier Typical Evangelism*, 5–6, 8. See W.R. Hutchison, *The Modernist Impulse in American Protestantism* (Cambridge: Harvard University Press 1976), 257–8 for the critique of liberal Protestantism advanced during the 1920s in the United States.

10 *NO*, 'the Quiet Hour,' 11 May 1932

11 Roberts Papers, file 114, 'Lecture on Preaching,' 28–9

12 W.G. McLoughlin, *Modern Revivalism: Charles Grandison Finney to Billy Graham* (New York: Ronald Press 1959)

13 Pidgeon Papers, file 115, 'My Quest,' 15 Jan. 1930

14 Roberts Papers, 'Normal Evangelism'

15 Pidgeon Papers, Radio Ministry file, Marjorie Whitney to Pidgeon, 25 March 1933

16 Pidgeon Papers, file 1230, 'Religion and Prosperity,' 8 Nov. 1931

17 Roberts Papers, file 143, 'Direct Overtures from God,' 1930

18 G.E. Jackson, 'Man Made Remedies for a Man Made Depression,' Address to the Empire Club of Canada, 23 Feb. 1933. See also University of Toronto Archives, Gilbert Jackson file, *Toronto Telegram*, 11 Dec. 1934

19 A.L. McCrimmon, 'Evangelism in the Convention: An Epitome,' *CB*, 4 Feb. 1932

20 For accounts of the evangelistic activity see the columns of the *CB* for the months of January through April. One detailed account is 'Walkerville Deeply Moved at Revival,' *CB*, 18 Feb. 1932.

21 Pidgeon Papers, file 174, 'Report on the Proposed Simultaneous Movement for the Evangelization of Canadian Life,' 25 Oct. 1932

22 Pidgeon Papers, file 174, Canon A.P. Stratford to Pidgeon, 31 Oct. 1932; Pidgeon to Canon C.W. Vernon, 17 Nov. 1932

23 *Ottawa Citizen*, 8–11 Nov. 1932

24 Pidgeon Papers, file 174, Pidgeon to Rev. J.H. Eikert, 23 Nov. 1932

25 *Montreal Herald*, 2 Nov. 1932

26 *Ottawa Citizen*, 7 Nov. 1932

27 *Montreal Witness*, 26 Oct. 1932; 9 Nov. 1932; 18 Jan. 1933

28 The similarity of the testimonies can be established by reading newspa-

per reports of the meetings across Canada. See *Ottawa Citizen*, 6 Nov. 1932; *Toronto Star*, 9 Dec. 1932; *Vancouver Sun*, 31 March 1933; *Edmonton Journal*, 28 April 1933; *Regina Leader-Post* 11 May 1933; *Winnipeg Free Press*, 14 May 1933.

29 UCA, R.B. Cuming Papers, file 15, 'Oxford Group House Party, Alma College,' 2 July 1934

30 *Toronto Globe*, 12 Dec. 1932

31 *Montreal Witness*, 27 Sept. 1933; 8 Nov. 1933; 27 Nov. 1933; 3 Jan. 1934

32 Pidgeon Papers, Radio Ministry file, Miss M. Elemitey to Pidgeon, 24 March 1933

33 L. Grayson and J.M. Bliss, *The Wretched of Canada* (Toronto: University of Toronto Press 1971), xxv

34 *NO*, 21 Dec. 1932

35 'A Protest,' signed by G.C. Pidgeon and five other clergymen, *NO*, 28 Dec. 1932. Pidgeon also published a protest in the *Toronto Globe*, 22 Dec. 1932.

36 Pidgeon Papers, file 402, Manley F. Miner to Pidgeon, 25 Jan. 1933

37 Pidgeon Papers, file 401, the Rev. A.G. Jones to Pidgeon, 22 Dec. 1932

38 'What Is Divine Guidance?' *CB*, 26 Jan. 1933; 'What Is Sharing?' *CB*, 23 Feb. 1933

39 'A Minister's Confession,' *CB*, 26 Jan. 1933. See the articles in the *CB*, 8–15 Dec. 1932 for similar responses.

40 Pidgeon Papers, file 404, the Rev. G.P. McLeod to Pidgeon, 14 June 1933

41 *Edmonton Journal*, 25 April–1 May 1933

42 *Regina Leader-Post*, 16 May 1933

43 Pidgeon Papers, file 405, W.E. McNiven to Pidgeon, 19 Sept. 1933

44 Pidgeon Papers, file 405, the Rev. J.W. Clarke to Pidgeon, 18 Sept. 1933

45 The activities of the local Oxford groups in Canada were reported in the *Montreal Witness* throughout 1933 and early 1934.

46 UCA, C.E. Silcox Papers, box 9, file 4, 'The Oxford Group Movement,' Toronto, 31 July 1934

47 *Montreal Witness*, 8 Nov. 1933

48 *Toronto Globe*, 21 Dec. 1932

49 *Regina Leader-Post*, 10 May 1933

50 D.L. Ritchie, 'The Oxford Group Movement,' *CJRT*, Nov.–Dec. 1932

51 This point is developed by N.K. Clifford, 'Religion in the Thirties: Some Aspects of the Canadian Experience,' in D. Francis and H. Ganzevoort, eds., *The Dirty Thirties in Western Canada* (Vancouver: Tantalus Research Ltd 1980)

52 Committee of Thirty, *The Challenge of the Oxford Group Movement: An*

Attempt at Appraisal (Toronto: Ryerson 1933)

53 *Western Recorder*, Jan. 1933

54 Roberts Paper, file 114, 'Lecture on Preaching'; R. Roberts, 'The Oxford Group,' *Christian Century*, 1 Feb. 1933. For an account of a house-party, see Cuming Papers, box 5, file 15, 'Notes on the Alma College House Party,' 4–5 July 1933.

55 T.J. Jackson Lears, *No Place of Grace: Antimodernism and the Transformation of American Culture, 1880–1920* (New York: Pantheon Books 1981), 47–58

56 Pidgeon Papers, file 179, D.N. McLachlan to the Ministers of the United Church of Canada, 3 Jan. 1934

57 Pidgeon Papers, file 175, Joint Committee for the Evangelization of Canadian Life, 'God in National and Personal Life,' n.d.

58 'The Statement on Evangelism,' *Record of Proceedings, Sixth General Council of the United Church of Canada* (1934), 6, 11

59 McLoughlin, *Modern Revivalism*, 528

9 STUMBLING TOWARDS A THEOLOGICAL REFORMULATION

1 J.W. Grant, *The Church in the Canadian Era* (Toronto: McGraw-Hill Ryerson 1972), 138

2 Alvyn Austin, *Saving China: Canadian Missionaries in the Middle Kingdom, 1888–1959* (Toronto: University of Toronto Press 1986), 102. For an analysis of the decline and reassessment of foreign missions in American society see William R. Hutchison, *Errand to the World: American Protestant Thought and Foreign Missions* (Chicago: University of Chicago Press 1987), 125–75.

3 *The United Church of Canada Yearbook* (1936), 173

4 UCA, GC4, C6 E24, Papers of the Fourth General Council, Committee on the Economy, file 11, 'The Offices of the General Council and the Departments of the Church'

5 UCA, Board of Evangelism and Social Service Papers, box 7, file 87, 'Report of the Committee on Recruits for the Ministry to the Board of Christian Education,' April 1937

6 *United Church Record and Missionary Review*, Nov. 1931

7 *The United Church of Canada Year Book* (1928–36)

8 *Reports of Proceedings, Eighth General Council, United Church of Canada* (1938), 182–97

9 On the rise of the welfare state in Canada and its social and intellectual underpinnings see James Struthers, *No Fault of Their Own: Unemployment and the Canadian Welfare State, 1914–1941* (Toronto: University of Toronto

Press 1983); and Doug Owram, *The Government Generation: Canadian Intellectuals and the State, 1990–1945* (Toronto: University of Toronto Press 1986).

10 *Reports of Proceedings, Eighth General Council, United Church of Canada,* 195–6

11 UCA, George Campbell Pidgeon Papers, file 1406, 'The Social Outlook of the United Church of Canada,' 2 June 1935

12 UCA, E.H. Oliver Papers, file 45, 'Report of Visit ... to Dried Out Areas of Southern Saskatchewan,' Summer 1931

13 UCA, National Emergency Relief Committee Papers, 'Extracts from Letters Received from the West' n.d.; *Board of Evangelism and Social Service Annual Report*, 1931–8

14 E.H. Oliver Papers, file 45, A.S. Orton, 'Report of M & M Visitation,' Saskatoon, 7 July 1931

15 E.H. Oliver Papers, file 45, 'Report of Visit ... to Dried Out Areas of Southern Saskatchewan'

16 Quoted in C. Mackinnon, *The Life of Principal Oliver* (Toronto: Ryerson 1938), 35

17 UCA, National Emergency Relief Committee Papers, Correspondence, n.d.

18 E.H. Oliver, *His Dominion of Canada* (Toronto: Board of Home Missions of the United Church of Canada 1932), 264–83

19 *NO*, 20 Jan. 1932

20 E.H. Oliver Papers, files 98–9, 'Sharing in the Bible,' n.d.

21 E.H. Oliver, *Tracts for Difficult Times: Christian Literature of Comfort, Challenge, and Reconstruction* (New York: Round Table Press 1933)

22 On the central characteristics of neo-orthodoxy see W.R. Hutchison, *The Modernist Impulse in American Protestantism* (Cambridge: Harvard University Press 1976), 289–98; Donald B. Meyer, *The Protestant Search for Political Realism* (Berkeley: University of California Press 1960); and Paul A. Carter, *The Decline and Revival of the Social Gospel, 1920–1940* (Ithaca: Cornell University Press 1956).

23 M. Horn, *The League for Social Reconstruction: Intellectual Origins of the Democratic Left in Canada, 1930–1942* (Toronto: University of Toronto Press 1980), 31, 62–3

24 'Report No. 2 of the Commission of Evangelism and Social Service,' *Minutes of Toronto Conference* (10 June 1933), 23

25 *Record of Proceedings, Ninth General Conference,* Montreal-Ottawa, 8 June 1933, 821

26 John Line, 'Modern Knowledge and the Christian Idea of God,' *NO*, 17 Aug. 1932

27 Pidgeon Papers, file 278, 'Dissent from Action of Conference'

28 C.E. Silcox, 'The Next Ten Years,' *NO*, 12 Sept. 1933

29 UCA, Richard Roberts Papers, 'Lectures on Preaching,' 106–12

30 Silcox, 'The Next Ten Years'

31 *Toronto Telegram*, 13 June 1933

32 Pidgeon Papers, file 274, J. Cowan to Pidgeon, 13 June 1933

33 Roberts Papers, 'Lectures on Preaching,' 107

34 Pidgeon Papers, file 408, Russell Harris to Pidgeon, 24 Jan. 1934

35 Roberts Papers, 'Lectures on Preaching,' 94

36 UCA, Commission on Christianizing the Social Order Papers, file 1, J. Dow, 'The Gospels,' Toronto, 17 March 1933

37 Ibid., J. Hugh Michael, 'The Social Teachings of St. Paul,' Toronto, 15 May 1933

38 Dow, 'The Gospels,' and from the same commission see James A. Thomson, 'The Teaching and Influence of Christianity on Social Questions during the Nineteenth Century,' Halifax, 13 Sept. 1933

39 Board of Evangelism and Social Service, *Christianizing the Social Order: Statement Prepared by the Commission and Delivered to the Sixth General Council of the United Church of Canada* (1934), 5–6; 'The Significance of the Report of the Commission on Christianizing the Social Order,' *Tenth Annual Report of the Board of Evangelism and Social Service*, 26

40 E.J. Urwick and I. Biss, 'Modern Industry: A Short Analysis of Some Outstanding Dangers in the Present Situation,' *Supplement to 'Christianizing the Social Order*, Section 2, 14

41 'Modern Industry,' 14–22

42 *Christianizing the Social Order*, 8–9

43 Ibid., 10–11

44 Ibid., 13

45 Advocates of the traditional social gospel position submitted a minority report suggesting that the commission support a clearly socialist platform. See Commission on Christianizing the Social Order Papers, file 4, John Line, 'The Church and the Social Order,' 3. For further evidence of debate within the commission see file 3, Minutes, Christian Social Order Commission, 12 May and 11 June 1934.

46 'The Statement on Evangelism,' *Record of Proceedings, Sixth General Council* (1934), 11

47 R. Roberts, *The Contemporary Christ* (New York: Macmillan 1938), 143–5

48 Pidgeon Papers, file 189, 'A Message to the Congregation of Winnipeg,' 11 Oct. 1936

49 Roberts Papers, file 11, Roberts to Gwen, 7 Nov. 1936

50 G. Stanley Russell, 'The Church at Bay,' *Queen's Quarterly* 44, no. 2 (Summer 1937)

51 *Record of Proceedings, Sixth General Council* (1934), 64

CONCLUSION

1 Suzanne Zeller, *Inventing Canada: Early Victorian Science and the Idea of a Transcontinental Nation* (Toronto: University of Toronto Press 1987), 269. For a superb analysis of the transformation from an understanding of the human body as the 'pinnacle of divine creation' to a physiological understanding see S.E.D. Shortt, *Victorian Lunacy: Richard M. Bucke and the Practice of Late Nineteenth-Century Psychiatry* (Cambridge: Cambridge University Press 1986), 4–25, 71, 91–3.

2 Keith Thomas, *Religion and the Decline of Magic* (London: Weidenfeld and Nicolson 1981), 765–800

3 Jeffrey Cox, *The English Churches in a Secular Society Lambeth, 1870–1930* (New York: Oxford University Press 1982), 93–5

4 UCA, George Campbell Pidgeon Papers, file 1032, 'The Liquor Question in Ontario,' 28 Nov. 1926

5 This issue is raised by George Rawlyk, 'A.L. McCrimmon, H.P. Whidden, T.T. Shields, Christian Higher Education and McMaster University,' in G.A. Rawlyk, ed., *Canadian Baptists and Christian Higher Education* (Kingston and Montreal: McGill-Queen's University Press 1988), 31–62; and N.K. Clifford, *The Resistance to Church Union in Canada, 1904–1939* (Vancouver: University of British Columbia Press 1985), 236–41. This question was also suggested in the debate following the publication of Pierre Berton's highly controversial *The Comfortable Pew: A Critical Look at Christianity and the Religious Establishment in the New Age* (Toronto: McClelland and Stewart 1965). See especially Peter Berger, 'The Relevance Bit Comes to Canada,' in William Kilbourn, ed., *The Restless Church: A Response to the Comfortable Pew* (Toronto: McClelland and Stewart 1966), 75–9.

Note on the Sources

Full bibliographic references to the sources appear in the Notes; here the major archival and primary sources consulted will be described, as well as the secondary material that relates most directly to the subjects of Canadian religious history and secularization. Readers should consult the Notes for references to material on specialized themes or questions.

This book is largely based on collections in the United Church Archives in Victoria University at the University of Toronto. The most important sources are the numerous collections of personal papers of Methodist and Presbyterian clergymen. The most valuable are those that contain a variety of material diaries, memoirs, correspondence, sermons, and addresses – and that cover most of a clergyman's life. The most extensive collections include those of Henry Flesher Bland, Nathanael Burwash, Albert Carman, S.D. Chown, John Maclean, George Pidgeon, Richard Roberts, James Robertson, Alexander Sutherland, and F.H. Wallace. Less extensive collections in the United Church Archives include the papers of Salem Bland, William Case, R.B. Cumming, Alfred Gandier, W.H. Hincks, George Jackson, G.G.D. Kilpatrick, Robert Milliken, Charles E. Silcox, Alfred Livingston Taylor, and Thomas Webster. The papers of Nathanael Burwash, F.H. Wallace, W.H. Hincks, and S.D. Chown include valuable unpublished memoirs. The Crossley-Hunter scrapbook is also in the United Church Archives. The rich and extensive C.W. Gordon Papers are in the archives section of the Elizabeth Dafoe Library at the University of

Manitoba. The originals of the E.H. Oliver Papers are held in the
University of Saskatchewan Archives. The Walter Bryden Papers are
in the Presbyterian Church Archives at Knox College in Toronto, and
William Cochrane's diary is in the Archives of Ontario.

Equally valuable are the numerous publications by Canadian clergymen. The Victorian clergy, in particular, published widely. Their
publications include books of sermons and addresses, novels, historical accounts, and pamphlets on controversial questions. Among the
more prolific clergymen-authors, whose writings formed the basis for
much of this book, were Nathanael Burwash, Albert Carman, William Caven, S.D. Chown, William Cochrane, E.H. Dewart, George
Grant, C.W. Gordon, D.J. Macdonnell, Richard Roberts, and Alexander
Sutherland. Two important lay persons who wrote extensively on
religious questions of the day were Agnes Machar and John George
Marshall. The National Library of Canada, the United Church Archives, and Emmanuel College Library of Victoria University in
Toronto have extensive book and pamphlet collections. Many pamphlets that were published for a particular congregation and are de-
posited in local libraries have been reproduced by the Canadian Institute of Historical Microreproductions.

A great deal of clergymen's writings appeared in the various de-
nominational journals and newspapers. The most valuable newspapers
are the *Christian Guardian, Presbyterian Witness, Presbyterian Review,
Canadian Baptist,* and *New Outlook,* as well as the *Westminster* and
Western Recorder. Theological journals include *Earnest Christianity,
Canadian Methodist Quarterly, Canadian Methodist Review, Knox College
Monthly and Presbyterian Magazine,* and *Canadian Journal of Religious
Thought.* The *Canadian Methodist Magazine* was more of a general interest magazine with a strong religious and missionary content. These
newspapers and journals are in the United Church Archives. College
journals, such as *Acta Victoriana* and the *Queen's College Journal,* are also
good sources. The *Lord's Day Advocate,* originals of which are located
in Emmanuel College Library, is indispensable for the Sabbatarian
movement, and the *Montreal Witness* is an important general paper
for evangelical religion. During the late nineteenth century *Saturday
Night Magazine* and the *Week* covered religion and the churches, especially in Toronto, from an outsider's point of view.

For more specific issues or themes the papers and records of different
church boards and committees in the United Church Archives can be

consulted. General information regarding the activities of various boards can be found in *Acts and Proceedings of the General Assembly of the Presbyterian Church*, *Journal of Proceedings of the General Conference of the Methodist Church*, and the *Reports of Proceedings of the United Church of Canada*. Of particular interest are the reports of the various committees on church life and work, which canvassed the clergy about the condition of religion and church-going within their parish. Important collections of records are in the massive Church Union collection, the Methodist Church Army and Navy Board Papers, the various boards of evangelism and social service, and the United Church of Canada Christianizing the Social Order Papers. The records of the Lord's Day Alliance and the papers of John Charlton, a central figure in the movement, are in the University of Toronto's Thomas Fisher Rare Book Library. The war service records of the chaplains are in the National Archives of Canada.

There is a rich tradition of biographical and autobiographical writing in the Canadian Methodist, Presbyterian, and Baptist churches. It began with John Carroll's five-volume *Case and His Cotemporaries; or, The Canadian Itinerants' Memorial: Constituting a Biographical History of Methodism* (Toronto 1867–77). The most helpful biographies of figures who were active in the Methodist, Presbyterian, or Baptist churches between the 1850s and 1930s include Jones H. Farmer, ed., *E.W. Dadson, B.A., D.D.: The Man and His Message* (Toronto 1902); C.W. Gordon, *The Life of James Robertson: Missionary Superintendent in Western Canada* (Toronto 1908); C.W. Gordon, *Postscript to Adventure: The Autobiography of 'Ralph Connor'* (Toronto 1937); R.N. Grant, *Life of Rev. William Cochrane* (Toronto 1899); T.A. Higgins, *The Life of John Mockett Cramp, D.D., 1796–1881* (Montreal 1887); J.G. Hodgins, ed., *'The Story of My Life' By the Late Rev. Egerton Ryerson, D.D., LL.D.* (Toronto 1883); George Leslie Mackay, *From Far Formosa: The Island, Its People, and Missions* (Toronto 1896); J.F. McCurdy, *Life and Work of D.J. Macdonnell* (Toronto 1897); John McDougall, *George Millward McDougall: The Pioneer, Patriot, and Missionary* (Toronto 1888); J.H. MacVicar, *Life and Work of Donald Henry MacVicar* (Toronto 1904); George Patterson, *Missionary Life among the Cannibals: Being the Life of John Geddie, D.D.* (Toronto 1882); J.E. Wells, *Life and Labours of Robert Alex Fyfe, D.D., Founder and Many Years Principal of the Canadian Literary Institute* (Toronto 1885); George Young, *Manitoba Memories: Leaves from My Life in the Prairie Province, 1868–1884* (Toronto 1897); *The Last Martyrs of Eromanga: Being a Mem-*

oir of the Rev. George N. Gordon and Ellen Catherine Powell, His Wife
(Halifax 1863); and Memoir of Daniel Arthur MacGregor, Late Principal
of Toronto Baptist College (Toronto 1891).

In Canadian historiography there have been numerous studies in
social and intellectual history that discuss certain aspects of the secularization question. The ground-breaking studies are Carl Berger, Science, God, and Nature in Victorian Canada (Toronto 1983); Ramsay Cook,
The Regenerators: Social Criticism in Late Victorian English Canada
(Toronto 1985); and A.B. McKillop, A Disciplined Intelligence: Critical
Inquiry and Canadian Thought in the Victorian Era (Montreal 1979). Re-
cent works in the history of religion in Canada that discuss the question
of secularization are Michael Gauvreau, The Evangelical Century: Col-
lege and Creed in English Canada from the Great Revival to the Great
Depression (Montreal and Kingston 1991); John Webster Grant's A
Profusion of Spires: Religion in Nineteenth-Century Ontario (Toronto 1988);
William Westfall, Two Worlds: The Protestant Culture of Nineteenth-
Century Ontario (Kingston and Montreal 1989); and Marguerite Van
Die, An Evangelical Mind: Nathanael Burwash and the Methodist Tradition
in Canada, 1839–1918 (Kingston and Montreal 1989).

More general histories of religion that form a foundation for studying secularization include John Bossy, Christianity in the West, 1400–
1700 (Oxford 1985); Hugh McLeod, Religion and the People of Western
Europe, 1789–1970 (Oxford 1981); and Keith Thomas, Religion and the
Decline of Magic: Studies in Popular Beliefs in Sixteenth and Seventeenth
Century England (London 1971). On the history of the Bible and biblical
criticism see The Cambridge History of the Bible, especially volume 3,
edited by S.L. Greenslade, The West from the Reformation to the Present
Day (Cambridge 1963); and Stephen Neill and Tom Wright, The Interpretation of the New Testament (Oxford 1964). There is a vast literature
on the science-versus-religion debate. A full bibliography appears in
James R. Moore, The Post-Darwinian Controversies: A Study of the Protestant Struggle to Come to Terms with Darwin in Great Britain and America
1870–1900 (Cambridge 1979), one of the leading books in the field.

Related studies in the British context include Owen Chadwick's
two-volume masterpiece The Victorian Church (London 1966, 1970).
Chadwick's The Secularization of the European Mind in the Nineteenth
Century (Cambridge 1975) is a central work. Other more specialized
studies of religion and secularization in England include Jeffrey Cox,
The English Churches in a Secular Society (Oxford 1982); A.D. Gilbert,
Religion and Society in Industrial England (London 1976); A.D. Gilbert

The Making of Post-Christian Britain (London 1980); and Ian Sellers, *Nineteenth-Century Nonconformity* (London 1977). For Scotland, the two volumes by Andrew Drummond and James Bulloch, *The Church in Victorian Scotland* (Edinburgh 1975) and *The Church in Late Victorian Scotland* (Edinburgh 1977), are the central texts and indispensable for understanding Presbyterianism in Canada. A briefer, but important, study is A.C. Cheyne, *The Transformation of the Kirk: Victorian Scotland's Religious Revolution* (Edinburgh 1983). Two important books on the transatlantic character of evangelicalism in the nineteenth century are Richard Cawardine, *Trans-Atlantic Revivalism: Popular Evangelicalism in Britain and America, 1790–1865* (Westport 1978); and John Kent, *Holding the Fort: Studies in Victorian Revivalism* (London 1978).

For religion and secularization in the American context, see especially Paul Carter, *The Spiritual Crisis in the Gilded Age* (Illinois 1971); William R. Hutchison, *The Modernist Impulse in American Protestantism* (Cambridge, Mass. 1976); Martin Marty, *Modern American Religion, Volume 1: The Irony of It All, 1893–1919* (Chicago 1986); and James Turner, *Without God, Without Creed: The Origins of Unbelief in America* (Baltimore 1985). On the character of American religion see Ann Douglas, *The Feminization of American Culture* (New York 1977); Nathan Hatch, *The Democratization of American Christianity* (New Haven 1989); W.G. McLoughlin, *Revivals, Awakenings, and Reform* (Chicago 1978); and Sidney Mead, *The Lively Experiment: The Shaping of Christianity in America* (New York 1976). Of course, the concept of 'religious declension' was introduced in historical literature in Perry Miller's masterpiece *The New England Mind* (Cambridge, Mass. 1939, 1953).

More specialized studies on the history of religion in the United States that were helpful for this book include Whitney R. Cross, *The Burned-Over District: The Social and Intellectual History of Enthusiastic Religion in Western New York, 1800–1850* (Ithaca 1950); William R. Hutchison, *Errand to the World: American Protestant Thought and Foreign Missions* (Chicago 1987); T.J. Jackson Lears, *No Place of Grace: Antimodernism and the Transformation of American Culture, 1880–1920* (New York 1981); George R. Marsden, *Fundamentalism and American Culture: The Shaping of Twentieth Century Evangelism, 1870–1925* (New York 1980); Colleen McDannell, *The Christian Home in Victorian America, 1840–1900* (Bloomington 1986); David S. Reynolds, *Faith in Fiction: The Emergence of Religious Literature in America* (Cambridge 1981); Ernest R. Sandeen, *The Roots of Fundamentalism: British and American Millenarianism, 1800–1930* (Chicago 1970); Timothy L. Smith,

Revivalism and Social Reform in Mid-Nineteenth Century America (New York 1957); and Susan Tamke, *Make a Joyful Noise unto the Lord: Hymns as a Reflection of Victorian Social Attitudes* (Athens, Ohio 1978).

The literature on consumer culture is fairly recent. The ground–breaking studies include Rosalind Williams, *Dream Worlds: Mass Consumption in Late Nineteenth Century France* (Berkeley 1982); and T.J. Jackson Lears, *The Culture of Consumption: Critical Essays in American History* (New York 1983). Similar studies do not exist for Canada, but Joy Santink's study on retailing, *Timothy Eaton and the Rise of His Department Store* (Toronto 1990), is a solid beginning.

There is a rich tradition of Canadian church history that begins in the 1870s. The best of the early histories are I.E. Bill, *Fifty Years with the Baptist Ministers and Churches of the Maritime Provinces of Canada* (St John 1880); William Gregg, *Short History of the Presbyterian Church in Canada from the Earliest Times to the Present Time* (Toronto 1893); Egerton Ryerson, *Canadian Methodism: Its Epochs and Characteristics* (Toronto 1882); E.M. Saunders, *History of the Baptists of the Maritime Provinces* (Halifax 1902); T.W. Smith, *History of the Methodist Church of Eastern British America*, 2 vols. (Halifax 1877,1890); Alexander Sutherland, *Methodism in Canada: Its Work and Its Story* (Toronto 1904); Thomas Webster, *History of the Methodist Episcopal Church in Canada* (Hamilton 1870), and *Centennial of Canadian Methodism* (Toronto 1891). S.D. Clark's *Church and Sect in Canada* (Toronto 1948) introduced the declension thesis into Canadian historiography. More recent literature includes the volumes from the 'national school,' J.S. Moir, *The Church in the British Era* (Toronto 1972) and John Webster Grant, *The Church in the Canadian Era* (Toronto 1972). A model denominational history is John S. Moir, *Enduring Witness: A History of the Presbyterian Church in Canada* (Hamilton 1974). The Methodists and Baptists still await a similarly comprehensive treatment. The Baptist tradition in the Maritimes, however, has been analysed in two studies by George Rawlyk: *Ravished by the Spirit: Religious Revivals, Baptists, and Henry Alline* (Kingston and Montreal 1984); and *Champions of Truth: Fundamentalism, Modernism, and the Maritime Baptists* (Montreal and Kingston 1990).

On specialized topics or themes there is Richard Allen, *The Social Passion: Religion and Social Reform in Canada 1914–1928* (Toronto 1973); N.K. Clifford, *The Resistance to Church Union in Canada, 1904–1939* (Vancouver 1985); Brian Fraser, *The Social Uplifters: Presbyterian Progressives and the Social Gospel in Canada, 1875–1915* (Waterloo 1988);

and John Webster Grant, *Moon of Wintertime: Missionaries and the Indians of Canada in Encounter since 1534* (Toronto 1984). Recent historical literature on the foreign missionary movement in Canada includes Alvyn Austin, *Saving China: Canadian Missionaries in the Middle Kingdom, 1888–1959* (Toronto 1986); Ruth Compton Brouwer, *New Women for God: Canadian Presbyterian Women and India Missions, 1876–1914* (Toronto 1990); Stephen Endicott, *James G. Endicott: Rebel Out of China* (Toronto 1980); and A. Hamish Ion, *The Cross and the Rising Sun: The Canadian Protestant Missionary Movement in the Japanese Empire, 1872–1931* (Waterloo 1989).

The recent histories of Canadian universities are integral to any understanding of religion and the churches in Canada. A good general introduction is D.C. Masters, *Protestant Church Colleges in Canada* (Toronto 1966). For the institutions that were developed by the Methodist or Presbyterian churches see A.G. Bedford, *The University of Winnipeg: A History of the Founding Colleges* (Toronto 1976); Nathanael Burwash, *History of Victoria College* (Toronto 1927); Hilda Neatby, *Queen's University, Vol. 1, 1841–1917* (Montreal 1978); George Rawlyk and Kevin Quinn, *The Redeemed of the Lord Say So: A History of Queen's Theological College* (Kingston 1980); John G. Reid, *Mount Allison University*, 2 vols. (Toronto 1984); and C.B. Sissons, *A History of Victoria University* (Toronto 1952). For Baptist institutions of higher education see Charles M. Johnston, *McMaster University, Volume 1: The Toronto Years* (Toronto 1976); and George Rawlyk, ed., *Canadian Baptists and Christian Higher Education* (Kingston and Montreal 1988). A good survey of biblical studies in Canadian universities is John S. Moir, *A History of Biblical Studies in Canada: A Sense of Proportion* (1982).

There are numerous studies in various aspects of Canadian social and intellectual history that offer important insights regarding religion and secularization in Canada. These studies include C. Armstrong and H.V. Nelles, *The Revenge of the Methodist Bicycle Company: Sunday Streetcars and Municipal Reform in Toronto, 1888–1897* (Toronto 1977); Susan Houston and Alison Prentice, *Schooling and Scholars in Nineteenth-Century Ontario* (Toronto 1988); Alan Metcalfe, *Canada Learns to Play: The Emergence of Organized Sport, 1807–1914* (Toronto 1987); Douglas Owram, *The Government Generation: Canadian Intellectuals and the State* (Toronto 1986); Paul Rutherford, *A Victorian Authority: The Daily Press in Late Nineteenth-Century Canada* (Toronto 1982); S.E.D. Shortt, *The Search for an Ideal: Six Canadian Intellectuals and Their Convictions in an Age of Transition, 1890–1930* (Toronto 1976); S.E.D. Shortt,

Victorian Lunacy: Richard M. Bucke and the Practice of Late Nineteenth-Century Psychiatry (Cambridge 1986); Thomas Socknat, *Witness against War: Pacifism in Canada, 1900–1945* (Toronto 1987); Mariana Valverde, *The Age of Light, Soap, and Water: Moral Reform in English Canada, 1885–1925* (Toronto 1991); and Suzanne Zeller, *Inventing Canada: Early Victorian Science and the Idea of a Transcontinental Nation* (Toronto 1987).

Recent biographies of public figures who were deeply involved in the Church and matters of religious faith are Michael Bliss, *A Canadian Millionaire: The Life and Business Times of Sir Joseph Flavelle, Bart., 1858–1939* (Toronto 1978); James Greenlee, *Sir Robert Falconer: A Biography* (Toronto 1988); K.W. McNaught, *A Prophet in Politics: A Biography of J.S. Woodsworth* (Toronto 1959); and Margaret Prang, *Newton Wesley Rowell: Ontario Nationalist* (Toronto 1975).

Index

Acadia College 30, 58, 101
agnosticism 11–12, 192. *See also*
indifference
Alline, Rev. Henry 91
Ames, A.E. 241
Ames, Rev. William 241
Angel and the Star, The
(C.W. Gordon) 143–4
anti-clericalism 8
atheists 11–12
Austin, Alvyn 229–30
Avison, Rev. H.W. 241

Bangs, Rev. Nathan 34
Baptist church: doctrinal standards
of 58; and First World War 158;
and fundamentalist-modernist
controversy 195; liberalism of
57–8; preaching in 39; and
revivalism 212; theological
colleges 295n13
Baptists: on adult immersion 259n13;
on church-state relations 21; and
comparative religion 106–7;

critique of liberal Christianity 160;
and evolutionary thought 57–8;
and fundamentalism 81; and the
Oxford Group movement 220;
and religious liberty 195; separateness of 10; and union 289n83;
wartime preaching 160, 163–4
Barth, Karl 201–2, 233, 236
Belleville Seminary 29
Bible: authority of 74; and Christian
social teachings 241–2; divine
inspiration of 75, 81; dramatic
elements in 141; in family
worship 31, 136; fundamentalist
reading of 81–2, 192; modern
understanding of (*see* biblical
criticism); and popular culture
82–3, 151, 208; Revised Version
75; in theological curriculum 184–
5; as Word of God 27, 39, 74, 87,
91, 250
Bible colleges 193
Bible reading 82–3, 151
biblical criticism 17, 45–6, 62–7, 70,

74–7, 82–3, 104, 118, 143–4, 202,
235–7, 241–2; and comparative
religion 105–6; critique of 80, 82–4
biblical knowledge. *See* religious
knowledge
biblical stories, in C.W. Gordon's
fiction 121–2, 143–4
Bingham, Rev. E.E. 220
Biss, Irene 241, 243–4
Black Rock (C.W. Gordon) 120, 121–
3, 141–2
Blackstock, Rev. W.S. 54–5
Bossy, John 133
Boxer Rebellion (China) 107
Bramshott Camp 165, 169
Brandon College 195
British Association for the Advance-
ment of Science 55
Brouwer, Ruth 18, 103
Brown, Rev. Walter 241
Bryden, Rev. Walter 202–3
Buchman, Frank 213–14, 217, 223
Buddhism 101
Burpee, Rev. R.E. 100
Burwash, Rev. Nathanael: back-
ground 31–2; as biblical critic
64–6, 67; causes of doubt 46;
and Christian Perfection 33; on
Revised New Testament 75; on
science and religion 46, 55–6;
spiritual crisis 32–3
Butterfield, Herbert 22

Calvinism: and evangelicalism 20,
37–8; and evolutionary thought
54, 59; and fundamentalism 81;
liberalization of 37–9; orthodox
doctrines of 34–6, 39, 47, 113–14;
and war 177
Cameron, Rev. W.A. 170

Campbell, Rev. John 79–80
Canadian Army Medical Corps 164
Canadian Expeditionary Force 158
Canadian Forum 243
Canadian Journal of Religious Thought
201–2
Canadian Literary Institute
(Woodstock College) 22, 58, 163
Canadian nationalism 51, 186
Carman, Rev. Albert: background
28–9; and Christian Perfection 33;
conservatism of 72; as a controversialist 110; conversion
experience 29; on divine inspiration of the Bible 75; doubt 29;
'Gospel of Justice' 68–9; on
sabbath observance 133; on
theological education 79
Carroll, Rev. John 141
Case, Rev. William 20, 30
Caven, Rev. William: and biblical
criticism 63–4, 66; on doctrinal
standards 62–3; and Macdonnell
heresy trial 62; on preaching 72–
3, 96; on sabbath observance 137
Chadwick, Owen: on Darwin 46; on
liberalism 22; on secularization 6
Chambers, Rev. E. 169
chaplains: and church union 186; as
evangelists 167; faith of 164;
message to the churches at home
175–6, 178; in postwar Canada
183; preaching at the front 168–
73; on religion of soldiers 167–9,
253; soldiers' criticism of 174–5;
survey of religious conditions
176–8
Chown, Rev. S.D.: background 146;
and church union 186; and crisis
of faith 182; on decline of

evangelicalism 206–8; overseas wartime tour 166, 179; postwar criticism of churches 180; reassessment of social gospel 152, 160, 179, 183–4; social gospel of 146–50; support of war effort 157–8

Christian evolutionism 57–9

Christian Perfection 33, 60–1, 148

Christianity: definition of 5–6; in secular society 4–5, 8, 255–6

Christianizing the Social Order 244–5, 247–8

Church and Sect in Canada (S.D. Clark) 14–16

church architecture, secular atmosphere of 128–30

church attendance. *See* churchgoing

Church in the Canadian Era, The (J.W. Grant) 15–16

church union 9–10, 254; historical analysis of 14–15; and liberal Christianity 153–4, 181, 203–4; Presbyterian non–concurrence 154, 202–3; and secularization 154–5

churches: decline of authority 180; prospects for 204, 246–7; in secular society 242–4, 255–6; secularization of 4, 128–9; social teachings 69

churchgoing 11, 73, 153, 188, 204, 254

church-state relations 21–3

Clark, S.D. 14–16

clergy: and doctrinal standards 40–5; and doubt 25, 28–33, 39–40, 45–7; as novelists 140–1; and ordination vows 7, 39–40; as pastors 83–4; role in society 4–5,

7–8; in the schools 22–3; and sense of crisis 19

clerical profession 7–8, 30, 39–41, 129, 149, 230; declining status of 185, 187

Cochrane, Rev. William: clerical life 30, 129; on muscular Christianity 131; on preaching 96

college life 32–3, 187–8, 229

Collins, Rev. J.E. 160–1

Colter, Rev. W.H. 233

Colwell, Rev. T.C. 170

comparative religion 17, 101–7, 251

Connor, Ralph. *See* Gordon, Rev. C.W.

conservatism 208–10

consumer culture 5, 97, 127–8, 145, 252; and churchgoing 188–9; and Grimsby Park 130–1; and the Oxford Group movement 206, 226; secular ethics of 248; and secularization 23–4, 48, 197–8, 254

conversion: in Crossley-Hunter meetings 92–4; description of 28–9; necessity of 27–8, 36, 88, 94, 171, 251; in Oxford Group meetings 216–17, 223–4

Cook, Ramsay 12, 17, 18

Coulter, Rev. J.M. 241

Cox, Jeffrey 253

Cragg, Rev. Charles 160

Cramp, Rev. John Mockett 30–1, 58

Creighton, W.B. 219

crisis theology 229

critical inquiry 7. *See also* biblical criticism

Croil, Rev. James 102

Cross, Rev. George 106–7

Crossley, Rev. H.T.: background 89; evangelicalism of 90, 92–3; on

novel reading 140; sermons of 90
Crossley-Hunter revival meetings
73, 90–8

Dadson, Rev. E.W. 21, 84
Dawn by Galilee, The (C.W. Gordon)
143
denominational affiliation, statistics
of 10
denominationalism 154, 186, 203;
critique of 181. *See also* church
union
Denovan, Rev. Joshua 81
devotional literature 11, 31, 142–3
Dewart, Rev. E.H.: background
50–1; as biblical critic 60–1, 67;
'Christianity and Skepticism' 3–4;
as a controversialist 110; 'Development of Doctrine' 59–62; editor
of *Christian Guardian* 52, 59–60,
78; on free thinkers 51–2; historical writing 13, 17; literary career
51; opposition to speculative
criticism 77; revival activity 86;
on science and religion 53, 56–7
diaries 30–1
diffusive Christianity 253. *See also*
indifference; religious knowledge
Dobson, Rev. Hugh 245
Doctor, The (C.W. Gordon) 144–5
doctrinal standards 39–45, 58, 62–3,
70–1, 79, 190–1, 193–4; disintegration of 70–1, 177–8, 238–40
Doran, George H. 131
doubt 3–4, 25, 31, 39, 42–7, 49, 51,
91, 100, 104, 106–7, 126, 249–51
Dougall, F.E. 216
Dow, Rev. John 241–2
Drummond, Henry 117
Drury, E.C. 241

Eaton's store 127–8
election 37–9
Emmanuel College (Toronto) 190,
199, 209, 238, 240
Endicott, Rev. James 245
Enduring Witness (J.S. Moir) 16
established church 21–2
evangelical tradition 207–8
evangelicalism: at the battlefront
170–1; in C.W. Gordon's novels
121–2, 141–3; character of 20, 26–
31; critique of 191; of Crossley-
Hunter 73, 90–3; decline of 25–6,
67–8, 84–5, 116–17, 150, 206–8,
227; and diaries 30–1; doctrines
of 25–8; on foreign mission
fields 38, 102; in gospel songs
92–3; and the Oxford Group
movement 215–17, 223–5; during
war 161–2
everlasting punishment, doctrine of
41–2, 45
evolutionary thought 17, 54–9

Falconer, Rev. J.W. 162
Falconer, Sir Robert 9, 241
Fallis, Rev. George 167, 168
family worship 11, 31–2, 94; decline
of 135–6
Farrell, Rev. A.C. 169, 222
First World War: aftermath of 174–
5, 179–80; battlefront worship
services 168–71; and the chaplains' survey 176–8; and crisis of
faith 156–7, 162, 168, 179–80;
impact on religion 209, 213, 247–
8, 253–4; moral conditions 166–7;
realism concerning 164–7; as
religious crusade 157–9; and the
social gospel 159–60; theology

during 160–4, 167, 171–3
Fitzpatrick, Charles (minister of justice) 138
Fleming, Sir Sandford 95
foreign missions 38; and crisis of faith 100; decline of 229–30; disillusionment with 102, 107–8; and popular culture 99; and the social gospel 103–4, 108; support for 100–1
Foreigner, The (C.W. Gordon) 145
Forsey, Eugene 237
Fraser, Brian 150
free thought 12, 43–4, 51–2
fundamentalism 78, 81–2, 154
fundamentalist-modernist controversy 191–5, 199–200
Fyfe, Rev. R.A. 58

Gandier, Rev. Alfred 153, 190
Gauvreau, Michael 18–19, 258n8, 267n42, 297n36
Geddie, Rev. John 38, 100, 102
George, Henry 147
Gibson, Rev. J.M. 37–8
God: changing understanding of 36–7, 40, 47, 59, 70–1, 163, 167–8, 199–200, 235–6; of Christianity 6; the Creator 54–6; declining belief in 160, 208, 235
Goforth, Rev. Jonathan 107–8
Good, W.C. 241
Gordon, King 237
Gordon, Rev. C.W. [pseud. Ralph Connor]: background 117–18; and church union 186; depiction of sinfulness 144; devotional literature 143–4; and dramatic rights to novels 131–2; evangelical views 118; historical writing

14; literary appeal 123, 141; and muscular Christianity 131, 140; novelist of the West 120–4; novels as secular sermons 140–3; on religious conditions in the West 117, 120, 122, 124; on sabbath observance 137
Gordon, Rev. Daniel Miner 58, 63
Gordon, Rev. George 38, 102
gospel songs 91–3; definition of 276–7n62
Graham, Rev. E.E. 165–6
Grant, John Webster 228; on missions 282n73; on secularization 15–16, 17
Grant, Rev. George: on biblical criticism 80–1; 'How to Read the Bible' 82–3; on Macdonnell heresy trial 44; on tolerance 43–4; on world religions 104–6
Gregg, William 39
Grimsby Park 130–1
Gwen: An Idyll of the Canyon (C.W. Gordon) 142

Harris, Rev. Elmore 106
Harrison, Rev. William 55
Hawkins, Rev. C.W. 9
heaven, as depicted in gospel songs 93
Henderson, Rev. James 147
heresy trials 13, 42–5, 62, 76–80, 154, 191–2, 289n86
Herridge, Rev. W.T. 158–9
Hincks, Rev. William H. 91
Hinduism 101, 105
historical criticism 45. *See also* biblical criticism
historiography 12–19
History of the Conflict between Religion

and Science (John W. Draper) 54–5

Hodge, Charles 113

home missions 109; disillusionment with 124–5

'How to Read the Bible' (George Grant) 82–3

Howarth, Rev. David 188–9

Huestis, Rev. C.H. 180

Hunter, Rev. John Edwin: background 89–90; conversion techniques 93–4

Hunter-Rose Publishing Co. 86

hymn singing 11, 91

hymns 276–7n62. *See also* gospel songs

immigration 108–9, 252

immortality 172–3; soldiers' belief in 172

indifference: of churchgoers 49, 53, 67–8, 107–8, 116–19, 124–6, 135–6, 153, 188–9, 198, 211; of soldiers 157, 169–70, 173, 175

individualism 7, 47

inquiry room 88, 93–4

institutional church 128–9

Inter-Church Forward Movement 229

inter-denominational cooperation 9, 95, 183, 229. *See also* church union

Islam 101, 105–6

Jackson, Gilbert E. 211–12

Jackson Lears, T.J. 189, 278n82

Jesus Christ: Christian understanding of 6; in gospel songs 92–3; life of 6, 46, 250; the Redeemer 172, 194; as Saviour 92–3, 161, 163–4; second coming of 81; as a social reformer 68–9, 71, 146–7;

soldiers' image of 171; teachings of 236–7, 241–2

Jesus the Messiah in Prophecy and Fulfillment (E.H. Dewart) 77

Joint Committee on the Evangelization of Canadian Life 212–13, 226–7

Jones, Sam 88–9

Jordan, Rev. W.G. 39

Kerr, Rev. A.E. 197

Kilpatrick, Rev. George 167–8

Kilpatrick, Rev. T.B. 162

Kingdom of God 148, 154, 156–7, 159, 182, 228, 239, 245

Kingdom of God and the Problems of Today, The (A. Sutherland) 147–8

Knox College (Toronto) 35, 62, 113, 153, 185, 203

Laird, Rev. Robert 241

Leacock, Stephen 8

League for Social Reconstruction 243

Leben Jesu (D.F. Straus) 46

leisure 7, 127, 130, 135; and secularization 197–8

liberal Christianity 49–50, 68, 69–71, 72, 193, 251, 253; and church union 153–4, 186; and comparative religion 104–7; critique of 73–6, 160–1; inadequacy of 152–3, 179–80, 184, 191, 199–203, 208, 229, 234, 245, 247, 255; persistence of 202, 248

Line, Rev. John 201, 237, 241

Living Epistles; or, Christ's Witness to the World (E.H. Dewart) 52–3

Lord's Day Alliance 136–8

McCosh, James 57

McCourt, Edward 144
McCrimmon, Rev. A.L. 212
Macdonald, Rev. James 120
Macdonnell, Rev. D.J. 80, 86;
  background 40–1; causes of
  doubt 46; on doctrinal standards
  70–1; on everlasting punishment
  42; heresy trial 42–5, 62; on
  sabbath observance 133
McDougall, Rev. George 109
MacGregor, Rev. D.A. 22, 48
Machar, Agnes 44, 85
Machar, Rev. John 40
McKillop, Brian 17, 18, 53–4
Mackinnon, Rev. Clarence 139, 204
McLachlan, Rev. D.N. 207
Maclean, Rev. John 182
MacLennan, Rev. D. 215
McMaster University (Toronto)
  106–7, 195
MacNeill, Rev. A.T. 163–4
McNiven, Rev. W.E. 222
McQueen, Rev. D.G. 119
MacVicar, Rev. D.H. 74, 207
Man from Glengarry, The
  (C.W. Gordon) 142, 144–5
Marshall, John George 38
materialism 23–4, 189, 211, 244.
  See also consumer culture
Methodism: and evangelicalism 20;
  and evolutionary thought 54, 56–
  7; and novel reading 140; passing
  of 182; and revivals 32–4; in the
  West 112
Methodism in Canada
  (A. Sutherland) 124–5
Methodist church: Army and Navy
  Board 157–8, 161, 165–6, 174–5;
  code of discipline 140, 166;
  Committee on the State of the

Church 84; Department of
  Temperance and Moral Reform
  148–9, 151; doctrinal standards of
  79; and First World War 157, 175,
  177; and professional revivalism
  86, 89; and the Salvation Army
  86; and the social gospel 146–50,
  184; and the Workman trial 78–9;
  worship in 35
Methodist Church and Missions, The
  (A. Sutherland) 125–6
Methodist Hymn and Tune Book 91
Metropolitan Methodist Church
  (Toronto) 87–8, 129–30
Michael, Rev. J. Hugh 241–2
Miller, Rev. J.S. 168
Milliken, Rev. Robert 123
Milne, Rev. J.W. 222
ministry: recruits for 185, 187, 204,
  230; wartime resignations from
  175
miracles. See supernatural, the
missionaries 102–3
missionary literature 14, 101, 103–4,
  109, 120–4
missions: declining strength of 107;
  to the natives 109, 112–13; and
  religious conviction 99–100; and
  secularization 125–6; as source of
  renewal 100–1, 109–11, 251–2
'Modern Industry' (Urwick and
  Biss) 243–4
modernism, accommodation with
  4, 7, 19, 49–50, 70–1, 154–5, 208,
  250–2, 254–6
Moir, J.S. 16, 21, 76; on secularization 264n64
Montreal Witness 42, 215–16, 226
Moody, Barry 58
Moody, Dwight 86–8, 118, 139, 247

Moody–Sankey revivalism 90–1
Moore, James R. 54
Moore, Rev. T.A. 186, 191
moral conditions, at the battlefront
166–7
Moral Man and Immoral Society
(Niebuhr) 243–4
Moral Rearmament 227. *See also*
Oxford Group movement
Morrison, Rev. Duncan 91–2
Mott, John R. 214
Murray, Rev. Walter 186
muscular Christianity 131
music 91–2

natural theology 45–6
neo-orthodoxy 203, 236
New Outlook 219–20
New Testament, critical approach to
64, 66
Niebuhr, Reinhold 243–4
novel reading 97; as profane activity
51, 140

Old Testament, moral content of
66–7
Oliver, Rev. E.H.: background 13;
on battlefront conditions 165; on
church union 14, 181, 186; and
Commission on Evangelism 245;
critique of church in wartime
176–7; historical writings 13–14,
235; as moderator 230; on
soldiers' religious indifference
177–8; support of war effort 158;
theological reformulation 233,
235–7; tour of Prairies 234; on
war experience 183
On Liberty (J.S. Mill) 22
ordination vows 7, 39–40

Origin of Species (Charles Darwin)
22, 46
orthodoxy, decline of 47, 66–7
Oxford Group movement 205–6;
appeal of 218–19; appraisal of
219–20, 221, 223–6; Canadian tour
213–27; decline of 226; and
evangelicalism 215–17; growth
218; 221–2; meetings 216–17; and
Methodism 215; principles of
214; secular ethics of 248, 255;
social ethics 223, 237

Pentateuch (Bishop Colenso) 46
Pentecostals 193
perfectionism, critique of 239–40
Pidgeon, Rev. George: background
206–7; battlefront sermons 170–1;
and church union 186; and
Commission of Evangelism 245;
conservatism of 153; on decline of
evangelicalism 206–7; on fundamentalism 193; as moderator
189–90; need for revival 204; and
the Oxford Group movement
214–15, 219, 226; postwar criticism
of churches 180; radio ministry
210; relief work 233; on seculariza-
ization 206, 254; on the social
gospel 150, 190, 238–9; support of
war effort 159; on theological
renewal 194–5; wartime sermons
163
piety 11, 26–7, 28, 29–30, 29–31,
30–1; lack of 116. *See also* doubt;
indifference
Pine Hill College (Halifax) 9, 184,
185
pluralism 21
popular culture 82–3, 127–8; and

foreign missions 99; and gospel songs 91–2; and preaching 96–7, 139–40; and secularization 19. *See also* consumer culture
popular religion 8–9, 86–98, 213–27
Post-Darwinian Controversies, The (James R. Moore) 54
post-millennial thought 81
Potts, Rev. John 86
prayer question 48, 208
preaching: at the battlefront 170–3; decline of 206; as entertainment 96, 139; evangelical style 9, 27–8, 36, 96, 139; indifference to 25–6, 67–8, 84–5; narrative style 139–40; secularization of 84–5, 96; during wartime 162–4. *See also* sermons
predestination 37–9
premillennial thought 78, 81
Presbyterian church: Board of Foreign Missions 102; Board of Social Service and Evangelism 150–1, 153; and the Campbell heresy trial 79–80; and the chaplains' survey 176–8; Commission on the War and the Spiritual Life of the Church 161–3; Committee on Church Life and Work 135; Committee on Religious Education 151; Committee on the State of Religion 133–4; doctrinal standards 41–5, 62–3; and First World War 158; missionary policy 118–19; preaching in 37–9; and the social gospel 150; and urban revivalism 86, 95–6; in the West 114–15; worship practices 43–4, 94–5
Presbyterian College (Halifax) 58

Presbyterian College (Montreal) 74, 79, 193
Presbyterian College (Winnipeg) 185
Presbyterianism. *See* Calvinism
Presbyterians (non-concurring) 154
Princeton University 113
Principles of Geology (Charles Lyell) 46
Profusion of Spires, A (J.W. Grant) 17
progressive revelation 59–62, 60–2, 65, 66–7, 79, 149
Prophetic Bible Conferences 81
Prophetic Bible movement 106
Prospector, The (C.W. Gordon) 120, 124
Providence: in daily life 26–7; declining belief in 15, 47–8; and evolutionary thought 58–9; and the Great Depression 211–12; in history 12

Queen's University (Kingston) 40, 185

radical Christianity 242, 245–8
Rauschenbusch, Walter 236
Rawlyk, George 17, 195, 258n9, 267n31
Recall of Love, The (C.W. Gordon) 143
recreation 127–31
redemption: doctrine of 210; and suffering 162–3
religion: definition of 5–6; and moral order 3–4; persistence of 18
Religions of the World, The (George Grant) 104–6
religious conditions: in cities 16, 52,

73, 86, 135, 147, 151, 197–8; at
colleges 32, 187–8; after First
World War 181–2; at the front
168–74, 177–8; during Great
Depression 210–11, 228–30; in
pioneer society 20–1, 34; in rural
society 188–9; on western frontier
112, 115–17, 119, 123–5
religious fiction 140–1. *See also*
devotional literature
religious knowledge 151, 172, 177–8
religious liberty. *See* tolerance
repentance 27–8, 88–90, 171. *See also*
conversion
respectability 73, 94, 130–1, 145, 251
revival, need of 182–3, 188, 205, 207,
210–11, 227, 254
revivalism: at the battlefront 170–1;
at Crossley-Hunter meetings 90–
8; decline of 34; in Methodism
32–4; opposition to 95–6, 209; and
Oxford Group movement 213–26;
popular resistance to 251; and
secularization 97–8, 247
Riddell, Rev. W.A. 151
Ritchie, Rev. D.L. 202, 223–4
Ritschl, Albrecht 40
rituals 9
Robb, Rev. A.D. 166
Roberts, Rev. Richard: background
196; and Commission on Evangelism 245–6; concept of sinfulness
225, 246; critique of liberal
Christianity 199–200; on decline
of evangelicalism 206; on decline
of worship 198; on fundamentalist-modernist controversy 199–
200; on impact of war 209–10;
member of the Commission on
Christianizing the Social Order

241; on modern revivalism 209;
opposition to social gospel
platform 238–9; outlook for
United church 246–7; on the
Oxford Group movement 225;
pastoral problems 197; on
secularization 198; support of
church union 196; on theological
depression 240; and theological
reformulation 246
Robertson, Rev. James: appointed
superintendent 115; background
113; conservatism of 116; on
indifference 116–17; and missionary recruits 115, 117, 119;
missionary tours 114–15; theological views 113–14, 116
Robertson College (Edmonton) 185
Rowell, Newton Wesley 241
Rundle, W.E. 241
Ryerson, Rev. Egerton: critique of
revivalism 34; on doubt 3; on
Methodist class meetings 266n27;
on religious liberty 21; on
repentance 28; and school
legislation 22–3

Sabbatarian movement. *See* Lord's
Day Alliance
sabbath desecration 20, 112, 135, 252
sabbath observance 21, 132–9;
legislation 132–3, 137–9
sacrifice 163–4
St Andrew's College (Saskatoon)
185, 235
salvation, doctrine of 27–8, 38, 90,
102
Salvation Army 85–6
Sanderson, Rev. J.E. 28
Santink, Joy 128

Saturday Night 84–5, 96, 129–30
scepticism 3–4, 157, 168. *See also*
  doubt; indifference
science 7, 13, 16, 231, 241
science and religion 45–7, 53–4, 249;
  reconciliation of 54–9
Sclater, Rev. J.R.P. 194, 197
Seaforth Camp 169
secular society 4–5, 8, 86, 242–4
secularization: and Canadian
  historiography 12–19; causes of
  4, 21–2, 24, 154–5, 198–9; and
  church union 154–5, 186; of the
  churches 128–9, 152–3, 190, 239;
  and consumer culture 17, 23–4,
  48, 127–8, 189, 197–8, definition
  of 3–4, 7; and liberal Christianity
  71; and materialism 23–4, 47, 244;
  of missions 102–4, 108, 125–6; and
  modern revivalism 97–8; and the
  Oxford Group movement 227;
  and pluralism 127; process of 7,
  249–56; of the pulpit 84–5; of
  religion 70–1, 247; of sabbath
  observance 135–9; and the social
  gospel 149; timing of 18–19, 155;
  and tolerance 21–2
sentimental religion 96, 144
sermons, content of 9, 68, 72, 84–5,
  96, 116, 139–40, 239
Shaw, Rev. J.M. 162–3, 193–4
Shearer, Rev. J.G. 120; and the
  Lord's Day Alliance 136–7
Sheppard, E.E. 84–5, 96
Shields, Rev. T.T. 158, 195
Silcox, Rev. C.E. 238–40
Simpson, Jimmy 241
sinfulness: as basis of theological
  reformulation 199–200, 210, 234,
  245–6; in C.W. Gordon's novels

144; as cause of Great Depression
  210–12; concept of 208, 210, 211,
  246, 253–4; evangelical consciousness of 29, 31–2; in evangelical
  preaching 27, 36, 38–9, 67–8, 88–9;
  exposed by war 161, 161–3, 162;
  in Oxford Group meetings 219,
  225; portrayed by Crossley-
  Hunter 94; preaching of 200–1;
  Sutherland on 110
Sky Pilot, The (C.W. Gordon) 120,
  121, 131, 141–2
Smith, Goldwin: on moral standards
  of the Old Testament 67; 'Prospect of a Moral Interregnum' 13,
  260n24; on secularization 4
social conditions: in cities 68–9, 73,
  127–8, 135, 151–2, 189, 197–8;
  during Great Depression 210–12,
  218–19, 232–3; industrial order
  243–4; material improvement of
  23–4, 34, 47; in pioneer society
  33–4; during postwar years 189;
  and secularization 3; in the West
  115, 125, 137, 234–5
social gospel 18, 68–9, 128, 146–50,
  156, 191, 202, 250–1, 252; on
  foreign mission fields 103–4, 108;
  impact of 152; opposition to 160–
  1, 179, 238–40; persistence of 161,
  248
Social Passion, The (Richard Allen)
  16–17
social surveys 151–2
social welfare 7, 249
sociology, and Christianity 149, 152
Solandt, Rev. D.M. 241
soldiers: and disillusionment with
  churches 173–5; religion of 157,
  164, 169–73, 177–8, 253

Some Causes of the Decline of Earlier Typical Evangelism (S.D. Chown) 207–8

Songs of Life (E.H. Dewart) 51

Songs of Salvation (H.T. Crossley) 92–3

Spence, Rev. R.E. 188

statistics: on church attendance 132, 134; on church membership 132, 134; on denominational affiliation 10; on Methodism's decline 145; on United church income 231–2

Strong–Boag, Veronica 189

Summer in Prairie Land, A (A. Sutherland) 111–12

Sunday schools 135

supernatural, the 5, 6, 7, 26, 70, 97, 149, 152, 203

supernaturalism, decline of 70, 152, 253, 254

Sutherland, Rev. Alexander 14; background 110; critique of social gospel 147–8; editor of *Earnest Christianity* 111; historical writings 12, 124–6; on indifference 125; *Methodism in Canada* 12, 124–5; on promise of the West 111–12; theological views 110–11

Taoism 105

Taylor, Rev. W.R. 241

temperance 21, 28, 41, 50, 128, 146, 150, 153, 154

theological colleges: curriculum 184, 187; enrolment 185; during wartime 158

theological depression 191, 195, 199–201, 210, 239–40

theology, end of 147

Thomas, Rev. Ernest 224–5, 241, 245

Thomas, Rev. H.E. 165, 167

Thomas, Rev. Jesse 96

Tillich, Paul 233

tolerance 7, 12, 23, 43–4, 249; and secularization 21–2; of world religions 104–7

Trades and Labour Congress 137

Turner, Federick Jackson 13

Union government 159

Union revival services. *See* Crossley-Hunter revival meetings

Union Theological Seminary 113

United church: and Barthianism 201–2; Board of Education 187; Board of Evangelism and Social Service 207, 227, 237, 240, 243, 245; Commission on Christianizing the Social Order 240–5, 247; Commission on Evangelism 245–6; Committee on Church Life and Work 188–9; Committee on Finance 231–2; Committee of Thirty 224–5; debate on social gospel 237–40; doctrinal standards of 193–4; doctrinal statement 190–1, 254; formation of 181, 186; fundamentalist critique of 192; and the Great Depression 228–33; as inclusive institution 192, 193–4, 194; modernism of 192; National Emergency Relief Committee 233; and the Oxford Group movement 219–20, 223–7; prospects for 240; Special Committee on Recruits for the Ministry 187; and theological depression 239–40

United Theological College (Montreal) 202, 237

urban churches 147, 197–8
Urwick, E.J. 241, 243–4

Van Die, Marguerite 17–18, 154
Van Paassen, Pierre 173, 175
Victoria College (Cobourg) 28, 32,
  55, 59, 64, 65
Victoria College (Toronto) 76, 79,
  158, 175
voluntarism 23, 137

Wallace, Rev. F.H.: background 34–
  5; as biblical critic 65–6; causes of
  doubt 46–7; on Revised New
  Testament 75; spiritual crisis 35–
  7, 39; on Workman trial 78
Walsh, H.H. 15
Webster, Rev. Thomas 12, 26
welfare state 231
Wentworth, Rev. F.H. 220
Wesley, John 33, 60, 148
Wesley College (Winnipeg) 174, 182
West, the: and church union 186;
  impact of Great Depression 230–
  1; promise of 109, 111, 115, 122,

125, 252; secular nature of 124–5
Westfall, William 17, 23
Westminster Confession of Faith 37,
  40–1. *See also* doctrinal standards
Westminster Hall (Vancouver) 184,
  185
Whidden, Rev. H.P. 195
Williams, Rosalind 23
Winning of the Frontier, The
  (E.H. Oliver) 13–14, 235, 336
Withrow, Rev. William 129, 141
Witley Camp 170
Woodsworth, Rev. James 14
Woodsworth, James Shaver 147
Workman, Rev. George C. 76–9
world religions 101–7
worship: at the battlefront 168–71;
  decline of 198; family 11, 31–2,
  94, 135–6; indifference to 49; in
  the Presbyterian church 43–4

YMCA 36, 164, 167, 170–1, 213, 272n3
Youmans, Harriet 130
Young, Rev. George 26–7, 28
YWCA 272n3